EDDEY & DARBYSHIRE
ON
THE ENGLISH
LEGAL SYSTEM

AUSTRALIA
Law Book Co
Sydney

CANADA and USA
Carswell
Toronto

HONG KONG
Sweet and Maxwell Asia

NEW ZEALAND
Brookers
Wellington

SINGAPORE and MALAYSIA
Sweet and Maxwell Asia
Singapore and Kuala Lumpur

EDDEY & DARBYSHIRE ON
THE ENGLISH LEGAL SYSTEM

By

PENNY DARBYSHIRE PH.D., M.A.
Senior Lecturer in Law,
Kingston Law School,
Kingston University

SEVENTH EDITION

LONDON
SWEET & MAXWELL
2001

First Edition 1971
Second Edition 1977
Third Edition 1982
Fourth Edition 1987
Reprinted 1990
Fifth Edition 1992
Sixth Edition 1996
Seventh Edition 2001
Reprinted 2003, 2004

Published in 2001 by
Sweet & Maxwell Ltd of
100 Avenue Road,
London NW3 3PF
Typeset by
Servis Filmsetting Ltd,
Manchester, England
Printed in England by
MPG Books, Bodmin, Cornwall

Free online updates are available at www.sweet&maxwell.co.uk/academic

No natural forests were destroyed to make this product;
only farmed timber was used and replanted

A CIP catalogue
record for this book
is available from
the British Library

ISBN 0421 787902

Preface

I wrote this book for law students everywhere. It helps in understanding English law if you have a grasp of the sources, the institutions, the people who populate them and the way cases progress through them. Studying the English Legal System should be stimulating. Our legal system is very old and very important, in worldwide terms. Its rich history is awesome so I hope I have not made the English Legal System seem dull. At the same time, the system is a living organism. It is transforming rapidly before our eyes. This edition has had to be entirely rewritten, such is the pace of change in the context of every Chapter. The way it develops raises intense political and moral issues. Above all, I hope it helps you to understand that the law exists in the real world, not in books.

Penny Darbyshire, October 2001.

Contents

PART VI: Access to Justice

Table of Cases

TABLE OF CASES

Table of Statutes

Table of Statutory Instruments

Table of International and European Conventions and Legislation

Part I: Sources

1. Understanding the English Legal System

1. What is Law?

Societies and their subcultures govern themselves by countless sets of rules of different types, written or unwritten. Without these codes of acceptable behaviour, there would be no society, no order, only chaos and anarchy. We conduct our lives according to all manner of learned or agreed rules of conduct. These include our own internalised moral code, unconsciously followed rules of etiquette and civilised behaviour. We may adhere to the tenets of a religion and a particular church. We may belong to a private organisation, such as a political party or a sports club with its own constitution and membership rules but none of the codes so far mentioned, however complex, carries the force of law. For instance, the constitution of the California Parent Teachers' Association is lengthier and much more complex than the English Courts and Legal Services Act 1990 but it is not law. It cannot be interpreted or enforced by a court. **1-001**

What then is special about legal rules? To commit a gross generalisation and without getting involved in heavy jurisprudence (the philosophy of law), a rudimentary definition of law, within the English legal system, is a rule that is backed by a sanction for its breach, ultimately enforceable by a court, a tribunal or arbitration. There is considerable overlap between non-legal rules and the law. For instance, the basic rules of most major religions are astonishingly similar. Most of them condemn murder and so do all legal systems, although what constitutes murder and the punishment imposed differs from one legal system to another. In another overlap, dropping litter in the street would be condemned by most English people as anti-social behaviour but it is also illegal and subject to a fine enforceable in a criminal court. Nevertheless, many forms of anti-social **1-002** behaviour, such as spitting in a crowded street, would shock most people, as a breach of the rules of civilised behaviour but are not illegal. Again, we must distinguish between the immoral and the illegal. Adultery is not illegal, though it is a breach of many people's religions or moral codes. Some M.P.s and peers think adulterous behaviour should have legal ramifications. They attempted but failed to amend the Family Law Bill 1996, to allow the judge to take account of such "faults" on the part of divorcing couples.

1-003   Sanctions for breach of the law take many forms, apart from the obvious example of sentences passed for breaches of the criminal law. When part of the Merchant Shipping Act 1988 was found by the European Court of Justice (ECJ), in the *Factortame* cases, to be in breach of the E.C. Treaty, the operation of the offending sections of the Act had to be suspended and the United Kingdom government had to compensate Spanish fishermen who had been prevented from plying their trade in British coastal waters. If I breach my contract with you, you can ask a civil court to impose a sanction on me by awarding damages against me or enforcing my obligations under the contract. If a minister makes a new set of regulations, they can be quashed by the High Court if she failed to follow procedure prescribed in the enabling Act of Parliament which gave her the power to make the regulations, such as consulting affected parties.

2. Distinguishing Between Different Types of Law

Substantive and Procedural

1-004   While the former prescribes, proscribes and regulates areas of human activity, the latter sets down rules for the manner of enforcing the law in relation to that activity. The Theft Acts and many leading cases define what conduct and mental elements constitute the offence of theft but the procedures for arresting the suspect, questioning, charging, and trying him are contained in several quite different statutes (Acts), cases and sets of procedural rules.

Private and Public

1-005   The former governs relations between private citizens or bodies, the latter applies to public bodies which are publicly regulated and usually publicly funded, such as the departments of local and central government and public services, such as the Highways Agency. Historically, the British constitution boasted that it did not recognise this distinction, since all public bodies were equally bound by the ordinary law of the land, enforceable in the ordinary courts. While it is true to say that the English legal system does not provide a separate court structure for adjudicating on disputes arising with public bodies, as does the French legal system, last century, especially the period since 1981, saw the massive growth in a body of law regulating the conduct of public bodies which all English lawyers would now acknowledge as public law. The study of public law is a requirement for entry to the legal profession and it covers such topics as regulating police behaviour and the judicial review (a check by the High Court) of the legality of decisions taken and rules made by public bodies.

Domestic and International

Our domestic law is applicable in and enforceable by the courts of England and Wales (or England or Wales separately) and, sometimes, throughout the United Kingdom. Public international law is contained in conventions and treaties devised and agreed to by groups of countries concerned to regulate activities in which they have a common interest or which take place across national boundaries, covering everything from air traffic to drug trafficking. Its interpretation and enforcement may be the task of an international court recognised in or established by such a treaty. Frequently, more detailed laws giving practical effect to treaty requirements are enacted into domestic law. Our Misuse of Drugs Act 1972 provides domestic law in accordance with the requirements of the international conventions on narcotics.

1-006

It is important to understand that E.C. law and the law of the European Convention on Human Rights are not foreign law, they have been incorporated into United Kingdom law but in different ways.

Civil Law and Criminal Law

Private civil law regulates relations between private persons or bodies and civil law is usually invoked only by those parties seeking to protect their private rights or interests. For instance, if I commit a tort against you, say, negligently backing my muckspreader over your gatepost, the State, as such, has no interest in taking me to court to sue for damages on your behalf but you may sue me in a civil court. Similarly, if I unfairly dismiss you, you may take me to an employment tribunal to ask for compensation but if you choose not to enforce your legal right to protection by the civil law, that is your prerogative. The State is not going to step in if you do not act. Having said that, elements of the State, such as government agencies, have a vast range of statutory and common law powers to invoke the civil law against private individuals and, of course, a private party may take a civil court action against an element of the State, such as suing the police over a death in custody but all of these activities between citizen and State are subject to the rules of public law as well.

1-007

By contrast, a criminal offence is a wrong against the State and punishable as such, in the criminal courts. Whereas the State has no interest

5

in pursuing your civil claim, if you are a victim of a crime, such as theft, the State may prosecute the offender, whether or not you wish to take action against him. The aim of taking a criminal case to court is to punish the wrongdoer, rather than to compensate, although our judges and magistrates may attach a compensation order to any sentence they pass. Just to confuse you, in English law, victims of crime retain the right of private prosecution so may prosecute the offender in the criminal courts, if the State chooses not to prosecute.

1-008　　I know that my explanation may have confused the distinction, rather than clarified it but, in studying law, you will soon be able to recognise the difference. Suffice it to say that virtually all the foundation subjects studied in a law degree, such as tort, contract, land law, equity, most of public law and E.C. law are elements of civil law. Most of the criminal law we study is taught under the heading of criminal law. A true story may help to distinguish.

A story from the student world: my bike

1-009　　When I was a law student, I was biking to college to sit the last of my finals when a car driver knocked me off my bike. The police arrived on the scene and took details of the accident and interviewed her and the witnesses. She was prosecuted in criminal proceedings in Kingston magistrates' court, pleaded guilty to the offence of careless driving and was fined. My solicitor, acting on my behalf, threatened to sue her in civil proceedings in Kingston County Court for damages for the losses I had suffered, as a result of her negligent driving. I needed the cost of a new bike and damages for the pain and shock of my injuries. Luckily, the driver's motor insurance company, acting on her behalf, agreed to settle out of court for the sum claimed by my solicitor. This was typical. As we shall see, the vast majority of civil disputes are settled out of court by the parties or their representatives. What is also typical was my solicitor's tactic of waiting for the outcome of the criminal case before threatening a civil action against her. A civil case is much easier to prove than a criminal one. The *quantum* (standard) of proof is lower so my solicitor knew that the driver's criminal conviction would make the civil case easy to prove. To help matters, the police had given him their file of statements, taken as criminal evidence, to use as civil evidence. (Incidentally, I still had to sit my private international law exam, in shock, with my right arm dislocated and my gashed knee bandaged. What cruel lecturers I had.)

Civil and criminal cases: getting the language right

1-010　　Here is a list of the correct terminology used in most civil and criminal cases. Try to get it right.

CIVIL	CRIMINAL
The claimant	The prosecutor
sues	prosecutes
the defendant	the defendant
in the county court or High Court.	in the magistrates' court or Crown Court.
Most cases are settled without a trial, as no defence is entered.	Most cases are heard without a trial as the defendant pleads guilty.
If a defence is entered, the case goes to trial and it is heard before a single judge, who decides on fact and law. In exceptional cases, a jury decides.	If the defendant pleads not guilty, the case goes to trial and is heard by a district judge (magistrates' court) or lay magistrates, who decide on fact and law. In the Crown Court, the jury decides issues of fact (the verdict) and the judge rules on points of law.
If the judge finds the case proven, he enters judgment for the claimant.	If the magistrates or jury find the case proven, they bring in a verdict of guilty and convict the defendant.
He may make an order, *e.g.* an award of damages, against the defendant.	The magistrates or judge may pass sentence on the defendant, *e.g.* a fine or a term of imprisonment.
If the judge does not find the case proven, he enters judgment for the defendant.	If they find the case is not proven, they acquit the defendant.

In either case, if the losing party appeals, she becomes "the appellant" and the other side "the respondent." If she seeks judicial review, she becomes the applicant.

3. *What is the English Legal System?*

The study of the English legal system applies to the powers, proce- **1-011**
dures and activities of the group of courts and statutory tribunals in
England and Wales and the people who work in them and/or whose job
it is to resolve legal problems. The legal systems of Scotland and
Northern Ireland are quite separate. They have distinct court structures,

7

different procedures and sometimes apply different rules of substantive law.

1-012 We speak of the English legal *system* as if it were a coherent structure with the constituent parts working in a smooth, interrelated fashion but it is very important to bear in mind that no-one has custom-designed it. Think of it more as a heap of *Lego* bricks, some of which are joined together, than a sophisticated piece of *Lego Technic*. It has been given to us in little boxes, over the last ten centuries and parts have been deconstructed and reconstructed from time to time. We fiddle with it. For instance, Lord Woolf has been concerned recently with how to improve access to civil justice and, in 1991–1993, the Royal Commission on Criminal Justice contemplated how the criminal process could be improved but no-one ever examines the workings of the whole structure. We take it for granted that we need two levels of first instance court (trial court). We take it for granted that we need both a Court of Appeal and the Appellate Committee of the House of Lords, because it has been that way beyond living memory. Only students in tutorials are tortured with such questions. The general issues paper of the Civil Justice Review, published in 1986, raised the radical question of whether we really need both the county courts and the High Court dealing with civil trials.

1-013 It is true to say, however, that, considering nothing much has happened in the English legal system since the 1870s, we have scrutinised and reconfigured an enormous number of bricks in our *Lego* pile since 1985, largely thanks to the Conservative Lord Chancellor, Lord Mackay and his Labour successor, Lord Irvine. Examining the English legal system with the eyes of an outsider, as he is a member of the Scottish Bar, no block of our system was, to Lord Mackay, sacrosanct. He was prepared to leave virtually no brick unturned, no question unasked. He made many enemies by his radical approach, daring to ask whether it is in the public interest that lawyers' monopolies should be protected and whether we should really assume that the litigant is better off being represented by a lawyer in an adversarial process. Another Scot, Lord Irvine continues with the same approach.

Hallmarks of the English Legal System

The Common law

1-014 The English legal system is a "common law" legal system. This means that many of our primary legal principles have been made and developed by judges from case to case in what is called a system of precedent, where the lower courts are bound to follow principles established by the higher courts in previous cases. The term "common law" historically distinguished the law made by judges in the royal courts in Westminster and commonly applicable in the whole of the kingdom, from the canon law (ecclesiastical law) or the local systems of customary law which predominated until 1066 and existed beyond.

Judge-made law is at least as important to us as the law made by Parliament. For instance, there is no statute telling us that murder is a crime and defining it for us. It is a common law crime. The required guilty act, of causing death and the necessary degree of guilt, malice afore-thought, have been prescribed and defined, over the centuries, by judges. Similarly, the law of negligence was the invention of a judge who wanted to find a remedy for a woman who had suffered gastro-enteritis when she drank from an opaque bottle of ginger beer, wherein lurked the decomposing remains of a stray snail. She was given the ginger beer and thus had no contract with the retailer or manufacturer and we can assume Mr. Slimey Snail was not a pet, endowed with his own third party liability insurance, so the Judge, Lord Atkin, decided that, as a matter of principle, she should have a right to damages against the manufacturer, as they owed her a duty of care. Thus, he invented what became the law of negligence.

Adversarial procedure

Another of the hallmarks of the English legal system and all common law systems is that basic trial procedure is essentially adversarial. This means that the two parties to the case are left to their own devices to prepare and present their cases unaided by the court. Crass comparisons are made between this typical common law procedure and the type of "inquisitorial" procedure, with officials of the court involved in the fact finding process, which is said to be a hallmark of continental European legal systems. As we shall see, however, our trial system has not always been adversarial and inquisitorial elements are appearing at many points in the system. Also, it is wrong to label European procedural systems as inquisitorial. **1-015**

Jury trial and orality

Historically, certainly since 1215, jury trial was central to the English legal system in both criminal and civil cases, although its use in civil cases is now rare and it is confined to the most serious cases in the criminal courts. The need to argue cases before a jury has certainly shaped our rules of evidence, procedure and our substantive law and has meant that, historically, most of each argument has been presented to the court orally, through oral argument by the parties and oral examination and cross-examination of witnesses by the parties. Again, the emphasis on orality is rapidly disappearing, with the admission of more and more written statements and documentary evidence in hard copy and electronically retrievable form. Since 1995, in civil cases, lawyers now have to present the court with a skeleton argument so the advocate's art of oral story-telling is being replaced by a scene in a typical High Court room where all bewigged heads are face-down in "the bundle" of pre-served documents, flicking through to make cross-references, incomprehensible to the casual observer. It has taken some fun out of court watching.

Lay magistrates

1-016   The bulk of criminal cases are heard in magistrates' courts, mostly by lay justices. There are over 30,000 of them and no other legal system makes such heavy use of laypeople as decision-makers. In exporting the common law, we exported the concept of magistrates but they tended to be professionals. When you add to them the use of lay arbitrators, tribunal panel members and jurors, you start to realise how many important decisions are taken by lay persons in the English legal system.

4. The Mother of All Common Law Systems

Just as the British Parliament has been called "the mother of parliaments," so I would call the English legal system the mother of all common law legal systems, worldwide. We exported the common law and our legal system, along with the English language, into our old colonies and the Commonwealth. The common law daughters of the English legal system include the United States, Canada, Australia and New Zealand but we maintain our direct link with the living common law of Commonwealth countries, both dependent and independent, through the judicial committee of the Privy Council. This Court sits in London and is the highest court of appeal for those jurisdictions. Since it is mainly composed of Law Lords you can see that this provides for harmonious development of principle throughout all of these common law jurisdictions. Decisions of the judicial committee are persuasive and not binding precedents on the English courts but they are heavily influential, since everyone realises that when those senior judges metamorphose back into Law Lords they are hardly likely to contradict legal principles which they carefully established when doing their job as privy councillors.

1-017   This common law cross-fertilisation is by no means confined to Commonwealth countries, however. Certain areas of the common law, such as tort and criminal law, have developed globally, with judges in the courts of one country regularly persuaded by the reasoning of their brethren in another jurisdiction. You only have to flick through the pages of an English text on criminal law to see how other countries tackle some of the interpretive problems facing our criminal courts. Where no precedent exists, English judges may well be persuaded by a precedent from America, Australia or Hong Kong. At the same time, English common law is still alive throughout the United States, even in forms which have been replaced in England. For instance, the actions constituting an attempted crime in California are determined by old English case law, replaced by the Criminal Attempts Act 1981. Throughout the USA, crimes are divided into felonies and misdemeanors, a distinction which we disposed of in 1967. They also chose to retain the harsh felony murder rule. Californian property law uses concepts straight out of medieval English property law, replaced by the English in the Law of Property Act 1925. If you buy property in the United States, you may be astonished by quaint concepts and language.

Apart from judicial borrowing of precedents, there is a ceaseless interchange between academics in the common law world, in terms of writing, thinking, teaching and research. If you want to read the best of English legal history these days, you have to turn to American journals and books. English legal history is American legal history.

The Comparison with Other European Systems

Since, in our popular rhetoric and our legal analysis, we are always **1-018** comparing ourselves with continental legal systems, notably the French and since we, along with all other European Union Member States, now all have to absorb E.C. law into our domestic legal systems, we students of the English legal system need to understand something more about another major "family" of laws, the "Romano-Germanic" family, as David and Brierley describe it, in *Major Legal Systems in the World Today*. Apart from Eire, a common law country, the legal systems of all our European Union partners are, historically, members of that other major family.

Different Roots

The Romano-Germanic family was developed by scholars in the **1-019** European universities from the Renaissance of the twelfth and thirteenth centuries. There was a need for an autonomous law, independent of canon (Church) law, to replace inadequate and bitty customary law. Scholars latched onto Roman law as a neat pre-existing body of rules and set about refining it. Law was seen as a fairly abstract body of principles of justice, and its teaching was linked to the teaching of philosophy, theology and religion. It emerged from France and Italy but was taught in this way in Spain, Portugal, Scandinavia, even Oxford and Cambridge. The teaching of national law was not taken up until the seventeenth and eighteenth centuries. The flexibility and abstract nature of this civil law refined and taught in Europe can be contrasted with the rigidity of the common law rules developing in the Westminster courts. Eventually, Roman law was translated into the basis of national laws for practical application. This could not be done in England because the rules of common law, devised and applied by the courts, were already too entrenched. From the thirteenth to the sixteenth centuries, the law as taught in the universities had considerable influence. Jurists, not governments, developed the law so the countries of the Romano-Germanic family had jurists and legal practitioners who took their concept of law, approach and reasoning from Roman law.

1-020   The study and refinement of Roman law naturally progressed to its codification. Codes were developed independently but the most influential of these was the Napoleonic Code of 1804. The French code was received in Belgium, the Netherlands, the Rhenish provinces, Luxembourg, Poland and Italy. Thanks to colonisation by the Spanish, Portuguese, French and Dutch, elements of Romano-Germanic law spread throughout South America, parts of North America (Louisiana, Quebec) and Africa. The French influence extends to Turkey, Egypt, Iran, Syria, Iraq, Japan, Taiwan, Vietnam and Cambodia. The Romano-Germanic family can, then be seen alongside the common law family, as populating a large part of the world. Certain countries have a mixture of the two. Examples are Scotland, Israel, South Africa, Zimbabwe and Botswana.

Because the French Napoleonic Code was absorbed into so many legal systems, too many to list here, this made France an even more fecund mother of legal systems than the English. Notice that Germany did not adopt the French code but devised one of its own so some comparativists talk of a French family and a German family.

And Different Branches

The same divisions of law can be found throughout the Romano-Germanic legal systems and some of them, such as "the law of obligations," are alien and incomprehensible to the common lawyer.

Written constitutions

1-021   The United Kingdom is one of very few countries, common law or Romano-Germanic, without a written constitution. As a consequence, we lacked any notion of fundamental rights until very recently. There is almost no awareness amongst the public at large of what the United Kingdom constitution amounts to. There is no talk of fundamental constitutional rights, as is common in Germany and France and as is drummed into each small child's memory in the United States, because we do not think we have any. Indeed, we have only spoken in terms of human rights in the last year, since the Human Rights Act 1998 came into force, in October 2000. In all our European partner states, along with all of England's common law daughters, the legality of the law of the land can be tested against a written constitution in a special constitutional court and struck down if determined to offend against some constitutional requirement. In the United Kingdom, on the other hand, we are used to the idea that the law of our land is untouchable. Parliament is supreme and, prior to 1973, only Parliament could undo what a previous parliament had done. Maybe it is this inability to conceptualise any law superior to that made by Parliament which partly explains why we reacted so badly to the affrontery of the ECJ's rulings in the *Factortame* cases, which resulted in the suspension of that part of the Merchant Shipping Act 1988 which flew in the face of the Treaty of Rome.

Public law and private law

Romano-Germanic legal systems all recognise the distinction between public and private law which, historically, English common law did not acknowledge. The French, for instance, have a separate set of courts, headed by the Conseil d'Etat, administering a separate body of public law developed by those courts to a sophisticated level by the first half of the twentieth century. French law has, in this respect, been highly influential over Belgian and Dutch law. Those countries also have courts which are modelled on the Conseil d'Etat. In the English legal system, however, the development of public law was stifled, until the Crown Proceedings Act 1947, by the rule that the Crown could not be sued and until 1981 by the difficulties in applying for judicial review. It is only since the 1960s that we have acknowledged the separate existence of a body of public law, worthy of being taught as an independent subject. We still do not have a separate set of public law courts, along French lines but at least we now list all applications for judicial review to be heard in the administrative court by specialist judges, with a simplified procedure, which has allowed the rapid development of a coherent body of public law.

1-022

The concept of law

The very way in which law is conceived of in the legal systems of the Roman-Germanic family is radically different from the way we approach it and it has developed in the common law countries and this goes a very long way towards explaining why E.C. law and the judgments of the ECJ were so much easier, in the early days, for our European partners to assimilate than for us. This is how David and Brierley, in their classic analysis, explain la différence:

1-023

> "In countries of the Romano-Germanic family, the legal rule is formulated, characterised and analysed in the same way. In this family, in which doctrinal writing is held in high esteem, the legal rule is not considered as merely a rule appropriate to the solution of a concrete case. It is fashionable to view with a certain disdain, and as casuistic, the opposite view which places the rule of law at the level of concrete cases only. Digests of decided cases, form books and legal dictionaries are certainly useful working instruments for practitioners, and they provide much of the raw material for jurists in their work. But these compilations do not

enjoy the high prestige associated with legal scholarship. The function of the jurist is to draw from this disorganised mass first the rules and then the principles which will clarify and purge the subject of impure elements, and thus provide both the practice and the courts with a guide for the solution of particular cases in the future."

1-024   In common law countries, just about the opposite is going on. The initial approach is one of pragmatism in individual cases, rather than abstract principle. The common law is developed, whether the judges are dealing with a judge-made law or interpreting a statute, on a case by case basis. The concern of the judge is to find the solution to the instant case. When a sufficient body of case law has developed, through the application and extension of judicial reasoning in the system of precedent, then it may be possible to elevate these judicial rulings to the level of principle. Examples of this abound. In public law, the principles of natural justice have developed in this way. The judges have, on a case by case basis, extended the right to a fair hearing in an unbiased tribunal from hearings in the inferior courts to all manner of decisions by administrative bodies. Because judicial reasoning is such an important source of law, we are heavily dependent on law reports. Academics certainly comment on judicial reasoning but they cannot be said, for the most part, to be the source of legal doctrine themselves. Indeed, there was a convention that judges did not cite living authors. The exception is that, where there is no precedent, the courts will resort to examining what are known as "books of authority" by the early writers in the common law, from the seventeenth and eighteenth century and it is now quite common, in certain areas of law, such as criminal law, for judges to refer to modern textbooks or articles.

Sources of law and the judicial approach

1-025   The primary source of law in the Romano-Germanic legal systems is undoubtedly codified law, the drafting and interpretation of which is influenced by or the task of academic jurists. In common law countries, we depend on a mixture of judge-made law (common law) and statute, as interpreted by judges, whose reasoned opinions we must read in the law reports. If we take the French legal system as a contrasting example, we can see that the judge is not considered to be a source of law. Indeed, following the revolution, judges' powers were curtailed and they were prohibited from creating binding rules of precedent, as Article 5 of the Code Civil now stipulates. Of course, this is constitutional theory but in reality, French judges have had to make law, to a certain extent, and some critics say that the notion that they do not make law is an academic myth. While even the judgments of the Cour de Cassation are not meant to form binding precedents, they are followed by the lower courts in most cases.

Certainly French public law is almost entirely judge-made since it was developed after the Napoleonic era of codification. The French ambivalence is illustrated by the way law is taught. Textbooks emphasise codified law, legislation, with cases relegated to footnote illustrations, yet tutorials concentrate on case commentaries. Because of the supposed insignificance of cases, they are not so easy to find as in our legal system. They tend to be numbered and named after the location of the court hearing, rather than entitled with the names of the parties, like English cases.

The nature of a judgment in French law could not be further from its English counterpart. Whereas some of our leading House of Lords decisions contain the reasoned opinions of five Law Lords, distinguishing and applying a long list of precedents and stretching through over 100 pages in the law reports, French judgments, even emanating from the Cour de Cassation, rarely amount to two pages. They are in the form of a syllogism: they set out the facts, the legal issue in context and the conclusion, without, usually, citing any previous case authority. Because judgments are so short, they are normally published accompanied by academic commentary. All this is explained by Dadamo and Farran, in *The French Legal System.*

Procedural differences

We most commonly see the English legal system contrasted with European systems in terms of procedure, notably criminal procedure. Broadly speaking, European systems were characterised as inquisitorial, with the examining magistrate, then the court, taking a significant part in fact-finding and examining witnesses. This caricature was contrasted with the adversarial or accusatorial system, which the common law population likes to emphasise is so much fairer, with the judge acting as an unbiased umpire, permitting both sides to prepare and present their cases and examine witnesses, independent of court interference. Both the English and continental legal systems have recently departed from the purity of their respective models, however, especially with the procedural changes of the 1980s and 1990s. One significant difference, which should be mentioned at this point, however, is that, whereas English barristers have been used to arguing most of their case orally in civil proceedings, until the requirement for written skeleton arguments in civil cases, from the 1990s, European advocates are much better trained in reducing their arguments into writing.

1-026

Bad Europeans

I have endeavoured to explain at some length the contrast between the English legal system and the Romano-Germanic systems of our European Union partners for two reasons. First, we need to see where the English legal system sits, in worldwide terms and secondly, we need to understand why E.C. law seems a bit more difficult for us to get used to

1-027

than for our European counterparts. E.C. procedural law and the concept of law is derived directly from the French legal system, the mother or sister of all the other European Union legal systems, apart from Eire. The Europhobe might say that, just as the Union seems to be in the political grip of the Franco-German alliance, so the French and Germans had sewn up E.C. law before we even got into the Common market because, just as E.C. procedure is French, so substantive E.C. law is based on German (and American) competition law.

The French influence can be seen in these aspects of E.C. procedure: French is the working language of the court; lawyers' oral submissions are strictly limited to 30 minutes' argument. Common lawyers, trained in the tradition of oral advocacy, have to be helped by the Court's staff to reduce their arguments into writing; the roles of the advocate-general and judge-rapporteur are modelled on the French. They have no common law equivalent; the system of references for preliminary rulings under Art. 234 EC bears a direct similarity to references of questions of law from the French inferior courts to the Cour de Cassation. Again, there is no common law equivalent; the early judgments of the ECJ looked just like French judgments, with very little reasoning and no precedents cited. This was one of the most difficult aspects of E.C. law for the common lawyer to comprehend but the ECJ has now changed. For the sake of consistency, it takes serious account of its own precedents and cites them in its judgments and reported decisions contain much more reasoning than they formerly did, thus looking much more like common law judgments.

1-028   To add to all this, the European Court of Justice certainly accepts and applies broad principle in the same way that a court in a Roman-Germanic legal system would so this must be more predictable to members of other Member States than they seem to be to us. To compound this, as I explained above, all other Member States have written constitutions which spell out the relationship of domestic law and E.C. law and citizens of all other Member States are used to having their statutes measured against a higher form of law, the constitution. We are not and, in the way in which British politicians reacted to some ECJ judgments, we showed that we simply did not appreciate that our enacting of the European Communities Act 1972 was a very significant derogation from the supremacy of Parliament.

5. Keeping up-to-date with the English Legal System

1-029   The English legal system is the fastest changing area of English law. Like all law books, this one, finished in October 2001, will be out of date by the time you read it. If you are a law student, do yourself some favours, to keep up to date in all your legal studies.

* Never buy out-of-date law books. They are as dangerous as last week's cream cakes

* Show tutors/examiners that you have kept up to date by reading a quality daily newspaper, such as *The Times*, *The Financial Times*, *The Guardian* or *The Independent*. *The Times* has the greatest legal content, with a law supplement on Tuesdays. It also contains brief reports of recent cases, to help you keep up with your other legal studies. They are produced much more quickly than any other hard copy set of law reports. *The Guardian* contains useful analysis of social issues in the legal system, as does *The Independent*. If you cannot buy a paper, you can read them online. For instance, if you enter *The Times* website www.thetimes.co.uk and click on law, you will see all the recent articles archived, as well as law reports. You can also search through old newspaper articles in various news databases, such as *Lexis-Nexis*, if your library has it, and on CD-Rom. Many newspapers are available at half-price for students (see their websites). By getting into the habit of reading the newspapers, you can also make the law more interesting for yourself by understanding how law is about real people, in the real world. Law is not just in books.

* Take yourself off to court. The courts are a free source of daily entertainment, Mondays to Fridays. Justice in England and Wales is meant to be open to the public. Courts and tribunals are everywhere. Go and see how law operates in the real world, in sorting out people's disputes and responding to their offences. In this way you will learn a lot about procedure, the court structure, lawyers, magistrates and judges.

* Regularly browse the legal news journals, such as *The New Law Journal*, *Legal Action*, the Law Society's *Gazette* or *The Lawyer*.

* Visit relevant websites and check on What's New? The most useful for ELS is the Lord Chancellor's Department, in charge of the courts, legal services and judges and magistrates, www.lcd.gov.uk. The Home Office is in charge of the police and the criminal justice system so visit its site periodically, www.home-office.gov.uk. The criminal justice system and Youth Justice Board have their own sites and the LCD site is swift and user-friendly and has useful links. A quick, efficient and accurate way of keeping up with legal news is to browse through the press releases from these departments and then you can choose which topics to pursue on the site in more detail.

* Read my updates to this book, related articles and updates on all your legal subjects on the FREE Sweet and Maxwell website for students, www.sweetandmaxwell.co.uk/academic.

2. Sources of English Law

The sources of English and Welsh law are statute law (Acts of Parliament **2-001** and Statutory Instruments), other delegated legislation, common law (case law made by superior judges), E.C. law, the European Convention on Human Rights, international treaties, the residuary royal prerogative and, less obvious nowadays, books of authority and custom. Some Welsh law is also derived from delegated legislation resulting from policy debated and decided on in the Welsh Assembly, acting under powers devolved onto them from the Secretary of State for Wales, under the Government of Wales Act 1998 (details in the statute and on the Assembly website).

The major problems with this multitude of sources today are lack of accessibility and the tremendous bulk of law being produced and the consequent confusion, even among lawyers and judges. The common law presumption that everyone knows the law is demonstrably false.

This Chapter is a mere outline. For those who wish to know more about any of these sources of law, I strongly recommend you explore *Exploring the Law* and *The Law Making Process*. The latter provides a great explanation of how law is made and the former provides excellent examples of how English law develops from these sources.

1. Legislation

The most obvious source of codified law is an Act of Parliament, the **2-002** United Kingdom Parliament. In the British constitution, a fundamental doctrine is that of parliamentary sovereignty which recognises that supreme power is vested in Parliament and that there is no limit in law to the law-making capacity of that institution. This is now massively tempered by membership of the E.C. since 1973 and the importation of the European Convention on Human Rights by the Human Rights Act 1998, in 2000. Nevertheless, unless it conflicts with E.C. law or the Convention, what

2-003

Parliament passes in the form of an Act will be put into effect by the courts. This acceptance by the courts of parliamentary supremacy is entirely a matter of history derived directly from the seventeenth century conflict between the Stuart Kings and Parliament. In that conflict, the courts took the side of Parliament and one result of their joint success was that, thereafter, the courts have been prepared to acknowledge the supremacy of Parliament within its own sphere, whilst Parliament has readily allowed the independence of the judiciary to become an acknowledged factor in the constitution. The contrast with countries with a written constitution (most countries) is, however, very marked in that their Supreme Courts have the power to overrule legislation as being "unconstitutional." No such power exists in the English legal system. In *British Railways Board v. Pickin* (1974) an unsuccessful attempt was made to persuade the courts to intervene, on the grounds that the Board had obtained powers in a private Act of Parliament by misleading Parliament. The only role of the courts is to "interpret" the statutory provisions to the circumstances of any given case. If there is an element of human rights in issue, they must, where possible, interpret Acts so as to give effect to Convention rights and they are obliged to recognise E.C. law as supreme, if it conflicts with English law.

The Queen in Parliament

2-004

The United Kingdom Parliament is made up of three constituent elements: the monarch, the House of Lords and the House of Commons. An Act of Parliament normally has approval of all three elements. It can be passed without the approval of the Lords, using the Parliament Acts. This has only been done five times and occurred in 1991 with the War Crimes Act. Jack Straw, Home Secretary in 2001, threatened to use the Act again, to push a third Mode of Trial Bill through the Commons, the first two Bills having been defeated in the Lords. The monarch's place in Parliament is a formality. She attends the opening of a new session of Parliament, as she does each autumn and after each General Election when a new government is elected, such as in June 2001. She reads the speech from the throne, which is the Government's statement of its legislative proposals for the coming session of Parliament. The speech is written by the Prime Minister and does not in any way reflect her personal views. All legislation must receive the Royal Assent before it becomes law. It has not been refused since the reign of Queen Anne in 1707 and will never be refused, such is the strength of the constitutional convention that the monarchy does not interfere in politics.

Procedure

An Act of Parliament starts off as a Bill. Most Bills are Government Bills. Their clauses will have been agreed by the "sponsoring" department which has instructed parliamentary counsel to draft the Bill.

Before the Bill becomes an Act of Parliament, and the clauses become **2-005** sections, it must undergo five stages in each House. It may start off in the Commons or Lords. Once the Bill with any amendments has been approved both by the House of Commons and, normally, the House of Lords, it needs only the Royal Assent to become an Act of Parliament. It comes into immediate effect unless it contains its own starting date, or it has a provision which allows different parts of the Act to be brought into force at different times, by a Minister making a statutory instrument to that effect. For instance, different parts of the Crime and Disorder Act 1998 and the Access to Justice Act 1999 are still being brought into force in 2001, the time of writing. The Human Rights Act 1998 came into force in 2000. If you want to know more about parliamentary procedure and how Bills progress, call the Commons information desk—they provide an excellent set of fact sheets which are free and *accurate*—or log on to the website. Even better, go and watch proceedings yourself, free. If you want to watch the Committee rooms you can skip the queue. While you are there, go and watch the Law Lords hearing a case. They hold their court in a room at the end of the Lords' Committee corridor.

The Form of an Act of Parliament

Language
Statutory language must be precise. Every Act must relate to existing **2-006** legislation on the subject so clauses often amend old Acts or cross-refer to others. Further, although the modern aim is to draft the law in plain English, the endeavour to close loopholes also makes Acts complex. In 1995, I watched an argument between a parliamentary draftsman and a tax lawyer, at a conference on legislation. The tax lawyer accused the draftsman of making the Finance Acts too complicated for ordinary people to understand. The draftsman retorted that if clients stopped paying tax lawyers like him large amounts of money to find loopholes, he could draft them in simpler language. Controversial or big Bills suffer many amendments, especially by the Government who introduced them. It is said that there is a tendency to introduce big Bills in outline and fill in the details as they pass through Parliament. These factors combine to make statutes complicated and notoriously difficult for the lay person to understand. Although the earliest statutes had long titles and preambles, since the Short Titles Act 1896, Acts of Parliament have been given a short title and preambles have become the exception.

Citation
From 1963 every Act is given a Chapter number for the year in which **2-007** it receives the Royal Assent. This abolishes the centuries-old system by which Acts were given a Chapter number for the session of the parlia-

ment in question designated by the regnal year of the monarch. This system could produce difficulties. For instance, 1937 under the former system was cited as "1 Edw. 8 and 1 Geo. 6." The present system is to refer to an Act by its short title and Chapter number for the year in question: for example, The Crime and Disorder Act 1998 (chap. 37).

Acts are published by Her Majesty's Stationery Office (HMSO). It is headed by a Controller and operates as part of the Cabinet Office. He is the Queen's Printer and responsible for all legislation of the United Kingdom legislatures and command papers. In practice, HMSO makes new legislation available for sale to the public as soon as it has been given the Royal Assent. It is available free online from the HMSO, with all public Acts from 1988. The Government's other publications, such as the Highway Code, Ordinance Survey Maps and reports of inquiries are published by The Stationery Office, privatised in 1996.

Public Bills and Private Bills

2-008 A Public Bill is legislation which affects the public at large, and applies throughout England and Wales. Most Bills are Public and sponsored by the Government. A Private Bill is legislation which affects a limited section of the population, either by reference to locality or by reference to a particular family or group of individuals. These are known respectively as Local and Personal Bills. A Private Member's Bill is a Public Bill introduced by a back-bench Member of Parliament, who has been successful in the ballot. A Hybrid Bill may cover work of national importance but in a local area. Examples are the Channel Tunnel Bills of the 1970s and 1980s.

Consolidation, codification and statute law revision

Consolidation is the process by which provisions in a number of Acts of Parliament are brought together and re-enacted in one Act. It is not a method for changing the law but it does make the law easier to find. In order to ease the passage of such measures, they go through Parliament in special procedure. In 2000 for example, the legislation concerning sentencing was consolidated in the Powers of the Criminal Courts (Sentencing) Act 2000.

Codification is the term used for an Act of Parliament which brings together all the existing legislation and case law and forms a complete restatement of the law. It can involve changes in the law and is thus one method of law reform. Recently, Lord Chief Justice Bingham added his weight to the academics' increasingly impatient demand for a codification of the criminal law and Professor Spencer added a persuasive and reasoned argument for codifying criminal procedure and the Government has included plans for a code in its legislative proposals announced in its 2001 white paper, *Criminal Justice: The Way Ahead*

(2001). See more discussion on codification in the Chapter on law reform.

The Law Commission, which was set up under the Law Commissions **2-009** Act 1965, has, as one of its responsibilities, to keep under review all the law with a view to its systematic development and reform including, in particular, the codification of the law. It is consequently working at the present time on possible legislation which will, at some future time, codify particular branches of the law.

Statute law revision is the procedure under which obsolete provisions in statutes are repealed and legislation is kept up to date. This is now a matter for the Law Commission which has overall responsibility for advising the repeal of obsolete and unnecessary enactments.

Since 1993/1994, a Special Public Bill Committee "fast-track" procedure has been used for legislation proposed by the Law Commission and other non-contentious Bills. This "Jellicoe procedure" employs a committee of specialists (*e.g.* judges and lawyers on The Arbitration Bill 1996) instead of a committee of the whole House. Lord Chancellor Mackay's ill-fated Domestic Violence Bill 1995 was supposed to be one such Bill. Unfortunately, it proved to be very controversial and was lost. We come back to the Law Commission in the Chapter on law reform.

Delegated Legislation

This is the name given to law made in documentary form by subordi- **2-010** nate authorities acting under law-making powers delegated by Parliament or the sovereign, acting under her prerogative. Parliament does not have time or expertise to fill in the details or technicalities of the law so most big Bills are mere frameworks. The big difference between Acts of Parliament (primary legislation) and subordinate or delegated legislation is that the courts can quash the latter if it is outside the remit of delegated power (substantively *ultra vires*) or has not been made in a procedurally correct way (procedurally *ultra vires*). The Court of Appeal confirmed that it was entitled to review subordinate legislation on the grounds of illegality, procedural impropriety or *Wednesbury* unreasonableness, even where it had been debated and approved by affirmative resolution of both Houses of Parliament. The Court was entitled to assess for itself the facts presented to Parliament as supporting the legality of the subordinate legislation. The extent to which a statutory power was open to judicial review on the ground of irrationality depended critically on the nature and purpose of the enabling legislation: *R. (Javed) v. S.S. for Home Department* and joined cases (2001).

Such legislation can take the following forms.

Orders in Council

Parliament sometimes permits the Government through Her Majesty **2-011** in Council to make law by way of an Order in Council. This is particularly true where an emergency is imminent. Orders in Council are sometimes issued under a prerogative power, as was the Order in Council concerned in the case of *C.C.S.U. v. Minister for the Civil Service* (1984), otherwise known as "the GCHQ case", which Margaret Thatcher used to issue a ban on trade union membership in GCHQ. An Order in Council requires the formality of a meeting of the Privy Council in the presence of the Queen. Practically, the decision to use prerogative power in this way is made by the Cabinet, or a small section thereof.

Statutory instruments

A more common form of delegated legislation is the power frequently given to ministers to make law for a specified purpose. The document containing this law is called a statutory instrument and thousands are issued every year. As each one is published it is given a number for the year, for example, the Area Fishing (Enforcement of Community Quota and Third Country Fishing Measures) Order 2001 (S.I. 2001 No. 1631). Statutory instruments have become of major importance as a source of law. Much more law is contained in them than in Acts. Almost all E.C. law comes into English law via statutory instruments, like the one just mentioned.

Byelaws

2-012   Parliament delegates to local authorities and other public bodies the power to make local laws or laws limited to their particular functions. Thus local authorities can make town laws, or byelaws, for their areas. For instance, there are often rules governing behaviour in parks or leisure centres. Even so the authority has to obtain confirmation of the byelaws from the named central government minister before the byelaws take effect. The power to make byelaws also belongs to public bodies such as the British Airports Authority. Byelaws can be quashed on judicial review by the Divisional Court of the QBD if they are *ultra vires*, or their illegality can be used as a defence where someone is prosecuted for infringing them. This happened to Lindis Percy, a protester against U.S. defence forces in this country. She appealed to the Crown Court against her conviction for breach of byelaws by repeatedly entering a secure defence installation and the Crown Court upheld her appeal, holding the byelaws to be *ultra vires* the Military Lands Act 1892, the enabling Act (facts in *S.S. for Defence v. Percy* (1999, HC)). Another example is *Boddington v. British Transport Police* (1998, HL), where B sought to defend himself from a charge of illegally smoking on a railway carriage on the ground that the posting of no smoking notices by Network South Central was *ultra vires*. He was convicted and the House of Lords dismissed his last appeal.

24

Comment on delegated legislation

Since the mid-point of the twentieth century, there has been increas-   **2-013**
ing concern that Acts are mere frameworks, giving substantial powers to
Ministers to fill in the details through delegated powers, usually using statutory instruments. For instance, the Access to Justice Act 1999 provides a
new framework for the provision of legal services but leaves it up to the
Lord Chancellor to devise a funding code to say what types of litigation
will be publicly funded and leaves it up to regional bodies to allocate priorities in spending their budget. Concern has repeatedly been expressed
that too much legislative power is being given to the executive. The Lords
raised this concern in a debate in 1991, citing the Child Support Act,
which gave over 100 regulation-making powers to the Minister and
others, most of which were subjected to the negative procedure, by which
a statutory instrument automatically becomes law, unless concerns about
it are positively raised in Parliament.

In recent years there has been concern over the frequent use of "Henry
VIII" sections in Acts which permit a Minister to amend primary legislation, an Act, through a statutory instrument. Such a power, for a Minister to "fast-track" an amendment to a piece of legislation incompatible
with the European Convention on Human Rights, is contained in the
Human Rights Act 1998. This caused concern in the passage of the Bill
through the Lords.

2. Statutory Interpretation

"Rules" for Statutory Interpretation

Inevitably, disputes arise as to the meaning or application of legislation   **2-014**
and the task of the judges in this context is, therefore, described as that of
statutory interpretation. Judges are not the only people who need to interpret statutes. Law lecturers and students and lawyers advising their clients
need to do so. Judges of the lower courts need to interpret statutes for
their own sake and sometimes for juries. Magistrates' clerks (legal advisers) need to know how to advise their bench. Civil servants and local
government officers need to know how to apply the law to us. Most
importantly, as ordinary citizens, all of us are presumed to know the law
so we need to understand the way our business and social lives are regulated and what our rights (*e.g.* as employee) and duties (*e.g.* to pay tax) are.
Before I describe the "rules" for this I should explain that two experts on
statutory interpretation, Cross and Bennion, insist that there are no such
"rules". Bennion said Cross wrote his book to prove there were no such
rules. In Bennion's own first edition, 1984, he said there are no such rules.
"Instead there are a thousand and one interpretive criteria." (See
Bennion's letter). Nevertheless, judges have developed a set of common

25

law principles to help them interpret statutes that are known as the rules of statutory interpretation. It is important to understand that judges do not articulate the application of these "rules" but they do tend to apply them sequentially. The labels of these "rules" are now simply a construct for academic analysis. Cross and other commentators argue that judges now take a "contextual approach". (See Cross, *Statutory Interpretation*). In doing this, judges claim to be searching for "the will of Parliament" and sometimes they articulate this. For instance, in *R. v. Chief Constable of the R.U.C., ex parte Begley* (1997), Lord Browne Wilkinson explained this limit on the House's role in developing the common law, as he saw it:

> "It is true that the House has power to develop the law. But it is a limited power. And it can be exercised only in the gaps left by Parliament. It is impermissible for the House to develop the law in a direction which is contrary to the expressed will of Parliament."

The first tactic judges use is to look for definitions of contentious words. The Interpretation Act is generally useful. One of its better-known sections provides that "unless the contrary intention appears (a) words importing the masculine gender include the feminine (and vice versa) (b) words in the singular include the plural, and words in the plural include the singular". Most statutes contain definitions of the words they use, especially if they are novel, so The Crime and Disorder Act 1998, s. 85 defines "action plan order" and "drug treatment and testing order", for example. Sometimes words are left undefined and it is for the courts to determine their application. The Harassment Act 1997 does not define harassment but the High Court decided it did not include the activities of Microsoft, intimidating a software counterfeiter by provoking police raids, conducting oppressive litigation and telephoning the claimants at night: *Tuppen v. Microsoft* (2000).

2-015   The first principle in interpretation is that the judge should apply the words according to their "ordinary, plain and natural meaning". In *Clarke v. Kato* (1998) the House of Lords held that as a matter of ordinary language, a car park did not qualify as a road for the purposes of the Road Traffic Act 1998 so as to be an area in respect of which a motor insurance policy had to provide cover.

Unfortunately, the courts sometimes find themselves bound by the literal words of an Act into an interpretation which they consider leads to a daft result. In *Horsman* (1997), the Court of Appeal decided it could not substitute a conviction for another offence, where a defendant had pleaded guilty because the Criminal Appeal Act 1968 clearly contemplated expressly a jury verdict and provided no other power. Lord Justice Waller said "the powers of the Court of Appeal flow only from statute, and however anomalous, if the words of the section are clear, there is no room for construing them in any other way . . . the question whether there should not be some amendment should be looked at with some haste". Sometimes judges are frustrated that a legislative oversight can produce a harsh result in unforeseen circumstances. A poignant example was *R. v. Human Fertilisation and Embryology Authority, ex parte Blood* (1996/1997). Diane Blood and her husband had decided to have a baby. Before she got a chance to conceive, her husband died of meningitis. While he was still in a coma, a sample of sperm was removed and frozen and his widow, Mrs Blood wanted to use it to conceive. The Human Fertilisation and Embryology Act required a man's written consent for the storage or use of his sperm in the United Kingdom. Much as the judge and the public had "universal sympathy" (Stephen Brown J.) for the weeping Mrs. Blood's "double bereavement", he could not surmount the clear requirement of the Act. Baroness Warnock, whose committee's finding led to the Act, blamed herself for not foreseeing such a case and Lord Winston, the famous fertility specialist, called the result "cruel and unnatural". The Court of Appeal too felt "all the courts . . . can do is give effect to the clear language of the Act" (*per* Woolf M.R.). Happily, they allowed her appeal on a point of E.C. law. They ruled that she had the right to take the sperm for insemination elsewhere in the E.C. She conceived in 1998.

Sometimes a case can be spared a bad outcome which would result **2-016** from a literal interpretation, because a second principle which has become known as the golden rule, is that the literal application need not be applied, if to do so would lead to absurdity or to inconsistency within the statute itself. An outstanding example of the golden rule occurred in *Re Sigsworth* (1935), where a man was found to have murdered his mother. In the statute dealing with the distribution of the mother's estate it was laid down that the estate was to be distributed amongst "the issue". The son was her only child. The judge held that the common law rule that a murderer cannot take any benefit from the estate of a person he had murdered prevailed over the apparently clear words of the statute.

A third principle is that if the so called literal or golden rules fail to assist, the judge is entitled to consider the "mischief" rule. This rule, which was first settled in *Heydon's Case* in 1584, allows the judge to consider (1) what was the common law, (2) what was the defect or mischief in the common law, (3) what remedy Parliament in the legislation has provided for the defect. Here, a judge is entitled to examine existing legislation and case law before coming to a decision, with the intention that the ruling will "suppress the mischief and advance the remedy." In *Bournemouth Community and Health NHS Trust, ex parte L* (1998), the House of Lords held that the statutory predecessor to section 131(1) of the Mental Health Act 1983 was designed to cure the mischief caused by the assumption that compulsory powers had to be used unless the patient could express a positive desire for treatment, and to replace that by the offer of care, without deprivation of liberty, to all who needed it and were not unwilling to receive it.

2-017   The court is not easily persuaded to reject the plain words of the statute. Lord Scarman in *Stock v. Frank Jones (Tipton) Ltd* (1978) explained that: "if the words used by Parliament are plain there is no room for the anomalies test, unless the consequences are so absurd that without going outside the statute, one can see that Parliament must have made a drafting mistake . . . but mere manifest absurdity is not enough; it must be an error (of commission or omission) which in its context defeats the intention of the Act".

Nevertheless, in *Inco Europe v. First Choice Distribution* (2000) the House of Lords said the courts must be able to correct obvious drafting errors. In suitable cases, the court can add, omit or substitute words. Before doing so, they must be abundantly sure of three matters:

1.   the intended purpose of the statute or provision in question;
2.   that by inadvertence, the draftsman and Parliament had failed to give effect to that purpose in the provision in question; and
3.   the substance of the provision that Parliament would have made, although not necessarily the precise words that it would have used, had the error in the Bill been noticed.

Drafting errors and omissions may occur because of the number of amendments made as a big Bill passes through Parliament. A famous example of this is section 16 of the Theft Act 1968, which became known as "a judicial nightmare" and remained uncorrected until the Theft Act 1978. Lord Goff closely examined *Hansard* and recounted its messy legislative history in *Preddy* (1996, HL) and commented:

> "hurried amendments to carefully structured comprehensive Bills are an accident-prone form of proceeding; and the new s.16 . . . proved to be so incomprehensible as to be unworkable in practice".

2-018   Sometimes legislation proves to be completely unworkable and this has repeatedly occurred in the area of criminal procedure and sentencing, which has been the subject of far too much legislation. For instance, the Criminal Justice and Public Order Act 1994 purported to do away with committals from magistrates' courts to the Crown Court and to replace them with transfer proceedings. When Epsom Magistrates' Court tried to use the new transfer scheme in September 1995, the bench and clerk found it did not work. Eventually, the section was abandoned and a new scheme created in 1998. Academics and the Law Commission get very frustrated when they have warned that there are gaps in a Bill or defects and Ministers just ignore or even ridicule them. This frustration is expressed by Ashworth in an editorial of the March 1996 *Criminal Law Review* and has frequently been complained of by Sir John Smith, especially when things go wrong, in the nature of "I told you so" comments in the *Criminal Law Review.*

Other "Rules" (Aids to Interpretation)

Where specific words are followed by general words, the general words **2-019** must be given effect in the light of the foregoing specific words. This is called the *"ejusdem generis"* rule. An example is *Hobbs v. C.G. Robertson Ltd* (1970) where the Court of Appeal had to construe the following phrase concerning the provision of goggles in the Construction (General Provision) Regulations 1961 "breaking, cutting, dressing or carving of stone, concrete, slag or similar materials" to circumstances where a workman injured an eye, through the splintering of brickwork from a chimney breast which he was required to remove. The Court applied the *ejusdem generis* rule in holding that brick was not "a similar material" to stone, concrete or slag; the provision of goggles was, therefore, not compulsory and the workman's claim failed. A connected rule is that where, in a statute, there is a list of specified matters, which is not followed by general words, then only the matters actually mentioned are caught by this provision of the Act. The Latin phrase for this is *"expressio unius est exclusio alterius"*. In *R. v. Inhabitants of Sedgley* (1831) a statutory provision for rating occupiers of "lands, houses, tithes and coal mines" was held not to apply to any other kind of mine and in *B. v. D.P.P.* (1998), the Court of Appeal applied the rule (not saying they were doing so) in interpreting the Sexual Offences Act 1956. The inclusion of a specific statutory defence in two sections demonstrated conclusively that Parliament did not intend that the defence should be available for other offences where a defence was not mentioned. The rule *"noscitur a sociis"* means that where two or more words follow each other in a statute, they must be taken as related for the purpose of interpretation. For example, in *Inland Revenue Commissioners v. Frere* (1965) the House of Lords held that in the relevant phrase of the statute "interest, annuities or other annual payments" the word "interest" meant annual interest.

It is accepted practice that a statute must be taken as a whole. **2-020** Consequently it follows that a judge must relate a word or phrase in a statute to its place in the context of the whole measure.

Other presumptions are that:
  (i)   there is no change in the existing law beyond that expressly stated in the legislation;
  (ii) the Crown is not bound unless the Act specifically makes it so. The Windsors can only be prosecuted for speeding because the Road Traffic Act binds the Crown;

(iii) legislation is not intended to apply retrospectively, unless this is expressly stated to be the case;

(iv) any change in the law affecting the liberties of the subject must be expressly and specifically stated;

(v) any liability for a criminal offence must be on the basis of fault, unless the words of the statute clearly intend otherwise;

(vi) the legislation applies throughout the United Kingdom unless an exemption for Scotland or Northern Ireland is stated. Because Scotland, in particular, has its own legal and local government system, it is common for Parliament to legislate for Scotland separately and now much of this legislative power has been passed to the Scottish Parliament;

(vii) if the provisions of two Acts appear to be in conflict, the court will endeavour to reconcile them, since there is no presumption of implied repeal. If reconciliation is not possible, logic demands that the later provision be given effect. For instance, *Padmore v. Inland Revenue Commissioners (No.2)* (2001, HC), the Court had to resolve a conflict between two inconsistent tax provisions. The Chancery Division held that where the Act being construed is a consolidating Act, it is only permissible to take into account the earlier legislation if the later language is ambiguous, obscure or would lead to an absurdity. Where there is a conflict between two sections in the same statute, the court must do its best to reconcile them and may read words into the statute, to give effect to plain legislative intent;

(viii) legislation must be construed so as not to conflict with E.C. law. (See Chapter on E.C. law);

(ix) legislation must be construed so as to give effect to the European Convention on Human Rights where possible. (See Chapter on the Convention);

(x) Parliament intends to give effect to international treaties to which the United Kingdom is a contracting party.

Extrinsic Aids

2-021   Judges decided that they would refrain from consulting *Hansard*, the report of debates on a Bill through Parliament and would only permit reference to preparatory documents to determine the mischief the Act sought to remedy. They set out guidelines in *Black-Clawson v. Papierwerke* (1975, HL). The reason for this rule is that people should be entitled to know the law by taking an Act at face value. Furthermore the intentions of, say, the Lord Chancellor, in introducing the Courts and Legal Services Bill may have differed from the "intention of Parliament", in passing the Act, after it had been debated and amended. Because of this rule the judge was unable, theoretically, to make use of Parliamentary debates, reports of committees or commissions or what the government Ministers involved had said about the measure as evidence of Parliamentary intent. This rule, that no extrinsic aids would be used, ensured that Parliament had a complete obligation to express itself precisely when making new law.

Serious inroads into this rule, significantly altering the judicial role in statutory interpretation, were made by the House of Lords in *Pepper v. Hart* (1993). In this case, the question arose whether, under the Finance Act 1976, Parliament had intended school teachers at private schools to be taxed on the full value of the benefit in kind of the private education offered to their own children. The House of Lords ruled, erroneously, that this had been Parliament's intention. Their Lordships' attention was later drawn to the statement of the sponsoring minister. From this, it became clear that the true intention was that the teachers should only be taxed on the cost to their employers, which was minimal, so an Appellate Committee of seven Law Lords was reconvened and the case reargued, with reference to *Hansard*.

2-022

Their Lordships held that Parliamentary materials should only be referred to where:

"(a) legislation is ambiguous or obscure or leads to an absurdity;
(b) the material relied on consists of one or more statements by a minister or other promoter of the Bill together if necessary with such other Parliamentary material as is necessary to understand such statements and their effect;
(c) the statements relied on are clear" (*per* Lord Browne-Wilkinson).

Despite their Lordships' warnings that this new activity was to be the exception, judges and counsel in cases since 1993 have made frequent use of the *Pepper v. Hart* principle, even where there is little ambiguity in a statute and case law has extended the rule to allow reference to preparatory material, such as green papers and white papers, and reports of the Law Commission and Royal Commissions. Even back in the 1970s, the Master of the Rolls, Lord Denning, and the Lord Chancellor, Lord Hailsham, said they always consulted *Hansard*. Drawing attention to the dangers of all this, the editors of *Cross on Statutory Interpretation* (1995 ed.) say it creates more work for lawyers, in advising clients and preparing litigation. Resorting to all these extrinsic aids, they comment, is no substitute for the clearest possible drafting of the text of the statute. Dame Mary Arden, when chairman of the Law Commission, warned of the dangers of *Pepper v. Hart*. Ministers might prefer to have Bills drafted in general terms and make good the deficiency with a speech in Parliament. The executive might try to take short cuts by failing to get legislation accurate and relying on departmental notes on clauses. This would strengthen

2-023

the power of the executive over Parliament. She said these dangers had been recognised. Departmental legal advisers scrutinised ministerial speeches in *Hansard* and if they were inaccurate, the Minister could correct a mistake at an appropriate point during further consideration of a Bill.

2-024   An example of the application of *Pepper v. Hart* appears in *Mullen* (1999, CA), where Lord Justice Auld resorted to parliamentary debates to interpret the Criminal Appeal Act 1995. The case appears in the Chapter on criminal procedure. Looking at *Hansard*, he decided that the meaning of "unsafe" conviction in the amended form of the Criminal Appeal Act 1968 was meant to be the same as before the 1995 amendment. In other words, to restate the practice of the Court of Appeal, over the years, in deciding what constituted sufficient grounds for quashing.

Different considerations apply in the case of a statute which incorporates an international convention. Here, exceptionally, the court must have regard to the full background and reference may be made to relevant material which explains the provisions in the convention. For a discussion of the approach of the English courts in interpreting international law in recent cases, including the *Pinochet* cases, see the very useful article by Qureshi.

Intrinsic Aids

The judge is, however, entitled to find assistance from the intrinsic aids contained in the statute itself; these include the long title, marginal notes, headings, which may be prefixed to a part of the Act, and Schedules, which are part of the Act although they do not affect words used in the body of the Act unless these are ambiguous. Preambles may also be used in statutory interpretation, although they are rarely used in modern statutes. E.C. legislation makes regular use of preambles. The famous "Eurobananas" Regulation of 1994, regulating standards of bananas, contains a preamble longer than the text. The European Court of Justice examines these preambles as a matter of course, in interpreting E.C. legislation.

Punctuation is referred to in interpreting the meaning of a sentence in the same way as we use it as an essential guide to the sense of normal everyday English.

Criticism

2-025   It can be gathered from the strictness of the approach articulated by some judges that if the words of a statute fail to deal with a particular situation, there is no power in a court to fill the gap, despite the fact that Lord Denning M.R. often claimed "We fill in the gaps." This absence of provision is known as "*casus omissus*", and in general the principle requires Parliament to pass a new statute to make good the deficiency. Lord Simonds in *Magor and St. Mellors R.D.C. v. Newport Corporation* (1952) said on this point "the power and duty of the court to travel outside them (the words of a statute) on a voyage of discovery are strictly limited. . . . If a gap is disclosed, the remedy lies in an amending Act."

This view is unrealistic. Generally Parliament, save in taxation cases, is very slow to amend faulty legislation. In recent years, however, the House of Lords seems to have grasped the nettle and become much more willing to give a purposive construction to legislation. In the *Fothergill* case (above) Lord Diplock is explicitly critical of Lord Simonds' approach and lays the blame for unsatisfactory rules of statutory interpretation on the judges' "narrowly semantic approach to statutory construction, until the last decade or so".

Criticism used to be made fairly often and somewhat more infrequently now of the inflexible attitude of some judges in the task of statutory interpretation. In view of the difficulty of using language with an exactness which covers every conceivable situation, including the future, critics claim that the task of construction would be better done if judges took off their blinkers and considered all the circumstances which are relevant to the interpretation of the legislation in the particular case. Judging from the wide application given to *Pepper v. Hart,* many modern judges agree with this criticism. Taking a broad, purposive approach, they apparently relish the opportunity to consult extrinsic aids. On the other hand, they may decline to do so in the face of clear language. An example is the *Cato* case above. Here Lord Clyde, speaking for the Law Lords, rejected an invitation to include car parks in the definition of "road" to give a purposive construction, because it would strain the word "road" beyond what it meant in ordinary usage. **2-026**

Recently, some commentators have made sweeping statements that judges now favour a broad purposive approach. This simply is not true in most cases, as the above cases demonstrate and as can be seen from any trawl through recent *Times* law reports. The reason is that judges cannot use the purposive approach to avoid clear words. Lord Steyn said in *IRC v. McGuckian* (1997, H.L.)

"During the last 30 years there has been a shift away from the literalist approach to purposive methods of construction. When there is no obvious meaning of a statutory provision the modern emphasis is on a contextual approach designed to identify the purpose of a statute and to give effect to it."

(See his application of the purposive approach in *R. v. A* (2001) which I analyse in depth in the Chapter on human rights.) But Dame Mary Arden, quoting him, added that the courts can only apply a purposive approach where the purpose is sufficiently clear.

Nevertheless, one can identify some cases where judges clearly articulate that they are taking a purposive approach and they explain why. In **2-027** one such case, judges were anxious to enforce safety on the railways and rejected the literal interpretation sought by Railtrack to excuse itself. Indeed, they even thought it regrettable that Railtrack had appealed the case, remarking that the sight of Railtrack engaged in litigation with its inspectorate was not likely to enhance public confidence: *Railtrack plc v. Smallwood* (2001, QBD). Another example is *R. v. Colohan* (2001), where the Court of Appeal interpreted the Protection from Harassment Act 1997, which leaves much in general terms for judges to interpret on a case by case basis. They mentioned the purpose of the Act but thought its wording "abundantly clear". Another excellent and explicit example of a purposive interpretation is *Callery v. Gray* (2001) where the Court of Appeal had to make sense of the Access to Justice Act's provisions as to costs in conditional fee agreement cases (see legal services Chapter).

Both the European Court of Human Rights and the ECJ take a broad purposive approach to interpretation, described as "teleological". English and Welsh judges are well aware of this and use it themselves in relevant cases but some of them have adopted the habit in their interpretive tasks, even where the case has nothing to do with E.C. law or the Convention. For a detailed analysis of the most important case so far applying the Convention in statutory interpretation, see my analysis of *R. v. A*, in the Chapter on the Convention.

Another, in some ways more serious, criticism is that there is a lack of consistency in the application of the rules. It is suggested that judges may use whichever rule leads to the result which they wish to achieve; on one occasion they will rely on the literal rule, whereas on another they will reject it.

2-028   In a 1992 critique, *Making The Law*, the Hansard Commission recommended that for every Act of Parliament, the relevant government department and Parliamentary Counsel should prepare "notes on sections", an updated version of the "notes on clauses" prepared for a Minister during the passage of a Bill. These should be published with the Act and used by the courts in interpreting it. See the research and critique by Sacks. She did research to try and ascertain whether judges are given sufficient guidelines to help them perform their task. She found that problematic wording in statutes did not always arise from careless drafting or because Parliament did not foresee a particular situation, as was commonly assumed. It was sometimes because "the Government either lacked clear objectives or, had deliberately intended to obfuscate in order to avoid controversy". References to *Hansard* did not help. "Time and again Members of Parliament pleaded for enlightenment." Worse, many difficult clauses received no debating time. She says this reflects badly on the parliamentary scrutiny process itself and calls for the adoption of a method used by the French. She warns of the dangers of selective reading from *Hansard* and the inconsistent use of background reports. She repeats the recommendation of the Renton Committee and others that a statement of intent be included in every Act. This was done in the Courts and Legal Services Act 1990 but not in some of the other major statutes cited in this book. A Bill, she recommends, ought to be accompanied by a very detailed explanatory memorandum, as it proceeds through Parliament. This is done in other parliaments.

At last, New Labour promised to make legislation more accessible and is attempting to fulfill that promise. Since the beginning of the 1998–1999 parliamentary session, Bills are being presented with fairly full "explanatory notes", written in clear and simple English. This is explained, and some of the difficulties of the drafter, by Christopher Jenkins, the First Parliamentary Counsel in an article which is well worth reading.   **2-029**

The attempt to make legislation more comprehensible has a long and somewhat fruitless history. The Statute Law Society was formed in 1968. Its main object was to procure technical improvements in the form and manner in which legislation is expressed and published so as to make it more intelligible. Its first report, in 1970, said procedures must be governed by the needs of the user. This was approved in 1975 by the Renton Committee. The Rippon Commission followed almost 20 years later and listed the following principles:

- Laws are made for the benefit of citizens.
- All citizens should be involved as fully and openly as possible in the way statute law is prepared.
- Statute law should be as certain and intelligible as possible for the benefit of citizens.
- Statute law should be rooted in the authority of Parliament and thoroughly exposed to democratic scrutiny.
- Ignorance of the law being no excuse, statute law had to be as accessible as possible.
- Although governments need to be able to secure the passage of their legislation, to get the law right and intelligible is as important as getting it passed quickly.

In the meantime, tax lawyers, among others, were still frustrated by the complexity of Finance Acts. In 1996, the Inland Revenue admitted tax law could be simplified and a rewrite project was launched. The Capital Allowances Bill 2001 was subjected to a four-stage consultative process involving users of tax legislation. Also in 2001, the Lords and Commons set up a Joint Committee on Tax Simplification Bills.

Tax lawyers and taxpayers are not the only people who get frustrated   **2-030**
by confusing legislation. The group which undoubtedly has the biggest struggle and suffers from the greatest volume of legislation, as well as some of the most ill-drafted, complex and often unworkable legislation,

are magistrates' clerks. The Justices' Clerks' Society tries to answer interpretive questions and frequently identifies lacunae in the law. They have formulated the policy that where there is a lack of clarity, any doubt should be resolved in the defendant's favour.

3. Case Law

2-031   Remembering that the English legal system is a common law system, indeed the mother of all common law systems, the significance of case law, *i.e.* common law in creating and, presently, refining our laws cannot be underestimated. The law produced by the courts can be just as important as the law produced by Parliament. For instance, in 1991, the House of Lords abolished the rule protecting a husband from criminal responsibility for raping his wife. By case law is meant the decisions of judges laying down legal principles derived from the circumstances of the particular disputes coming before them.

The Meaning of Precedent

2-032   The reason why such importance is attached to case decisions is explained by this doctrine of judicial precedent, which is also known as "*stare decisis*" (to stand by decisions). This doctrine, in its simplest form, means that when a judge comes to try a case, she must always look back to see how previous judges have dealt with previous cases (precedents) which have involved similar facts in that branch of the law. In looking back in this way the judge will expect to discover those principles of law which are relevant to the case under consideration. The decision which she makes will thus seek to be consistent with the existing principles in that branch of the law, and may, in its turn, develop those principles a stage further.

Because the branches of English law have been gradually built up over the centuries, there are now hundreds of thousands of reported case decisions available in hard copy, CD-Rom or online, with many more on databases such as *Lexis* so that the task of discovering relevant precedents and achieving consistency is by no means simple. The standing of a precedent is governed by the status of the court which decided the case. Decisions of the House of Lords are obviously to be treated with the greatest respect, whereas a decision of a county court judge has normally limited effect. This quite common sense approach has developed into a rigid system under which precedents of the superior courts, if found to be relevant to the facts of a particular case, are treated as "binding" on the lower courts, so that the judge in the lower court must follow the reasoning and apply it to the case in hand. The judge is thus obliged to decide the case in accordance with binding judicial precedent.

The Doctrine of Precedent in Operation

The system operates as a hierarchy.

The European Court of Justice and the European Court of Human Rights

Decisions of the former are binding on all English and Welsh courts. Decisions of the latter must be taken account of.

The House of Lords

Decisions of the House of Lords are binding on all the courts lower in the hierarchy. This is so not only where the facts of the later case are identical, which will be very rare, but also where the facts of the case call for the application of the same legal principle as in the House of Lords case. Until 1966, by reason of the binding nature of judicial precedent, a decision of the House of Lords, once made, remained binding on itself, as well as on all the courts lower in the structure. In 1966, by a formal Practice Statement, the House of Lords judges announced that in future they would not regard themselves as necessarily bound by their own previous decisions. The Practice Statement is worth quoting at length, as it gives us a neat summary of the arguments for and against a rigid system of binding precedent.

> "Their Lordships regard the use of precedent as an indispensable foundation upon which to decide what is the law and its application to individual cases. It provides at least some degree of certainty upon which individuals can rely in the conduct of their affairs, as well as a basis for orderly development of legal rules. Their Lordships nevertheless recognise that too rigid adherence to precedent may lead to injustice in a particular case and also unduly restrict the proper development of the law. They propose, therefore, to modify their present practice and, while treating former decisions of this House as normally binding, to depart from a previous decision when it appears right to do so. In this connection they will bear in mind the danger of disturbing retrospectively the basis on which contracts, settlements of property and fiscal arrangements have been entered into and also the especial need for certainty as to the criminal law. This announcement is not intended to affect the use of precedent elsewhere than in this House."

There have not been many instances since the 1966 Practice Statement of the House of Lords departing from a previous decision. In *Herrington v. British Railways Board* (1972) the Court revised a long-standing legal principle concerned with the duty of care owed to a child trespasser. In

R. v. Shivpuri (1986) the House of Lords departed from a decision given only one year earlier when reconsidering the law relating to criminal attempts.

The Court of Appeal

2-035   The Civil Division of the Court of Appeal by its decisions binds all the courts in the structure except the House of Lords. The Court of Appeal does bind itself for the future, according to the decision in *Young v. Bristol Aeroplane Co.* (1944) although it may escape if (i) a later decision of the House of Lords applies; (ii) there are previous conflicting decisions of the Court of Appeal; or (iii) where the previous decision was made "*per incuriam*", *i.e.* in error, because some relevant precedent or statutory provision was not considered by the Court. A great example of such a decision, which the Divisional Court of the QBD held was decided *per incuriam* and thus not even binding on a magistrate, was *Thai Trading* (1998, CA), on the legality of a contingency fee agreement entered into by a solicitor. The House of Lords authority of *Swain v. Law Society* (1983) had not been cited. It was obviously binding on the Court of Appeal and they decided wrongly, in ignorance of it, so *Thai Trading* is a *per incuriam* decision and not binding on any court. Note that the respondents in the case were unrepresented. With an increasing number of litigants in person, this problem is bound to occur, which is why Lord Justice Otton invented judicial assistants to do background research for judges in cases like this. See the Chapter on legal services.

2-036   Lord Denning, when Master of the Rolls, tried to avoid this rule. The Criminal Division of the Court of Appeal does not consider itself always bound by its own decisions. Where the liberty of the subject is concerned, the court feels itself free to overrule a previous decision if it appears that in that decision the law was misunderstood or misapplied "and if a departure from authority is necessary in the interests of justice to an appellant": *R. v. Spencer* (1985). An example of this occurred in *R. v. Shoult* (1996, CA). A court led by Lord Taylor, L.C.J., declined to follow *R. v. Cook* (1995, CA), in considering an appeal against a prison sentence for a drink-driving conviction. This will especially apply since October 2000, where the court chooses to modify the law in accordance with the European Convention on Human Rights and can clearly be seen in the case law on the Criminal Appeal Act discussed in the Chapter on procedure.

The High Court

2-037   Decisions of a single judge in the three divisions of the High Court are binding on the lower courts but not on other High Court judges. If a High Court judge is presented with a precedent from a previous High Court case he will treat the precedent as "persuasive", and not as "binding".

Decisions by a Divisional Court are binding on judges of the same Division sitting alone but not necessarily on future Divisional Courts: see *R. v. Greater Manchester Coroner, ex parte Tal* (1985).

The County Court, the Crown Court and magistrates' courts

The decisions of these courts are seldom reported and not binding.

Terminology

Binding and persuasive

It has already been explained that depending on the status of the court a precedent may be binding or it may be persuasive. Precedents which come from the Judicial Committee of the Privy Council or from countries within the common law jurisdiction, like Canada and Australia, are persuasive and the adoption of concepts from those foreign jurisdictions has led to developments in English common law, for instance, in criminal law and the tort of negligence. **2-038**

Other terms

Where a judge finds that a precedent to which he is referred is not strictly relevant to the facts of the case concerned, he is said to "distinguish" that case. As such, the case is not binding upon him. If, on the other hand, the judge holds that a precedent is relevant, and applies it, he is said to "follow" the reasoning of the judge in the earlier case.

When an appeal court is considering a precedent, it may "approve" the principle of law established in the case, or it may "disapprove" the precedent. It can "overrule" the principle of law established in a precedent if the case was decided by a court junior in status to it. A decision is said to be "reversed" when a higher court, on appeal, comes to the opposite conclusion to the court whose order is the subject of the appeal. **2-039**

Ratio decidendi and obiter dicta

The most important and binding element of a judgment is the legal principle which is the reason for the decision or "*ratio decidendi*" as it is known; and then the remainder of the judgment, statements which deal by way of explanation with cases cited and legal principles argued before the court, are called "*obiter dicta*" or things said by the way. The whole of a dissenting (disagreeing minority) judgment is "*obiter*". **2-040**

It is the "*ratio*" of a decision which constitutes the binding precedent; or "*rationes*" if there is more than one reason. So that when in a case a judge is referred to a precedent, the first task of the court is to decide what was the "*ratio*" of that case, and to what extent it is relevant to the principle to be applied in the present case. Whilst an "*obiter dictum*" is not binding, it can, if it comes from a highly respected judge, be very helpful in establishing the legal principles in the case under consideration.

So important is it that a judgment should be accurately recorded that, before publication in the "official" law reports, judges are asked to check for accuracy the court reporter's version of the judgment.

Advantages and Disadvantages of a System of Binding Precedent

2-041   The main advantages of the doctrine are that it leads to consistency in the application and development of the principles in each branch of the law, and by virtue of this characteristic it enables lawyers to forecast with reasonable certainty what the attitude of the courts is likely to be to a given set of facts. The system is flexible in that it can find an answer to any legal problem, and it is essentially practical in that the courts are perpetually dealing with actual circumstances. It must also be said that one result of the recording of cases over the centuries is that the tremendous wealth of detail leads to considerable precision in the principles established in each field of law.

Critics argue that restriction on judicial discretion can be undesirable, and can lead to a judge, who wishes to escape from a precedent, drawing illogical distinctions. Added to this is the difficulty, which can occur in some Appeal Court decisions, of discovering exactly what the *ratio decidendi* of a previous case is. This has been known to be the case when the House of Lords decides an appeal by a majority vote of three to two, and the three judges in the majority appear to arrive at their decision for different reasons. An example of this difficulty is *Harper v. National Coal Board* (1974) where the Court of Appeal was, for this reason, unable to discover the *ratio decidendi* of the House of Lords' decision in *Dodd's Case* (1973). A final factor, which is a practical problem, is that there are so many cases being dealt with each year that inevitably there is increasing complexity in each branch of the law. The sheer bulk of cases on commercial or criminal law is almost overwhelming and causes textbooks to become increasingly specialised and substantial. Even so, it can well happen that a case of importance is not reported, other than on *Lexis*, and so may go unnoticed for some considerable time. Such a case remains a precedent.

Law Reports

2-042   A system of binding precedent is dependent on the publication of reported cases. Law reporting dates back to the thirteenth century. The earliest case summaries were collected in manuscript form in what became known as the Year Books. These seem to have been prepared by students or practitioners and circulated among the judges and leading barristers. With the invention of printing, the production of law reports for sale to the legal profession, between the sixteenth and nineteenth centuries became common practice. They are published under the reporters' names. These reporters varied widely in their accuracy and reliability, but their law reports remain available, and have now been republished in a series called *The English Reports*, covering 1220–1865.

Since 1865, law reporting has been placed on a different basis, although it remains a matter for private enterprise. In 1870, the Incorporated Council of Law Reporting was established. It consists of representatives of the Law Society and the Inns of Court and publishes what have come to be treated as the Official Law Reports. (See Reeves' history of law reporting). The reports are published some considerable time after the judgment has been given, but are regarded as authentic. Approved judgments handed down in the High Court or Court of Appeal can be copied immediately. Unapproved judgments are only given to the parties involved (Practice Statement, L.C.J., November 1998). High Court and Court of Appeal decisions are available online, via the Court Service website and House of Lords decisions are available on the Lords' section of the Parliament website. *The Weekly Law Reports* (W.L.R.) and *All England Law Reports* (All E.R.), are available sooner and are published commercially by firms of law publishers. They are on hard copy and CD-Rom. All decisions of the Crown Court, High Court and above, whether or not reported elsewhere, are stored on *Lexis*, the best known law database. As well as these full reports, a number of law magazines carry summaries of recent case decisions, as do *The Times* and *The Independent*. Case summaries appear on another commercial database, Lawtel. Law reporting is done by barristers who attend the court throughout the hearing of the case.

Citation of Judgments

In order to control the multiple citation of precedents of different value   **2-043**
in reports of varying accuracy, the Lord Chief Justice recently issued three Practice Directions. Approved reserved judgments of the Court of Appeal and High Court (the Supreme Court) can be cited as soon as handed down (November 1998). If a case is reported in the official *Law Reports*, that one should be used. If not but it appears in the *Weekly Law Reports* or *All England Law Reports*, then they can be cited. If not reported in any of these, specialist private reports may be cited. Unreported cases may not be cited without permission (P.D., CA (Civ Div), 1999). In civil courts, county court judgments and those on applications may not normally be cited.

Advocates are now required to state, in their skeleton argument, the proposition of law demonstrated by each authority they wish to cite and must justify citation of more than one authority for each proposition. If advocates wish to cite foreign authorities they must justify doing so and certify that there was no English authority on the point.

2-044   Advocates have a common law duty to the court to achieve and maintain appropriate levels of competence and care: *Harley v. McDonald* (2001, PC). They still have a duty to draw to the attention of the court authorities which support their opponent's case (P.D. (Citation of Authorities) 2001, CA). Doubtless this attempt by the judges to limit citations stems from the uncontrolled growth in the number of precedents lawyers will incorporate in their arguments, as demonstrated by a small piece of statistical research by Zander. In 2000, Zander showed that the number of authorities referred to in judgments had almost doubled since Diamond's research in 1965, from an average of 8.9 to 15.6. The percentage of those authorities cited which were unreported had almost quadrupled and the percentage of overseas authorities cited had increased from 3.7 per cent to 7.5 per cent. From 2001, all High Court and Court of Appeal judgments are numbered and have numbered paragraphs, not pages. This neutral citation of judgments caters for those cited from electronic sources (P.D. (Judgments: Form and Citation) 2001, LCJ).

Do and Should Judges Make the Law?

2-045   Of course judges make law. That is the nature of the common law. To pretend otherwise is silly. They created the law of tort. They invented the basic rules of contract. Murder is a common law crime. When a statute protecting people from harassment does not define harassment, obviously, the Government who introduced the Bill and Parliament who passed it as an Act are expecting the judges to define it and thus make the law. When judges reinterpret English law in accordance with the Treaty of Rome or other E.C. treaties or the European Convention, they are making the law. When judges find themselves dealing with an entirely novel set of circumstances, such as whether silent phone calls constitute an assault (*Ireland* (1997, HL)) or when the House of Lords overrules outdated and undesirable common law "rules" such as the marital exemption in rape, they are making law (*R. v. R.*, 1991, HL and see especially CA judgments).

Nevertheless, the extent to which it is desirable to take this activity of rule creation has been the subject of endless debate. Many judges and academics have written on this subject but it is an argument of constitutional law and there is no space for it in this book. A good starting point for the reader would be Zander's *The Law Making Process*, Chapter 7. The approach of those who would prefer to leave as much rule creation as possible to Parliament is typified by Bennion's 1999 article.

4. Custom

2-046   The common law was derived from the different laws of the existing Anglo-Saxon tribal groups in, for example, Kent and Wessex. The term "common law" emphasises the point. As England became one nation, with one king and one government, so the laws of the Anglo-Saxon regions had to be adapted into a national law common to the whole country. Since the difference between the regions stemmed from their different customary laws it is no exaggeration to say that custom was the principal original source of the common law and in this historical sense, custom, as the basis of common law, continued to play a part over the medieval period.

Customs thus were absorbed into the legal system, sometimes in the form of legislation and sometimes, particularly in the earliest period, by the judges giving decisions which were based on custom. The gradual result was that custom virtually disappeared as a creative source of law. An exception exists at the present day on a limited scale for cases where the courts can be convinced that a particular local custom applies. Usually in such cases, custom is pleaded as a defence as permitting the conduct in question. It is unusual, nowadays, for an argument to be based on custom and the rules for its acceptance are strict. Recognised custom does, however, play a very important part in the interpretation of international law. See below.

5. Books of Authority

A distinction is drawn between books of antiquity and those of recent **2-047**
origin. Both categories are of importance and have a part to play in the system, but only the books of antiquity can strictly be regarded as a source of law.

In the first category fall certain ancient textbooks, any one of which by long-standing judicial tradition can be accepted as an original source of law.

The following works, most of which were written by judges, are accepted as books of authority—

Glanvill, *De Legibus et Consuetudinibus Angliae* (c. 1189): authoritative on the land law and the criminal law of the twelfth century.

Bracton, *De Legibus et Consuetudinibus Angliae* (c. 1250): mainly commentaries on the forms of action with case illustrations. A major study of the common law.

Littleton, *Of Tenures* (c. 1480): a comprehensive study of land law.

Fitzherbert, *Nature Brevium* (c. 1534): a commentary on the register of writs.

Coke, *Institutes of the Laws of England* (1628): an attempted exposition in four parts of the whole of English law.

Hale, *History of the Pleas of the Crown* (1736) (60 years after Hale's death): the first history of the criminal law.

Hawkins, *Pleas of the Crown* (1716): a survey of the criminal law and criminal procedure.

Foster, *Crown Cases* (1762): authoritative within its scope, which is concerned with the criminal law.

Blackstone, *Commentaries on the Laws of England* (1765): a survey of the principles of English law in the mid-eighteenth century intended for students. From the time of Blackstone on, writers of legal textbooks have fallen into the second category, that is those of recent origin.

2-048   Modern textbooks are not treated as works of authority although they are frequently referred to in the courts. Counsel are permitted to adopt a textbook writer's view as part of their argument in a case. Judges will often quote from a modern textbook in the course of giving judgment; for example, *Re Ellenborough Park* (1956) the Court of Appeal adopted the definition of an easement as defined in *Cheshire's Modern Real Property*. Sometimes the judge will decide that a statement in a textbook on a particular point is incorrect.

In *R. v. Moloney* (1985) the House of Lords held that the definition of "intent" in *Archbold*, the virtual bible of criminal court practice, was "unsatisfactory and potentially misleading". The reason why no textbooks, since *Blackstone's Commentaries* were published in 1765, have been accepted as works of authority seems to be that (i) case reports have become fuller and much more easily accessible and (ii) by that time the principles of the common law were fully established, so that there was no question of a later textbook being itself a source of law.

2-049   One old rule which seems to have died out is the rule that a living person could not be an authority in his own lifetime. Under the present arrangements a living textbook writer can be quoted in court, and occasionally the court may refer with advantage to articles in learned law periodicals. For instance, in *R. v. Shivpuri* (1986) the House of Lords paid tribute to an article in the *Cambridge Law Journal* by Professor Glanville Williams. This article had a considerable influence on the court in persuading it to reverse its previous ruling.

6. International Law as a Source of English Law

2-050   There are two types, private and public international law. The former deals with such things as family law—what happens when there is a divorce between nationals of two different jurisdictions, who has care and control of the children and what happens if one kidnaps the children and takes them abroad. It also determines, for instance, what law should govern a dispute arising out of a car accident between nationals of two different states which takes place in a third. Private disputes between individuals or commercial organisations, such as those arbitrated in London, discussed in the Chapter on alternatives to the civil courts, may also be governed by elements of international law. Public international law (PIL) governs relations between states and the entities of states and creations of states such as the United Nations and the World Bank. Over the decades of the twentieth century and even before, we have created a number of fora to resolve international disputes. In the news at the moment is the War Crimes Tribunal for the former Yugoslavia. As I write, in summer 2001, the former President Milosovic is being indicted before it, in the Hague, Netherlands. If you want to keep up-to-date with the Milosovic case or other indicted war criminals, or the progress of the War Crimes Tribunal dealing with Rwanda, then go to the U.N. website, have a look round it then click on the links to those two. PIL regulates such matters as the carriage of goods by air and sea, use of illegal drugs and war crimes. As individuals become more mobile in their domestic, social and working lives and with globalisation of the market place, so United Kingdom governments sign up to more and more treaties obliging us to enact domestic legislation (such as the Misuse of Drugs Act 1972) governing the lives of the citizenry and so we see more international litigation in the English courts. Qureshi's very useful contemporary article examines the attitude of the English courts to PIL issues, as manifested in recent case law, most famously, the *Pinochet* cases. One fascinating aspect of PIL this article explains is the recognition of custom in PIL. We bind ourselves to the explicit obligations of treaties but are also bound by the tacit rules of custom. Customary international law (CIL) is law which is a product of consensus amongst the community of nations. States regard it as binding in their dealing with other states. He quotes Lord Lloyd in the first *Pinochet* case (2000, HL) on the effect of CIL in English law:

> "The application of international law as part of the law of the land means that, subject to the overriding effect of statute law, rights and duties flowing from the rules of (customary international law) will be recognised and given effect by the English courts without the need for any specific act adopting those rules into English law."

In applying and interpreting international conventions, the courts will **2-051** apply a purposive construction, as the House of Lords did in *Sidhu and Others v. British Airways plc* (1997). This case also determined that domestic common law cannot override a convention to which the United Kingdom is a contracting party. In this case, the parties sought to sue for damages at common law but the Lords held that their remedies were limited to those available for international carriage by air according to the Warsaw Convention. It provided a comprehensive code with a uniform international interpretation which could be applied in the courts of contracting parties, exclusive of any reference to domestic law.

2-052   Do not forget that the European Convention on Human Rights and the treaties of the European Union have a massive effect on English law as well as generating rights and liabilities in public and private international law. They are such a significant source of English law that they merit separate Chapters of this book.

FURTHER READING

2-053   Public Information Offices, House of Commons: 0207 219 4272. Lords: 0207 219 3107.

Parliament:www.parliament.uk

Welsh Assembly:www.assembly.wales.gov.uk

Scottish Parliament: www.scottish.parliament.uk

Her Majesty's Stationery Office: www.hmso.gov.uk

The Stationery Office: www.thestationeryoffice.com

C. Manchester, Salter and P. Moodie, *Exploring the Law* (2nd ed., 2000).

M. Zander, *The Law Making Process* (5th ed., 1999).

The Right Honourable Lord Bingham of Cornhill, L.C.J., "A Criminal Code: Must We Wait Forever?" [1998] Crim.L.R. 694.

J.R. Spencer, "The Case for a Code of Criminal Procedure" [2000] Crim.L.R. 519.

J. Bell and G. Engle, *Cross on Statutory Interpretation* (1995).

F. Bennion, *Statutory Interpretation.*

F. Bennion, letter, (1997) 147 N.L.J. 684.

www.francisbennion.com

The Statute Law Review

Articles on the Diane Blood case in *The Times* October 18, 1996.

V. Sacks, "Towards Discovering Parliamentary Intent" (1982) 3 Statute Law Review 143.

C. Jenkins, "Helping the Reader of Bills and Acts" (1999) 149 N.L.J. 798.

Dame Mary Arden, "Modernising Legislation" [1998] P.L. 65.

P. Reeves, "Law Reporting from the 13th to the 21st Century" (2000) 164 Justice of the Peace 1023.

M. Zander, "What precedents and other source materials do the courts use?" (2000) 150 N.L.J. 1790.

F. Bennion, "A Naked Usurpation" (1999) 149 N.L.J. 421.

K. M. Qureshi, "International Law and the English Courts" (2001) 151 N.L.J. 787.

Brownlie, *Public International Law* (2000).

Harris, *Cases and Materials on Public International Law.*

Dicey & Morris, *Conflict of Laws.*

Cheshire & North, *Private International Law.*

United Nations: www.un.org

3. E.C. Law: Its Impact on English Law and the English Courts

1. E.C. Law is Part of United Kingdom Law

Membership of the European Community has dramatically curtailed **3-001** the sovereignty of Parliament in the British constitution. It is simply unrealistic to consider the English legal system, or English sources of law, in isolation from the E.C. year by year, as the ambit of Community power is extended and now Union power, so the bulk of substantive law accelerates in growth and it is no longer appropriate to consider E.C. law as a single subject. Apart from the Treaties and Regulations, which are directly applicable in all Member States without further ado (and made binding in United Kingdom law by the European Communities Act 1972, s.2), most statute law comes into the United Kingdom "by the back door", through the medium of delegated legislation but it is scrutinised in Parliament by committees in both Houses. For detail of parliamentary scrutiny of E.C. law, see the free factsheets available from the Lords and Commons' information offices and available from the Parliament website.

The interpretive and other judgments of the ECJ are also a source of **3-002** E.C. law and they and the E.C. Treaties and secondary legislation have to be interpreted by the English and Welsh courts. All our magistrates, judges and other adjudicators must treat questions as to the meaning or effect of the Treaties and Community instruments as questions of law to be determined in accordance with principles laid down by the ECJ. On any such question, they must take judicial notice of the Treaties, the Official Journal of the Communities and decisions or opinions of the ECJ

47

or Court of First Instance (European Communities Act 1972, s.3, as amended). This means all ECJ rulings are binding precedents to be applied in the English and Welsh courts. (See below).

Here, I provide a simple and very basic guide to the institutions of the E.C. and the sources of E.C. law. It is essential, however, for every student of English and Welsh law to understand that they cannot ignore E.C. law. Regrettably, English lawyers, until the late 1990s suffered an appalling ignorance of E.C. law, which reflects the insularity of the wider British community.

3-003   This Chapter is the most basic of introductions. For a simple, well written and accurate account of E.C. law, I strongly recommend Steiner and Woods *EC Law*, to which I am indebted for much of the content of this Chapter. To this you need to add the Treaty of Nice 2000, which may have been ratified by the time you read this book. Forster's *Blackstone's EC Legislation* is updated annually and an indispensable accompaniment to any E.C. law textbook. We are lucky to have a collection of brilliant textbooks on E.C. law written in the English language. My favourite is Weatherill and Beaumont, *EU Law*, which I have used here, and Craig and de Burca's *Text, Cases and Materials* for a comprehensive materials collection.

2. The Treaties

3-004   The E.C. was created by the signing of the Treaty of Rome in 1957 and the Treaty remains an essential source of E.C. law, as well as the Community's constitution. Incorporation of this and the other E.C. Treaties into English law was effected by The European Communities Act 1972. The other major instruments with which we must concern ourselves are the Single European Act of 1986, which created the single European market, which was in effect by the end of 1992, and the Treaty on European Union (TEU, Maastricht Treaty), ratified in 1993, which extended the scope of community competence and provided for economic and monetary union and Union citizenship, and the Treaty of Amsterdam, signed in 1997 and in force in 1999.

3-005   The Union consists of three pillars: the E.C., which is the central law making and law enforcing unit and the two outside pillars, Justice and Home Affairs (JHA) and Foreign and Social Policy. Decision-making in the outside pillars is largely a matter for the Council. It gives much more freedom to the Member States and involves fairly slow policy negotiations. Following the Treaty of Amsterdam (ToA), some policy areas were shifted from Justice and Home Affairs to the E.C., such as immigration and asylum and border checks (passport control). New elements have been added to the E.C. Treaty, such as the Protocol on Social Policy. The

Amsterdam Treaty thus added a further dimension to the E.C., based on fundamental rights. Very importantly, the ECJ's jurisdiction was extended beyond the E.C. into the JHA pillar but in a very restricted manner. (The pressure group JUSTICE considers co-operation in this third pillar ineffectual. They consider the lack of democratic and judicial control over the third pillar has "profound implications for human rights".) The Amsterdam Treaty also introduced closer co-operation between States. See Steiner and Wood's very interesting analysis of whether this shift in the powers of the E.C., by Amsterdam, moves the E.U. in the direction of a federal superstate. The Union now has 15 Member States. In October 1991, the European Economic Area was created, including States subjected to Community law on the internal market and competition but not represented in the institutions. Thirteen countries have applied to join the E.U. The Union could have 27 members by 2010. The Treaty of Nice (2000) contains a protocol on enlargement from 2005. Notice that the contents and likely effectiveness of the Treaty of Nice are somewhat doubtful at the time of writing, 2001, as Eire's citizens have voted not to ratify it. Each Treaty is debated and signed at an Inter Governmental Conference (IGC). The next IGC, on enlargement, is due in 2004.

3. Institutions

The basic four E.C. institutions are the Parliament, the Council, the Commission and the Court of Justice. The other institution which necessitates a brief mention is the Court of First Instance. Notice the ToA altered the Treaty Article numbers so the old ones appear bracketed.   **3-006**

Parliament (Article 190 (137))

Members of this large assembly are directly elected by their Member   **3-007**
States. It is essential to grasp that, unlike conventional Parliaments on the Westminster model, this is not the legislature of the Community, although its powers have been massively enhanced by the 1986 Single European Act and by the Treaty on European Union 1992, as explained below. This has gone some way to remedy the institutional imbalance in the Community and to remedy the "democratic deficit", complained of by critics, that the unelected Council is the primary legislature. The ToA extended its powers of co-decision. Parliament now has a legislative role on several levels, advisory and consultative, a right to participate in conciliation and co-operation procedures and a right of co-decision in certain defined areas. (See Steiner and Woods, Chapter two or any other E.C. law textbook for explanation.)

The Council (the Council of the European Union) Arts 202–210 (145–154)

3-008   This body is composed of one representative minister from each Member State. These delegates change according to the nature of the subject under discussion. For instance, on agricultural policy, states will send their agriculture ministers. On economic issues, finance ministers will attend. When the Council is composed of heads of state or government it is known as The European Council. They meet at least twice a year, with the Commission President, assisted by foreign ministers and a Commissioner (Single European Act 1986, Art. 2).

3-009   The Council's job is to ensure the Treaty objectives are attained. It has the final say on most Community secondary legislation but, in most cases, can only act on a proposal from the Commission. If the E.C. can be said to have a legislature for its secondary legislation, this is it. Since it is not a permanent body, much of the Council's day to day work, initially scrutinising Commission proposals, is delegated to COREPER, the committee of permanent representatives.

The Commission (Arts 211–219 (155–163))

3-010   The Commission's 20 members are drawn from Member States, two from some, one from others, but must act independently of state control. They are appointed for five years, renewable. If the Treaty of Nice is ratified, it will consist of up to 27 but they will sit in rotation. Its functions are as follows:

The motor

3-011   It takes the initiative because the Council can only take important decisions following proposals of the Commission but it may request the Commission to undertake studies and submit appropriate proposals. Nevertheless, this power of initiative makes it very powerful in setting the agenda of the Council and Parliament.

The watchdog

3-012   The Commission enforces the Member States' Treaty obligations and may take an errant Member State to the ECJ, under Article 266 (169), should persuasion fail. It can also impose fines and penalties on those in breach of E.C. competition law, or who ignore decisions taken against them. Accordingly, the Commission has extensive investigatory powers. For instance, because Germany failed to comply with rulings on water purity and protection of birds, it imposed a daily fine of £350,000 while the infringement continued.

The executive

3-013   The Commission is, effectively, the Community executive. Policies formed by the Council need detailed implementation by the

Commission. Much of this is effected by legislation, which requires a final decision by the Council. The Commission has its own decision-making powers and enforces competition policy.

Negotiator

In relation to the E.C.'s external policies, the Commission acts as a negotiator, leaving agreements to be concluded by the Council, after consulting the Parliament, where this is required by the Treaty.   **3-014**

The Court of Justice (Arts 220–245 (164–188))

Composition

The Court consists of 15 judges (Art. 221): one for each Member State. They are assisted by eight Advocates General (Art. 222 (166)), whose task it is to assist the Court, individually, by making a detailed analysis of all the relevant issues of fact and law in a case before the Court and submitting a report of this, together with recommendations, to the Court. Thus, they can express their personal opinions, which the judges cannot, and they can examine any related question, not brought forward by the parties. Article 233 (167) of the Treaty stipulates that both judges and A.G.s "shall be chosen from persons whose independence is beyond doubt and who possess the qualifications required for appointment to the highest judicial offices in their respective countries or who are jurisconsults of recognised competence" (*e.g.* academic lawyers). Each judge and Advocate General is appointed for a term of six years.   **3-015**

Procedure

The Court's workload has increased massively since 1970. Then, 79 cases were brought before it and now hundreds of cases per year are lodged, with hundreds more being lodged before the Court of First Instance (CFI). The latter was created to deal with this increased workload but, still, it has proved necessary to devise another coping mechanism. This has been the tendency to hear cases before a chamber of three or five judges, reserving the plenary sessions of seven, nine, 11, or 13 judges for the more important cases. The grand plenum (now of 15 judges) is reserved for the most important cases, where issues of fundamental principle are considered, such as the *Faccini Dori* case on horizontal direct effect of directives (see below).   **3-016**

The case for each party is submitted in written pleadings, oral argument being strictly limited to about half an hour per party. The common lawyers appearing before the Court from Eire and the United Kingdom find more difficulty in adjusting to this procedure than do lawyers from continental Europe. The President allocates one of the judges to act as a judge-rapporteur to each case. She prepares a public report after the   **3-017** written procedure, ready for the oral hearing. It contains a summary of the facts and legal argument. She prepares a private report to the judges, containing her view of whether the case should be assigned to a chamber.

Meanwhile, an Advocate General will also have been assigned to the case. They are not assigned to cases brought by or against their native Member State. The A.G. prepares an opinion which is delivered orally, at the end of the oral hearing. It contains a full analysis of relevant E.C. law, which may give a more complete and accurate account than that produced in argument by the parties, since the lawyers appearing in the case may appear before the ECJ only once in their legal careers.

3-018   The Advocate General also gives his opinion as to how the Court should decide the case. Whilst it is true that the Court follows this opinion in most cases and it is thus a good indicator as to how the Court is likely to decide, as well as providing an essential explanation of the reasoning behind the Court's decision, after the event, this opinion should never be referred to as a "ruling", as is frequently misreported by the British news media.

After this, the Advocate General drops out of the picture and the judges deliberate in secret, without interpreters, in French, the working language of the Court. (Since Finland and Sweden joined the E.C. in 1995, it has been argued that the Court should adopt English as a second official language, since this is the second language of Scandinavians but the cost of double translation would be prohibitive.) After deliberations, the judge-rapporteur will draft and refine the decision.

Function

3-019   Under Art. 220 (164), the task of the Court is prescribed as to "ensure that in the interpretation and application of this Treaty the law is observed". It is the supreme authority on all matters of Community law. In its practices and procedure, it draws on continental models, notably French procedure but in substantive law, it borrows principles from all Member States.

The E.C. Treaty is a framework, generally speaking, with few of its provisions spelled out in detail. This gives the Court massive latitude as a court of interpretation, in effect creating E.C. law and jurisprudence. Its boldness has been a matter of controversy but since we are watching the emergence of a whole new legal system and body of law, it is hardly surprising that the Court's decisions contain sweeping statements of principle, especially given that the E.C. Treaty is silent, even on such fundamentals as the relationship between E.C. law and national law (see *Costa v. E.N.E.L.*, 1964, below).

3-020   When developing new legal principles, the Court's first reference point is the objectives of the Community and the Articles of the Treaty. Over the years, it has built up a massive body of reported decisions. Like our House of Lords, the Court is not bound by its own previous decisions but usually follows them. The judgment is a single one, rather like that of the Privy Council but without much indication of the reasoning behind it (especially in the older cases). This is where the submission of the Advocate General comes in useful, as an explanation.

Jurisdiction

The Court's work consists mainly of the following: **3-021**

- determining whether or not a Member State has failed to fulfil a Treaty obligation. Actions may be brought by the Commission or another Member State (Arts 226 (169) 227; (170));
- exercising unlimited jurisdiction in reviewing penalties (*e.g.* fines imposed by the Commission). Actions may be brought by natural and legal persons (Art. 229 (172));
- reviewing the legality of an act, or failure to act, of the Council or Commission or Parliament. A request for review may be made by a Member State, the Council, the Commission, or Parliament or, where it concerns them, by the Court of auditors or ECB. Any natural or legal persons may challenge regulations or decisions which are addressed to them or concern them (Art. 230 (173));
- deciding over compensation for damage caused by the institutions. Actions can be brought against the Community by Member States and natural or legal persons (Arts 235 (178); 288 (215));
- acting as a court of appeal on points of law from the Court of First Instance (Art. 225 (168));
- giving preliminary rulings at the request of a national court or tribunal (Art. 234 (177)).

This last point is most important for our purposes, as this is the mech-   **3-022**
anism through which E.C. law is developed and interpreted in its domestic context, in English case law. Any case may be referred to the Court from any English court or tribunal, under Article 234, where there is an item of E.C. law to be interpreted. The Court gives its interpretation and then remits the case to the domestic court, leaving them to apply that interpretation and then decide the case accordingly.

Note that the ToA provided for a very important extension of the Court's jurisdiction. Hitherto, it has only had power over E.C. law, emanating from the Community, the central pillar. It now has power to rule on decisions made in the Justice and Home Affairs pillar, subject to agreement by the Member States. In these policy areas, however, only courts of last instance may refer from the Member States.

If the Nice Treaty is eventually ratified and the Union enlarges, then the Court will need to sit in chambers more often.

Court of First Instance (Art. 225 (168a))

3-023   The Single European Act (1986) provided for the establishment of a new Court of First Instance and it began its work in 1989. Its 15 judges usually hear cases in chambers of three or five, any of whom, apart from the President, may be called upon to act as Advocate General. Its jurisdiction was limited to disputes between the Community and its servants, cases involving E.C. competition law and applications for judicial review and damages in certain matters under the European Coal and Steel Community. In 1992, however, the TEU amended Article 168a to provide that the Council, acting on a request from the European Court, could transfer any area of the Court's jurisdiction to the Court of First Instance, except for Article 234 (177) preliminary rulings. Accordingly, a lot of work was transferred down in 1993, to relieve pressure on the Court. By 1996, the Court of First Instance was hearing as many cases as the Court of Justice. There is a right of appeal from this Court, on matters of law, to the ECJ. If the Treaty of Nice is ratified and put into effect, judicial panels will be attached to the CFI and it will be given jurisdiction in certain Article 234 references.

Article 234 (177) Preliminary Rulings

3-024   Article 234 enables any court or tribunal in any Member State to refer a point of E.C. law in a pending case to the Court for their interpretation. The Court's ruling on the point is then sent back to the national court to be applied in the case, which will have been suspended in the meantime. These references are a significant volume of the Court's workload and they have proved to be the essential vehicle for the Court to develop its principles and precedent. Article 234, provides:

"The Court of Justice shall have jurisdiction to give preliminary rulings concerning:
  (a)   the interpretation of this Treaty;
  (b)   the validity and interpretation of acts of the institutions of the Community and of the ECB;
  (c)   the interpretation of the statutes of bodies established by an act of the Council; where those statutes so provide.
     Where such a question is raised before any court or tribunal of a Member State, that court or tribunal may, if it considers that a decision on the question is necessary to enable it to give judgment, request the Court of Justice to give a ruling thereon.
     Where any such question is raised in a case pending before a court or tribunal of a Member State against whose decision there

is no judicial remedy under national law, that court or tribunal shall bring the matter before the Court of Justice."

Paragraph (b) includes all Article 249 (189) legislative acts, described below and the Court has ruled that it also includes non-binding recommendations and opinions. The Court cannot rule on questions of national law so cannot rule that a national provision is incompatible with Community law but has said it will provide the national court with all necessary criteria to enable it to answer such a question. It will not rule on how law is to be applied by the domestic court but will offer guidance. It has interpreted international treaties entered into by the Community.

Although the reference procedure has been the major case law tool by which the ECJ has developed its general principles and coloured in the sketches of E.C. instruments by interpreting them, all references are bogged down in a frustrating backlog. The ECJ and CFI have now got a backlog of over 2,000 cases and the average time taken to deal with a case is 21 months. The Court's procedures will be reformed if the Nice Treaty 2000 is ratified; a third tier of courts will be added and making procedural changes will be easier but the status of the Nice Treaty is in doubt, as I write, in 2001.

3-025

National Courts or Tribunals that can Refer

If parties have contracted to arbitrate, the arbiter is not a court or tribunal within Article 234 (177) but where the law imposes an arbitrator to resolve disputes, then a question can be referred to the ECJ. Even a body exercising functions preliminary to its judicial function may refer. In *Pretore di Salo v. Persons Unknown* (1987, ECJ), an Italian public prosecutor, who would later act as examining magistrate, was allowed to refer. In *El-Yassinin v. Secretary of State for the Home Department* (1996), the Court permitted a reference from an Immigration Adjudicator, because "the body" was a permanent officer, appointed by statute, hearing and determining disputes according to statutory powers. An independent arbitrator to whom parties had voluntarily submitted their dispute was not allowed to refer, however, in *Nordsee Deutsche Hochseefischerei GmbH* (1981).

3-026

The Discretion to Refer

The Court originally took a strict view that it was for the national courts and not for them to decide when a reference was necessary for the decision but it has emphasised that it will not answer hypothetical questions or act on references from non-genuine disputes which have been contrived simply to test E.C. law by means of an Article 234 (177) reference.

3-027

The Court has specified that, for it to assume jurisdiction, it is essential for the national court to explain why it considers a preliminary ruling to be necessary and the national court must define the factual and legislative context of the question it is asking.

3-028   The question of the timing of a reference is left to the national court but the Court has requested that facts and points of national law be established in advance. A national court or tribunal cannot be prevented from making a reference by a national law that it is bound to follow the decision of a higher court on the same question of Community law. In other words, our Court of Appeal could still make a reference, if they considered it necessary, despite the existence of a House of Lords precedent on the same question of Community law. The Court emphasised in the *Rheinmuhlen-Dusseldorf* case (1973) that, as the object of Art. 234 is to ensure that the law is the same in all Member States, domestic law cannot limit the lower court's power to make a reference if it considers the superior court's ruling could lead it to give judgment contrary to Community law.

"Necessary"

3-029   Note the use of the word "necessary" in the discretionary power to refer. The Court must consider a reference necessary. The ECJ defined this in *CILFIT* (1981). There is no need to refer if:

(a)   the question of E.C. law is irrelevant; or
(b)   the provision has already been interpreted by the ECJ, even though the questions at issue are not strictly identical; or
(c)   the correct application is so obvious as to leave no scope for reasonable doubt. This matter must be assessed in the light of the specific characteristics of Community law, the particular difficulties to which its interpretation gives rise and the risk of divergences of judicial decisions within the Community.

The approach of the United Kingdom courts to the discretion to refer

3-030   In *Bulmer v. Bollinger* (1974, CA) Lord Denning M.R. set out guidelines for English courts, other than the House of Lords, for deciding when it was necessary to make an Article 177 reference (now 234). They were influential in a number of cases but did not meet with uncritical approval. Mr Justice Bingham warned that the European court was in a better position to determine questions of Community law because, for instance, of their expertise, their unique grasp of all the authentic language texts of that law and their familiarity with a purposive construction of Community law. Once he became Master of the Rolls, he set out this important dictum, in *R. v. International Stock Exchange, ex parte Else* (1993, CA):

"if the facts have been found and the Community law issue is critical to the court's final decision, the appropriate course is ordinarily to refer the issue to the Court of Justice unless the national court can with complete confidence resolve the issue itself. In considering whether it can with complete confidence resolve the issue itself the national court must be fully mindful of the differences between national and Community legislation, of the pitfalls which face a national court venturing into what may be an unfamiliar field, of the need for uniform interpretation throughout the Community and of the great advantages enjoyed by the Court of Justice in construing Community instruments. If the national court has any real doubt, it should ordinarily refer."

Commenting on this case, Weatherill and Beaumont, in *EU Law*, praise **3-031** Sir Thomas for doing a great service in creating a presumption that national courts and tribunals should make a reference if they are not completely confident as to how the issues can be resolved.

"This is a *communautaire* approach consistent with the spirit of judicial cooperation that is needed if the Article 234 system is to do its job of ensuring uniform interpretation of Community law throughout the Community."

It is, nevertheless, a rebuttable presumption so the English law reports have many examples of the courts declining to refer. An example is *R. v. Ministry of Agriculture, Fisheries and Food, ex parte Portman Agrochemicals Ltd* (1994). Brooke, J., in declining to refer, took account of the guidelines in previous case law but was influenced by the fact that neither of the parties wished for the case to be referred and that, given the usual 18-month delay to be expected in receiving the Court's interpretation, the answer would be redundant by the time they would receive it.

Some judges have warned that English courts should exercise great caution in relying on the doctrine of "*acte clair*" in declining to make a reference. The Court accepts that national courts will apply this doctrine, borrowed from French law, when the interpretation of a provision is clear and free from doubt (see below).

It is possible, in the English legal system, for an appeal to be made **3-032** against a lower court's decision to refer. Such an appeal was successfully made in *ex parte Else* (above), the Court of Appeal holding that it was not necessary to refer.

The Obligation on National Courts of Last Resort to Refer

Two questions arise here. Firstly, when is a court a court of last resort? **3-033** There are two theories, abstract and concrete. Under the former, only the

57

House of Lords would be obliged to refer. Under the more practical concrete theory, any court from whom there is no appeal or from which appeal has been refused should be obliged to refer. The rulings of the ECJ seem to support the latter: *Costa v. ENEL* (*obiter*). This seems to be fairer to the parties, especially where they have been refused permission to appeal and it seems more likely to achieve the harmonisation of law Art. 234 is aiming at. The matter may be resolved by *Lyckeshog*, a 2000 reference. The second question relates to the circumstances in which the obligation to refer arises.

Although the wording of this paragraph looks mandatory, as if courts like the House of Lords must refer every point of E.C. law to the ECJ, the Court has ruled, in the *Da Costa* case (see below) that this is not necessary where the question raised is materially identical to a question which has already been the subject of a preliminary ruling in an earlier case. In *CILFIT v. Italian Ministry of Health*, above, the Court spelled out what they consider to be the discretion available to courts of last resort, as above, despite the wording of Article 234. They said that courts of last resort have the same discretion as others, to decide whether a reference is necessary and that there is no obligation to refer if the criteria laid down are satisfied.

3-034   Satisfying the conditions for the application of the third *CILFIT* criterion will not, however, be easy, as the Court laid down the condition that the national court must be convinced that the matter is equally obvious to the courts of the other Member States and to the ECJ and they reminded courts that, in satisfying themselves of this criterion, they should bear in mind the plurilingual nature of that law and the Court's use of purposive and contextual construction. While many English judges would not shy away from a purposive and contextual approach, I am at a loss to see how the House of Lords has the facilities to delve into the domestic law reports of the other 14 Member States to see how a point has been variously interpreted by other national courts, in their many national languages.

There are modern examples of the House of Lords refusing to refer a case to the ECJ, mainly relying on the first *CILFIT* exception, that the Community law point was irrelevant, including a case in which they refused to follow the *Von Colson* principle: *Finnegan v. Clowney Youth Training Programme Ltd* (1990, HL) Nevertheless, in recent years, the House seems to have been more prepared to refer to the ECJ and seems more ready to apply European Court case law where it does not refer, such as in *Webb v. EMO Air Cargo (No. 2)* (1995, HL). The case is illustrative of the fact that, had the House not made a reference, it would have come to the opposite conclusion from that reached by the ECJ and would have refused an appeal which it was ultimately persuaded to allow.

3-035   There is now a practice direction, issued by the ECJ in 1999, stating when it is appropriate to make a reference but it really states the existing principles, as set out by ECJ case law. It was repeated as a Supreme Court Practice Direction in our Supreme Court, for the guidance of all domestic courts and tribunals.

4. Sources of E.C. Law

The sources of E.C. law are as follows, in addition to the general principles and decisions of the ECJ: **3-036**

> *The E.C. Treaty and Protocols*, as amended by further treaties, such as the Single European Act 1986 and Treaty on European Union 1992.
> *E.C. secondary legislation* (Regulations, Directives and Decisions).
> *International agreements* entered into by Community institutions on the Community's behalf, using their powers under the Treaty.
> *Decisions* of the ECJ and Court of First Instance. This includes the vast body of law and principle established by the ECJ.

Article 10(5) of the Treaty obliges all Member States to "take all appropriate measures, whether general or particular, to ensure fulfilment" of all these obligations.

Secondary Legislation (Legislative Acts)

The law-making powers of the Community institutions are laid down   **3-037**
in Article 249 (189) of the Treaty (as amended by the TEU). They are set out very clearly and students of English law need to know and understand this Article:

> "In order to carry out their tasks and in accordance with the provisions of this Treaty, the European Parliament acting jointly with the Council, the Council and the Commission shall make regulations, issue directives, take decisions, make recommendations or deliver opinions.
> A regulation shall have general application. It shall be binding in its entirety and directly applicable in all Member States.
> A directive shall be binding, as to the result to be achieved, upon each Member State to which it is addressed, but shall leave to the national authorities the choice of form and methods.
> A decision shall be binding in its entirety upon those to whom it is addressed.
> Recommendations and opinions shall have no binding force."

These are all called "acts". Distinguish between binding and non-binding acts. Only the first three are binding.

- *Regulations* are generally applicable and designed to apply to all situations in the abstract. Since they are binding in their entirety and directly applicable in all Member States, they may give rise to rights and obligations for states and individuals without further enactment.
- *Directives* are binding as to the result to be achieved, upon each Member State to which they are addressed. The State thus fills in the details by enacting domestic law in accordance with the principles it is directed to effect.
- *Decisions* are individual acts, addressed to a specified person or persons or States. They have the force of law and, therefore, have effect without further expansion.

Acts which do not conform with procedural safeguards may be annulled.

- *Recommendations and opinions* have no binding force in law, although they are of persuasive authority.

5. *Direct Applicability and Direct Effect*

3-038   To understand the application of E.C. law, it is necessary to have a basic grasp of the distinction between the principles of direct applicability and direct effect. It is also necessary to draw attention to the distinction between horizontal and vertical direct effect, that is, between provisions directly effective between individuals, giving rise to rights or obligations enforceable between individuals and provisions giving rise to rights of individuals against the Member States. When the European Communities Act 1972 took the United Kingdom into the E.C., or Common Market, as it then was, E.C. law became directly applicable, in international law terms, as if it were domestic English law. The terminology becomes confusing, however, because provisions of international law which are found to be capable of application by national courts at the suit of individuals are also termed directly applicable. To spare confusion, therefore, all British writers on E.C. law have adopted the term "directly effective" to express this second meaning, that is, to denote provisions of E.C. law which give rise to rights or obligations which individuals may enforce before the national courts.

3-039   Whether a particular provision of E.C. law gives rise to directly effective, individually enforceable rights or obligations is a matter of construction, depending on its language and purpose. Since principles of construction vary from State to State, the same provision may not be construed as directly effective everywhere. For lawyers in the English legal system, whether a provision is directly effective is crucially important because, thanks to the concept of primacy of E.C. law, a directly effective provision must be given priority over any conflicting principle of domestic law. The E.C. Treaty specifies, in Article 249, that regulations are directly applicable but it has been left to the ECJ to set out, in a group of leading cases, which and when other E.C. provisions can have direct effect.

Treaty Articles

The issues of whether and when a Treaty Article could have direct effect was first considered in the *Van Gend en Loos* case of 1962. The question arose as to whether Article 12 of the Treaty, which prohibited States introducing new import duties, could confer enforceable rights on nationals of Member States. The ECJ held that it could because the text of the Article set out a clear and unconditional duty not to act. The prohibition was, thus, perfectly suited by its nature to produce direct effects in the legal relations between Member States and their citizens. The ECJ clearly thought it desirable that individuals should be allowed to protect their rights in this way, without having to rely on the E.C. Commission or another Member State to take action against an offending Member State.

3-040

This case involved a flouted prohibition but ECJ case law soon extended direct effect to positive Treaty obligations, holding that an Article imposing upon a Member State a duty to act would become directly effective once a time-limit for compliance had expired. The ECJ has found a large number of Treaty provisions to be directly effective, in relation to free movement of goods and persons, competition law and discrimination on the grounds of gender or nationality.

3-041

The ECJ applies the following criteria to test whether a provision is amenable to direct effect. It must be:

- clear and precise, especially with regard to scope and application;
- unconditional; and
- leave no room for the exercise of implementation by Member States or community institutions.

The ECJ has, however, applied these conditions fairly liberally, with results as generous as possible to the individual seeking to rely on the Article.

Although the *Van Gend* case involved vertical direct effect, that is, a citizen enforcing rights against a State, later case law, notably *Defrenne v. Sabena* (1975, ECJ) demonstrated that Treaty Articles could also have horizontal direct effect, that is, could be relied on between individuals, such as private employer and employee. A good recent example of the invocation of *vertically* directly effective Treaty Articles is the *Factortame* case, discussed below.

3-042

Regulations

3-043   Regulations are, as stated above, designed to be directly applicable and, thus, directly effective. It is important to understand that this means both vertically and horizontally.

Directives

3-044   Directives are an instruction to Member States to enact laws to achieve a certain end result, so it was originally assumed they could not be directly effective. Nevertheless, in *Grad v. Finanzamt Traunstein* (1970, ECJ) the ECJ held that no such limitation applied. Here, a German haulier was allowed to rely on a Directive and decision on VAT which the German government had ignored.

The conditions for effectiveness are the same as those applied to test Treaty provisions: clarity, precision, being unconditional, leaving no room for discretion in implementation. Once a time-limit for implementation has expired, the obligation to implement it becomes absolute but a directive cannot be directly effective before that time-limit has expired: *Ratti* (1978, ECJ). Where a State has implemented a directive inadequately, it is still possible for it to be declared directly effective, to make up for that inadequacy (*U.N.O.* (1976, ECJ)). These conditions for making a directive directly effective were applied by the Court of Appeal in *Marks and Spencer plc v. Commissioners of Customs and Excise* (2000, CA).

3-045   If they can be interpreted as directly effective, directives of course then have to be interpreted and applied by our courts and tribunals and the citizens and their lawyers affected by them, as if they were, say, a statute. Unlike statutes, however, we are given lengthy preambles to help us. If you take a look at any directive, you will see what I mean. Take Directive 2000/78, passed in November 2000 but not yet in force at my time of writing. It provides us with a preamble of over five pages.

Horizontal or vertical direct effect?

3-046   One of the most significant but difficult issues before the ECJ in recent years has been the issue of whether directives can be declared effective horizontally, that is, to enforce private rights and obligations between private parties. All the case law referred to above relates to the enforcement of private rights against a State, giving vertical direct effect to a directive. The ECJ has no problem in declaring vertical direct effect since this is merely enforcing rights and obligations against a State which that State has omitted to effect in its own domestic legislation. It is not so keen, however, to hold private parties bound by a directive which a State has neglected to implement, when the default is clearly the State's.

3-047   The leading case on this issue is *Marshall v. Southampton & South West Hampshire Area Health Authority (Teaching)* (1984, ECJ) but, as we shall see, subsequent case law, in particular the *Marleasing* case and *Foster v. British Gas*, leave the law in a position which is far from clear. The decision in the *Marshall* case is clear enough.

Mrs Marshall was an employee of the Area Health Authority and she **3-048** challenged their compulsory retirement age of 65 for men and 60 for women as discriminatory and in breach of the E.C. Equal Treatment Directive 76/207. Different retirement ages were permissible in domestic English law, under the Sex Discrimination Act 1975. On a reference from the Court of Appeal, the ECJ held that the different retirement ages did indeed breach the Directive and that Mrs Marshall could, in the circumstances rely on the Directive against the State (here represented by the Area Health Authority) regardless of whether they were acting in their capacity as a public authority or her employer. The issue of horizontal and vertical effect of directives had been fully argued before the ECJ and they determined that:

". . . a Directive may not of itself impose obligations on an individual and that a provision of a Directive may not be relied upon as such against such an individual."

This looks like a very straightforward refusal to permit directives to have direct effect but problems remain.

1. Here, Mrs Marshall could rely on the Directive against her employers because they were a part of the State so how is "State" to be defined? The wider the definition, the more individuals will be allowed to rely on directives as directly effective.
2. Is the time now ripe for directives to be given horizontal direct effect?
3. Has the ECJ permitted individuals to avoid the harshness of this ruling against horizontal effect by requiring domestic courts to apply directives indirectly, as a matter of interpretation (the *Von Colson* principle)?

What is the State?

In the *Marshall* case, then, an Area Health Authority was regarded as **3-049** an arm of the State, as was the Royal Ulster Constabulary in *Johnson v. RUC* (1984, ECJ), but what of other publicly funded organisations such as universities or publicly run corporations? The House of Lords sought a preliminary ruling from the ECJ on the status of the British Gas Corporation and in their response, in *Foster v. British Gas* (1989, ECJ), the ECJ took the opportunity to provide a definition, although it is not, I am afraid, definitive. The Court ruled that a directive may be relied on as having direct effect against:

"a body, whatever its legal form, which has been made responsible, pursuant to a measure adopted by the State, for providing a public service under the control of the State and has for that purpose special powers beyond those which result from the normal rules applicable in relation between individuals."

The ECJ ruled that:

1. It was up to them to rule which categories of body might be held bound by a directly effective directive.
2. It was up to the domestic court to decide whether a particular body fell within that category.

On the first of these points, it is still unclear which bodies will be classed as part of the State.

On the second point, the refinement of the concept of State is laid open to differences of interpretation by Member States' domestic courts.

3-050   The United Kingdom's definition of a state body was addressed in the 1992 case of *Doughty v. Rolls Royce* (1992, CA). Here, the Court of Appeal ruled that Rolls Royce did not qualify as part of the State, within the Foster definition because they did not provide a public service, nor possess any special powers, despite being wholly owned by the State. The issue as to what is an emanation of the State was addressed again by the ECJ in *Kampelmann v. Landscaftsverband Westfalen-Lippe* (1997) and seems to have been expanded. The Court defined it by repeating the exact words they had used in Marshall but then added "or other bodies which irrespective of their legal form, have been given responsibility, by the public authorities and under their supervision, for providing a public service". See comment by Tayleur.

Should Horizontal Direct Effect now be Extended to directives?

3-051   In three cases in 1993 and 1994, Advocates General separately argued that the Court should reverse its decision in *Marshall* and give horizontal direct effect to directives. In the *Faccini Dori* case of 1994, an Italian student sought to rely on a 1985 Directive, unimplemented by Italy, to cancel a contract she had entered into with a private company and now regretted. A number of reasons had been put forward by the Advocates General in these cases and academic commentators for an extension of the concept. For instance, the Court is prepared to give horizontal direct effect to Treaty Articles, despite the fact that, like directives, they are addressed to Member States. Secondly, the emergence of the single market in 1993 necessitated enforcing equality of the conditions of competition and the prohibition on discrimination. Thirdly, the TEU had amended the E.C. Treaty to require publication of directives in the Official Journal (so private persons had less excuse not to know their responsibilities under a directive). A full ECJ of 13 judges nevertheless declined to adopt this reasoning and extend the concept of horizontal direct effect. They reiterated that the distinguishing basis of vertical direct effect was that the State should be barred from taking advantage of its own failure to comply with Community law.

Decisions

The *Grad* case, discussed above, confirmed that decisions could be directly effective, provided they meet all the required criteria. This does not pose any of the moral problems of horizontal direct effect of directives, since decisions are, in any event, only binding on the addressee.   **3-052**

International Agreements to which the E.C. is Party

The ECJ has shown an inconsistent approach to the question of which international agreements to which the E.C. is a party can be directly effective. The full picture can only be painted by the ECJ on a piecemeal basis, from case to case.   **3-053**

6. *The* Von Colson *Principle and* Marleasing

Where individuals seeking to rely on a directive cannot show that their opponent is a branch of the State, all may not be lost, because of a principle developed in *Von Colson and Kamann* (1983, ECJ). Miss Von Colson was claiming that the German prison service had rejected her job application in breach of the Equal Treatment Directive and German law provided inadequate compensation. At the same time, another claimant, Miss Hartz, was making the same claim against a private company. Thus, the issue of horizontal/vertical direct effect and the public/private distinction was openly raised in a reference under Article 177 (now 234) before the ECJ. The ECJ avoided opening up these distinctions by ingenious reliance on Article 5 (now 10) of the E.C. Treaty. Article 10 requires States to "take all appropriate measures" to ensure fulfilment of their community obligations. This obligation falls on all parts of a State, said the Court, including its courts. Thus, the courts in a Member State must interpret national law in a manner which achieves the results referred to in Article 189 (now 249), *i.e.* the objectives of a directive. The German courts were obliged, then, to interpret German law in such a way as to enforce the Equal Treatment Directive. The ECJ added, however, an important qualification to this obligation: "it is for the national court to interpret and apply the legislation adopted for the implementation of the Directive in conformity   **3-054** with the requirements of Community Law, in so far as it is given discretion to do so under national law." These qualifying words were, however, moderated in *Marleasing* (below) to "as far as possible".

3-055
The significance of this case is that it provides horizontal effect in an indirect way. Even though E.C. law is not applied directly, it may still be applied indirectly through the medium of domestic interpretation. As one might expect, the application of the *Von Colson* principle very much depends on the interpretation of the domestic courts.

The principle was extended in a very significant way by the case of *Marleasing SA v. La Comercial Internacional de Alimentacion SA* (1990, ECJ). The Court held that a national court was required to interpret its domestic legislation, whether it is legislation adopted prior to or subsequent to the Directive, as far as possible within the light of the wording and purpose of a directive, in order to achieve the result envisaged by it. To extend the principle even to legislation adopted prior to a directive is a large extension and, some would argue, may perhaps have an unfortunate effect in holding parties bound by a directive which was different in scope from the domestic legislation with which they are dutifully complying. Some argue this case is a large step towards accepting the horizontal direct effect of directives. The end result of such interpretation certainly appears to be the same, as far as the individual litigants are concerned.

3-056
Further comments on this principle are necessary at this point: first, the Court declined to apply the principle to extend criminal liability (*Pretore di Salo v. Persons Unknown* (1986, ECJ). Secondly, it is unclear to what extent national courts are required to depart from national law in order to achieve the result sought by the Directive. To achieve such a result may involve the national court departing significantly from the wording of national law. For instance, in the *Von Colson* case, the national law clearly limited the compensation payable to the two women to a nominal amount, whereas the ECJ held that the Directive required the amount to be effective. It does seem, however, that the national court is not required to override the clear wording and intent of national law in order to make it comply with the Directive which cannot be construed as directly effective *Euo Bus Austria GmbH v. Nouog* (1997, ECJ).

Thirdly, the ECJ has no jurisdiction to construe national law itself. It can only interpret the Directive and must leave it to the national court to construe national law in conformity with that interpretation. Commentators, such as Weatherill and Beaumont, in *EU Law* warn, in strong terms, of the dangers of the *Von Colson* principle:

> "it is dangerous to include national courts within the concept of a 'member state' for the purposes of Article 249. It is inappropriate constitutionally to require judges to implement directives into national law; this is a matter for the executive and the legislature."

7. Damages from a Tardy State: The Francovich Principle

Yet another remedy is available for a citizen who has suffered as a result **3-057** of the non-implementation of a directive but where the conditions for direct effect are not satisfied. In another case giving a bold interpretation to Article 5 (now 10), the ECJ held that, in certain conditions, the aggrieved citizen may have a remedy against the State in damages.

In *Francovich v. Italy* (1991), the applicants were employees of businesses **3-058** which became insolvent, leaving substantial arrears of unpaid salary. They brought proceedings in the Italian courts against Italy, for the recovery of compensation provided by Directive 80/987, which Italy had not implemented. The Directive guaranteed payment of unpaid remuneration in the case of insolvency by the employer. The applicants could not rely on the concept of direct effect, however, because the Directive's terms were insufficiently precise. The ECJ, nevertheless, held that the applicants were entitled to compensation from the State. Inherent in the Treaty, they said, was the principle that a Member State should be liable for damage to individuals caused by infringements of Community law for which it was responsible. Their interpretation rested, in particular, on Article 5 (now 10), which places a duty on Member States to take all appropriate measures to ensure the fulfilment of Treaty obligations. The ECJ argued that to disallow damages against the State in these circumstances would weaken the protection of individual rights. The Court laid down three conditions for an individual claiming damages against a Member State for failing to implement or incorrectly implementing a directive:

1. The result laid down by the Directive involves the attribution of rights attached to individuals.
2. The content of those rights must be capable of being identified from the provisions of the Directive.
3. There must be a causal link between the failure by the Member State to fulfil its obligations and the damage suffered by the individuals.

The ECJ has left it up to each Member State to determine the compe- **3-059** tent courts and appropriate procedures for legal actions intended to enable individuals to obtain damages from the State. The procedures must be not less favourable than those relating to similar claims under domestic law and must not make it difficult or practically impossible to obtain damages from the State. In *Becker v. Finanzamt Munster-Innestadt* (Case 8/81), in clarifying the above conditions, the ECJ held that provisions of directives can be invoked by individuals insofar as they define rights which individuals are able to assert against the State. Only a person with a direct interest could invoke a directive but this might include a third party: in *Verholen*, a husband could bring a claim where his wife was discriminated against in a social security benefit, as it disadvantaged him.

Damages from a State whose Legislature Flouts E.C. Law

3-060   In *Factortame 4*, properly known as the joined cases *Brasserie du Pecheur SA v. Federal Republic of Germany and R. v. Secretary of State for Transport, ex parte Factortame Ltd and Others (No. 4)* (1996, ECJ), the Court extended the principle it had developed in *Francovich* to permit a claim of damages against a State, to instances where its national legislature had passed a law which was in serious breach of E.C. law. In the first case, French beer manufacturers were claiming damages against Germany for passing beer purity laws that effectively excluded the import of their beer. In the second case, the United Kingdom Parliament had passed the Merchant Shipping Act 1988, which effectively excluded foreign fishing vessels, notably Spanish, from their right to fish in British coastal waters, by laying down registration conditions of residence, nationality and domicile of vessel owners. Spanish fishermen complained that the Act offended against Art. 52 (now 43), which guarantees freedom of establishment. In prior cases, the Court had already ruled the domestic legislation to be in breach of E.C. law. What was now at issue was whether the aggrieved parties could claim damages against the respective states in the national courts. The *Factortame* case had been referred by the Queen's Bench Divisional Court for an Art. 177 (now 234) preliminary ruling. The ECJ decided the following (paraphrased):

1.   The *Francovich* principle, making states liable for loss or damage suffered by individuals and caused by the State's breach of E.C. law, applied to all state authorities, including the legislature.
2.   The conditions of a claim of damages in this context were:

   a.   that the rule of Community law breached was intended to confer rights on the individuals who had suffered loss or injury;
   b.   that the breach was sufficiently serious: the Member State had manifestly and gravely disregarded the limits on its discretion;
   c.   that there was a direct causal link between the breach and the damage sustained by the individuals.

The State must make good the consequences of the damage, in accordance with its national law on liability but the conditions laid down must not be less favourable than for a domestic claim and must not make it excessively difficult or impossible to make a claim. (Comment: in the context of English law, it was virtually impossible for the Spanish fishing vessel owners to claim damages in the English courts, because we have no substantive or procedural law enabling a claim for damages against Parliament.)

3. Such a claim could not be made conditional on establishing a degree of fault going beyond that of a sufficiently serious breach of Community law.

4. Reparation must be commensurate with the damage sustained and this might include exemplary damages, where a public authority had acted oppressively, arbitrarily or unconstitutionally. It was left to the domestic legal system of each Member State to set the criteria for determining the extent of reparation.

5. Damages could not be limited to those sustained after a judgment finding such an infringement of Community law.

The upshot of these cases was, in 1996, that the onus was on the United **3-061** Kingdom to find some procedure, in the English courts, for making a claim against the State for a breach of E.C. law by Parliament. Not only must we find a procedure but we must devise some substantive cause of action in damages. Neither the ground nor the procedure had to be too difficult to allow the Spanish claim. In 1997, the Spanish brought their claim through the Queen's Bench Divisional Court and were awarded damages. This was upheld by the Court of Appeal then the House of Lords so the Secretary of State for Transport lost in all three courts. The House found that the Government, in introducing this legislation had acted carefully and deliberately to discriminate on grounds of nationality in the face of a clear and fundamental provision of the Treaty, former Article 7. This was done in good faith and to protect British fishing communities rather than to harm the Spanish but inevitably it took away or seriously affected their rights to fish. There was a fundamental breach of Treaty obligations. It was a sufficiently serious breach to entitle Factortame and 96 others to compensation in damages: *R. v. S.S. for Transport, ex parte Factortame Ltd And Others (No. 5)* (1999, HL).

Notice that *Factortame 4* was swiftly followed by a case which clarified **3-062** how bad the breach of E.C. law had to be before damages could be claimed. In *R. v. H.M. Treasury, ex parte British Telecommunications plc* (ECJ, 1996), the Court ruled that damages could be claimed by individuals who had suffered loss as a consequence of a State's enacting a directive incorrectly (this much was not new). The important point about this case, however, was that they ruled that the breach of E.C. law was not sufficiently serious to merit damages. The United Kingdom had acted in good faith and simply made a mistake in its enactment into U.K. law of the relevant Directive. The wording of the Directive was ambiguous and several other Member States had also misinterpreted it so there was no manifest and grave breach of E.C. law, as required by *Factortame 4*.

Steiner and Woods point out quite rightly, however, that in the cases after this, the ECJ's application of the *Factortame-Brasserie du Pecheur* principles is inconsistent, despite their clarity. For instance, the result in *R. v. Ministry of Agriculture, Fisheries and Food, ex parte Hedley Lomas Ireland Ltd*, two months after the BT case, was "surprising", because it found that a State's "mere infringement" of Community law might be sufficient to warrant an action for damages, where the State was not "called upon to make any legislative choices or has a considerably reduced choice, or none". In this case and *Dillenkofer*, the Court did not list and apply the principles listed in *Factortame-Brasserie du Pecheur* but did revert to its approach in the BT case, in *Denkavit* and other cases, then applied the stricter *Hedley Lomas* principles in another case against the United Kingdom MAFF.

8. General Principles of Law

3-063   Over its relatively short lifetime, the ECJ has built up and interpreted a body of general principles. They must be applied in interpreting E.C. law, including E.C. elements of domestic law. They can be invoked by States and individuals to challenge community action or inaction, to claim damages against and they can be used to challenge a Member State. These general principles, developed by the ECJ as the English courts have developed the common law, should be distinguished from the fundamental principles of the E.C. Treaty (*e.g.* free movement of goods and persons; non-discrimination). In part, the general principles are derived from fundamental right in individual Member States. The ECJ could not be seen to be taking these away, nor could it leave E.C. law in a state conflicting with constitutional rights in any Member State so in *Internationale Handelsgesellschaft mbH*, the ECJ, while asserting the primacy of E.C. law, pointed out that respect for fundamental rights was part of E.C. law. The Court looks for principles common to Member States' constitutions and is guided by international treaties to which Member States are signatories, the most obvious and important being the European Convention on Human Rights. The rights include, for example:

- proportionality: administrative authorities must not use means more than appropriate and necessary to achieve their ends;
- legal certainty: includes the principle of legitimate expectation (same as English law) and the principle of non-retroactivity;

- natural justice: the right to a fair hearing (same as English law), the duty to give reasons, due process;
- the right to protection against self- incrimination;
- equality;
- subsidiarity (in the E.C. Treaty, now Art. 5): the Community can only act if its objectives cannot be achieved by the Member States.

9. The E.U. and the European Convention on Human Rights

All the Member States are signatories of the Convention so one would **3-064** think the obvious way for the ECJ to guarantee rights would be for the E.C. to be a signatory of the Convention. An attempt to do this was, however, declared invalid by the ECJ. The 1996 Intergovernmental Conference failed to have accession incorporated into the Treaty of Amsterdam. The ECJ will continue to apply the Convention rights within its jurisdiction. What happens in the Union, outside the E.C. and the relationship between Union law and the Convention is much more complex and was explored in the *Matthews* case (1999, ECHR). In this case, Ms Matthews, a British resident of Gibraltar, applied in 1994 to register as a voter in the European Parliamentary elections. Her application was denied. She then brought an action on the basis of the Convention, Article 3, Protocol 1 which provides that that the State will provide for elections by secret ballot to ensure free expression of the people in the choice of legislature. The ECHR upheld her claim. The ECHR drew a distinction between acts of the E.U., which could not be challenged before it, as the E.U. is not a State party to the Convention, and acts of Member States of the E.U. Contracting States of the Convention remain responsible for ensuring that Convention rights are guaranteed and their obligation could not be set aside by subsequent Treaties entered into by the States. The ECHR noted the ECJ's jurisprudence in which it recognised and protected Convention rights. Legislation emanating from the E.U. institutions had the potential to affect the citizens of Gibraltar to the same extent as Gibraltar's domestic legislation and the United Kingdom would thus be obliged to secure for the citizens of Gibraltar the rights guaranteed by Article 3, Protocol 1 of the Convention, irrespective of whether they were elections to the domestic or European Parliament. Further, Gibraltar was affected by the supremacy of E.C. law, as much as any other E.C. territory. The problem for the United Kingdom, however, is that, for the vote to be granted to Gibraltarians to the E.U. Parliament, a unanimous vote of the Council is required and Spain refuses to co-operate. As Nash and Furse remark, this case demonstrates that the current position is unsatisfactory. For an explanation, see their comment and Steiner and Woods at 127–129.

10. Direct Effect of Community Law in the United Kingdom

3-065   The European Communities Act 1972 gave legal effect to E.C. law in the United Kingdom. Pay close attention to the wording of section 2(1):

> "All such rights, powers, liabilities, obligations and restrictions from time to time created or arising by or under the Treaties, and all such remedies and procedures from time to time provided for by or under the Treaties, as in accordance with the Treaties are without further enactment to be given legal effect or used in the United Kingdom shall be recognised and available in law, and be enforced, allowed and followed accordingly; and the expression 'enforceable Community right' and similar expressions shall be read as referring to one to which this subsection applies."

In the *Factortame (No. 1)* case of 1990, the House of Lords interpreted "enforceable Community right" to mean directly effective legal right. This section gives effect to all directly effective Community law, whether made prior to or after the passing of the Act.

3-066   Section 3 binds all our courts to interpret matters of E.C. law in accordance with the rulings of the ECJ and requires our courts to take judicial notice of E.C. legislation and the opinions of the ECJ. Our courts have had no problem in applying directly effective provisions. They seem to have been reluctant in some cases, however, to apply the *Von Colson* principle. In *Duke v. Reliance Systems Ltd*, Duke complained that she had been forced to retire at 60, despite her male colleagues' being permitted to work until 65. Equal Treatment Directive 76/207 was not enacted into domestic law until the Sex Discrimination Act 1986. Duke could not rely on the Directive as directly effective because her employer was a private company. She argued that the English courts should construe the unamended Sex Discrimination Act 1975 in a manner consistent with the Equal Treatment Directive, treating her enforced retirement as unlawful dismissal. The House of Lords considered the case of *Von Colson* but opined that it did not provide a power to interfere with the method or result of the interpretation of national legislation by national courts. They noted that the Equal Treatment Directive postdated the Sex Discrimination Act 1975 and thought it would be unfair on Reliance to "distort" the construction of the Act to accommodate it. The House of Lords later applied the same objections in relation to the Northern Ireland legislation, despite the fact that it was passed after the Directive (*Finnegan*, 1990, HL).

Nevertheless, the House is prepared to make a distinction when con-   **3-067**
struing national legislation that has been passed in order to implement a
directive. In *Pickstone v. Freemans plc* (1989, HL) the House adopted a purposive construction in interpreting an amendment to the Equal Pay Act
1970, in order to make it consistent with the United Kingdom's obligations under the Equal Pay Directive. The same purposive approach was
taken in *Ulster v. Forth Dry Dock & Engineering Co. Ltd* (1990, HL). In this
case, Lord Templeman said he thought the *Von Colson* principle imposed
a duty on the United Kingdom courts to give a purposive construction to
United Kingdom legislation which had been passed to give effect to directives. In *Webb v. EMO Air Cargo (U.K.) Ltd* (1992, HL), Lord Keith, giving
the opinion of the House, said it was the duty of the United Kingdom
court to construe domestic legislation in accordance with the ECJ's interpretation of a relevant Community Directive "if that can be done without
distorting the meaning of the domestic legislation". He noted that,
according to the ECJ, this obligation on the domestic courts only arises
where domestic law is open to an interpretation consistent with a directive. In this case the House agreed with the Court of Appeal, the
Employment Appeal Tribunal and an industrial tribunal that the applicant had not suffered discrimination under English law. They nevertheless asked the ECJ to construe the relevant directive and the application
of the principle of equal treatment to the circumstances of the case. The
ECJ sent back its interpretation, flatly disagreeing with the House and
ruling that the facts of the case disclosed discrimination. The House
applied the ECJ's ruling in October 1995. The report provides an interesting example of how the House had to construe an English statute in
accordance with E.C. law in a way which seemed to run contrary to the
instincts of domestic courts at all levels.

11. Supremacy of Community Law in the United Kingdom

Curiously, the founding Treaty of the European Community, the   **3-068**
Treaty of Rome 1957, did not prescribe the supremacy of Community
law over national law. It was left to the embryonic ECJ in developing its
limbs, to describe the conception of its supremacy in *Costa v. E.N.E.L.*
(1964, ECJ). This quotation is as oft-cited and as jurisprudentially significant as Lord Atkin's famous neighbour principle, which did so much
more than just resolve the problems caused when a snail was left to
decompose in a bottle of ginger beer. In addition, the words below are so
constitutionally significant, they should be learned and absorbed by every
British citizen, let alone every student of English law:

"By creating a Community of unlimited duration, having its own institutions, its own personality, its own legal capacity and capacity of representation on the international plane and, more particularly, real powers stemming from a limitation of sovereignty or a transfer of powers from the States to the Community, the Member States have limited their sovereignty rights, albeit within limited fields, and have thus created a body of law which binds both their nationals and themselves.

The integration into the laws of each Member State of provisions which derive from the Community, and more generally the terms and the spirit of the Treaty, make it impossible for the States, as a corollary, to accord precedence to a unilateral and subsequent measure over a legal system accepted by them on a basis of reciprocity."

By 1970, the Court had asserted the supremacy of E.C. law, even over Member States' constitutions (the *Internationale Handelsgesellschaft* case, 1970, ECJ). By 1977, in *Simmenthal*, the Court had explained that this meant that every court, however lowly, was under a duty to disapply national law in favour of Community law, where there was a clear conflict. Furthermore, in the *Factortame* case of 1990, the Court added that national courts must be capable of protecting claimed Community law rights in the face of clear contrary provisions in national law, pending the ECJ's final ruling on the precise nature of those rights.

The Effects of E.C. Sovereignty Within the United Kingdom

3-069   In the European Communities Act 1972, the British Parliament effectively gave away its legislative sovereignty in matters within the E.C.'s sphere of activity, recognising the principle of supremacy of directly effective E.C. law over domestic legislation. The crucial words of section 2(4) are both retrospective and prospective:

". . . any enactment passed or to be passed . . . shall be construed and have effect subject to the foregoing provisions of this section".

This means that, where domestic law conflicts with directly effective E.C. law, the latter must be applied and the only way of altering this position is to repeal this subsection. The House of Lords recognised that this was the effect of this subsection in *Factortame* (1990) when they disapplied part of the Merchant Shipping Act 1988, the clear words of which flew in the face of established Community law rights, including freedom of establishment and non-discrimination.

In this case, as explained above, Spanish owners of fishing vessels sought to register as British so that they would have access to the British Fishing quota under the common fisheries policy. The 1988 Act attempted to limit registration to British managed vessels. *Factortame* and others sought a judicial review in the High Court of the legality of the Act. The High Court referred the question of E.C. law to the ECJ but, meanwhile, the procedural question of how to grant interim relief found its way up to the House of Lords. The House declined to grant an interim injunction against the Crown as an injunction cannot, in English law, bind the Crown. Furthermore, they objected, the applicants' Community law rights were "necessarily uncertain" until determined by the ECJ and appeared to run directly contrary to Parliament's sovereign will. They sought a preliminary ruling from the ECJ. The Court answered by saying that where the sole obstacle preventing a national court from granting interim relief based on Community law is a rule of national law, that rule of national law must be set aside. Not surprisingly, when the ECJ ruled on the substantive question, they upheld *Factortame*'s complaint that part of the Merchant Shipping Act ran contrary to E.C. law.

In *Equal Opportunities Commission v. Secretary of State for Employment* (1994, **3-070** HL), the House of Lords confirmed that the *Factortame* case had established that a declaration could be obtained in judicial review proceedings that an Act of Parliament is incompatible with Community law. In this case the House accepted the EOC's complaint that part of the Employment Protection (Consolidation) Act 1978 was in breach of Community law. The Act was subsequently amended by Parliament.

A Comment on *Factortame 4*

The United Kingdom media reacted especially badly to the *Factorame* **3-071** *4* ruling, affronted at the thought of having to pay retrospective damages to the Spanish for stopping them coming and raiding "our" fish stocks. What is so ridiculous is that we reacted as if the ruling were a surprise. When we passed this piece of protectionist legislation in 1988, we were warned formally by the Commission, in 1989, acting under their former Article 169 powers, that we were in breach of the Treaty so we might have guessed that the ultimate punchline would be that we would have to pay damages to the Spanish. We reacted with the same indignant horror to *Factortame 1*, in 1990, which effectively ruled that a part of the Merchant Shipping Act would have to be suspended, as if we were shocked at this assault on the legislative sovereignty of Parliament. Apparently many of us had not noticed, or worked out that we had given this away, on joining the common market, as it then was, in January 1973. As if to rub salt into the wound made by *Factortame 4*, in March 1996, the beef crisis broke out within days of the judgment. We entered the hypocritical position of arguing that the Court's powers should be curbed, by the 1996 Intergovernmental Conference (the renegotiation of Maastricht), yet at the same time lodging a claim before the Court against the Commission for losses caused by the export ban on British beef.

12. The Charter of Fundamental Rights (2000)

3-072   This was signed at the end of 2000. It is declaratory only and therefore its legal status seems to be "soft law" but it has already been referred to, in 2001, by the ECJ in the *BECTU* case. It is addressed to the Community institutions and Member States when implementing E.C. law. It put social and economic rights on the same footing as civil and political rights. The rights include dignity, freedoms (*e.g.* liberty, freedom of expression, equality, solidarity, good administration and justice). Art. 21 (1) declares against any form of discrimination. As a *Times* journalist commented, however, in October 2000, "(o)pponents will portray the document as an embryonic European Constitution that will bring a European "superstate" a step closer, be seized on by the European Court of Justice and roll back the British labour reforms of the 1980s". Notice the ECJ prediction was proved correct within six months.

13. The Future of the E.U.: The Nice Treaty 2000; The Corpus Juris Project

3-073   The Nice Treaty resulted from the Inter Governmental Conference of 2000 but whether it will ever be ratified in its present form is now open to doubt, as the citizens of Eire voted, in 2001, not to ratify it. If it is ever validated, this is what it provides for:

- enlargement from 2005 but expectation that there will be no new accession States
- alterations to the Council and Commission
- increasing the Assembly
- judicial panels attached to the CFI
- some Article 234 references heard by the CFI
- a protocol on the ECJ re. procedural rules.

The *corpus juris* Project

3-074   The Commission is pressing for a greater measure of control over criminal investigation and prosecution within Member States. It is thought this is needed to combat organised crime. The aim is to protect the financial interest of the E.U. (protecting the budget; tax evasion). It is directed at eight crimes: fraud, market rigging, abuse of office, misappropriation of funds, disclosure of secrets derived from office-holding, money laundering and receiving and conspiracy. Consequences may include a Community police force, customs service and courts and ultimately a legal service.

FURTHER READING

www.europa.eu.int comprehensive links to European institutions. **3-075**

www.parliament.uk for excellent factsheets on E.C. institutions and law and details of how E.C. law and E.U. policy are scrutinised in both Houses.

J. Steiner and L. Woods, *EC Law* (7th ed., 2000). New edition every two years.

N. Foster, *Blackstone's EC Legislation* (new edition annually).

S. Weatherill and P. Beaumont, *EU Law* (3rd ed., 1999).

P. Craig and G. De Burca, *EU Law, Text Cases and Materials.*

JUSTICE "Justice in Europe", 1997.

T. Tayleur, "Emanations of the State" (2000) 150 N.L.J. 1292.

M. Fletcher, "Fresh row brews over European rights Bill", *The Times*, October 2, 2000.

S. Nash and M. Furse, "Human Rights Law Update" (1999) 149 N.L.J. 891.

4. The European Convention on Human Rights and English Law

1. Incorporation into United Kingdom Law

The European Convention on Human Rights was drafted over 50 years **4-001** ago by British lawyers. It grew out of a disgust with fascism and an anxiety to protect basic freedoms. It is a Treaty of the Council of Europe. The United Kingdom, led by a Labour government, was the first signatory (1951). From 1966, the Government allowed individuals to bring claims against the United Kingdom. By 1998, 99 cases had been taken against the United Kingdom, more than any country except Italy, and the United Kingdom had been found to be in violation of the Convention 52 times. The United Kingdom was a very frequent defendant before the European Court of Human Rights, partly because we lack a written constitution. Prior to 1998, the individual could not assert their Convention rights through the domestic courts. Judges of the United Kingdom were powerless to apply it. The courts, in any event, took a fairly conservative approach, despite "ingenious and persistent invitations by counsel" to depart from domestic law (Bingham L.C.J. in his maiden speech in the Lords, 1996). The Lord Chief Justice made a speech urging incorporation of the Convention and in the Court of Appeal he and his fellow judges expressed dissatisfaction with their powerlessness to allow appeals in a case which raised Convention issues: *R. v. Morrissey* (1997). The Conservative administrations of the early 1990s had grown hostile to the ECHR, especially because of decisions such as that against Home Secretary Michael Howard in relation to sentencing juveniles and against the United Kingdom and in favour of the IRA families in the Death on the Rock case (which Michael Heseltine called "ludicrous") and called for an alteration to its powers. They urged on the Court the recognition of a greater "margin of appreciation", the principle by which the ECHR permits latitude to the law in the contracting states, and wanted the Court to pay greater heed to domestic circumstances and traditions. They sought a new fact-finding procedure and vetting of potential judges. They were dilatory in enforcing the judgments of the ECHR which they did not like (see Bindman). In 1996, the Labour opposition issued a consultation paper on their plans to incorporate Convention rights should they be elected. The Lords had a two-day debate on the Constitution, in which, despite Lord Bingham's entreaties, the Conservative Lord Chancellor Mackay expressed the view that United Kingdom citizens were adequately protected by the common law. Enacting a Bill of Rights would, he feared, give the courts wide discretion over matters which were properly the preserve of Parliament. The generalised wording of the Convention would leave too much scope for judicial interpretation and litigation. Lord Irvine, then Shadow Lord Chancellor, opened the case for the Opposition, pointing out that Britain was virtually alone amongst the major nations of Western Europe in failing to give its citizens the means to assert Convention rights in the courts (see Hudson). Once in Government, New Labour swiftly published a white paper, *Bringing Rights Home*. In the Tom Sergeant Memorial Lecture in 1997, Lord Chancellor Irvine said

> "The Human Rights Bill . . . will be a constitutional change of major significance, protecting the individual citizen against erosion of liberties, either deliberate or gradual. It will promote a culture where positive rights and liberties become the focus and concern of legislators, administrators and judges alike".

The Human Rights Bill would require judges to produce a decision on the morality of conduct, not simply its compliance with the bare letter of the law. He thought the traditional common law approach to the protection of liberties, described as a negative right (the right to do anything not prohibited by law), offered little protection against creeping erosion of individual liberties by a legislature. The Human Rights Act 1998 incorporated the Convention into English law on October 2, 2000. This means the Convention rights become part of United Kingdom law and thus English law and can be enforced by English and Welsh courts and tribunals.

4-002   Once the Act was about to come into force, the point was made that our judiciary would become the guardians of individuals' rights as the Lord Chancellor called them in the Paul Sieghart Memorial Lecture, 1999. The newspapers carried a number of articles expressing concern about the judicial appointment system, manifesting a distrust of the Oxbridge white, male judiciary it produced to enforce Convention rights. Liberals like Lord Lester had campaigned for over 30 years for incorporation but the Conservative Lord Kingsland reiterated traditional fears about the Act, like those expressed above. (See their views in the special *Times* supplement.)

The Human Rights Act 1998, in Force October 2, 2000

The best explanation of the Convention in the English legal system is **4-003** by Robin White in his excellent 1999 book, *The English Legal System in Action*. You would do yourself a big favour by visiting the Government's two very informative websites, the Home Office Human Rights Unit and the LCD Human Rights site, with their excellent links to other Human Rights sites. While in one of the websites, click on the Act itself and take a look at it or go directly to the statute on the HMSO website. Look at the Schedule to the Act, as that lists the Convention rights.

Section 1 and Schedule 1 restate Conventions and Protocols as part of United Kingdom law with the exception of Article 13. Article 13 would have given a remedy for violation in any court or tribunal. The Government did not want to give them sweeping, new, inappropriate powers. People will have to seek remedies elsewhere, such as on appeal or in judicial review proceedings.

Section 2 provides that when a court or tribunal is determining a ques- **4-004** tion in connection with a Convention right it "must take into account" judgments, decisions or declarations of the ECHR, or opinions or decisions of the Commission or the Committee of Ministers. Notice this does not mean the ECHR decisions are binding, as the White Paper explained. This is in distinct contrast with the binding decisions of the ECJ, as provided by the European Communities Act 1972. Section 3 of the Human Rights Act says "(s)o far as possible, primary legislation and subordinate legislation must be read and given effect in a way which is compatible with the Convention rights". Notice two things: this applies to all of us in interpreting legislation, not just the courts but the obligation is qualified. This is important. Section 6 makes it unlawful for any public authority, including any court or tribunal, to act in a way incompatible with a Convention right. Notice the meaning of "public authority" has already been criticised by academics and others as too vague. Any party to any legal proceedings can rely on a Convention right. This means, for example, it can be used to apply for a stay (stop) of proceedings, as a defence, a ground of appeal or to found an application for judicial review. If a court or tribunal is satisfied of a violation, they may award anything appropriate within their jurisdiction. Damages or compensation may only be awarded by those courts or tribunals empowered to do so (s.8).

Where courts cannot interpret a piece of legislation as compatible, then **4-005** certain courts may make a declaration of incompatibility, under section 4(2) but in the English legal system, only these courts have this power: HC, CA, HL, PC and the Courts Martial-Appeal Court. A lesser court or tribunal must apply the incompatible law and the case will have to be taken on appeal until one of these courts is reached. This may take two levels of appeal. For instance, the Employment Appeal Tribunal and Social Security Commissioners do not have this power. The declaration of incompatibility does not affect validity and is not binding on the parties (s.4). In any case where a court is considering making a declaration of incompatibility, the Crown is entitled to notice and to be joined as a party to the proceedings (s.5). Section 11 provides for a fast track legislative procedure designed to remove the incompatibility, as described in the Chapter on sources so a Minister can use a statutory instrument to amend offending primary legislation and, as explained in that Chapter, this "Henry VIII" section of the Act is controversial. People can still apply to the Strasbourg Court but they will have to show they have exhausted all domestic remedies.

Section 19 obliges the sponsoring minister to make a written statement that a new Bill is compatible or decline to make a statement but indicate that the Government wishes to proceed. A Joint Parliamentary Committee on Human Rights has been created.

4-006   The Act necessitated the biggest project in training judges and magistrates ever managed by the Judicial Studies Board. The Board has an H.R. Working Group. Like the ECJ, the European Court of Human Rights takes a highly purposive approach to legislative interpretation. This will have to permeate down to our judiciary. This will be an obvious impact on precedent and existing judicial interpretations of statute. In order to effect a Convention right, the Court of Appeal may consider itself not to be bound by previous binding precedents which are incompatible with Convention rights. This was explained in the 1997 White Paper *Rights Brought Home.* This can be seen in relation to criminal procedure and criminal appeals, as explained in the Criminal procedure Chapter. A very interesting illustration of a High Court judge deciding that the Convention overrode a clear common law principle occurred in *The Sunday Mirror* case, in 2001, below, under Article 10.

The Privy Council has held that provisions of constitutional human rights legislation "call for a generous interpretation, avoiding what has been called 'the austerity of tabulated legalism', suitable to give individuals the full measure of the fundamental rights and freedoms referred to", *Ministry of Home Affairs v. Fisher* (1980).

A number of extra judges were created to deal with what the Government predicted would be a heavy workload generated by the HRA 1998. The statistical bulletin on the LCD website analysing court business in the first three months after the implementation of the Act discloses that its impact was not as significant as predicted during that period. By October 2001, however, when the Act had been in force for a year, the Convention had been considered in 167 cases in the High Court and above. See Starmer. Many far-fetched claims have failed. In *R. v.*

Commissioner of Police of the Metropolis (2001), the High Court warned lawyers that the Convention should not be invoked when the deprivation of rights was merely theoretical or illusory.

JUSTICE has recommended a Human Rights Commission to educate **4-007** the public and take cases and provide information and assistance to individuals and bodies affected by the Act.

The Justices' Clerks' Society welcomed the Bill but warned that it provided scope for considerable time to be spent in argument at the magistrates' court which will not affect the result of the case at that stage. The Justices are obliged to take account of Convention rights but are powerless to make a declaration of incompatibility. This could lead to cumulative delay in contested hearings.

2. The Convention Rights

These are appended to the HRA 1998 as Schedule 1, where they are **4-008** spelled out in full. Briefly, they are, by Article:

2. Right to life.
3. Prohibition of torture.
4. Prohibition of slavery and forced labour.
5. Right to liberty and security.
6. Right to a fair trial.
7. No punishment without law.
8. Right to respect for private and family life.
9. Freedom of thought, conscience and religion.
10. Freedom of expression.
11. Freedom of assembly and association.
12. Right to marry.
13. Not incorporated into English law. See above.
14. Prohibition of discrimination.
16. Restrictions on political activity of aliens.
17. Prohibition of abuse of rights.
18. Limitation on use of restrictions on rights.

Some rights are absolute, such as 3. Some admit exceptions, such as 2 and most are subject to restrictions to ensure respect for other rights and freedoms.

3. The European Court of Human Rights

Until the 1990s, there was a part-time two-stage system for dealing with **4-009** applications. Cases would first be determined by the Commission and then by the Court. Not infrequently, the latter disagreed with the former. Following a special meeting of the Council of Europe's Committee of Ministers, in 1993, the new full-time single Court was opened, in 1998, with the hope that it would be quicker and more efficient. Three judges filter applications and those deemed admissible go to panels of seven judges. Exceptionally, a grand chamber of 17 will hear the most difficult cases and cases where their decision may be inconsistent with a previous one.

The Committee of Ministers

4-010   This is the decision-making organ of the Council of Europe and is composed of the foreign Ministers of the 40 contracting States. It supervises the execution of the Court's judgments and can check that a State has taken steps to amend offending legislation.

4. The Approach of the European Court of Human Rights

4-011   A.T.H. Smith explains the principles upon which the ECHR has acted:

1. A generous approach is taken when determining what comes within the scope of the rights.
2. There are four requirements for a conditions can be imposed on a right:

    *   interference must be lawful;
    *   it must serve a legitimate purpose;
    *   it must be necessary in a democratic society;
    *   it must not be discriminatory.

3. The Convention is a "living instrument", which means that the older a decision, the less value it may have as a guide to construction.

4-012   The Court has held that the Convention, not the domestic court, determines whether proceedings are civil or criminal, thus questions are currently hanging over the status of fine defaulters' courts (see other Chapters of this book) and Anti Social Behaviour Orders, which the Government presumed were civil when it introduced them in the Crime and Disorder Act 1998 (*R. (McCann and Others) v. Manchester Crown Court* (2001, CA). In *Georgiou v. U.K.* (2001) the ECHR held that penalty assessments for VAT were criminal matters (see discussion of domestic consequences by

McFarlane) and in *King v. Walden* (2001) the Chancery Division held the same applied to determinations of the tax commissioners to penalise defaulting taxpayers.

One practical drawback in the Court's functioning is its backlog, like the ECJ. In 2000, it had over 12,600 applications waiting to be heard. Another is the fact that the Court does not award compensation itself. The Council of Europe's Parliamentary Assembly is becoming increasingly critical of the reluctance of some States to execute the Court's judgments and proposes to introduce a system of fines for persistent offenders. The Court's primary principle in assessing compensation is that victims should, as far as possible, be placed in the same position as if the violation of their rights had not occurred. There are some points where the structure of damages differs from that of the United Kingdom courts. For details, see *Damages Under the HRA*, a Law Commission Report. Following a finding of a breach of the Convention, the State is legally obliged to make reparation for the consequences of the violation. Where the domestic law affords only partial reparation, Article 41 provides that the Court can award an applicant "just satisfaction" for pecuniary and non-pecuniary damage.

5. Examples of the Convention's Application in English Law

It should be understood that cases against any State before the ECHR are of equal value to the English and Welsh courts in assisting them to apply the Convention. Below I list just a few recent cases which involved the United Kingdom as a respondent. This is only a sample, not a comprehensive list so you can start to understand the impact of Human Rights law on English law. **4-013**

Article 2 Right to Life

- Where an applicant was diagnosed with leukaemia, having been born in 1966, eight years after her father was present during four nuclear tests, there was no breach by the Government in failing to warn her parents or monitor her father's dose levels, in the light of information available to the national authorities at the time. There was no evidence of a causal link: *LCB v. U.K.* (1998). **4-014**

- Failure to conduct a proper investigation into the circumstances of the deaths of persons killed in the fight against terrorism in Northern Ireland, in circumstances which "cried out for explanation" was a violation: *Jordan v. U.K.* and three joined applications (2001, ECHR). These applicants were all families of alleged victims of the United Kingdom's "Shoot to Kill" policy against Northern Ireland terrorists, including an innocent bystander. Damages were not awarded for the deaths as the facts were disputed. The procedural deficiencies were: the police investigation lacked independence; the DPP's decision not to prosecute was unexplained; the inquests were futile because the coroners (unlike English coroners) could not give opinions on civil or criminal liability; the inquests were not prompt; legal aid was not available and documents were not disclosed in advance of the inquests. As a result of this case, changes are proposed, at my time of writing, to coroners' powers in Northern Ireland, to allow the compelling of suspects believed to be responsible for deaths to attend hearings and the power to state that the death was unlawful.

- In 1995, the Court found a violation of the right to life in the notorious "Death on the Rock" case, where the SAS had shot dead three IRA members in Gibraltar, suspected of having planted a car bomb. This ruling provoked a hostile reaction from Michael Heseltine, a Conservative minister. See above. For a full account see *The Guardian* and other newspapers of September 28, 1995.

- An application by parents of Argentinian victims of the sinking of the *General Belgrano* in the Falklands war was struck out as out of time. It should have been within six months of the incident: *Rosas etc. v. U.K.* (2000).

- In the cases arising out of the shoot to kill policy operated by the United Kingdom Government in Northern Ireland, the Court held that the procedural aspects of Art. 2 had been violated.

Article 3 Inhuman and Degrading Treatment

4-015
- The United Kingdom's failure to provide children with protection against serious long-term neglect and abuse was a breach: *Z. v. U.K.* (2001, ECHR)

- The Court held the United Kingdom to be in breach for allowing the defence of lawful chastisement in criminal law to a stepfather who used a cane.

- Where a prisoner committed suicide, after manifesting suicidal tendencies, the Court found a breach because of lack of medical records of the detainee's mental state and treatment by a doctor who lacked specialist psychiatric knowledge. Further, the imposition of an additional sentence, close to his release date, was incompatible with the required standard of treatment in respect of the mentally ill: *Keenan v. U.K.* (2001).

- Expelling an asylum seeker to a country where there were clear human rights problems and where the applicant had given evidence of ill treatment, leading to the death of his brother, was a potential breach of Art. 3. See also *Chahal v. U.K.* (1996).

Article 5 Liberty and Security

* See Chapter on criminal procedure on bail, etc.   **4-016**
* Mental Health Review Tribunal procedure was held by the Court of Appeal to be in breach, because it placed the burden of proof on the restricted patient to show he was no longer suffering from a mental disorder: *R. (H) v. MHRT etc.* (2001).
* The continued detention of a person no longer suffering from mental illness was a violation: *Johnson v. U.K.* (1997).
* The treatment of the applicants, sentenced indeterminately "at Her Majesty's pleasure", as juveniles, was a breach, since, after the expiry of the fixed "tariff" part of their sentence, they were unable to have the lawfulness of their continued detention reviewed by a court. For instance, the Parole Board had considered and recommended the release of one applicant but the Home Secretary informed the applicant that he had not accepted the recommendation. The lack of adversarial proceedings prevented it from being a court or court-like body: *Hussain v. U.K., Singh v. U.K.* (1996). Similarly, the 15-year tariff set by the child killers of Jamie Bulger was later declared to breach the Convention.

Article 6 Fair Trial

Per Lord Steyn in *Kebilene*, above, "when article 6 of the Convention   **4-017**
becomes part of our law, it will be the prism through which other aspects of our criminal law may have to be re-examined".

* See Chapter on criminal procedure.
* The Court has repeatedly found against the United Kingdom in relation to courts-martial proceedings, for instance, in *Findlay v. U.K.* (1997); *Coyne v. U.K.* (1997). Since a defendant's commanding officer and other officers participated in proceedings, they were insufficiently independent. It paid compensation in a friendly settlement of six applications in 2000. Parliament swiftly passed the Armed Forces Discipline Act 2000 to amend the systems to make them compatible with the Convention. Systems of military adjudication which had been in place for over 600 years had to be altered. At the time of the *Findlay* case, there were 50 others outstanding, which are costing millions of pounds to settle. In response to *Findlay*, the Conservative Government had introduced the Armed Forces Bill (later Act) of 1996 but it was inadequate to remedy the defect.

- The ECHR has frequently ruled that in cases where it takes a long time to bring proceedings to a conclusion, there has been a breach. They delivered 248 judgments against Italy in the first eight months of 2000. In *Howath v. U.K.* (38081/97) the Court of Appeal had substituted a sentence of imprisonment for a community service order two years after the original sentence. The Court held there had been a breach. Similarly, in the *Robins* case of 1997, the Court held four years was an inordinate delay in settling costs in a civil case but, ironically, it took four and a half years for the application to be resolved by the ECHR.

- The denial of a public hearing and pronouncement on judgment in public in child custody proceedings was not a breach: *B. v. U.K.*, *P. v. U.K.* (2001, ECHR).

- The Road Traffic Act 1988, s.172, which requires a registered owner to reveal the identity of the driver of a car is not a breach of the privilege against self-incrimination: *Brown* (2000, PC). This case put an end to hundreds of speeding drivers thinking they could get away with not responding after being caught on speed cameras.

- The nature of judicial review proceedings which restricted the court to examining the quality of the decision-making process rather than the merits of the decision meant that an applicant alleging bias had not had a fair hearing: *Kingsley v. U.K.* (2001, ECHR). Here, the problem was that the Court of Appeal had held that the Gaming Board of G.B. had taken a biased decision but had no power to remit it to the Board.

- There are many cases in the history of the ECHR where applicants claim a breach of Article 6 because of the unavailability of legal aid.

- The domestic planning process ground to a halt by February 2001, by many challenges in the High Court that it breached Article 6. Some of those challenges had been upheld by the High Court and all planning appeals were suspended while cases were hastily sent up to the House of Lords using the leapfrog procedure. The House of Lords put paid to all such claims by upholding the Secretary of State's appeals in *R.v. Secretary of State for the Environment Transport and the Regions, ex parte Holding and Barnes plc* and joined cases (2001). The Minister's powers under the Town and Country Planning Act were not incompatible with the Article 6(1) right to have civil rights determined by an independent and impartial tribunal. Lord Slynn relied on previous decisions by the ECHR which recognised that some administrative law decisions which affected civil rights were taken by Ministers answerable to elected bodies.

- Very importantly, the House of Lords ruled that the presumption of innocence in Art. 6(2) did not apply retrospectively. The applicant could not rely on a Convention right in a national court in respect of a conviction before the 1998 Act came into force (October 2, 2000): *R. v. Lambert* (2001, HL).

Article 7 No Punishment Without Law

- The Court found inadmissible an action under Arts 7 and 8 challeng-   **4-018**
ing the sex offenders register. The Court held that registration was not a "penalty" but aimed at preventing re-offending and was not severe. The measure pursued legitimate aims. Taking into account the gravity of the harm that could be done to victims, the requirement to register was not disproportionate: *Adamson v. U.K.* (1999).

Article 8 Private and Family Life

- The Court considered that military investigations into the sexual-   **4-019**
ity of gay members of the armed forces and their subsequent dismissal were grave breaches: *Lustig-Prean and Becket v. U.K.* and joined applications (1999).
- In gender reassignment cases, where applicants born as males sought to be re-registered as females, the Court held that the Government was under no positive duty to amend its system of birth registration: *Sheffield and Horsham v. U.K.* (1998).
- The Court held there was no violation, nor of Article 14, when measures were taken against gypsies to enforce planning measures when they stationed caravans on their land without planning permission: *Chapman v. U.K.* and four joined applications (2001).
- The Court held there was a breach where a mother was not properly informed of the facts in an allegation of child abuse and thus not properly involved in the decision-making process on the care of her daughter: *TP and KM v. U.K.* (2001).
- A conviction for gross indecency under the Sexual Offences Act 1956 constituted an unnecessary interference with the right to respect for private life. Following a search of his premises, police had seized photos and videos of the applicant and other consenting men engaging in oral sex and mutual masturbation. The acts took place in the applicant's home and did not involve physical harm. There was no evidence the tapes were available for wider distribution: *ADT v. U.K.* (2000). The opposite and somewhat surprising, result was reached by a nine-judge court in *Laskey, Jaggard and Brown v. U.K.* (1997). This involved another consenting group of homosexuals who, in private, engaged in sado-masochistic maltreatment of the genitals with nettles and staples, ritualistic beating and branding. They had been convicted under the Offences Against the Person Act 1861, which, it was agreed, was an interference in their right to respect for private life but it was

carried out "in accordance with the law" and pursued a legitimate aim of "protection of health or morals". The only issue before the Court was whether the interference was "necessary in a democratic society". The Court observed that there was a significant degree of injury and wounding and the State authorities were entitled to consider the potential harm. They concluded the authorities were entitled to consider this interference "necessary in a democratic society" for the protection of health.

- The Court of Appeal held that English law recognised a right to personal privacy, grounded in the equitable doctrine of breach of confidence, in *Douglas and Others v. Hello! Ltd* (2001). Here, Michael Douglas and Catherine Zeta-Jones had a contract with *O.K.* magazine giving the latter exclusive rights to their wedding photographs. They all sought to bar the rival magazine from publishing their illicit photos. They succeeded in obtaining an injunction preventing publication but *Hello!* were successful in the Court of Appeal in having the injunction discharged. The Court attempted to strike a balance between rights to privacy and freedom of expression, under Art. 10. The Court thought that, on balance, the Douglases were likely to succeed at the eventual trial in establishing a breach of their privacy BUT for *Hello!* the injunction would kill the issue. It might suffer a loss of readership and lucrative advertising contracts. The balance of convenience favoured *Hello!* and the injunction would be discharged.

- Article 8 rights did not apply retrospectively to allow third parties to join in proceedings on the basis that their rights had been infringed in relation to a lease entered into before the 1998 Act came into force: *Biggin Hill Airport v. Bromley L.B.C.* (2000, CA).

- A policy that prisoners must be absent when privileged legal correspondence held in their cells was examined by prison officers was unlawful. The House of Lords reached this conclusion by applying the common law but it was supported by the Art. 8(1) right to respect for correspondence (*Daly*, 2001). This case is very important as the House ruled that the courts must apply a proportionality test in judicial review cases, including Human Rights cases, as proportionality is a principle of English law. See Plowden and Kerrigan.

Article 10 Freedom of Expression

4-020
- A court order to a journalist to reveal his sources was held by an eighteen-judge Court to constitute a violation. The interference in this freedom was not justified in a democratic society. Indeed, the Court set out some general principles. Freedom of expression constituted one of the essential foundations of a democratic

society: the safeguards afforded to the press were of particular importance, as reflected in the professional codes and laws of several of the contracting states. Without such protection sources could be deterred from assisting the press in informing the public on matters of public interest.

• Where the British Board of Film Classification refused to grant a certificate for the applicant's video, *Visions of Ecstasy*, which depicted the erotic visions of St Teresa, on the ground that it was blasphemous, there was no violation. It was undisputed that the refusal was an interference with the right of freedom of expression. The aim of the interference was to protect Christians from offence and although blasphemy only protected Christians, this did not detract from the legitimacy of the aim and it was not for the European Court to rule in the abstract on this. It was fully consonant with Article 9 on freedom of thought, conscience and religion. Blasphemy legislation was still in force in various European countries. In 1982, for the same reasons and upholding the application of blasphemous libel, the Commission had rejected *Gay News'* application in *Gay News v. U.K.*

• The High Court held that the Article overrode a clear common law rule of defamation in *O'Shea v. MGN Ltd* (2001). *The Sunday Mirror* published an advertisement for a pornographic website, promoted by a glamour model who looked like the claimant. Under English common law, a claimant may sue for libel if defamatory words or pictures can be understood to refer to her by ordinary, sensible readers. It is a strict liability rule because it does not matter if the publisher did not intend it. The Judge decided that at common law the claimant was able to bring a valid claim in relation to the look-alike. But applying Article 10, he had to decide whether the common law principle went beyond what was necessary for the protection of the reputation of others. He decided it would place an impossible burden on the publisher if he were required to check every photograph, including photographs of street violence or looting, in case they proved to be look-alikes of other people. Article 10 thus provided a defence. See Bays.

Article 12 Right to Marry

• In gender reassignment cases (above), the Court held that the restriction on the right to marry those not of the opposite biological sex did not remove the very essence of the right.   **4-021**

Article 13 Effective Remedy

• In *Keenan v. U.K.*, above, the Court found the bereaved parent was not provided with an effective remedy because the inquest did not   **4-022**

provide a remedy in determining the liability of the authorities for
mistreatment and did not provide for compensation.
- In the child abuse case, proceedings for negligence and breach of
statutory duty had been struck out in the United Kingdom court
and this was a denial of an effective remedy.

Article 14 Prohibition against Discrimination

4-023
- Bereaved fathers were equally entitled to the "widowed mother's
allowance", conceded the United Kingdom Government, agree-
ing to pay arrears of benefit to two male applicants. Accordingly
the ECHR agreed to strike out both cases: *Cornwell v. U.K.* and a
joined application (2000, ECHR).
- Note that a new addition to the Convention, Protocol 12, provides
a free-standing right to equality, because Article 14 is too limited.
It was open for signature from the Member States from
November 2000. Ten States must sign and ratify before it comes
into force in the ratifying States. The United Kingdom
Government has indicated it has no plans at present to ratify.
JUSTICE, the lawyers' pressure group, believes the United
Kingdom Government should ratify it and incorporate it into the
Human Rights Act 1998. See Niaz.

It has been predicted that Convention rights will have a big impact on
companies and businesses. See articles in *The Times*, in 1998–2000 and
the *New Law Journal* in 2000–2001

6. The Approach of English Courts to Convention Rights and Interpretation of Domestic Law

4-024
Prior to the implementation of the HRA 1998, the Government
sought to stop fears that the courts would be swamped with claims by
pointing out that the Convention had been in force in Scotland since May
1999 and 98 per cent of challenges had failed.

At the time of writing, 2001, it is too soon to make any generalisations
on how our courts will approach their task of applying common law precedents and interpreting statute to incorporate the Convention but there
has already been a great deal of speculation in the Parliamentary debates
of the Human Rights Bill in 1998 and in law journals as to how the courts
might or should approach the Convention.

Emmerson is reported as predicting "a major shift of power from
Parliament to judges. They will, in effect, be able to rewrite sections of
Acts by reading into them words that are not there and by massaging

away any potential conflicts with the Constitution." *The Times*, November 26, 1998. Nevertheless, in 1999, the House of Lords was swift to point out, in *Kebilene* (below) that the Convention gave way to Parliamentary sovereignty. In the words of Lord Steyn,

> "It is crystal clear that the carefully and subtly drafted Human Rights Act 1998 preserves the principle of Parliamentary sovereignty. In a case of incompatibility, which cannot be avoided by interpretation under section 3(1), the courts may not disapply legislation. The court may merely issue a declaration of incompatibility which then gives rise to a power to take remedial action: see section 10."

As for common law remedies, Lord Chancellor Irvine said in Parliament

> "In my view, the courts may not act as legislators and grant new remedies for infringement of Convention rights unless the common law itself enables them to develop new rights and remedies. I believe that the true view is that the courts will be able to develop the common law by relying on the existing domestic principles of trespass, nuisance, copyright, confidence and the like, to fashion a common law right to privacy."

As is plain to see from the judgments in the Catherine Zeta-Jones and Michael Douglas privacy action, the Court of Appeal did exactly that, by building on the equitable doctrine of breach of confidence. Kearns considers this "lamentable". He would prefer European privacy rights to be "holistically imported as a welcome, clear and logical privacy law system" ((2001) 151 N.L.J. 377.

In October 1999, the House of Lords refused to accept an argument **1-025** that a defendant had a legitimate expectation that the DPP would take account of Article 6 when deciding whether to prosecute. There was "clear statutory intent to postpone the coming into effect of central provisions of the Act" (*per* Lord Steyn in *R. v. D.P.P., ex parte Kebilene*).

If you want to read a great example of modern interpretative techniques of domestic legislation and the House of Lords' prescribed methods of interpreting it against the Convention, then one case provides that opportunity. By May 2001, the House of Lords was already asked to construe a new statute which appeared to conflict with Convention rights. This is a landmark precedent because it demonstrated how to interpret and apply the court's duty under section 3 of the HRA. It will be cited for many years to come. The case was *R. v. A (Complainant's Sexual History)*. They had to construe section 41 of the Youth Justice and Criminal Evidence Act 1999, restricting evidence and questioning about the victim's sexual history, which had just been brought into force. They applied their interpretive duty under section 3 of the HRA and gave proper regard to the protection of the complainant, the victim.

4-026   I shall analyse Lord Steyn's interpretive methods sequentially, with my explanations italicised:

1. *He plunged straight into a purposive construction of the 1999 Act*: in the criminal courts, outmoded beliefs about women and sexual matters lingered on. *Referring to another common law*, in Canadian jurisprudence they had been referred to as the discredited twin myths.

2. *Statement of moral principle*: "such generalised, stereotyped and unfounded prejudices ought to have no place in our legal system". It resulted in an absurdly low conviction rate in rape cases. The Sexual Offences (Amendment) Act 1976 did not achieve its object.

3. *Conclusion on purpose of Act*: "(t)here was a serious mischief to be corrected".

4. *Statement of problem before the House*: the blanket exclusion of prior sexual history between the complainant and the accused posed an acute problem of proportionality. *(Not articulated but a principle applied by the ECHR)*

5. *Applying what he called* "common sense": a prior relationship *between accused and accuser* might be relevant to the issue of consent *in rape.*

6. *Statement of principle of interpretive duty, based on his interpretation of his court's duty under the HRA 1998*: when a question arose whether in a criminal statute, Parliament adopted a legislative scheme which made an excessive inroad into the right to a fair trial, the court was qualified to make its own judgment and had to do so.

7. *Application of ECHR jurisprudence*: it was well established that the guarantee of a fair trial under Article 6 was absolute. A conviction obtained in breach could not stand. The only balancing permitted was in respect of what the concept of a fair trial entailed. Applying proportionality, in determining whether a limitation was arbitrary or excessive a court should ask itself whether:

   (i)   the legislative objective was sufficiently important to justify limiting a fundamental right;

   (ii)   the measures designed to meet that objective were rationally connected to it, and

   (iii) the means used to impair the right or freedom were no more than necessary to accomplish the objective.

8. Two processes of interpretation had to be distinguished.

   • Ordinary methods of purposive and contextual interpretation might yield ways of minimising the "exorbitant breadth" of the section.
   • The interpretative obligation of HRA, section 3(1). (*i.e.*, so far as possible, primary legislation had to be given effect in a way compatible with the Convention).

9. *He applied the first method, looked at the wording of the section and relevant domestic cases on evidence prior to the 1998 Act and concluded this could not solve the problem.*

10. *Interpreting section 3 of the 1998 Act:* cited *Kebilene*. The section 3 obligation went far beyond the rule which enabled the courts to take the Convention into account in resolving any ambiguity in a legislative provision. Parliament specifically rejected the legislative model requiring a reasonable interpretation. It placed on a court a duty to strive to find a possible interpretation compatible with Convention rights. It was much more radical than than the ordinary method of interpretation which permitted a departure from language of an Act to avoid absurd consequences. In accordance with the will of Parliament, it would sometimes be necessary to adopt an interpretation which linguistically might appear strained. The techniques to be used would not only involve the reading down of express language in a statute but also the implication of provisions.

11. *Interpreting section 4 of the HRA 1998*: a declaration of incompatibility was a measure of last resort.

12. *Conclusion, implying Parliamentary intent*: the legislature, if alerted to the problem, would not have wished to deny the accused the right to put forward a full defence by advancing probative material. It was possible to read into section 41 of the 1999 Act the implied provision that evidence or questioning required to ensure a fair trial under Article 6 should not be inadmissible.

13. *Implications for future trials*: sometimes logically relevant evidence of sexual experience might be admitted but where the line was to be drawn was up to the trial judge.

7. Is the HRA Applicable Horizontally?

There have been many weighty academic articles on whether the Act provides rights against private bodies. This debate is fuelled by the ambiguous and cryptic nature of the Act itself. If you read the wording of the **4-027** statute you can see this for yourself. On the one hand, as I pointed out above, section 3 requires primary and subordinate legislation to be read as far as possible in a way which is compatible with Convention rights but this instruction is not limited to public authorities or just the courts. It appears to apply to all of us. Under section 2 courts and tribunals must take into account ECHR jurisprudence. The Government could have specifically excluded private parties from the scope of the Act, as other jurisdictions have done but did not. On the other hand, sections 6 and 7 only allow challenge to actions of public authorities. We are not helped by the statements made by the Lord Chancellor who sponsored the Bill through the House of Lords. In the second reading, on the illegality of contravening a Convention right he said:

"We decided first of all that a provision of this kind should apply only to public authorities . . . and not to private individuals. . . . The Convention had its origins in a desire to protect people from the misuse of power by the State, rather than from the actions of private individuals."

On the other hand he said:

"We have taken the view that . . . excluding Convention considerations altogether from cases between individuals . . . would have to be justified. We do not think that would be justifiable; nor indeed do we think that it would be practicable" (cited in a JUSTICE bulletin, autumn 1998).

The articles on this subject are too long and too many to summarize here. The contributors are Sir William Wade, Markenisis, Buxton L.J., Hunt, Leigh, Singh, Cooper and Phillipson. Nevertheless, they are all speculative as they all written before the courts have had a chance to interpret the Act.

FURTHER READING

4-028   G. Bindman, "Contempt of European Court" *New Statesman*, November 15, 1996.
LCD press release 100/99 on the Paul Sieghart lecture or see the full text, LCD website, www.lcd.gov.uk.
R. Hudson, (1996) 146 N.L.J. 1029.
Special law supplement of *The Times*, September 26, 2000.
R. White, *The English Legal System in Action*, 1999.
Home Office Human Rights Unit: www.homeoffice.gov.uk/hract.
LCD Human Rights site: www.lcd.gov.uk/human rights.
HMSO statutes: www.hmso.gov.uk/acts.

A lengthy bibliography is provided on the Home Office Human Rights Unit website.

A. T. H. Smith, "The Human Rights Act and the Criminal Lawyer: The Constitutional Context" [1999] Crim.L.R. 251 and see other articles in the same issue.

Law Commission, *Damages Under the Human Rights Act*, www.lawcom.gov.uk.

G. McFarlane, "EU and World Trade Brief" (2001) 151 N.L.J. 55.

The Court's judgments: www.echr.coe.int.

S. Nash, Human Rights Law Update, regular columns in the N.L.J.

The Times law reports.

K. Bays, "What a difference a judge makes?" (2001) 151 N.L.J. 842.

A. Niaz, "An independent right to equality" (2000) 150 N.L.J. 1609. See also (2001) 151 N.L.J. 65.

Supplements to *The Times*, September 26, 2000 and October 2, 2001.

G. Phillipson, "The Human Rights Act, 'Horizontal Effect' and the Common Law: a Bang or a Whimper?" (1999) 62 M.L.R. 824. Footnote 1 gives references to the previous articles. See also Loveland at (2000) 150 N.L.J. 1595 and citations therein.

Plowden and K.Kerrigan, "Judicial review—A New Test?" (2001) 151 N.L.J 1291.

K.Starmer and others, articles in *The Times*, October 2, 2001, reviewing the Act's first year.

A. O'Neill, "Judicial Politics and the Judicial Committee: the Devolution Jurisprudence of the Privy Council" (2001) 64 M.L.R 603.

S. Fredman, "Judging Democracy: The role of the Judiciary under the HRA 1998" (2000) 53 C.L.P. 98.

5. Law Reform and the Changing Legal System

1. The Inevitability of Change

The one certainty in the study of any area of law is that it will be char-   **5-001**
acterised by change. New governments want to make their mark and a
government with a powerful majority like New Labour will succeed in
having most of the Bills affecting their policy passed by Parliament. As we
can see from the jury Chapter, the notable exception and frustration for
them at the time of writing is the double rejection by the House of Lords
of the Mode of Trial Bills, seeking to abolish the defendant's choice of
trial venue.

Every branch of the law, together with the legal system which lies
behind it, is constantly undergoing change. Indeed, in recent years, the
complaint has been made that Parliament is choking with the sheer
volume of legislation it is expected to scrutinise. This makes life difficult
for the rest of us, keeping up with change. As can be seen from a comparison of this book with the 1996 last edition, most of it has been rewritten.

To the piles of domestic legislation we can barely digest, we have to add   **5-002**
E.C. legislation: Treaties and Regulations over which the United Kingdom
Parliament has no control but bind all of us and directives, most of which
the United Kingdom Parliament enacts through statutory instrument.

Equally, the superior courts develop the common law and change the
law. There are no more obvious and dramatic examples of this than, for
instance, changes to statutory interpretation in the Court of Appeal by
taking account of the European Convention on Human Rights since
October 2000 and developments in domestic law wrought by the courts'
application of E.C. law since 1973. There are today more judges and
more cases to be tried, than ever before.

Inevitably, the more complex the society, the more complex the law and the more complicated the cases which arise. Nineteenth century leading cases concerned with the sale of horses have given way to involved transactions between large commercial corporations, via fax and email.

There is substantial and constant campaigning by pressure groups like JUSTICE, Liberty, the Statute Law Reform Society and the Legal Action Group, as well as the Bar Council and Law Society, for changes in the legal system. These changes may relate to criminal procedure, to evidence, to the form of legislation or to such matters as legal aid and advice.

2. Methods of Law Reform

Parliament

5-003 Most Acts result from Government Bills, sponsored by the relevant Minister. The Minister, in turn, will be under pressure from government colleagues. Education legislation, for example, will be introduced by the Secretary of State for Education and will have been prepared initially by that department. Only a very few private Members of Parliament succeed each year in getting a Public Act on to the Statute Book. This is because parliamentary time is so valuable that the Government tends to demand almost all of it. Often the pressure for the legislation has come from interest groups, unions or pressure groups. Some, like the CBI, the National Farmers' Union, currently vocal (2001) on the foot and mouth crisis or the County Councils' Association, are very powerful organisations with wide national support but sometimes pressure from a small organisation can have the desired effect. In July 2001, the teachers' unions were lobbying the newly appointed Secretary of State for Education to scrap the system of AS levels introduced in 2000.

Very often legislation will be introduced following the report of a Royal Commission or an ad hoc review body. For example, the Royal Commission of Criminal Justice and Lord Woolf's scrutiny of civil procedure resulted in significant changes, as we can see from the criminal procedure Chapter. The report of a lone civil servant, Martin Narey, in his 1997 *Review of Delay in the Criminal Justice System* resulted in the enactment of large chunks of the Crime and Disorder Act 1998. There are many more examples throughout this book.

The Judiciary

5-004 Judges, whilst being bound by precedent, can nevertheless effect quite dramatic changes in the law through the medium of statutory interpretation and reinterpretation of the common law. This happened in 1991 when the lower courts and finally the House of Lords abolished the rule that a husband cannot be guilty of raping his wife: *R. v. R.*

Ostensibly, judges are not concerned with law reform but it is not uncommon for them to draw attention to anomalies and to call for change. A classic example appears in the 2001 case of *R. v. Kansal.* The Court of Appeal, in interpreting the powers of the Criminal Cases Review Commission under the Criminal Appeal Act 1995 and taking account of the retrospective provision of the Human Rights Act 1998, decided "with no enthusiasm whatever" that it had no option to declare a conviction unsafe, in any case referred to it by the Commission, if evidence obtained in breach of the European Convention or after a change in common law rendered the verdict unsafe, however old the case. This would mean the workload for the Commission and Court would be alarming. If that was not what Parliament intended, said the judges, then the sooner the matter was addressed, the better. Also, the Law Lords, retired Law Lords and the Lord Chief Justice have often spoken in law reform debates in the House of Lords. They turned out in force in the debate on the Human Rights Bill, including some former Law Lords I had assumed to be dead. Lord Chief Justice Bingham made a powerful speech on justices' clerks' powers, which made the Government think again, in the debate on the Crime and Disorder Bill 1998. Lord Chief Justice Lane and others made provocative speeches opposing Lord Chancellor Mackay's proposals to take away the Bar's monopoly on rights of audience, in the late 1980s. This and the famous judges' "strike", in 1989 resulted in such a watering down of the Courts and Legal Services Act 1990 that almost no progress was made in opening up rights of audience in court in the 1990s, a situation which in turn was deplored by the present Lord Chancellor in a 1998 consultation paper on rights of audience preceding the more draconian Access to Justice Act 1999. The senior judges have the Judges' Council as a vehicle for discussion of administrative and legislative proposals. They produce reports as a vehicle for lobbying Government with their views. For instance, they produced a response to the recent Government paper, *Modernising Civil Justice* (2001).

The Law Commission—a Story of Frustration and Wasted Taxpayers' Money

The Law Commission is an independent body established in 1965 to **5-005** keep the law of England and Wales under review "with a view to its systematic development and reform, including in particular the codification of such law, the elimination of anomalies, the repeal of obsolete and unnecessary enactments, the reduction of the number of separate enactments and generally the simplification and modernisation of the law".

The commissioners are distinguished lawyers seconded full-time from their employment for a five-year period. The chairperson is always a

High Court judge. The others are barristers, solicitors, judges or academics. Despite criticism, there are no laypeople. They have a secretary and about 15 members of the Government Legal Service, four or five Parliamentary Counsel, to draft Bills for them, 15 research assistants (highly qualified new law graduates), a librarian and administrative staff.

They conduct 20–30 projects at any one time. They research an area of law, which has been criticised by judges, lawyers, government departments or the public, to identify defects then issue proposals in a consultation paper, which they publish in hard copy and on their website. Once responses have been considered, they publish a report, usually with a draft Bill appended. Uncontentious law reform measures can be speeded through Parliament in the "Jellicoe" procedure which allows the use of a Special Public Bill Committee, without using parliamentary time allocated to normal Bills. The procedure was used for the Public International Law Act 1994 which implemented three Law Commission reports. Full lists of their consultation papers and reports appear on their website, as do a description of their work and their annual reports.

5-006   One of their jobs is consolidation of statutes and they have achieved this in a number of instances. Another job is statute law revision. Good progress has been made in the repeal of obsolete statutes. By means of Statute Law (Repeals) Acts, they have repealed 5,000 redundant Acts since 1965.

Codification is inevitably a long-term plan, since in each case the ultimate objective is a single self-contained code, which will be "the statement of all the relevant law in a logical and coherent form" but they are especially frustrated in their lack of progress in persuading governments to allocate parliamentary time to Bills designed to enact their Draft Criminal Code, which they published in 1989.

In the white paper published by the Labour Government in advance of the introduction of the Law Commissions Bill, the point was made that there was an urgent need for a review body. This was substantiated by the fact that there were said to exist some 3,000 Acts of Parliament dating from 1234, many volumes of delegated legislation and some 300,000 reported case decisions.

5-007   The annual report of the Law Commission contains an appendix which shows whether or not its reports have been given effect. Their website claims, in 2001, that more than two thirds of their reports have been implemented but there is still widespread frustration in Commissioners and other lawyers at the lack of progress on the rest and the inability of successive governments to at least codify the criminal law (see below). In the 1990s successive chairmen of the Commission complained bitterly at the log-jam of their reports ignored by governments. Only four were implemented in 1990–1994. The 1994 Annual Report complained of "serious unease among many people" that the work of the

Commission was being neglected. In a 1994 interview, then Chairman Sir Henry Brooke said there were 36 reports "stuck in the log-jam" and he was anxious to publicise this and put it to an end.

The Jellicoe procedure for speeding Bills through was introduced in 1994 and Hudson commented "(h)ow it can have taken until now to devise such an obvious procedure beggars belief" ((1994) 144 N.L.J. 1668). Disappointingly, the next chairman, Dame Mary Arden, commented in 1998 "the procedure has not worked quite as had been hoped as it makes very heavy demands on the time of members of the committee and of ministers and their officials". In the 1996 Annual Report, in an open letter to the Conservative Lord Chancellor, she accused the Government of wasting taxpayers' money by delaying implementation of law reforms. One of the reports ignored was on conspiracy to defraud, noting defects in the law. In *Preddy* (1996), the House of Lords ruled that mortgage fraud was not covered by the law of theft. Eleven prosecutions had to be dropped and many others were not brought. Another scandal relates to the state of offences against the person, embodied in the decrepit, inappropriate, contradictory and archaically-worded Offences Against the Person Act 1861, which the Commission reported on in 1993. Commissioner Stephen Silber Q.C. complained of inaction in 1996 and still in 2001, thousands of cases per year are being prosecuted under this anachronistic Act. He illustrated it with the example of stalking. Had their proposals been implemented, there would have been none of the uncertainty that arose in the courts as to whether it was a criminal offence.

One would think the Commission's work so uncontroversial that it would provoke no criticism but in 1995, *The Daily Mail* launched a campaign against its Family Violence Bill, calling the Commission a "trendy, left-wing academic quango" of "(l)egal commissars subverting family values" (quoted by Cretney). The Bill was introduced by the Jellicoe procedure but proved far from uncontroversial and was dropped. Conservative Lady Olga Maitland said the Commissioners were "living on another planet".

5-008

Advisory Committees

For ensuring that improvements are made in the law as circumstances demand, certain standing committees have been set up with responsibility for reporting on particular matters in need of reform.

5-009

1. *The Criminal Law Revision Committee* was established in 1959 to advise the Home Secretary. Its terms of reference are "to examine such aspects of the criminal law of England and Wales as the Home Secretary may from time to time refer to the committee to consider whether the law requires revision and to make recommendations". It produced on average one report a year; again it is a part-time body, and these reports have led to such legislation as the Suicide Act 1961 and the Theft Acts of 1968 and

1978. Its reports have sparked considerable controversy, from time to time.

2. *Other bodies.* The Lord Chancellor, in particular, is advised by several standing and many ad hoc committees. One of the most obvious is the Legal Services Commission. In addition, he currently has working parties considering various topics and the Research Secretariat of the Department sets an agenda for future research, which you can read on the LCD website, and funds projects conducted by academics which fit into its agenda.

3. *Royal Commissions.* These are appointed ad hoc, to conduct major reviews of the law or legal system. For instance, the Royal Commission on Assizes and Quarter Sessions (1969) recommended the creation of the Crown Court. The Royal Commission on Criminal Procedure (1980) produced recommendations which led to the passing of PACE. The Royal Commission on Legal Services (1979) was singularly unsuccessful, in that many of its recommendations have been ignored. In 1991 the Home Secretary and Lord Chancellor established the Royal Commission on Criminal Justice, at the height of public concern over famous miscarriages of justice. It reported in 1993 and some of its recommendations have been followed, such as those on appeals, in the Criminal Appeal Act 1995. Others have been ignored, such as those on the right to silence and yet others are still under consideration (mode of trial).

4. *Green papers and white papers.* All government departments may publish green papers setting out their proposals for legislative change. These are open invitations for comment by the interested public at large. Once gathered in, these responses help to modify final legislative proposals which are set out in a white paper. The present LCD does not work through green papers so much as consultation papers, available in electronic form, which you can see in their dozens on the LCD website. It produces just about too many consultation papers for one person to keep up with.

Statute Law Revision

5-010   Dame Mary Arden provides an interesting account of this. The Renton Committee on the Preparation of Legislation, in 1995, made detailed recommendations on the drafting of statutes, parliamentary procedure and statutory interpretation. In 1992 the Hansard Commission reported on the legislative process. Dame Mary quoted a 1987 Report of the Law Reform Commission of Victoria. It said:

- Badly drafted legislation encouraged litigation and was, therefore, expensive.
- Unclear legislation transferred the power to determine the law from an elected legislature to the courts.

- It is a fundamental civil liberty that people should be able to know and understand the laws that govern them.

She told the story of the Tax Law Rewrite. In 1995, the Inland Revenue published two documents listing criticisms of the 6,000 pages of tax legislation, including:

- Complicated syntax, long sentences and archaic or ambiguous language.
- The principles underlying the rules are not apparent. This forces the courts to interpret strictly according to wording.
- Too much detail, covering every conceivable situation.
- Many sections cannot be understood in isolation.
- Some rules are wide and, therefore, uncertain.
- It is difficult to find all the rules.
- Definitions are inconsistent and spread throughout different statutes.
- There is an imbalance between primary and secondary legislation.
- Lack of consultation and openness in drafting statutes.

The Revenue decided to organise a project themselves, a five-year plain English rewrite, consulting representative bodies and taxpayers and employing 40 lawyers. A special joint committee of the Lords and Commons will scrutinise Bills.

Consolidation and Codification

The work of the Law Commission and other reforming bodies leads **5-011** on to a consideration of the actual process by which legislation is simplified. Under the Consolidation of Enactments (Procedure) Act 1949, a system was introduced by Parliament under which, where the bringing together of separate statutory provisions, known as "consolidation", was deemed to be desirable, the Lord Chancellor could arrange to have prepared a memorandum showing how these various provisions would take effect in the proposed consolidating Act. Thus, for example, the whole of the legislation concerned with tribunals and inquiries was brought together and updated in the Tribunals and Inquiries Act 1992.

The consolidating procedure is not possible where the Bill involves changes of substance in the law, known as "codification". A codifying measure brings together the existing statute and case law, in an attempt to produce a full statement as it relates to that particular branch of law. The main examples of successful codification date from the end of the nineteenth century when the following four statutes were passed: the

Bills of Exchange Act 1882, the Partnership Act 1890, the Sale of Goods Act 1893 and the Marine Insurance Act 1906. The Bills of Exchange Act 1882, which was prepared by Sir M.D. Chalmers, involved the consideration of 17 existing statutes and some 2,500 decided cases. These were compressed to make a statute 100 sections long. After these Acts were passed, there was no more codifying legislation until the Theft Act 1968. The codification of arbitration law in the Arbitration Act 1996 was discussed in the Chapter on sources. It was partly codifying and partly consolidating and was subject to a special Jellicoe procedure, described above and in the Chapter on sources.

5-012   The difference between consolidation and codification is classically illustrated by the modern example of The Powers of Criminal Courts (Sentencing) Act 2000, designed to pull together all the legislative strands of sentencing, which has been such a struggle in application for judges and an even greater struggle for justices' clerks and other magistrates' legal advisers. The problem is, however, that this neat fabric is already unravelling, with a new statute in 2001. Doubtless, the Government will never resist the temptation to pick away at sentencing and criminal procedure as it does every year. What the Law Commission, Criminal Law Revision Committee, Lord Chief Justices and academics are clamouring for is a proper criminal code, which would include all substantive criminal statute law, criminal procedure and sentencing, like the California Penal Code. Then all we need do is buy or download the latest version every year. When the Government is tempted to pick away at procedure, it will have to weave its amendments into the existing cloth, instead of unravelling it by adding a new statute.

5-013   The Law Commission, frustrated at inaction on a criminal code, points out on its website (2001) that we are almost the only country in the world without one. Lord Chief Justice Bingham tells this pathetic history of English criminal law in exasperated tones. "The plea for such a code cannot, I fear, startle by its novelty":

- 1818, both houses petitioned the Prince Regent to establish a Law Commission to consolidate statute law.
- 1831, Commission established to inquire into codifying criminal law.
- 1835–1845, it produced eight reports, culminating in a Criminal Law Code Bill, ultimately dropped.
- 1879, Royal Commission recommended code containing 550 clauses.
- 1844–1882, Lord Brougham and others made eight parliamentary attempts to enact a code.
- 1965, Law Commission established.

- Criminal Code Team established including Professor Sir John Smith "the outstanding criminal lawyer of our time" (Bingham).
- Code published 1985, revised and expanded 1989.

Lord Bingham concluded:

"even the most breathless admirer of the common law must regard it as a reproach that after 700 years of judicial decision-making our highest tribunal should have been called upon time and again in recent years to consider the mental ingredients of murder, the oldest and most serious of crimes".

Cambridge Professor J.R. Spencer adds a plea for a code of criminal procedure, where English inaction looks even more pathetic in the face of a 1995 Scottish code;

". . . the sources are at present in a shocking mess, as a result of which the law is not readily accessible to those who have reason to discover it . . . dispersed among . . . some 150 statutes . . . even the modern ones are mainly messy and unsystematic and hard for the user to find his way around: a succession of Criminal Justice Acts, each a disparate jumble of new rules, or of new amendments to old ones".

He adds that almost all the law of evidence is uncodified and our haphazard way of creating rules results in "all sorts of astonishing contradictions". He, the Law Commission and others will doubtless be pleasantly surprised by the government announcement, in their 2001 white paper, *Criminal Justice: The Way Ahead* that they intend to introduce a criminal code.

3. Change and the English Legal System

The 1980s, 1990s and 2000s will go down in history as producing the **5-014** most dramatic changes in the English legal system since the Supreme Court of Judicature Acts of the 1880s merged law and equity and created the Supreme Court.

In the criminal justice system, the 1980s started with the work of the Royal Commission on Criminal Procedure which resulted in several pieces of legislation. Most notable was the Police and Criminal Evidence Act 1984, strengthening the rights of suspected persons. The Prosecution of Offences Act 1985 created a national prosecution service, the Crown Prosecution Service. The spate of miscarriages of justice which came to light in the late 1980s and early 1990s, notably the Guildford Four and Birmingham Six cases, provoked the establishment of the Royal

Commission on Criminal Justice, whose terms of reference charge it with the astonishingly bold task of assessing the desirability of importing inquisitorial elements of procedure from civil law countries. It produced a highly controversial report in 1993 which resulted in some sections of the Criminal Justice and Public Order Act 1994, the Criminal Appeal Act 1995, the Criminal Procedure and Investigations Act 1996 and, doubtless, further legislation on matters such as mode of trial. 2001 saw the publication of Sir Robin Auld's Criminal Justice Review. Depending on how attractive his suggestions prove to be, we can expect some radical changes to the court structure and jury trial, at the very least.

5-015   As far as civil procedure is concerned, equally radical changes have taken place. The Civil Justice Review of 1988 raised the question of whether a redistribution of civil work and a change in pre-trial procedure and the costs regime could cut out undesirable facets of English civil procedure, notably cost and delay in the High Court. Its recommendations led to Part I of the Courts and Legal Services Act 1990, which gave county courts almost the same jurisdiction as the High Court, allowing for a very significant shift of work down into the county court. The Heilbron-Hodge Report then the Woolf report of 1996 effected very significant changes in civil practice, then the Civil Procedure Rules 1998.

As for the court structure, the Children Act of 1989 gave parallel jurisdiction, in matters affecting children, to the three first instance courts, the county court, magistrates' court and High Court. Lord Chancellor Mackay said he saw this Act as paving the way towards a family court. The 1980s saw a massive growth in applications for judicial review to the High Court, following a simplification of procedure, and the practice of their being listed in the Crown Office list. By 2000, this list had transformed into the Administrative Court.

5-016   As far as members of the legal profession are concerned, they are still to feel the real impact of the Government's attack on their monopolies. The Administration of Justice Act 1985 effectively destroyed the solicitors' conveyancing monopoly by establishing a system of licensed conveyancers. This, however, posed no serious threat, in comparison with the Court and Legal Services Act 1990, which empowered the Lord Chancellor to open up competition to banks and building societies. Neither has the other side of the profession been spared from threat. Again, the CLSA 1990 destroys the barristers' monopoly over rights of audience in the higher courts, effectively allowing anyone to apply to be licensed for rights of audience in the various levels of court. As a corollary of this, judicial and other similar appointments are no longer limited to barristers and the CLSA substitutes rights of audience as the qualification. It had not had much impact however by 1998, so the new Lord Chancellor Irvine introduced the Access to Justice Act 1999, which finally abolishes the restrictive practices of the Bar.

The Legal Aid Act 1988 took the administration of civil legal aid out of the hands of the Law Society and gave it to a new Legal Aid Board. It allowed the Lord Chancellor wide and controversial powers to establish a franchising system for the provision of legal advice. Throughout the 1990s, the legal aid system came under increasing scrutiny. Lord Chancellor Mackay wanted to reform it but his successor, Irvine has scrapped it and replaced it with a radically new structure provided for in the Access to Justice Act 1999, which takes a holistic approach to the funding of and distribution of all legal services, not just those provided by lawyers in private practice.

FURTHER READING

Law Commission website: www.lawcom.gov.uk. Contains information, **5-017** Annual Reports, consultation papers and reports.

Interview with Sir Henry Brooke, *The Magistrate*, February 1994.

Dame Mary Arden, "Modernising Legislation" [1998] P.L. 65.

S.M. Cretney, "The Law Commission: True Dawns and False Dawns" (1996) 59 M.L.R. 631 (historical).

Rt. Hon. Lord Bingham of Cornhill L.C.J., "A Criminal Code: Must We Wait for Ever?" [1998] Crim.L.R. 694.

J.R. Spencer, " The Case for a Code of Criminal Procedure" [2000] Crim.L.R. 519.

THE COURT STRUCTURE

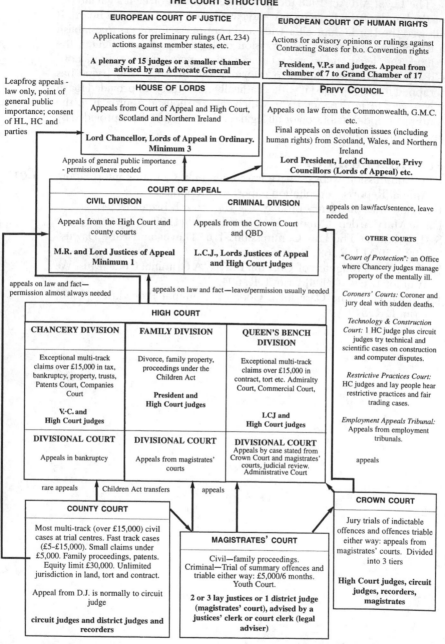

EUROPEAN COURT OF JUSTICE

Applications for preliminary rulings (Art. 234) actions against member states, etc.

A plenary of 15 judges or a smaller chamber advised by an Advocate General

EUROPEAN COURT OF HUMAN RIGHTS

Actions for advisory opinions or rulings against Contracting States for b.o. Convention rights

President, V.P.s and judges. Appeal from chamber of 7 to Grand Chamber of 17

Leapfrog appeals - law only, point of general public importance; consent of HL, HC and parties

HOUSE OF LORDS

Appeals from Court of Appeal and High Court, Scotland and Northern Ireland

Lord Chancellor, Lords of Appeal in Ordinary. Minimum 3

PRIVY COUNCIL

Appeals on law from the Commonwealth, G.M.C. etc.

Final appeals on devolution issues (including human rights) from Scotland, Wales, and Northern Ireland

Lord President, Lord Chancellor, Privy Councillors (Lords of Appeal) etc.

Appeals of general public importance - permission/leave needed

COURT OF APPEAL

CIVIL DIVISION

Appeals from the High Court and county courts

M.R. and Lord Justices of Appeal Minimum 1

CRIMINAL DIVISION

Appeals from the Crown Court and QBD

L.C.J., Lords Justices of Appeal and High Court judges

appeals on law/fact/sentence, leave needed

OTHER COURTS

"Court of Protection": an Office where Chancery judges manage property of the mentally ill.

Coroners' Courts: Coroner and jury deal with sudden deaths.

Technology & Construction Court: 1 HC judge plus circuit judges try technical and scientific cases on construction and computer disputes.

Restrictive Practices Court: HC judges and lay people hear restrictive practices and fair trading cases.

Employment Appeals Tribunal: Appeals from employment tribunals.

appeals

appeals on law and fact— permission almost always needed

appeals on law and fact—leave/permission usually needed

HIGH COURT

CHANCERY DIVISION

Exceptional multi-track claims over £15,000 in tax, bankruptcy, property, trusts, Patents Court, Companies Court

V.-C. and High Court judges

DIVISIONAL COURT

Appeals in bankruptcy

FAMILY DIVISION

Divorce, family property, proceedings under the Children Act

President and High Court judges

DIVISIONAL COURT

Appeals from magistrates' courts

QUEEN'S BENCH DIVISION

Exceptional multi-track claims over £15,000 in contract, tort etc. Admiralty Court, Commercial Court,

LCJ and High Court judges

DIVISIONAL COURT

Appeals by case stated from Crown Court and magistrates' courts, judicial review. Administrative Court

rare appeals   Children Act transfers   appeals

COUNTY COURT

Most multi-track (over £15,000) civil cases at trial centres. Fast track cases (£5-£15,000). Small claims under £5,000. Family proceedings, patents. Equity limit £30,000. Unlimited jurisdiction in land, tort and contract.

Appeal from D.J. is normally to circuit judge

circuit judges and district judges and recorders

MAGISTRATES' COURT

Civil—family proceedings.
Criminal—Trial of summary offences and triable either way: £5,000/6 months. Youth Court.

2 or 3 lay justices or 1 district judge (magistrates' court), advised by a justices' clerk or court clerk (legal adviser)

CROWN COURT

Jury trials of indictable offences and offences triable either way: appeals from magistrates' courts. Divided into 3 tiers

High Court judges, circuit judges, recorders, magistrates

Part II: Institutions

6. Civil Courts

As with the rest of the legal system, the work and jurisdiction of the civil courts is currently in a state of massive upheaval. Following the recommendations of the Civil Justice Review (1988), the Lord Chancellor was given sweeping powers under the Courts and Legal Services Act 1990 to reorganise the civil business of the High Court and the county courts. The Review recommended a significant shift of work down to the county courts, as it found that the High Court was clogged up with trivial cases. The Woolf report, *Access to Justice* was published in 1996 and recommended a radical overhaul of civil procedure. Lord Woolf's recommendations were effected in the Civil Procedure Rules 1998, which came into effect in 1999.

6-001

Detailed descriptions of judges' jurisdictions are provided in the documents on judges on the LCD website. Details of the courts' work are provided in the annual *Judicial Statistics*, also on the website. Not only does it provide statistics, for instance, on how many trial days occupied full-time judges and how many occupied deputies, but the report also gives very straightforward and useful descriptions of each court. For instance, the Chapter on "Family Matters" provides an excellent account of the family courts, their powers and procedures, which are a mystery to those of us who are not family law practitioners or lecturers and for which there is no space in this book or most other ELS textbooks.

Most courts are now administered by the Courts Service which is an independent government agency. One major exception is magistrates' courts. They are administered locally by magistrates' courts committees, which are described in the Magistrates Chapter.

1. Magistrates' Courts

Lay magistrates sit usually in threes, or sometimes as a pair. District judges (magistrates' courts) sit alone or, rarely, with two lay justices (see

6-002

113

Chapter on magistrates). Under the 1989 Children Act, implemented in October 1991, their domestic proceedings courts were renamed "family proceedings courts" and the specially trained magistrates who adjudicate are selected from "the family panel". They can make and enforce financial provisions following a family breakdown and can make orders protecting adults and children. Unlike the county courts and High Court, they cannot grant divorces. Under the 1989 Act, they share jurisdiction in children cases with the High Court and county courts and those cases are allocated according to complexity. They can make a range of orders relating to children, including care and supervision orders, adoption orders and contact and residence orders. Other civil work includes Council Tax and VAT enforcement.

2. County Courts

6-003   Since their establishment by the County Courts Act 1846, they have provided a local and inexpensive alternative to the High Court for the trial of civil cases. They do not follow county boundaries. Their name is historical. There are around 220 county courts in England and Wales, each with at least one circuit judge and one district judge. Circuit judges can hear all types of case and hear the more important work. District judges' jurisdiction to assess damages is now unlimited, unless otherwise directed. They preside over the small claims court, where the limit is £5,000. They are procedural judges so deal with pre-trial case management and they deal with 80 per cent of the contested trials in the county court. Recorders sit part time and their jurisdiction is similar to that of circuit judges. They also exercise case management powers. Deputy district judges sit part time. All types of judge sit alone although circuit judges may sit with a jury of eight, in categories of case described in the Chapter on the jury. The Lord Chancellor nominates a number of all these types of judge to sit proceedings under the Children Act 1989. There are some specialist circuit judges, for instance, those in the mercantile courts; Designated Civil Judges who are responsible for judicial management of civil judges in their area and Designated Family Judges who sit at care centres and are responsible for the judicial management of the centres' work.

County Court Jurisdiction
6-004   Under the Courts and Legal Services Act 1990, s.3 the county court was given almost all the powers of the High Court, with some restrictions. Nevertheless, county courts try the vast bulk of civil cases, such as tort, contract, property, insolvency and bankruptcy with the High Court reserved for a few special cases, in accordance with the recommendations of the Civil Justice Review 1988 and the Woolf Report 1996. Under the Civil Procedure

Rules 1998, cases are divided into small claims, fast track and multi-track and the county courts hear all small claims, virtually all fast track claims and most multi-track claims. Virtually all divorces are heard in county courts and very few are heard in the High Court. County courts share jurisdiction under the Children Act 1989 with the magistrates' courts and the High Court. Public law care cases involve parties other than just the parents, such as the local authority or NSPCC and are heard at certain special county courts called care centres. Family hearing centres hear private family proceedings, where only the parents and children are involved. County Courts include five specialist mercantile courts and a patents county court, all of which have specialist circuit judges. A few circuit judges have special jurisdiction to hear cases under the Race Relations Act 1976.

3. The High Court of Justice

The High Court of Justice and the Court of Appeal were brought into being as the Supreme Court of Judicature under the Judicature Acts 1873–1875. At that time, the High Court consisted of five Divisions, the Queen's Bench, Chancery, Probate, Divorce and Admiralty, Exchequer and Common Pleas. The last two Divisions were merged in the Queen's Bench Division in 1880 and the remaining three Divisions continued unaltered from then until the Administration of Justice Act 1970 redistributed the functions of the Probate, Divorce and Admiralty Division and created the Family Division.
6-005

The High Court sits at the Royal Courts of Justice in the Strand and, for the convenience of litigants and their solicitors, there are a number of district registries and trial centres in the larger cities in England and Wales. There are 107 High Court judges appointed to the three Divisions, 17 in Chancery, 17 Family Division judges and the rest in the Queen's Bench (source: *Monthly Judicial Statistics* on the LCD website). Trials are also conducted by deputy High Court judges (retired judges or specially appointed practitioners who the Lord Chancellor is testing out—see the Judges Chapter of this book) and circuit judges authorised under the Supreme Court Act by the Lord Chancellor to sit part time in the High Court. In 2000, around 351 circuit judges were so authorised, 174 for the Queen's Bench and Chancery Divisions and 147 for the Family Division. In 2000, there were 201 deputy High Court judges, authorised by the Lord Chancellor under the Supreme Court Act (Source: *Judicial Appointments Annual Report*, LCD website).
6-006

The Queen's Bench Division

This, the great common law court, takes its name from the fact that the early royal judges sat on "the bench", "en banc", at Westminster. This
6-007

Court absorbed the whole common law jurisdiction, when the High Court was reformed, as described. The present jurisdiction of the Division is thus both civil and criminal, original and appellate and the QBD is much larger than the other two Divisions.

In terms of its civil jurisdiction, most cases are contract or tort. Cases are heard in the Royal Courts of Justice or at provincial district registries of the High Court, located at county court centres. Interlocutory hearings (case management) are held by Masters of the High Court in London (in a part of the Royal Courts of Justice called "the Bear Garden") and by district judges outside London. The Division contains the Commercial Court and the Admiralty Court, hearing cases relating to ships, such as shipping collisions and damage to cargo. A specialist Administrative Court was added in 2000. The QBD administers the Technology and Construction Court (formerly Official Referees Court) which hears such things as technical construction disputes, computer and sale of goods litigation and torts relating to the occupation of land. Most QBD judges spend half their time sitting on circuit hearing serious Crown Court cases or civil cases heard outside London. Specialist QBD judges also sit in the Restrictive Practices Court and the Employment Appeal Tribunal. Judges generally sit alone, with the exception of certain judicial review cases and commercial arbitrations. Jury trial is permitted in five torts and at the discretion of the judge but very rare in other cases. The most common and well publicised jury trials are defamation actions involving prominent people such as the Geoffrey Archer libel case, whose outcome was under scrutiny and condemned in Geoffrey Archer's criminal trial for perjury in the Old Bailey in 2001.

The Divisional Court of the Queen's Bench Division

6-008   In its appellate jurisdiction, the Queen's Bench, like the other two Divisions, has what is rather confusingly called a Divisional Court. This is, in most instances, an appeal court. In the Queen's Bench Division its jurisdiction is:

- Appeals on a point of law by way of case stated from magistrates' courts, tribunals and the Crown Court.
- The supervisory jurisdiction of the High Court over inferior courts and tribunals and, most importantly, over governmental and other public bodies. Specialist judges of the Administrative Court, created in 2000 hear applications for judicial review. For instance, challenging the closure of a hospital, or challenging the Government's handling of the foot and mouth crisis of 2001. The Administrative Court also sits in Cardiff, to hear judicial review cases from Wales. Planning appeals and appeals from magistrates' courts can also be held in Wales.

- Applications for habeas corpus (challenging the legality of detention).
- Appeals and applications on planning matters.

The judicial review work of the Administrative Court is expected to expand significantly as actions are brought, from 2001, to test the boundaries of the Human Rights Act 1998 and the practical meaning of the European Convention on Human Rights in English law. The Convention became part of English law in October 2000. Accordingly, the Lord Chancellor asked Parliament to create extra QBD judicial posts, to cope with the workload.

The Chancery Division

This Division is the direct descendant of the Lord Chancellor's equity **6-009** jurisdiction, and it is thus substantially concerned with those matters which, before the Judicature Acts 1873–1875, belonged to the Court of Chancery. It has also had allocated to it by statute the responsibility for such matters as the winding-up of companies and revenue cases. Its specialist judges are headed by the Vice-Chancellor. The Lord Chancellor also has jurisdiction but never sits. Interlocutory matters are heard by High Court Masters in London and district judges outside. Some trials are heard by deputy High Court judges. Its jurisdiction can be summarised as:

- disputed intellectual property, copyright or patents;
- the execution or declaration of trusts;
- the redemption and foreclosure of mortgages;
- conveyancing and land law matters;
- partnership actions and other business and industrial disputes;
- the administration of the estates of deceased persons (contested probate);
- revenue issues, *i.e.* taxation cases;
- insolvency;
- professional negligence claims against solicitors, accountants surveyors and others.

It also contains two specialist courts: the Patents Court, dealing with patents and registered designs and the Companies Court, which deals mainly with company insolvency and it has administrative responsibility for the Restrictive Practices Court. The Chancery Division sits at the Royal Courts of Justice and eight provincial High Court centres. The Divisional Court of the Chancery Division hears tax appeals from the Commissioners of Taxes, from the county courts in bankruptcy cases and from the High Court in insolvency. Because of its intellectual property

117

and copyright jurisdiction, the litigants we are most likely to hear of in Chancery are pop and rock stars, such as the Spice Girls, Bruce Springstein and George Michael. In a 2001 case, in which Arsenal Football Club claimed a company was infringing the clothing trademarks, Mr Justice Laddie could not resist waving an Arsenal scarf above his head and offering to decorate his colleagues' rooms with Arsenal wallpaper.

The Family Division

6-010   This Division shares family jurisdiction with the magistrates' court and the county court. Its specialist judges are headed by a President. The main responsibilities of the Family Division are:

- complex defended divorce cases, either in London or district registries with divorce jurisdiction.
- complex applications relating to children, under the Children Act 1989: for instance applications for care orders, adoptions, wardship, residence and contact orders. Jurisdiction under the Children Act is concurrent with that of the county court and magistrates' court. Cases may be transferred. Only this court may deal with wardship applications, in which the court orders a child to be made a ward of court and subject to its control.
- the grant of probate or letters of administration to authorise the disposal of a decreased person's estate where the matter is uncontested. This work is done at the Principal Registry in London and 11 District Probate Registries in England and Wales.

The Divisional Court of the Family Division hears appeals from decisions of magistrates in a wide variety of domestic matters including orders made under the Children Act. It also deals with judicial review of family issues, as illustrated by the Diane Blood case, described in the Chapter on sources. 1998 saw a sudden increase in the work of the Probate Service of the Family Division, supplying copies of the will of the late Diana, Princess of Wales.

4. The Court of Appeal (Civil Division)

6-011   The Court of Appeal was created by the Judicature Acts 1873–1875, together with the High Court of Justice, to form the Supreme Court of Judicature. It was at first intended that the Court of Appeal should be the final appeal court, but a change of plan led to the Appellate Jurisdiction Act 1876, under which the House of Lords in its judicial capacity was retained as the supreme appeal court.

Thirty-five Lords Justices sit in the CA. The Master of the Rolls heads the Civil Division of the CA and the President of the Family Division and the Vice-Chancellor sit occasionally. It hears appeals on fact and law from the High Court, including divisional courts, the county courts and certain tribunals. Until recently, the Court was composed of three Lords Justices but, after the Access to Justice Act 1999, section 54, the Court may be composed of one or more judges, depending on the importance and complexity of the case. The rationale behind this was "proportionality and efficiency", explained in the 1998 Government white paper *Modernising Justice*, the same as the principles underlying the Civil Procedure Rules 1998. In a case of great importance (see *Ward v. James* (1966)) a "full court" of five judges is convened. It sits in the Royal Courts of Justice in the Strand but sat in Cardiff for the first time in 1999 and will sit in Wales at regular intervals. Latterly, the Lord Chief Justice, Lord Woolf has a habit of sitting in the Civil Division to hear cases interpreting the Civil Procedure Rules 1998, since it was he who devised them and oversaw their implementation, as Master of the Rolls. An example is *Callery v. Gray* (2001), analysed in the Chapter on legal services.

5. The House of Lords

The Appellate Committee of the House of Lords is the final court of appeal in civil matters from all courts in England, Wales and Northern Ireland and Scotland. It assumed its present jurisdiction under the Appellate Jurisdiction Act 1876. There is now a maximum of 12 Lords of Appeal in Ordinary, known as the Law Lords. At least two of the judges will be from Scotland and one from Northern Ireland. In addition to the Lords of Appeal in Ordinary, other judges who can take part in the work of the House are the Lord Chancellor, ex Lord Chancellors, the Master of the Rolls and peers who have held high judicial office. By constitutional convention, lay peers do not take part in the hearing of appeals.

6-012

Normally, five judges hear an appeal. The case is heard in a committee room of the House of Lords at Westminster. The judges wear lounge suits, although counsel are in wigs and robes, and the atmosphere is comparatively informal. The cases heard always raise a point of law of general public importance, which is the sole ground for obtaining leave to appeal to the House of Lords. In English appeals, leave may be granted by the court below. This may be the Court of Appeal or the Queen's Bench Divisional Court. If leave is refused by the court below, it is still possible for a party wishing to appeal to ask the Appeal Committee of the House of Lords itself to give leave to appeal. Under the Administration of Justice Act 1969, it is possible for an appeal to "leapfrog" the Court of Appeal and go direct to the House of Lords provided:

119

(i)   the trial judge is prepared to grant a certificate;
(ii) the parties agree to this course;
(iii) a point of law of general public importance is involved, which relates wholly or mainly to the construction of a statute or statutory instrument; or the judge was bound by a previous decision of the Court of Appeal or the House of Lords; and
(iv) the House of Lords grants leave.

In view of these stringent conditions not many successful applications are made (one only in 2000).

6-013   Each side, in any appeal to the House of Lords, must submit a "printed case", drawn up by counsel, which must contain a succinct statement of their argument. The oral hearing follows.

Their Lordships, after hearing the appeal, will take time to prepare their "opinions", or "speeches" as their Lordships' judgments are called. It is open to all five judges to give individual opinions and then the majority view prevails. The Court finally gives notice of its decision to the House of Lords itself, in the chamber. Judgments of the House of Lords are almost always reported, because every one adds some new principle to, or clarifies some existing principle of, law. As the supreme court, the decisions of the House of Lords are binding on all lower courts, and they thus form the most important precedents in domestic law. There are only around 60 such decisions in civil cases per year.

6. The European Court of Justice

6-014   The European Court of Justice consists currently of 15 judges, each of whom must be qualified to hold the highest judicial office in their own country, appointed for a six-year term by the governments of the Member States. The judges are assisted by eight Advocates General who prepare reasoned conclusions on the cases submitted to the Court. They sit in odd number chambers with the most important cases being heard by all 15. The Court is not bound by judicial precedent and has a flexible approach to the interpretation of the Treaties. It hears:

- applications from Member States for preliminary rulings on points of E.C. law, under Article 234 of the Treaty of Rome;
- direct actions against Member States or E.C., institutions;
- requests for opinions on international law and the E.C. treaties;
- tort claims;
- actions for judicial review.

There is a European Court of First Instance, described in the Chapter on E.C. law.

7. The European Court of Human Rights

In 1951 the United Kingdom was the original signatory to the **6-015** European Convention on Human Rights. The European Court of Human Rights sits in Strasbourg and hears actions for advisory opinions and rulings against contracting states. It is composed of a President, Vice President and judges elected by the Parliamentary Assembly of the Council of Europe and nominated by the 42 Member States of the Council of Europe, for a six-year period. Judges sit in their individual capacity and need not be nationals of Member States.

The staff filter out about two thirds of applications because the Court lacks jurisdiction. Applicants must first exhaust all domestic remedies and since 2000, the Human Rights Act 1998 provides United Kingdom residents with a set of remedies to enforce the Convention through our courts. A three-judge committee decides whether the application meets the Court's admissibility criteria. The Court has a duty to secure a friendly settlement where possible. An appeal may be taken from a ruling of a chamber of seven to a Grand Chamber of 17. It deals mainly with political and civil rights. For more details, see the Chapter on Human Rights.

8. The Judicial Committee of the Privy Council

This Committee was established in 1833, by the Judicial Committee **6-016** Act, which, as amended, remains the basic statute. It is primarily the ultimate appeal court from some Commonwealth countries and from certain of the independent Commonwealth states which have retained this form of appeal (around 27 in total). An example of the PC defining its own jurisdiction in such cases was *Gairy v. A.G. for Grenada* (2001). The Committee also hears appeals from Jersey, Guernsey and the Isle of Man and from certain domestic tribunals in England and Wales, such as the General Medical Council (*e.g. Ghosh v. GMC*, 2001 on Article 6 Convention rights before the GMC). It recently acquired a new significant jurisdiction over devolution issues under the Scotland Act 1998, the Northern Ireland Act 1998 and the Government of Wales Act 1998. It decides on the competences and functions of the legislative and executive authorities established in Scotland and Northern Ireland and questions as to the competence and functions of the Welsh Assembly. The PC made it clear in *Hoekstra and Others v. H.M. Advocate* (2000) that it only has jurisdiction over devolution issues and has not been given a general power to review the proceedings of the High Court of Justiciary in Scotland but devolution issues include Human Rights issues (*e.g. HM Advocate and Another v. McIntosh* (2001)). In the debate on the Scotland Bill 1998, some

121

peers called for a proper constitutional court. They thought the Judicial Committee of the Privy Council was inappropriate to review decisions from Scotland, because it is geographically imbalanced, consisting mainly of English Law Lords. The Privy Council's jurisdiction is derived from statute but its history derives from its medieval role as the body of the monarch's closest advisers.

6-017   The Judicial Committee is composed of Privy Councillors who have held or now hold high judicial office. Each case must be heard by not more than five and not less than three members of the Committee. In practice, the Court usually consists of three or five Lords of Appeal in Ordinary, sometimes assisted by a senior judge from the country concerned. It sits in Downing Street. Over the last decade, the Judicial Committee has provoked the impatience of the governments of independent Caribbean countries who send appeals to it in death penalty cases. The Committee frequently allows appeals against conviction, where the death penalty has been imposed (*e.g. Boodram v. State of Trinidad and Tobago* (2001)), or against the imposition of the death penalty. In one decision in 2000, it ruled that hundreds of death row prisoners in the Caribbean should be released (*The Times*, July 9, 2000) Consequently. Caribbean countries see the Privy Council as a group of unduly liberal judges who undermine their efforts to tackle high murder and violence rates and drug trafficking on their islands. They have long debated whether to abolish the Privy Council's jurisdiction and replace it with a regional court of appeal. See discussion by Lehrfreund at (1999) 149 N.L.J. 1299.

9. Other Civil Courts

Ecclesiastical Courts

6-018   These courts at the present time exercise control over clergy of the Church of England. In each diocese there is a consistory court, the judge of which is a barrister appointed by the bishop, and known as the Chancellor. For example, in 1995, a consistory court was convened to hear allegations of sexual impropriety made against the Dean of Lincoln. Appeal lies from the consistory court to, depending on the diocese, the Arches Court of Canterbury or the Chancery Court of York, and from either court a further appeal is possible to the Judicial Committee of the Privy Council.

Court of Protection

6-019   Under the Mental Health Act 1983, a judge of the Chancery Division can sit as a Court of Protection to administer the estate of a person suffering from mental disability. This "court" is a misnomer as it is, in law, an office of the Supreme Court.

Restrictive Practices Court

This court was set up by the Restrictive Trade Practices Act 1956 to **6-020** examine agreements which restrict prices or the conditions of supply of goods. For instance, applications may be made by the Director-General of Fair Trading. Sittings of the court consist of one High Court judge and at least two lay members. Judges may sit alone on appeals on law. Although not part of the High Court it is a superior court of record. Appeal lies to the Court of Appeal.

The Coroner's Court

The Coroners' Court is used to inquire (by an inquest) into unex- **6-021** plained deaths. The coroner may, and sometimes must, call a jury of from seven to 11 persons to return a verdict as to the cause of death. Coroners' Courts also inquire into the ownership of treasure trove, for instance, the discoveries of metal detector enthusiasts. The coroner must be legally or medically qualified.

The Employment Appeal Tribunal

This Court was established by the Employment Protection Act 1975 to **6-022** hear appeals from decisions of Industrial Tribunals (now employment tribunals), in particular those relating to unfair dismissal, equal pay and redundancy. The composition of the Court for a hearing is one High Court judge sitting with two lay people who have specialised knowledge of industrial relations. Appeals from the Employment Appeal Tribunal on points of law go direct to the Court of Appeal.

Offices of the Supreme Court

These include the Official Solicitor's Department, whose job it is to **6-023** protect the interests of minors and mental patients under a legal disability; the Tipstaff who delivers people to court or prison on the order of a Supreme Court judge and the Public Guardianship Office (formerly Public Trust Office), which holds private money held in court pending a case and handles the private money of some mentally disabled persons incapable of handling their own affairs.

FURTHER READING

Judicial *Guides for Applicants*, especially job specifications, LCD website, **6-024** www.lcd.gov.uk. Click on the "Judges" button.
Judicial Appointments annual reports, on the same site.
Annual *Judicial Statistics*, same site.
Monthly *Judicial Appointments* statistics, same site.
"Stage Fright for Baby Spice at High Court", *The Times*, February 10, 2000.
The Privy Council website, for very useful info. on the PC: www.privy-council.org.uk.

The Parliament website for House of Lords judgments and information on the House of Lord Appellate Committee: www.parliament.uk.

Civil Justice Review, Report of the Review Body on Civil Justice (1988).

The General Council of the Bar and The Law Society, "Civil Justice On Trial—The Case For Change" (known as The Heilbron Hodge Report) (1993).

Lord Woolf, *Access To Justice* (1996) and his interim report, 1995.

Robin White, *The English Legal System in Action* (1999), especially Chapter 2, "European Influences".

A. Le Seur and R. Cornes, "What do the top courts do?" (200c) 53 C.L.P. 53.

7. Criminal Courts

There is a basic division of modes of criminal trial in the English legal system into summary trial and trial on indictment. To complicate the matter there are now four categories of offence. These distinctions will be explained later but the English criminal court structure is based on the simple division into the two types of trial, summary trial and trial on indictment. The description applies to adult proceedings but 10–17-year-olds are dealt with in the youth court.

7-001

Note that at the time of writing, 2001, Lord Justice Auld has completed a review of the criminal courts and produced his Review in October 2001. He favours a unified criminal three-tier court. The middle tier would be composed of a mixed bench of professional and lay magistrates, with greater sentencing powers than the existing magistrates' court. Readers should refer to his summary report on his website. This idea of a mixed bench has been discussed before, by Seago, Walker and Wall, in 1995 and Darbyshire, in "Neglect", (1997). It was then discussed, after evidence was received by Auld L.J., by Sanders, in 2001. These are cited and discussed above in the Magistrates Chapter.

1. Summary Trial

The Magistrates' Court

Summary trials are held at magistrates' courts. Until 1949 they were known as police courts and many magistrates' courts are situated close to police stations. This is unfortunate since it conveys the impression that the court sits at the convenience of the police to distribute punishment in accordance with police evidence. As the police inevitably figure prominently in the magistrates' court, it is not surprising that the public has tended to think of it as the police court (see Darbyshire, "Concern", 1997, cited below). Happily, there are not so many uniformed police

7-002

officers in today's courts as there were prior to 1985. The Prosecution of Offences Act 1985 replaced police prosecutors with Crown Prosecutors and the 1990s saw private security officers replacing police court security officers. For most people who appear in a criminal court, as a defendant, witness or victim, the court involved will be the magistrates' court. All summary offences are statutorily defined. They include the vast bulk of traffic offences, the most trivial of which many people wrongly assume not to be normal criminal offences. Even a parking offence is a criminal offence, in English law. We do not have a third species of law, "violations", as they do in the United States. Common assault is a summary offence, as are many regulatory offences, prosecuted by government departments.

7-003   The category of offences of medium seriousness is called "triable either way". Here, the defendant may elect trial in the magistrates' court or in the Crown Court, unless the magistrates insist on a Crown Court trial or, in certain instances, where the prosecutor can and does so insist. Most defendants opt for summary trial.

Magistrates' jurisdiction is statutory. They can send an offender to prison for up to six months, or a maximum of 12 for more than one offence and/or impose a fine of up to £5,000 (fixed by the Powers of the Criminal Courts (Sentencing) Act 2000). If, after conviction, the bench feel their powers of sentence are inadequate, they may commit to the Crown Court for sentencing. A district judge (magistrates' court) sitting alone has the same powers as a bench of two or three lay justices. At the hearing of any case, the bench is assisted by the justices' clerk or, more usually, a court clerk. The former is legally qualified. The magistrates' clerk may advise the magistrates on the law and controls the administration of the court.

Throughout the nineteenth and twentieth centuries, more and more work has been shifted down onto the shoulders of the magistrates, by reclassifying offences as summary only or by shifting them out of the indictable category into the triable either way category. The result is that magistrates deal with over 97 per cent of all criminal cases and 95 per cent of all sentencing. It is a big mistake, therefore, to think of this court as dealing with trivia. For discussion see Darbyshire ("Importance and Neglect", 1997).

The Crown Court

7-004   The Crown Court hears appeals against conviction and/or sentence from those convicted in the magistrates' court. Appeals are usually heard by a circuit judge and two magistrates. Where an appellant is appealing in a licensing matter from a magistrates' court, four justices may sit with a judge. Note that licensing is not a criminal matter. It is an administrative function of the justices. The Crown Court also sentences defendants who have been committed for sentencing by magistrates, after having been summarily convicted of an either-way offence.

The Divisional Court of the Queen's Bench Division
7-005

This court hears prosecution and defence appeals by way of case stated on points of law from the magistrates' courts and conducts judicial reviews of the legality of proceedings in magistrates' courts. In doing this it is exercising the High Court's prerogative power to review the legality of proceedings in inferior tribunals. As explained in the Chapter on civil courts, an Administrative Court was created in 2000.

House of Lords
7-006

Where the case stated raises a point of law of general public importance, provided leave is given by the Divisional Court or by the Appeal Committee of the House of Lords, prosecution or defence may appeal to the House. This is known as a "leapfrog" appeal, described in the Chapter on civil courts.

2. Trial on Indictment

Indictable offences are recognised at common law, or by statute, and are generally the more serious forms of crime. As well as indictable offences, "triable either way" offences can also be tried at the Crown Court, at the option of the defendant or magistrates or because of the nature of the prosecution (see above). Additionally, since the Criminal Justice Act 1988, a summary offence may be added to an indictment in the Crown Court. The word "indictment" means a document which sets out in writing the charges against the accused person. Each separate charge is called "a count" of the indictment.
7-007

The Crown Court

The Courts Act 1971, which abolished the courts of quarter sessions and assizes, created in their place one unified Crown Court. It forms part of the Supreme Court and under the 1971 Courts Act, England and Wales are divided into six circuits based on London, Bristol, Birmingham, Manchester, Cardiff and Leeds. There are 90 Crown Court Centres of three types. *First tier* centres are visited by High Court judges for serious Crown Court work and High Court civil business. *Second tier* centres are visited by High Court judges for Crown Court criminal business only. *Third tier* centres are not normally visited by a High Court judge. Circuit judges and recorders sit at all three. Two presiding High Court judges are appointed to each circuit and are responsible for the organisational arrangements of the Crown Court. By Practice
7-008

Directions of 1995, 1998, 2000 and 2001, the Lord Chief Justice directs that offences should be classified into one of four categories and should be tried accordingly:

Class 1: The most serious offences are generally tried by a High Court judge, unless released by the presiding judge to a circuit judge. They include treason and murder.

Class 2: These are generally also tried by a High Court judge unless released to a circuit judge or a recorder. They include manslaughter and rape.

Class 3: These may be listed for a High Court judge but shifted to a circuit judge or authorised, trained recorder, if the listing officer, with general or particular directions by the presiding judge, so decides. They include all indictable offences other than those falling within classes 1, 2 and 4, for example, affray, aggravated burglary, kidnapping and causing death by dangerous driving.

Class 4: These offences are normally tried by a circuit judge or recorder but can be by a High Court judge, with the consent of that judge or the presiding judge. This class includes all "triable either way" offences and certain others, for example conspiracy, robbery, grievous bodily harm.

Judge-only Courts, "Bench Trials" as an Alternative to Judge and Jury

7-009   Note that when the defendant pleads not guilty, a jury of twelve sits with the judge or recorder. They decide on guilt and innocence and the judge does the sentencing. The defendant may not opt out of this and be tried by judge alone, which he can in some of our common law daughter jurisdictions, such as the United States. Latterly, there have been calls for the defendant to be allowed to opt for a judge-only trial (Darbyshire 1991, "Importance and Neglect", 1997 and see especially, Jackson and Doran, "The Case for Jury Waiver" and *Judge Without Jury*). There seems no logic in forcing a defendant to be tried by jury where he would be content to be tried by judge alone. Some of us have made the same recommendation to Auld L.J. and are glad he adopted our recommendation in his 2001 report.

The Court of Appeal (Criminal Division)

7-010   The Court of Appeal (Criminal Division) was established under the provisions of the Criminal Appeal Act 1966 to replace the former Court of Criminal Appeal. The Court's jurisdiction is contained in the Criminal Appeal Act 1968, as amended by the Criminal Appeal Act 1995.

It usually sits only in The Royal Courts of Justice in the Strand but in 1999, Lord Chief Justice Bingham took it to sit in Liverpool and in Bristol. The Court is made up of the Lord Chief Justice, the Vice-President of the Criminal Division, Lords Justices of Appeal and a number of Queen's Bench Division judges specially nominated by the Lord Chief Justice. Normally, three judges sit, except on rare occasions when five sit. In a well publicised speech in 1992, the outgoing Lord Chief Justice attacked the Lord Chancellor for a shortage of Lords Justices of Appeal, resulting in important criminal appeals being heard, in the main, by High Court judges. This is part of the ongoing concern by the judiciary at the over use of lower level judges to hear serious cases and appeals. To add fuel to the fire of judicial anger, the Criminal Justice and Public Order Act 1994, s.52 permits circuit judges to sit in the Court of Appeal (Criminal Division). The first one sat in 1995. The jurisdiction of the Court of Appeal (Criminal Division) is:

(i) to hear appeals against conviction on indictment with the leave of the Court of Appeal or if the trial judge certifies that the case is fit for appeal (Criminal Appeal Act 1995, s.1).

(ii) to hear appeals against sentence pronounced by the Crown Court provided that the sentence is not one fixed by law and provided that the court grants leave. An application for leave may be determined by a single judge, but if leave is refused, the appellant can require a full court, *i.e.* two or more judges to determine the matter.

(iii) to hear appeals referred to it by the new Criminal Cases Review Commission, under the Criminal Appeal Act 1995.

(iv) to hear appeals against a verdict of "not guilty by reason of insanity" or against findings of fitness and unfitness to plead.

(v) to hear an appeal by the prosecution against an acquittal on a point of law at the trial in the Crown Court. This provision involves an application by the Attorney-General for the opinion of the Court on the point of law and is known as an "Attorney-General's Reference". The result cannot affect the acquittal and the defendant is not named in the appeal.

(vi) to hear an appeal by the prosecutor, again as an "Attorney-General's Reference" against a lenient sentence. In this case the Court will set out sentencing guidelines for the future but may also increase the actual sentence imposed.

House of Lords

This hears appeals from the Court of Appeal and those which have leapfrogged from the High Court. Either prosecutor or defendant may appeal, provided the Court of Appeal certifies that a point of law of general public importance is involved and that either court feels that the point should be considered by the House and grants leave. The House, in disposing of the appeal, may exercise any of the powers of the Court of Appeal, or remit the case to it (Criminal Appeal Act 1968.) It is described more fully in the previous Chapter.

7-011

The European Court of Justice and the European Court of Human Rights

7-012   These are described in the Chapter on civil courts.

3. *The Youth Court*

7-013   In the United Kingdom, the age of criminal responsibility is 10. Ten to 17-year-olds are almost all tried in the youth court, which is a special court within the magistrates' court. This is a very important court, since the peak age of offending in England and Wales is around 17–18 (source *Annual Criminal Statistics*), although the majority of young offenders are diverted from the criminal process by the official cautioning scheme, put on a statutory basis by the Crime and Disorder Act 1998. As explained in the Magistrates' Chapter, the bench comprises specially trained magistrates, who usually sit in mixed gender threesomes. The predecessor of the court, the juvenile court, was formed in 1908, by the Juvenile Offences Act. It was thought desirable to keep adult defendants separate from juveniles. Ideally, the Act's progenitors would have liked to have seen a separate system of courts for young offenders. Separate courts have never been developed, except in large cities like London, Nottingham, Birmingham and elsewhere, where the caseload warranted it. Instead, it became the habit at smaller courts to convene the juvenile court on a separate day from the adult court. Eventually, this was whittled down to an hour's gap between adult and juvenile courts but the problem with this is that they sometimes overlap, or the morning court drags on through lunchtime so young and adult defendants are waiting around together and this defeats the whole purpose. The Court originally dealt with the "deprived" as well as the "depraved". In other words, it heard civil applications, often from the local authority, to take the child into care for its own welfare. This work was given away to the family proceedings court when the youth court was created by the Children Act 1989 so it now has a purely criminal jurisdiction. Importantly, the public are excluded from the youth court and procedure is more informal than that of the adult court. The youth court has a variety of powers. For example, as well as fining the child and/or parent, it can impose a supervision order, which is like a probation order for children, or order detention and training for up to two years so magistrates are more powerful in this court than in the adult court.

7-014   Only those youngsters who commit "grave crimes", under the Children Act 1933 or those tried with an adult are meant to be sent up for trial in the Crown Court. A "grave crime" means something like murder or rape. Jamie Bulger's killers, Thompson and Venables, were tried in the Crown Court. They successfully asked the European Court of

Human Rights to declare that their trial had been inappropriate but that case will be examined in the Chapter on criminal procedure. In 2001, Auld L.J. recommended, in his Criminal Courts Review, that grave crimes should be heard in a youth court composed of a judge and two youth panel magistrates.

FURTHER READING

Annual *Judicial Statistics*, LCD website, www.lcd.gov.uk.　　　　　**7-015**

Lord Justice Auld, *Criminal Courts Review*, 2001, www.criminal-courts-review.org.uk.

Darbyshire, "The Lamp That Shows That Freedom Lives—is it worth the candle?" [1991] Crim.L.R. 740 and see citations of 1997 and 1999 articles in the Magistrates Chapter.

John Jackson and Sean Doran, *Judge Without Jury*, 1995 and "The Case for Jury Waiver" [1997] Crim.L.R. 155.

8. History

1. Continuity

The British system of government, and the legal institutions which form part of it, are only explicable in terms of history. The Inns of Court, the Queen's Bench and Chancery Divisions of the High Court, the Justice of the Peace and the jury—these institutions, like many in the system, all have a long history. **8-001**

One important factor is that whereas most continental legal systems rely heavily on legal principles derived from Roman Law, the English legal system has remained comparatively uninfluenced by this source. The reasons for this would seem to be connected with the unbroken historical development of the system in England, where at no time was it felt necessary to look outside the principles of common law or equity for assistance. Inevitably, through the ecclesiastical courts in particular, some Roman Law influence can be traced but in general terms this is very limited, and especially when comparison is made with systems elsewhere. Indeed, the reason why England resisted the "invasion" of Roman Law, which forms the base of European civil law systems, was that a unified common law system was already growing in strength from the period prior to the Norman Conquest.

2. Early History

Anglo-Saxon Laws

The earliest English laws of which there is documentary evidence date from the Anglo-Saxon period of English history before the Norman Conquest. These laws are not strictly English laws; more accurately they are the laws relating to a particular tribal area such as Kent, Wessex or **8-002**

133

Mercia. In practice these laws are based on what seems to have been the original customs of the settlers in question. Not unnaturally there are marked discrepancies in the details of the laws remaining from the different areas. They clearly derive from the time before England emerged as a national unit.

The Norman Conquest (1066)

8-003   The Anglo-Saxon divisions were just giving way to a national entity when the Norman invasion of England occurred. The result of the Battle of Hastings in 1066 led to William the Conqueror ascending the English throne determined on a process of centralisation. William's tactics were to impose strong national government and this he did by causing his Norman followers to become the major land-owners throughout the country. The system used was "subinfeudation" under which all land belonged to the monarch and was by him granted to his followers on certain conditions. In turn they could grant their land to their tenants. Again subject to conditions, those tenants could make similar grants and so on, down the ladder. This method of granting land created the complete feudal system under which tenants owed duties to their lord, whilst he in turn owed duties to his lord and so on up to the monarch, as the supreme point of the feudal pyramid. However, the system never became as firmly entrenched in this country as it did, for instance, in France.

Feudal Courts

8-004   In the development of the feudal system a characteristic benefit to the feudal lord was the right to hold his own court. From the holding of this court he would obtain financial benefits, whilst at the same time it gave him effective power over the locality. So far as the ordinary individual was concerned this local manor court was the one which affected him most. Bearing in mind that the concept of central authority in law and government was still comparatively new, it was to take a long time before the royal courts were able to exercise control over these local courts. Although the passage of centuries did see the transfer of real power from local to national courts, these feudal courts remained in being in many instances down to the property legislation of 1925. Until 1925 there was a tenure of property called "copyhold", which involved the registration of the transaction in the local court roll so that the person held the land by "copy" of the court roll. This was a survival of a feudal court responsibility.

Royal Courts

8-005   Following the Norman Conquest, succeeding monarchs soon realised that besides the need for strong national government there was also a need for the development of a system of national law and order. To this end the closest advisers of the monarch—the "*curia regis*", or "King's

council", as it was called—encouraged, over a period of time, the establishment of three separate royal courts which sat at Westminster. These
were:

(i)   the Court of Exchequer, which as the name applies was mainly
concerned with cases affecting the royal revenue, but which also
had a limited civil jurisdiction;

(ii)   the Court of King's Bench, which taking its name from the original concept of the monarch sitting with his judges "*in banco*"—
on the bench—at Westminster, dealt with both civil and criminal
cases in which the King had an interest; and

(iii)   the Court of Common Pleas, which was established to hear civil
cases brought by one individual against another.

Each of the courts had its own judges. In the Court of Exchequer sat
judges called Barons, with a presiding judge known as the Chief Baron.
This Court appears to be the oldest of the three, emerging in recognis-
able form in the early thirteenth century having developed out of the
financial organisation responsible for the royal revenues. The Court of
King's Bench had its own Chief Justice and separate judges, and was
closely linked with the monarch and the Great Council for a very long
time. This was due, in particular, to the original understanding that this
was the court which followed the King's person. The Court of Common
Pleas had its own Chief Justice and judges and left records from the early
thirteenth century.

All three courts seem to have been required by the monarch—Stow in
his survey of London says in 1224—to make their base in Westminster
Hall and there arose continuing conflicts between them over jurisdiction.
The importance of getting more and more work was largely brought
about by the fact that the judges were paid out of the court fees. At any
rate these three royal courts, later added to by the introduction of a Court
of Chancery, survived five centuries before being reconstructed into the
present High Court of Justice in the Judicature Acts 1873–1875. The ultimate merger of Exchequer and Common Pleas into the Queen's Bench
Division came about in 1880.

3. *The Common Law*

Origin

As a centralised system of law and order gradually developed, so it   **8-006**
became necessary for the various customary laws of the different regions
to give way to national laws. This national law came to be known as the
common law. It was called "common" because it was common to the

whole country, as opposed to the local customs which had previously pre-dominated in the different regions. Since inevitably the different customs at times turned out to be in conflict, the decisions of the judges, absorb-ing certain of these customs and rejecting others, came to be of first-rate importance. They were creating "the law of the realm". Consequently, a feature of the original establishment of the common law is that it was derived entirely from case law.

Development

8-007   The Norman Kings, in attempting to weld the country together, made use of royal commissioners to travel the country to deal with governmen-tal matters of one kind and another. The production of the "Domesday Book", as a property and financial survey, is the best known example of this system. The extension of these activities to the judicial field seems to have arisen not long after the Conquest, when the King would appoint judges as royal commissioners, charged with certain royal powers, to travel different parts of the country to deal with civil and criminal matters in the locality in which they arose.

The sending of judges, or, as they were originally called, "itinerant jus-tices in Eyre", around the country, dates from not long after the Conquest; but the assize system, as later developed, really dates from the reign of Henry II (1154–89). The assize system only came to an end with the passing of the Courts Act 1971.

It was an important part of the work of these judges to formulate the common law. A task which over a lengthy period of time they did, by meeting together formally and informally to resolve problems which had arisen in the cases coming before them. The principles of law thus laid down, once accepted and developed, formed the common law. As these judges were linked with the courts meeting in Westminster Hall, the build-ing up of a national system grew apace. However, the common law never completely abolished local custom. In fact, as we have seen in the Chapter on Sources, custom has remained a source of law to the present time, even though it rarely applies today.

Forms of Action

8-008   In addition to settling principles of law which were to be followed nationally, the courts also began to establish formal rules relating to the procedure to be adopted in cases coming before them. These rules laid down early that actions were to be begun by the issue of a royal writ, and that the claim made was to be set out in an accepted fashion. This was called a form of action and over a period of time the system took on rigid-ity in that the judges came to take the view that unless a claimant could find an appropriate form of action their claim was not one known to the law. The court officials responsible for the issue of writs tried initially to satisfy the demands of claimants by drawing up a new form of action, but the judges frowned on this course and the practice was stopped by the Provisions of Oxford 1258. So great was the resulting dissatisfaction that 30 years later by the Statute of Westminster 1285 this strict approach was slightly relaxed, so that the officials could issue a new writ, where the new situation was closely related to that covered by an existing writ. The new writs so issued became known as writs "*in consimili casu*". The effect which the writ system had on the development of the legal system is seen below in the section concerning Equity.

Common law remains in being today in that the decisions of judges are still adding to it and in theory the legislation produced by Parliament is supplementing it. Every development in the system operates on the basis that its foundation is the common law. Some confusion has arisen because there are several different meanings attaching to the term:

(i) In the historical sense which has already been examined, common law refers to the national law of this country as opposed to local law or custom. It is the law "common" to England and Wales.

(ii) Sometimes the term is used to mean the law as made by the judges, in contrast to the law as made by Parliament. In this context, common law is limited to case decisions or precedents coming from the courts of common law and equity and so does not include legislation. It must not be overlooked that, as a result of the doctrine of parliamentary supremacy, legislation can always change or overrule the common law.

(iii) As the next section will show, there were, for centuries in England and Wales, two parallel systems of law, one known as the common law and the other as equity. In some contexts the term common law does not include the law derived from the courts of equity.

(iv) Finally the term common law may be used to draw a contrast to systems of foreign law. Here common law takes in both equity and legislation in that it means the complete law of England and Wales. When referring to an overseas country which has derived its legal system from England and Wales the term common law system or jurisdiction is used. This explains why sometimes an English judge will find case decisions from such countries contain persuasive arguments.

4. Equity

Origin

The difficulty which was experienced in the common law courts in relation to the use of writs and the forms of action led to increasing

8-009

dissatisfaction with the system. Litigants who were unable to get satisfaction from the courts turned to the monarch and petitioned him to do justice to his subjects and provide them with a remedy. The monarch handed these petitions on to the Lord Chancellor, who, as Keeper of the King's Conscience and an ecclesiastic, seemed to be a suitable person to deal with them. He set up his own Court of Chancery where he, or his representative, would sit to dispose of these petitions. In doing this work the Lord Chancellor would be guided by equity, or fairness, in coming to his decisions. Consequently, the legal decisions which succeeding Lord Chancellors made came to be known collectively as equity. The system seems to have become well established in the course of the fifteenth century.

Because of the rapid increase in the judicial nature of the work, it was soon found necessary to have a lawyer as Lord Chancellor. The discretion vested in early Lord Chancellors gradually gave way to a system of judicial precedent in equity, but it was a long time before the common law joke died, about equity being as long as the Chancellor's foot. In practice both common law and equity came to operate as parallel systems, with each set of courts regarding itself as bound by its own judicial precedents.

Development

8-010   Having once begun to remedy the wrongs brought about by the rigidity and technicality of the common law system, equity soon found itself establishing a jurisdiction over matters where the common law had failed, and continued to fail, to recognise legal rights and duties. The law relating to trusts, for example, was entirely based on decisions of the Court of Chancery. Nonetheless Equity was always a "gloss" on the common law; it always presumed the existence of the common law and simply supplemented it where necessary. That it continued to exist for some five centuries is an indication of the unchanging nature of English legal institutions, as well as of the important contribution which equity made to the development of English law.

Examples of new rights

8-011   The whole of the law of trusts, which was to become an important aspect of property law, owed its existence entirely to the willingness of equity to recognise and enforce the obligation of a trustee to a beneficiary.

Equity accepted the use of the mortgage as a method of borrowing money against the security of real property, when the common law took a literal view of the obligation undertaken by the borrower. It introduced the "equity of redemption" to enable a borrower to retain the property which was the security for the loan, even where there was default under the strict terms of the mortgage deed.

Examples of new remedies

At common law the only remedy for breach of contract was damages, **8-012** a money payment as compensation for the loss suffered. Equity realised that in some cases damages was not an adequate remedy, and therefore proceeded to introduce the equitable remedies of injunction and specific performance. An injunction is used to prevent a party from acting in breach of their legal obligations; a decree of specific performance is used to order a party to carry out their side of a contract. These remedies mean that a party to a contract cannot just decide to break it and pay damages.

Other equitable remedies are the declaratory order or judgment; the right to have a deed corrected by the process known as rectification; and the right to rescind (withdraw from) a contract. The willingness of equity to intervene where fraud was proven and its preparedness to deal with detailed accounts in the law of trusts and the administration of estates, also gained it wide jurisdiction. The appointment of a receiver is another solution to the problem of the management of certain financial matters, and was introduced by equity.

Examples of new procedures

In contrast to the rigid system of common law remedies equity **8-013** favoured a flexibility of approach. Consequently it was prepared, by a *"subpoena"*, to order witnesses to attend, to have them examined and cross-examined orally, to require relevant documents to be produced, known as discovery of documents, to insist on relevant questions being answered, by the use of interrogatories, and to have the case heard in English, where the common law for centuries used Latin. In the event of a failure to comply with an order, equity was prepared to impose immediate sanctions for this contempt of court.

Another classification sometimes employed is to define the jurisdiction of equity as exclusive, concurrent and auxiliary. In the exclusive jurisdiction sense, equity recognised actions, as in trusts and mortgages, where the common law would provide no remedy; in the concurrent jurisdiction sense equity would add to the remedies provided by the common law, as by the introduction of the injunction and the decree of specific performance; in the auxiliary jurisdiction sense equity employed a more flexible procedure than the common law. It will be seen that these three terms simply emphasise the ways in which equity can be seen to be related to, but to be different from, common law.

Maxims of Equity

As a result of its supplemental role, it became possible over the years **8-014** for an observer to point to certain characteristics of equity. These became so well known as to be called the maxims of equity. Among the most famous are:

He who comes to equity must come with clean hands;
Equity will not suffer a wrong to be without remedy;
Delay defeats equity; and
Equity looks to the intent rather than to the form.

The maxims emphasise that equity, being based in its origins on fairness and natural justice, attempted to maintain this approach throughout its later history. Certainly, the judges retained their personal discretion so that equitable remedies were not, and are not, obtainable as of right. It is very important to understand, for example, that remedies obtainable following judicial review are equitable, and thus discretionary.

Relationship between Common Law and Equity

Early history

8-015   Naturally, as might be presumed, in the early stages of their respective development relations between the two systems were comparatively strained. The common law lawyers regarded equity as an interloper, lacking the firmly-based legal principles with which they were familiar. They were unable, unlike the modern observer with the advantage of hindsight, to see that equity was invaluable in remedying deficiencies in the common law and in encouraging the latter to develop its substantive law and procedure.

As the Court of Chancery built up its jurisdiction and the two systems could be seen to be operating on a parallel basis, inevitably the question arose, what was to happen in the unusual instance when there was a conflict? This problem was solved by James I, in the *Earl of Oxford's* case (1615), by a ruling that where there was a such a conflict, the rules of equity were to prevail.

The later history of equity was dogged in the eighteenth and nineteenth centuries by the courts of Chancery becoming overburdened with work, with increasing reliance being placed on judicial precedent and consequent delays. Dickens' attack in his novel, *Bleak House*, on the delays and costs in the system, seems to have to been thoroughly justified, with some examples of cases awaiting judgment dragging on for scores of years until both parties were dead. Parliament in the 1850s endeavoured by legislation—the Common Law Procedure Acts 1852–1854 and the Chancery (Amendment) Act 1858—to ease the position, but the dual systems continued in being, to the sometimes substantial detriment of litigants, until the Supreme Court of Judicature Acts 1873–1875.

5. Nineteenth Century Developments

The Supreme Court of Judicature Acts 1873–1875

This legislation reorganised the existing court structures completely **8-016** and, in the process, formally brought together the common law courts and the courts of Chancery. In the Supreme Court of Judicature set up by the Acts, the three original royal courts became three divisions of the new High Court of Justice, the Court of Chancery which administered equity became the fourth division, *i.e.* the Chancery Division of the High Court, and a fifth division, dealing with those matters not within common law or equity, namely Probate, Divorce and Admiralty, completed the new arrangements. By Order in Council in 1880, the three royal courts were merged to form the Queen's Bench Division, thus leaving the three Divisions of the High Court — Queen's Bench, Chancery and Probate, Divorce and Admiralty — which were then to remain unchanged for 90 years.

The Judicature Acts 1873–1875 placed on a statutory basis the old rule that where common law and equity conflict, equity shall prevail. At the same time, it gave power to all the courts to administer the principles of common law and equity and to grant the remedies of both, as circumstances in a case demanded. Consequently, the old conflict no longer arises, although common law and equity principles still exist.

By bringing the two systems together administratively, and allowing the High Court judge to exercise the principles, procedures and remedies of common law and equity in a single case in the one court, it seemed to many people that the two systems had merged. That this was somewhat superficial is borne out by the exclusive jurisdictions left to the Queen's Bench and Chancery Divisions. In practice the work formerly done by the Court of Chancery is exactly that dealt with in the Chancery Division; equally it has its own judges selected from those barristers practising at the Chancery bar. A Chancery case remains something quite unlike a common law case, and the same can be said of the procedure.

The whole of the legislation has now been consolidated in the Supreme Court Act 1981.

Probate, Divorce and Admiralty Jurisdiction

The Supreme Court of Judicature Acts 1873–1875 in their recon- **8-017** struction of the court system established a separate Division of the High Court of Justice called the Probate, Divorce and Admiralty Division. Why was it that these three branches of the law merited a division of their own?

The answer is that these three important legal topics fell neither within the common law nor equity jurisdictions, since Probate (which is

141

concerned with wills) and divorce were, for centuries, treated as ecclesiastical matters, and there was a separate Admiralty Court inevitably influenced by international shipping practices.

Probate and divorce were transferred from the ecclesiastical courts to the ordinary civil courts in 1857 by the setting up of a Court of Probate and a separate Divorce Court.

The High Court of Admiralty although of great age historically gradually lost its widest jurisdiction to the common law courts, but it retained powers over collisions at sea, salvage and prize cases. All other aspects of the law merchant, that is the law affecting traders, had over the centuries been transferred to the common law courts.

Appeal Courts

8-018   The Supreme Court of Judicature Acts 1873–1875, in creating a Court of Appeal alongside the new High Court of Justice, had intended that this Court with its specially designated Lords Justices of Appeal should be the final appellate court for civil matters. Political considerations intervened, however and the proposal to remove judicial functions from the House of Lords was shelved. The Appellate Jurisdiction Act 1876 provided for the retention of the House of Lords as the final appeal court in civil cases and for the creation of special judges, Lords of Appeal in Ordinary, as life peers to staff the court.

6. Twentieth Century Developments

Criminal Courts

8-019   In 1907, the Criminal Appeal Act established the Court of Criminal Appeal to provide for the first time a general right of appeal for persons convicted and sentenced in indictable criminal cases. A further appeal in matters of general public importance lay to the House of Lords. The Court of Criminal Appeal became the Court of Appeal (Criminal Division) by the Criminal Appeal Act 1966.

The role of the Queen's Bench Divisional Court in ruling on points of law arising by way of case stated in summary criminal cases was amended by the Administration of Justice Act 1960. This Act enabled an appeal in a case of general public importance to be taken to the House of Lords if the divisional court grants a certificate to that effect and leave is obtained from the divisional court or the appeal committee of the House of Lords.

The court structure for trying indictable criminal cases was substantially changed by the Courts Act 1971 which abolished the historically derived Court of Quarter Sessions and Assizes and replaced them with a court called the Crown Court. The Crown Court was to be organised on a six circuit basis so as to achieve a much needed flexibility to lead to the prompt trial of indictable criminal cases.

Civil Courts

The Administration of Justice Act 1970 created a Family Division of **8-020** the High Court and amended the jurisdiction of the Queen's Bench and Chancery divisions, redistributing the functions of the former Probate Divorce and Admiralty Division. One novel change in appeal provisions was the introduction by the Administration of Justice Act 1969 of a possible "leapfrog" appeal from the High Court to the House of Lords, bypassing the Court of Appeal. The procedure was, however, made subject to stringent conditions which in practice limit its use.

Part III: Procedures

Part III: Procedures

9. Civil Procedure

Procedure, or the way a case is brought to court and put through the system, is very important in the English legal system, as anyone commencing training as a barrister or solicitor rapidly finds out.

9-001

If you think procedure is boring and so can be ignored, you are only fooling yourself. This Chapter explains civil procedure, normally activated when one private citizen or enterprise seeks to bring another to court for a civil wrong against them, such as a breach of contract, or a tort. Remember, it is up to the claimant to bring a case, not the State and the State has no interest in the outcome of the case. It just provides the courts to enable resolution of a private dispute. At the end of this Chapter we examine a procedure that can be used in civil or criminal cases, judicial review, where an aggrieved person may challenge the procedural legality or powers of an inferior court but where most cases involve challenging the way in which Government, central or local, has exercised its discretion.

In the next Chapter we then go on to examine criminal procedure, where a case is normally prosecuted by the State, the Crown, but may be brought by a private person. Here, the State, charged with controlling crime, does have an interest in the outcome so these courts are empowered to impose punishment on behalf of the public. We next examine the adversarial process and its recent erosion.

Before we examine the formal rules for taking a civil action through the courts, we have to bear in mind that the vast majority of people who could have a civil law remedy to their problem do not take it to court or even to any alternative forum. Civil disputes resolved through trial are and have been for centuries, only a tiny fraction of those where proceedings are issued. In turn, all of these are the tip of a much bigger iceberg of cases settled between solicitors but even then, most people do not get round even to seeing a solicitor. All this was well known even before its confirmation by Genn's *Paths to Justice*. This has led Michael Zander to conclude that most people simply cannot be bothered to go to court,

9-002

however much you simplify procedure and make the courts more accessible:

> "When a dispute occurs, most people are prepared to complain and
> many are prepared to go so far as to take advice, but on the whole, for
> a great variety of understandable reasons, they show little interest in
> using any of the forms of civil justice.
>   I believe that this is not to be regarded as necessarily a bad thing,
> there is probably very little that can be done to change the situation."
> (2000, at 38).

1. The Reformed System of Civil Procedure

9-003   "There was a time when there was a premium on ambush and taking
your opponent by surprise: litigation was a sport and the outcome
turned very much on who you could afford to instruct as your advocate
and champion." (Mr Justice Lightman, 1999).

Thankfully, after centuries of complaint that English civil litigation was
an embarrassment, conducted as a lawyers' Dickensian game and was
slow, expensive and complex, the Civil Procedure Rules 1998 were
passed, in the hope that one simplified set of rules for the High Court and
county courts, drafted in plain English and introducing judicial case management, would rid us of some of these problems. The Rules were drafted
according to the recommendations of Lord Woolf, in his famous 1996
report, *Access to Justice*. The Civil Procedure Rules 1998 and over 50 practice directions replaced two separate sets of rules for the High Court and
county court, in April 1999. They embodied a radically different
approach to civil procedure from what had gone before. The background
to this "new scenario" is explained below, after the description of the new
procedure. One of the major problems with the old system is that an
adversarial system, where the parties are left to battle it out, uncontrolled
by the court, is inherently unfair, where the parties are not equally
matched in terms of resources, information or wealth, such as where a
patient who suffered negligent surgery sues a health authority or a consumer sues a large company.

2. Civil Procedure Act 1997

9-004   Section 1 provided for one set of practice rules for the Court of Appeal,
High Court and county courts, "with a view to securing that the civil
justice system is accessible, fair and efficient".

Section 2 provided a Civil Court Rule Committee to include people "with experience in and knowledge of" consumer affairs and lay advice.

Section 6 established a Civil Justice Council comprising the Master of the Rolls (which, in 1999, was Lord Woolf), judges, lawyers, consumer/lay advice and litigant representatives, to keep the civil justice system under review (including alternative dispute resolution (ADR) and tribunals), advise the Lord Chancellor and suggest research.

3. The 1998 Rules and the New Regime

The overriding objective is set out in Rule 1.1:   **9-005**
The rules enable the court to deal with a case justly—

a.   ensuring the parties are on an equal footing
b.   saving expense
c.   dealing with the case in a way which is proportionate

- to the amount of money involved
- to the importance of the case
- to the complexity of the issues
- to the financial position of parties

d.   ensuring that it is dealt with expeditiously and fairly and
e.   allotting to it an appropriate share of the court's resources.

The court must apply the objective in

- interpreting the rules
- exercising their powers.

(The overriding objective is not waffly sentiment. It has repeatedly been applied by the Court of Appeal. The CA has held that there is no need to refer to Article 6 of the European Convention on Human Rights because of the court's obligation in the Rules to deal with cases justly: (*Daniels v. Walker*, 2000).)

Pre-action protocols have been issued for personal injury litigation and clinical disputes, construction and engineering, professional negligence and defamation. These are statements of best practice in negotiation, encouraging exchange of information and putting the parties into a position to settle fairly. A new draft protocol on judicial review cases has just been published (2001) and many more are being drafted. To see that negotiations are conducted fairly at this stage is very important because only a small fraction (under 20 per cent) of civil disputes are ever brought to court (see Genn, 1999, Zander, 1999 and 2000).

Starting proceedings The claimant (formerly plaintiff) or court issues and serves the claim on the defendant. This must include particulars of the claim (statement of case) or they must be served within four months. They may include points of law, witness lists and documents and must include statements of truth and value and specify the remedy sought. The 2001 Court Service consultation paper *Modernising the Civil Courts*, proposes that people should soon be able to issue a claim online, by telephone or digital TV. More of this below. Have a look at the forms for yourself on the Court Service website. The claimant then has four months to serve the claim form on the defendant.

9-006   The defendant must, within 14 days:

- admit the claim or
- file a defence (statement of case) or
- acknowledge.

If he files a defence, the case is automatically transferred to his home court. If not, the claimant may request a *default judgment* (Part 12). This means asking the court to grant his claim as the defendant has not entered a defence. Most cases end at this point. Over three quarters of county court claims are "default actions" where the claimant, usually a company is collecting a debt from a customer and, in the absence of a defence, judgment is automatically issued, without the involvement of a judge. Most are bulk claims issued at the centralised Claims Production Centre, in Northampton, by claimants such as banks, credit/storecard issuers mail order catalogues and utilities. Most are then enforced by warrants issued at the County Court Bulk Centre.

The defendant may issue a claim against a co-defendant or third party or make a counterclaim (Part 20). The claimant may reply and defend. The parties may write direct to others requesting further information (formerly known as "further and better particulars", now Part 18).

Interim orders
The parties may apply for the interim orders listed below. This should be less necessary than before 1999, because of case management—the court may now act on its own initiative. There is an obligation to apply early. Hearings may be by telephone and since February 2001, applications may be made online at Preston County Court, experimentally. Parties may file court documents by fax.

- pre-action remedies if urgent
- applications without notice (formerly called *ex parte*)
- extensions or shortening of time
- requiring attendance
- separating or consolidating issues or excluding issues
- deciding the order of issues
- staying (pausing) all or part of the case, hoping for settlement
- interim injunctions/declarations
- freezing injunctions (formerly called *Mareva* injunctions), which can also be made against a third party and search orders (formerly *Anton Piller* orders) may only be ordered by a HC judge or authorised judge
- pre-action disclosure (formerly discovery) or inspection, including against non-parties
- interim payments and payments into court
- a summary assessment of costs

Summary judgment may be initiated by the claimant, defendant or court, where the claim or defence "has no real prospect of success". The court may enter judgment, dismiss the case, strike out a claim, or make a conditional order. **9-007**

The court's duty to manage cases had already been introduced from 1994 in practice directions, including timetabling, the requirement for skeleton arguments and limitation of oral argument. The duty now includes:

- encouraging parties to co-operate
- identifying issues at an early stage
- deciding promptly which issues can be disposed of summarily
- deciding the order of issues
- encouraging ADR
- helping parties settle
- fixing timetables
- considering cost benefit
- grouping issues
- dealing with a case in the absence of one or more parties
- making use of IT
- directing the trial process quickly and efficiently.

Sanctions for failure to comply with case management include striking out, costs and debarring part of a case or evidence. Trials will only be postponed as a last resort. Sanctions should be designed to prevent rather than punish non-compliance with rules and timetables. The Court of Appeal suggested there are more flexible ways of controlling claimants' default and delay rather than a draconian strike-out: *Biguzzi* (1999).

Procedural judges manage cases. This means masters in the Royal Courts of Justice and district judges in the county court and High Court district registries.

Allocation: defended claims are allocated to one of three tracks, once the defendant has completed the allocation questionnaire. The judge may transfer a case to another court.

Small claims: for most actions under £5,000, except:

- personal injuries over £1,000
- disrepair over £1,000
- landlord harassment or unlawful eviction
- allegations of dishonesty

Claims over £5,000 may be allocated to the small claims procedure, by consent.

Fast track: for most cases £5–15,000, which can be tried in a day. Oral expert evidence is limited to two fields and one expert per field.

Multi-track: claims over £15,000 or over one day's trial. The High Court can only hear claims exceeding £15,000 or, in personal injury claims, over £50,000.

9-008 *Claims with no monetary value*, such as applications for injunctions, are allocated where the judge considers they will be dealt with most justly.

Discretionary factors: the procedural judge must have regard to:

- the nature of the remedy sought
- the complexity of facts, law and evidence
- the number of parties
- the value of the counterclaim
- oral evidence
- the importance of the claim to non-parties
- the parties' views
- the circumstances of the parties.

The Woolf Report suggested the following cases for the multi-track:

- those of public importance (an example of such a case was that of a dyslexic suing her local education authority for failure to diagnose her condition: *Phelps v. Hillingdon L.B.C.* (1998, CA));

- test cases: an example was successful negligence litigation by ex-miners, suffering from respiratory diseases against British coal, which encouraged many others to claim compensation, in 1998;
- clinical disputes (formerly medical negligence);
- cases with the right to jury trial.

Multi-track cases will normally be transferred out to trial centres but some must stay in the Royal Courts of Justice, *e.g.*:

- specialist cases
- defamation
- fraud
- contentious probate
- claims against the police (remember that many of these are jury trials).

District judges have unlimited jurisdiction to assess damages, unless otherwise directed. They should not deal with complex cases: *Sandry v. Jones* (2000, CA)

Small claims procedure: hearings are meant to be in public (European Convention on Human Rights, Article 6, fair trial) but will normally be held in the district judges' chambers. Costs are low and fixed so, however much the litigant spends on her side of the case, she cannot expect to recoup extravagant expenses. The district judge may adopt any procedure she considers fair, including hearing lay representatives. Baldwin's research indicated differences in procedure from one judge to another. See his various publications on this subject, such as *Small Claims in the County Court in England and Wales: The Bargain Basement of Civil Justice*, 1997 and *"Small Claims Hearings: The "Interventionist" Role Played by District judges"* (1998). Immediately after Baldwin's research, I shadowed a number of district judges. I too found that they all had idiosyncratic ways of conducting small claims. They were all aware of Baldwin's research and sensitive about whether their way of doing things was the "correct" one. Baldwin is continuing to research the effects of increasing the small claims limit to £5,000 and litigants' levels of satisfaction with small claims. Prior to the reforms, he found that at least three quarters of small claims litigants were contented with the way their cases had been handled in court, whereas, of those involved in county court open court trials, 40 per cent considered them inappropriate and disproportionately expensive. Baldwin found small claims tended to be used by professional people or businesses and had not provided the poor with an avenue for redress (summaries: LCD website/research and *Legal Action*, February 1998 and see discussion in Zander, 2000).

9-009   Incidentally, the first small claims courts were developed outside the court system, in London and Manchester, in 1971, primarily to deal with small consumer complaints, for which county court procedure was too elaborate and expensive. Although they were thus a type of privately accessible ADR (alternative dispute resolution), they proved so popular they were absorbed into the county court system, which developed the small claims procedure. It has remained important for costs to be low and fixed so litigants will know in advance the cost of bringing an action. Procedure has always been kept simple, with district judges permitted great leeway to assist the parties so that people can represent themselves. The vast majority of litigants are unrepresented and so what was meant to provide cheap DIY justice seems to have succeeded.

Fast track procedure: the intention is for the court to maintain "proportionality", which means limiting the costs recoverable from the unsuccessful party. For instance, where counsel is briefed, the court cannot normally order costs for a solicitor to accompany her. The aim is to increase access to justice by removing uncertainty. The fast track aims to help the parties to obtain justice speedily. The court directs the timetable and fixes the trial date no more than 30 weeks ahead. The intention is to provide little scope for either party to create extra work to gain a tactical advantage. Lord Woolf said it was important for the court to protect the weaker party against oppressive or unreasonable behaviour by a powerful party. Standard directions now include disclosure, the exchange of witness statements, expert evidence, and fixing the trial date. Parties are encouraged to use a single expert, or a court-appointed expert. The standard timetable is nine months from the issue of proceedings to trial. An indexed, paginated bundle must be produced to the court three to seven days pre-trial and may include an agreed case summary. The judge pre-reads the bundle. Judges may have Fridays off for pre-reading. Trial costs are fixed according to the amount recovered. Other costs are assessed summarily by the judge after the trial. See below.

9-010   *Multi-track procedure* varies. Simple cases are treated like fast track ones. Complex ones may have several directions hearings:

- a case management conference attended by lawyers familiar with the case, which may require a 500-word case summary
- a pre-trial review of the statement of issues
- other directions hearings.

Disclosure (formerly known as discovery). Lord Woolf thought one of two major generators of unnecessary cost was uncontrolled discovery so the automatic obligation to disclose documents is replaced by standard disclosure which requires only documents on which a party relies and documents which:

- adversely affect his case
- adversely affect another party's case
- support another party's case
- are required by a practice direction.

The court's power to control evidence (Rule 32): the court has power to control the issues, the nature of the evidence and its delivery: whether it is prepared to hear oral, hearsay, or written evidence, *etc.* The court has a great deal of control over what evidence it is prepared to hear and the format in which it is prepared to hear witnesses. Lord Woolf was of the strong opinion that over use of *expert witnesses* by both sides had made litigation costly and unduly adversarial. He denounced the development of the "large litigation support industry. . . . This goes against all principles of proportionality and access to justice." (Final Report). The assumption is now that one witness will do or, if more than one is permitted, that they will agree a statement pre-trial. Under Part 35, the expert's duty is to help the court and no party may call an expert or use a report without the court's permission.

Offers to settle (Part 36): this procedure encourages the parties to settle by financial incentive. It replaces pre-1999 payments into court and *Calderbank* letters. Under the old rules, the defendant could make a payment into court and force the plaintiff to take a gamble: take the money or proceed to trial and risk paying both sides' costs since the time of the payment in, which could be a Pyrrhic victory for a winning plaintiff. This happened to Albert Reynolds, former Irish Prime Minister, in 1996, when he won a libel action against the *Sunday Times* but had to pay over £1 million in costs. The intention of the new rules is that allowing the claimant to make an offer to settle alters the balance of power. It includes pre-action formal offers, the claimant's or defendant's offer to settle and the defendant's Part 36 payments into court. Incidentally, the trial judge knows nothing of the payment in, otherwise the gamble would not work. The money is looked after the Public Guardianship Office (formerly Public Trust Office). For commentary on the case law arising out of Part 36, see Hughes. He draws attention to a surprising interpretation of the rule in *Petrograde Inc. v. Texaco Ltd* (2000, CA), where the Court held that the Part 36 offers do not apply to summary judgment, only to judgments made "at trial".

9-011

Costs: under the old regime, in most cases costs would "follow" the event so the outcome would amount to "winner takes all". Under the new rules, the judge must assess costs in accordance with which party won different issues and the judge's view as to how reasonably the parties behaved. The court may make a wasted costs order against a representative if she has acted improperly, unreasonably or negligently and her conduct has caused unnecessary costs to the other party. Throughout the proceedings, costs must be kept down to a proportionate level. A 2000 appeal held that the emphasis was now on proportionality. Here the claimant was awarded £4,300 in damages plus interest but asked for £4,700 in costs. The district judge dismissed the claim and was upheld by a circuit judge. He reasoned that it was necessary for the parties to make an assessment at the outset of the likely value of the claim, or its importance and complexity and then plan in advance the necessary work, the appropriate level of person to carry it out, the overall necessary and appropriate time and the likely overall costs: *Steven v. Watts* (2000, Birm. County Court, unreported, cited by Gold). The essence of a summary assessment of costs is that the court should focus on the detailed breakdown of costs actually incurred by the party in question. If the judge considered the total unreasonable, he should examine the detail again, not substitute his own tariff: *1–800 Flowers v. Phonenames Ltd.* (2001, CA). In *Griffiths v. Solutia U.K. Ltd* (2001, CA), a group action, the claimant's costs were £210,000, as against £90,000. The Court of Appeal suggested that Civil Procedure Rules (CPR) management powers enable a court to impose a limitation on costs.

9-012 *A group litigation order* may be made (Civil Procedure Amendment Rule 19) to allow for case management in multi-party actions.

General points The reforms are intended to cut the length of trial but may increase the number of trials, as going to trial should become simpler and less expensive. Suitable cases may be disposed without a hearing (Rule 1.4 (2)). The statutory right to jury trial is unaffected in deceit, libel, slander, malicious prosecution and false imprisonment cases. Generally, hearings must be in open court. Practice Direction 39 refers to the European Convention on Human Rights. There are exceptions where hearings may be in private (formerly known as *in camera*, in chambers), *e.g.*:

- if the hearing involves a child
- mortgage possession cases.

Witness statements count as evidence-in-chief in the trial. Supplementary questions may be asked only for "good reason". Money judgments must be complied with within 14 days.

Family procedure is the subject of a special set of rules, not covered by this book. The CPR do not apply to most family proceedings but there are certain exceptions. For instance, the cost rules do apply. It is sometimes said that elements of the CPR were copied from existing family procedure. Family judges were well aware already of the need to keep costs and delay down and experts were only used with the court's permission.

The Woolf Reforms and ADR: encouraging and facilitating ADR (see Chapter on alternatives to the civil courts) forms part of case management.

Enforcement of civil court orders: a review commenced in 2000 to look at how   **9-013** enforcement can be made more effective. The Government plans to publish a white paper on enforcement in both civil and criminal proceedings: press notice 282/00, July 2000.

Other Points

- The overriding objective means that technical errors should   **9-014** not be regarded as incurable: *Law v. St. Margarets's Insurance* (2001, CA).
- The defendant may submit to the court there is "no case to answer" at the end of the claimant's evidence in the trial, where he considers the claimant's case has no real prospect of success. If the court agrees it will hold up that submission: *Brown v. Bennett* (2000) but the Court of Appeal called for caution in doing this because if the claim was dismissed and an appeal was successful, a retrial could result in more expense: *Boyce v. Wyatt Engineering* (2001, CA).
- The judge has a duty to give reasons, which is a function of due process. Parties should know why they had won or lost; the losing party would know whether there was a ground of appeal; giving reasons concentrates the mind so the decision is more likely to be soundly based on the evidence. *Flannery v. Halifax Estate Agencies Ltd.* (1999, CA).
- A judge can change his mind after giving judgment at any time before the order is drawn up. In *Kirin Amgenv. Transkaryotic Therapies Inc.* (2001), Mr. Justice Neuberger so held, having discovered there was a binding authority he had overlooked.
- The doctrine of *res judicata* imposes the principle that there should be finality in litigation. An adjudication by a court in a case will bar a second claim *Henderson v. Henderson* (1843), unless there is ignorance of the first claim or an agreement between the parties or for various other reasons. The doctrine was considered in *Johnson v. Gore Wood & Co.* (2001, HL). The house held that, although a second claim was normally an abuse of process, to say it was necessarily an abuse was too dogmatic. Lack of funds was relevant as an excuse for not adding a claim to an original action

against the defendant, especially if the lack of funds was caused by the party claimed against. The doctrine was applied by the Court of Appeal in *Lennon v. Birmingham City Council* (2001, CA). An employee brought proceedings against her employer before a tribunal which were dismissed on her withdrawal. She was estopped from bringing the same proceedings in the county court.

- Advocates have a common law duty not to mislead the court: *Vernon v. Bosley* (1997, CA) and a duty to keep up-to-date with recent law reports: *Copeland v. Smith* (2000, CA).

- The common law right of a litigant to be represented by lawyers of her choice survives the rules: *Maltez v. Lewis* (1999, Ch D). Rules permit a lay representative to act at a small claim hearing but such a person (a "Mackenzie friend") may be excluded from a private hearing by the judge (*R. v. Bow County Court, ex parte Pelling* (1999, CA). See also *Izzo v. Ross* (2001).

- A court has both inherent (common law) jurisdiction and power under the Supreme Court Act 1981 to prevent a vexatious litigant from bringing proceedings without leave of the court: *Ebert v. Birch* (1999, CA). On the court's inherent jurisdiction generally, see Dockray. The growth of litigants in person has seen an increase in such people who launch multiple actions against a number of targets and often try suing judges and all their lawyers.

- The 1990s also saw the massive growth in the use of expert witnesses: see (1996) 146 N.L.J. 1730.

- For a ghastly story of a 20-year legal battle, see the story of Patricia Eaton's case: (2001) 151 N.L.J. 429.

- Remember that civil jury trial is available in six torts. See Chapter on the jury. In *Tate v. Safeway* (2000), the CA ruled that the 1998 procedural rules could not be used to deprive a libel defendant of his right to jury trial.

Appeals from the High Court and County Court from 2000

9-015   As with most of its newest reforms of the English legal system, the Government explained the rationale behind its new regime, Part 52 of the CPR 1998, in force in May 2000, in its 1998 white paper, *Modernising Justice*. The resulting procedure is contained in the Access to Justice Act 1999, in the Civil Procedure Rules 1998, the amended Rules of the Supreme Court and in various practice directions. The whole regime is explained by the Court of Appeal (Civil Division) in *Tanfern Ltd. v. Cameron-Macdonald and Another* (2000). The Government explained, in *Modernising Justice*, that they planned to achieve their objectives of proportionality and efficiency (the same as in the rest of civil procedure) by:

- Diverting from the Court of Appeal those cases which, by their nature, do not require the attention of the most senior judges in the country;
- Making various changes to the working methods of the Court, "which will enable it to deploy its resources more efficiently and effectively", to enable the Court to deal with the increased workload which would result from the Human Rights Act 1998 (brought into force in 2000).

Their guiding principles are now:

- Permission to appeal will only be given where the court considers that an appeal would have a real prospect of success.
- In normal circumstances, more than one appeal cannot be justified.
- There should be no automatic right to appeal. Leave (now called permission) is be required in virtually all appeals to the Court of Appeal.

Jurisdiction

The Government, after consultation, decided routes of appeal should be as follows: **9-016**

- In fast track cases heard by a district judge, appeal lies to a circuit judge.
- In fast track cases heard by a circuit judge, appeal lies to a High Court judge.
- In multi-track cases, appeals against *final orders* lie to the Court of Appeal, regardless of the original judge.
- In multi-track cases, appeals against a *procedural decision* of a district judge will be to a circuit judge; decisions by a master or circuit judge lie to a High Court judge and from procedural decisions of a High Court judge lie to the Court of Appeal.
- Exceptional cases involving important points of principle or which affect a number of litigants may go straight to the Court of Appeal.

Composition

Changes to the composition, procedures, working methods and management of the Court of Appeal (Civil Division) are designed to help it **9-017** operate more efficiently. Under the Access to Justice Act 1999, the Court of Appeal can now consist of any number of judges, according to the importance and complexity of the case. If there are two judges and they cannot agree, the case may have to be re-argued before a new court of three or the original two plus a third: *Farley* (2000).

Procedure (Practice Note, CA, 1999)

9-018   Trial judges should routinely ask parties if they want permission to appeal but if in any doubt whether the appeal would have a real prospect of success or involves a general point of principle, should decline permission and let the litigant seek it from the CA. Permission can be granted if, though there is no real prospect of success, there is a public interest issue. On a point of law, permission should not be granted unless the judge thinks there is a real prospect of the CA coming to a different conclusion on a point of law which will materially affect the outcome of the case. A point of law includes an appeal on the ground that there was no evidence to support the finding. On an appeal on a question of fact, the CA will rarely interfere with a decision based on the judge's evaluation of oral evidence but permission is more appropriate where a party challenges the judge's inference from primary facts or where the judge has not benefitted from seeing witnesses. Where there is a lot of evidence, the judge should give reasons for refusing permission. Skeleton arguments should be submitted (1995, PD). There will be more emphasis on case management and a more coherent IT infrastructure.

Approach

9-019   Generally, every appeal is limited to a review of the decision of the lower court, unless Practice Direction provides otherwise or the court considered that in the circumstances of an individual appeal, it would be in the interests of justice to hold a rehearing. (Unfortunately, even experts such as Professor Jolowicz are uncertain what this means: (2001) 20 C.J.Q. 7.)

Grounds: the appeal court will only allow an appeal where the lower court was wrong (in substance) or where it was unjust because of a *serious* procedural or other irregularity. Under the new procedure, the decision of the lower court attracts a much greater significance.

Recording decisions: the new emphasis on the importance of the first instance decision makes it all the more important for decisions to be recorded accurately.

Powers

9-020   The general rule is that an appeal court has all the powers of the lower court. It also has the power to affirm, set aside or vary any order or judgment of the lower court, to refer any claim or issue for determination by the lower court, to order a new trial or hearing and to make a costs order. The CA is very reluctant to overturn a trial judge's findings of fact, because she has seen the witnesses or their statements and they consider her to be in a better position than themselves. They are even more reluctant to overturn a jury's decision. As we can see from the quotation from *R. v. Killkenny*, in the Criminal Division, cited below, this is mainly because judges accord juries a special constitutional position, which they are reluctant to usurp, as a matter of principle. Also, as juries do not give reasons, that makes it all the more difficult to draft an appeal or reconsider their findings of fact. The last word on the conditions in which the CA will overturn a civil jury's decision is in the new leading authority. In *Grobbelaar v. News Group Newspapers* (2001), it overturned an £85,000 damages award to a former Liverpool goalkeeper for a defamation action in which the jury were persuaded that he had been falsely accused of match fixing, despite strong video and audio-taped evidence (repeatedly shown on TV) of his taking bribes and boasting of a previous conspiracy. Simon Brown L.J. warned: "the court must inevitably be reluctant to find a jury's verdict perverse and anxious not to usurp their function" but he had satisfied himself, on the authorities, that the CA had the jurisdiction to entertain an appeal on the ground of perversity, if the verdict, on all the evidence, was not properly and reasonably open to the jury. A lengthy and detailed examination of the facts led the court "inexorably to the view that Mr Grobelaar's story is, quite simply, incredible. All logic, common sense and reason compel one to that conclusion." The verdict was an "affront to justice". The case is well worth reading for its entertainment value and as a study in precedent.

Second Appeals

The Court of Appeal in *Tanfern* said Parliament had made it clear in the Access to Justice Act 1999 that second appeals would now be a rarity. The decision of the first appeal court should be given primacy, unless the Court of Appeal itself considered that the appeal would raise an important point of principle or practice, or that there was some other compelling reason for it to hear a second appeal. Only the CA can grant permission for a second appeal from the county court or High Court: *Clark v. Perks* (2000, CA).

9-021

Appeals from Small Claims Hearings from 2000

An appellant must obtain permission to appeal but grounds are not restricted, as they used to be. Appeal lies to a circuit judge and there is a guarantee of an oral hearing, which is a review, not a rehearing.

9-022

Civil Justice under a Microscope—the Background to the Woolf Reforms

The problems of English civil procedure have been the subject of scrutiny for centuries. Prior to the Civil Justice Review 1988, there had been 63 reports, since 1900. With tedious and frustrating repetition, they

9-023

all identified the same core problems so that the opening words of Chapter two of Lord Woolf's interim report, 1995, gave commentators a frisson of déjà vu: "The process is too expensive, too slow and too complex." His Lordship said these problems militated against the provision of an accessible system of civil courts which is necessary for people to enforce their rights. Indeed, the very title of the Woolf report, *Access to Justice*, seems like an ironic cliché, after years of concern over the lack of it.

The Civil Justice Review was remarkable for the breadth and depth of its scrutiny of the system, its radical approach and its success rate, in that many of its recommendations were soon translated into law, in the Courts and Legal Services Act 1990 and subsequent delegated legislation. It recommended merging the jurisdiction of the county court and High Court and enabling the Lord Chancellor to make rules allowing for flexible distribution of the caseload between them. This was done, as was the shifting down into the county court of most cases, leaving the High Court for procedurally or evidentially complex cases and judicial review. Yet, despite the fact that its reforms were potentially the most radical since the Judicature Acts of 1893–1895, they did not satisfy critics. The two sides of the legal profession swiftly produced a 1993 report (Heilbron-Hodge) on the continuing problems of civil justice and their proposals for dealing with them so the Lord Chancellor commissioned Lord Woolf to carry out yet another scrutiny. In the meantime, the Heads of Division took matters into their own hands by issuing new and fairly radical Practice Directions for the conduct of litigation in the High Court. Listed are some of the recommendations and procedural reforms consequent upon them, which preceeded the Woolf reforms:

The Heilbron-Hodge Report 1993

9-024   The report started with the working premise that:

"It is axiomatic that in any free and democratic society all citizens should be equal before the law. This means that all litigants, rich and poor, however large or however small is the subject matter of their litigation, should have access to a fair and impartial system of disputes resolution."

They complained that:

- "An air of Dickensian antiquity pervades the civil process;"
- "Procedures are unnecessarily technical, inflexible, rule-ridden, formalistic and often incomprehensible to the ordinary litigant for whom they are ultimately designed";
- lawyers and judges were reluctant to change;

- progress of actions lay with the parties and their lawyers rather than the courts; causing avoidable delay;
- fear of costs of litigation deterred people from using the courts;
- most people wanted their dispute resolved rather than their "day in court".

The principles underlying their recommendations were:

- litigation should encourage the early settlement of disputes;
- litigants should have imposed upon them sensible procedural time-frames;
- judges should adopt a more interventionist role to ensure that issues are limited, delays are reduced and court time is not wasted;
- since court time is costly, a balance should be struck between the written and oral word and what can be achieved out of court rather than in court;
- justice should, where possible, be brought to the people;
- a widespread introduction of technology is urgently required;
- facilities for the litigant urgently need improving;
- additional resources must be found to improve the system.

Amongst others, here are some of their main recommendations. Some reforms were effected by the 1994/5 Practice Directions. My comments are bracketed:

1. merger of QBD and Chancery (not accepted);
2. High Court listing should be computerised;
3. common procedural rules for the High Court and county court (repeating the Civil Justice Review);
4. judicial review cases to be heard on circuit and more specialist county court trial centres;
5. revival of an ethos of public service amongst court staff and assistance to litigants;
6. plain English court documents;
7. a more interventionist approach by judges at trial and on appeal;
8. limits on discovery, provision of skeleton arguments and bundles and on appeal;
9. judicial intervention at trial to avoid time wasting;
10. promotion of ADR and training of lawyers therein.

The 1994/1995 Practice Directions

The Heilbron-Hodge Report doubtless prompted these Practice Directions and the establishment of Lord Woolf's scrutiny of civil procedure. Directions were issued for all three High Court divisions. They emphasised the importance of reducing cost and delay and threatened that "failure by practitioners to conduct cases economically will be visited

9-025

by appropriate orders for costs". The court should limit discovery of documents, oral submissions, examination of witnesses, the issues on which it wishes to be addressed and reading aloud from documents and authorities. Witness statements will generally stand as evidence-in-chief and the parties must, pre-trial, limit the issues. Bundled, photocopied documents and skeleton arguments must be lodged in court pre-trial. Opening speeches must be succinct and, where appropriate, lawyers must verify that they have considered the possibility of ADR with their client. These directions had a significant impact on the shape of the civil trial. The parties and the judge read most of the arguments and documentation in advance of trial, thus departing radically from the oral tradition characteristic of the common law, adversarial procedure. The directions also encouraged the judge to control the nature and content of the cases presented to her, again signifying a departure from the traditional judge's role as a non-interfering umpire.

The Interim Woolf Report 1995

9-026   This repeated many of the recommendations of its predecessors, the Civil Justice Review and the Heilbron-Hodge Report. Amongst Lord Woolf's main recommendations were these:

- an effective system of case management by the court, instead of allowing the parties to flout rules and run the cases;
- an expanded small claims jurisdiction of £3,000 (introduced, in 1996, then expanded to £5,000) and a fast track for cases up to £10,000. Judicial, tailored case management for cases over £10,000;
- encouragement of early settlement, assisted by enabling either party to make an offer to settle, replacing the system of payment into court;
- the creation of a new Head of Civil Justice;
- a single set of High Court/county court rules;
- court appointment of single, neutral expert witnesses;
- promotion of the use of IT for case management by judges and use of video and telephone conferencing.

Almost all of this was repeated in the final report, *Access to Justice* in 1996, then translated into the law, in the statute and 1998 Rules and Practice Directions, as set out above. There were minor amendments, as you can see. Safeguards were introduced in certain types of litigation, such as housing cases.

Reactions to Woolf

9-027   Commenting not on Woolf but on the increase in court fees imposed in 1997, Sir Richard Scott V.-C. said the idea the civil courts should be self-financing was "indefensible from a constitutional point of view" (speech quoted widely, *e.g.* in (1997) 147 N.L.J. 750).

Zander said the overwhelming majority of cases settled so did not need management; "we have virtually no information about either delays or costs" and Woolf had not commissioned research on his proposals; they had been trying to reform the system in the U.S. for 20 years without success; English judges had no familiarity with case management; many studies showed pre-trial hearing designed to make trials shorter made them longer and added to cost; U.S. research showed litigants were interested in an unbiased, careful hearing, not informal hearings ((1995) 145 N.L.J. 154). Zander feared increasing judicial discretionary powers of case management would create inconsistent decisions, making the process arbitrary and unpredictable. "My own view is that training can do little to deal with the problem because inconsistency stems from legitimate differences in philosophy as to how a judge should go about the business of judging" ((1996) 146 N.L.J. 1590). He also said lawyers would be unable to stick to time-limits. Case management was a common theme throughout Canada, the U.S. and Australia. A 1997 study of 10,000 U.S. cases by the Rand Corporation found some U.S. judges considered case management an attack on judicial independence and believed it emphasised speed and efficiency at the expense of justice. The study also found case management added to costs because lawyers spent an extra 20 hours responding to court directions, even in cases which would have settled anyway. Costs would become front-loaded ((1997) 147 N.L.J. 353 and 539). Lord Woolf called Zander's criticisms "strident . . . misleading and inaccurate" ((1997) 147 N.L.J. 751). Zander defended himself in a lecture to the Chancery Bar Association ((1997) 147 N.L.J. 768 and *Civil Justice Quarterly*). See responses to Zander and other critics by Greenslade at (1996) 146 N.L.J. 1147. Zander had the last word in 2000 (below).

A Law Society survey of litigation solicitors found only a third considered litigation too adversarial and a third thought case management would improve litigation. 62 per cent thought judges should encourage earlier settlements (*Gazette*, May 21, 1997). **9-028**

Zuckerman (1996) argued that the cause of excessive cost lay not in the complexity of procedure but in the incentives lawyers had to complicate litigation. Much of what he said applied to the old legal aid system, since abolished.

Comments on the Woolf Reforms Since Implementation in 1999

The Civil Justice Council's annual reports have generally concluded that implementation of the reforms has gone well. In their first report, 1999, they were concerned about delay in introducing new IT into the courts. *Modernising the Civil Courts* promises to deal with the latter. **9-029**

Nigel Foster, a law lecturer, gave a condemnatory personal account of his experience bringing a small claim under the new rules ((2000) 150 N.L.J. 318). His claim took nine months, involved four court appearances and at least six judges. Evidence rules were applied inconsistently. The trial judge had neither pre-read the papers nor managed the case. Similarly, Sarah Rowlands tells a hideous tale of the palaver she went through in recovering £260 from a travel agent, in *The Times*, March 17, 1998.

Richard Harrison ((2000) 150 N.L.J. 541) commented that processing cases brusquely, efficiently and driving litigants away from the system did not mean that they were enjoying "access to justice". Increased cost and frustration was caused by the courts' inflexibility in preventing the parties from managing the cases themselves. This would clash with the requirements of the Human Rights Act. Constant amendments to the rules rendered them very complex, the opposite of one of Woolf's major objectives.

9-030   On the other hand, Robert Turner, Senior Master in the High Court, welcomed the new rules ((2000) 150 N.L.J. 49). The pervading adversarial approach had gone and been replaced by a degree of co-operation. Settlements were achieved earlier, procedures were defining the real issues between the parties and solicitors would find the quicker rate of disposal allowed them to do more work. In the short term, however, the new rules had not succeeded in attacking cost, delay and complexity because the new system was costly at the commencement of the action ("front loaded"); the new procedures with pre-action protocols, allocation and listing questionnaires and case management conferences, etc. were more complex and many county courts were struggling with implementation so delays were occurring.

A survey of heads of legal departments of United Kingdom companies by Eversheds, lawyers, found 54 per cent of respondents considered civil litigation improved in 1999–2000. Fifty-two per cent found litigation quicker but only 22 per cent considered it cheaper. Forty-three per cent were settling cases earlier. Clients no longer sought aggressive, uncompromising lawyers. Disputes were handled differently and 41 per cent had used ADR. Only 24 per cent thought litigants were getting better justice. Forty-four per cent said they were not. Nineteen per cent said costs had risen.

A MORI survey of 180 firms after the first year of the reforms, found that 76 per cent said there had been faster settlements and less litigation, although most respondents thought the outcome would have been the same under the old system. The early-settlement offer, bringing heavy penalties to those refusing to settle, had had the biggest impact on litigation, according to two thirds of private practice lawyers. Mediation had significantly increased. (See Chapter on alternatives to the civil courts.)

The Civil Justice Audit, comprised of this and a CEDR survey of 30 civil judges found: 80 per cent of lawyers were satisfied with the CPR; 36 per cent believed litigation had decreased; 47 per cent reported settling cases faster; 60 per cent thought judges should initiate settlement discussion; 58 per cent thought cases should be stayed for mediation and 78 per cent of in-house lawyers thought mediation should be required before a business dispute went to court ((2000) 150 N.L.J. 531).

Another survey by Wragge & Co. of in-house commercial lawyers found 81 per cent of respondents thought courts did not have enough resources. Eighty-nine per cent liked the changes and found litigation quicker, 41 per cent found costs cut and 80 per cent found ADR had proved popular. (Both surveys are summarised in *The Times*, May 2, 2000.)

Richard Burns, barrister and recorder, ((2000) 150 N.L.J. 1829) con-   **9-031**
cludes the reforms have been a relative failure. The pre-action protocols, use of single experts and sensible openness have all encouraged parties to settle out of court but litigation is now much more expensive because of "front loading", as many had predicted. The Rules compel the litigants to spend time and money progressing the case to trial. Paradoxically, this front-end loading of expense may lead to more trials. Since most cases still settle just before trial, all the expense of case summaries, skeleton arguments and preparing bundles is wasted. Case management is excessively bureaucratic and demanding and the courts remain under-resourced in staff, judges and IT. Although cases come for trial more quickly, the overall delay is probably just as bad, as litigants delay issuing proceedings. The notion of a level playing field is a cruel deception because with the abolition of legal aid, the gap between rich and poor litigants is wider than ever. Because judges have been given a wide discretion and they inevitably interpret the rules variously, this produces rough justice. He suggests some reforms.

Master John Leslie commented on "a new spirit of co-operation abroad". He found around 50 per cent of cases stayed for a settlement attempt did settle. He too complained of a lack of IT, though: *Counsel*, 2000.

Zander, in 2000, described the Woolf reforms in a more tempered way than before, praising some elements but he reiterated his criticism of front loading of costs, in the manner of "I told you so" and penalties for non-compliance and the inconsistent approach of judges when given discretion.

LCD Minister David Lock introduced *Emerging Findings: An Early Evaluation of the Civil Justice Reforms* (2001), with a claim that the rules are working well. He claims that all of the Woolf objectives are being broadly realised. There has been a drop in claims. Settlements are being reached earlier, thus avoiding trials. There has been a rise in cases where ADR is used. Case management conferences are successful and proving to be a key factor in making litigation less complex. The time taken from claim to trial has decreased and the number of appeals in the course of proceedings has fallen sharply. The time taken between claim and hearing in small claims has increased but that may be because of the increase in the small claims limit. Baldwin is researching the experiences of litigants and his report is due in late 2001. Pre-action protocols are working well and reducing the number of ill-founded claims. The use of single joint experts has contributed to a less adversarial culture, earlier settlements and may cut costs. The picture on costs is unclear. Statistics are hard to obtain. The views of litigants in person are also hard to obtain.

Developments from 2001

9-032   The LCD commissioned research into the effect of the Civil Procedure Rules by Nottingham Law School, reporting in 2003.

In 1998, the Lord Chancellor admitted that what many critics were saying was true—the courts would not be ready to cope fully with the Woolf reforms of 1999, because they did not have the technology in place ((1998) 148 N.L.J. 1835) but the Court Service published a consultation paper, in January 2001, *Modernising the Civil Courts*. It builds on the reforms already made and expands on plans announced in *Modernising Justice*, the 1998 white paper. Much of it is about IT: the "virtual court", issue of claims and enforcement procedures online or from a digital TV; "Court on Call", enabling court processes to be dealt with over the telephone; "gateway partnerships" between advice agencies and court staff, enabling the client to access the court and advice at the same time. Once this is done and they centralise information and advice via the internet, call centres and advice kiosks, the Court Service will cut the county courts down to a network of hearing centres. They plan to rationalise their estate (buildings) and share more courts with magistrates. In July 2000, the programme of reform started, with video conferencing from Cardiff, Leeds or a private VC suite, to the CA in the Royal Courts of Justice, London, for civil applications for permission to appeal. Further, people involved in any civil case at the pilot courts are able to choose to give evidence or make submissions via video link. The Cardiff and Leeds courts are also testing the use of video conferencing in civil and criminal matters and tribunal cases.

In December 2000, another phase started, with interim applications in civil (including family) cases being made by solicitors by email and the district judge considering them on screen. See also, "*Civil Justice 2000: A vision of the Civil Justice System in the Information Age*" (LCD website).

9-033   The Bar's response (2001) was to point out that the £43 million cost of all this might not enhance justice. IT is only a tool. It cannot furnish wisdom or sound judgment. Customer care is currently neglected when all cases are listed for 10.30 a.m., leaving people to hang around all day.

Worse, the plan to close most county courts (55 closed since 1994), leaving, say 50 trial centres, would deny public access to justice. District judges, now expected to deal with almost all cases up to £50,000 are also overburdened with "boxwork" in actively managing cases. In the meantime, recorders are inappropriately used.

The Legal Action Group (LAG) said extensive computerisation would disadvantage socially excluded court users, such as the elderly, people whose first language is not English and people without computers.

The first national consumer satisfaction survey of court users, in 2001, found 79 per cent were satisfied with the overall level of service. Eighty-six per cent were happy with the counter service, leaflets and forms and telephone responses.

Since the Woolf reforms were introduced, civil claims have plummeted in the High Court by 85 per cent and in the county courts by 17 per cent. QBD claims have dropped from 18,000 in June 1998 to a record low of 2,000 in November 2000.

Judicial Review

Historically, a person aggrieved with an error of law or the procedure **9-034** of an inferior court could petition the monarch to refer the proceedings for examination in the High Court. The High Court now exercises this residuary monarchical prerogative, in judicial review proceedings. The procedure is available in civil and criminal cases. Procedure is determined by CPR Part 54 and a new Practice Direction, both of which came into force in October 2000. The claim is made in the newly formed Administrative Court, in the QBD, or the new Administrative Court for Wales, at Cardiff. Judicial Review cases, since 2000, have titles like this: *R. on the application of Darbyshire v. Secretary of State for Education*. The question of permission is normally considered without a hearing. At the substantive hearing, the judge examines the legality and procedural correctness of the decision of the lower court or tribunal and whether the body has acted within its powers or *ultra vires*. The court may impose a quashing order on a defective decision (formerly *certiorari*), or make a mandatory order that a public body carry out its duty (formerly *mandamus*) or declare the law or order an injunction, preventing an illegality. This must be distinguished from an appeal on the merits. The judge has no concern with the merits of the case or with substituting a new finding of fact. Since the 1960s and especially since the procedure was made easier in 1981, there has been a massive growth in judicial review cases and most of them have been challenges to the legality of public bodies' decisions, mostly local or central government. Challenges have been made to a broad list of such decisions: planning, hospital closure, policing tactics, benefits which apply differently to men and women, decisions relating to the National Lottery and so on. It was thought that this court would be very busy with challenges under the Human Rights Act 1998. In *Kingsley v. U.K.* (2001, ECHR), the Court made a determination which may have a significant impact on the nature of judicial review proceedings. They held that if the process was restricted to examining the quality of the decision-making process rather than the merits of the decision, then an applicant alleging bias had not received a fair trial under Article 6(1) of the Convention.

FURTHER READING ON CIVIL PROCEDURE

9-035   H. Genn, *Paths to Justice*, 1999.

Mr Justice Lightman, "The case for judicial intervention" (1999) 149 N.L.J. 1819 (an excellent brief account of how massively different civil litigation used to be).

Summary of Lord Woolf's final report *Access to Justice*, 1996, in the Law Society's *Gazette* August 2, 1996.

Civil Procedure Act 1997, Current Law Statutes.

Civil Procedure Rules, LCD website www.lcd.gov.uk.

Civil Justice Council: www.open.gov.uk/civjustice.

Court service: www.courtservice.gov.uk.

District Judge Stephen Gold's witty column, "Civil Way" in *The New Law Journal*, is by far the best and funniest way of keeping up to date. Many of the case summaries cited above are derived from his work. The N.L.J. contained a very useful series in 1999, "Woolf Watch", giving detailed but clear explanations of elements of the rules.

Civil Justice Quarterly for updates, commentary, research and academic analysis.

A. Hughes, "Settlement Offers under the Civil Procedure Rules" (2001) 151 N.L.J. 962. (Procedure explained at (1999) 149 N.L.J. 194.)

J. Baldwin, "Small Claims Hearings: The 'Interventionist' Role Played by District Judges" (1998) 17 C.J.Q. 20.

J. Baldwin, "Increasing the Small Claims Limit" (1998) 148 N.L.J. 274.

I. Grainger & M. Fealy with M. Spencer, *The Civil Procedure Rules in Action*, Cavendish and *Introduction to the New Civil Procedure Rules*, Cavendish.

M.S. Dockray, "The Inherent Jurisdiction to Regulate Civil Proceedings" (1997) 113 L.Q.R. 120.

G. Applebey, "The Growth of Litigants in Person in English Criminal Proceedings" (1997) 16 C.J.Q. 127.

M. Rea, "England is a Model of Reform", *The Times*, November 19, 1996 (comparison with France).

CEDR Civil Justice Audit, 2000: www.cedr.co.uk.

LCD, *Emerging Findings; An Early Evaluation of the Civil Justice Reforms*, 2001, LCD website, www.lcd.gov.uk.

M. Zander, "The Woolf Report: Forwards or Backwards for the New Lord Chancellor?" (1997) C.J.Q. 208.

M. Zander, various N.L.J. articles, as listed in the text and (1998) 61
    M.L.R. 382
M. Zander, *The State of Justice* (2000), Chapter 2.
M. Zander, *Cases and Materials on the English Legal System* (8th ed., 1999).
A.A.S. Zuckerman and R. Cranston (eds), *Reform of Civil Procedure—
    Essays on Access to Justice* (1995). Review article by Zander at (1995) 145
    N.L.J. 1866 and (1996) n146 N.L.J. 29.
"The Court of Appeal (Civil Division) Proposals for Change to
    Constitution and Jurisdiction", L.C.D. consultation paper, 1998 and
    "Proposal to Extend the Requirement for Leave to Appeal to the Court
    of Appeal (Civil Division)", 1998.

10. Criminal Procedure

Criminal procedure seems to be constantly under review and each Home **10-001**
Secretary cannot resist making a list of statutory alterations *every* year. The
result is a complex mish-mash of statutes amended by sets of other statutes
which is a nightmare to apply for judges, magistrates' clerks and practising
lawyers. Spencer has called for a unified Code of Criminal Procedure.
Recently, procedure has been scrutinised by the Royal Commission on
Criminal Procedure 1981, which resulted in the Police and Criminal
Evidence Act 1984, then the Royal Commission on Criminal Justice 1993,
which resulted in the Criminal Justice and Public Order Act 1994, the
Criminal Appeal Act 1995 and the Criminal Procedure and Investigations
Act 1996 and the Narey Report 1997 (*Review of Delay in the Criminal Justice
System*), which resulted in the Crime and Disorder Act 1998. On top of this,
there have been a long list of white papers, especially on young offenders
and the New Labour set of white papers and consultation papers since 1997
resulted in a wholly new youth justice scheme, set up by the 1998 Act. In
2000, the Human Rights Act 1998 came into effect and has had and will in
future have a profound impact on criminal procedure, especially through
Articles 5 and 6, as described below. In 2000, Lord Justice Auld was asked
to conduct the Criminal Courts Review, to effect a similar scrutiny of the
criminal courts and procedure as effected by Lord Woolf on the civil courts
(above). He reported in October 2001 so readers should look out for this,
on the Review website, and for any consequent changes in the law.

1. European Convention on Human Rights, Articles 5 and 6

The Human Rights Act 1998 brought Convention rights into English **10-002**
law in 2000. The fundamental rights contained in Articles 5 and 6 have

become the yardstick against which all statute and case law on English criminal procedure must now be measured. The text of the Convention Articles is appended to the Human Rights Act 1998 and the Government's Human Rights Unit website is worth visiting for links and up to date information on changes in the law and new cases. The text of Article 6 is as follows.

Right to a Fair Trial

10-003
1. In the determination of his civil rights and obligations and of any criminal charge against him, everyone is entitled to a fair and public hearing within a reasonable time by an independent and impartial tribunal established by law. Judgment shall be pronounced publicly but the press and public may be excluded from all or part of the trial in the interests of morals, public order or national security in a democratic society, where the interests of juveniles or the private life of the parties so require, or to the extent strictly necessary in the opinion of the court in special circumstances where publicity would prejudice the interests of justice.

2. Everyone charged with a criminal offence shall be presumed innocent until proved guilty according to the law.

3. Everyone charged with a criminal offence has the following minimum rights:

    (a) to be informed promptly, in a language which he understands and in detail, of the nature and cause of the accusation against him;

    (b) to have adequate time and facilities for the preparation of his defence;

    (c) to defend himself in person or through legal assistance of his own choosing or, if he has not sufficient means to pay for legal assistance, to be given it free if the interests of justice so require;

    (d) to examine or have examined witnesses against him and to obtain the attendance and examination of witnesses on his behalf under the same conditions as witnesses against him;

    (e) to have the free assistance of an interpreter if he cannot understand or speak the language used in court.

10-004   Here is a paraphrase of Article 5. It appears in full, with the other Convention rights, appended as a Schedule to the Human Rights Act 1998.

Right to Liberty and Security

1. Everyone has the right to liberty and security of person. No one shall be deprived of his liberty save in the following cases and in accordance with a procedure prescribed by law:

- lawful detention after conviction;
- lawful arrest or detention for non-compliance with a court order or to secure fulfilment of a legal obligation;
- lawful arrest or detention, effected to bring someone before a competent legal authority on reasonable suspicion of having committed an offence or when it is reasonably considered necessary to prevent his committing an offence or fleeing after having done so;
- detention of a minor by lawful order for the purpose of educational supervision or lawful detention to bring him before a competent legal authority;
- lawful detention to prevent spread of infectious diseases, of persons of unsound mind, alcoholics or drug addicts or vagrants;
- lawful arrest or detention to prevent unauthorised entry into the country, or for extradition or deportation.

2. Everyone who is arrested shall be informed promptly, in a language which he understands, of the reasons for his arrest and of any charge against him.

3. Everyone arrested . . . shall be brought before a judge or other authorised officer to exercise judicial power and shall be entitled to trial within a reasonable time or to release pending trial. Release may be conditioned by guarantees to appear for trial.

4. Everyone who is deprived of his liberty by arrest or detention shall be entitled to take proceedings by which the lawfulness of his detention shall be decided speedily by a court and his release ordered if the detention is not lawful.

5. Everyone who has been the victim of arrest or detention in contravention of the provisions of this Article shall have an enforceable right to compensation.

In the text below, I examine how these two articles have already been used in interpreting the main elements of English criminal procedure. I come back to the Convention right at the end of the section to add other examples.

2. *The Prosecutors*

The Attorney General is a Government minister in charge of the prosecution process in England and Wales. He is appointed by the Prime Minister and so may change when the Government changes. His department is called the Law Officers' Department. His deputy is the Solicitor General. The Attorney is in overall charge of the prosecution process and

10-005

answerable to Parliament for decisions to prosecute or not to prosecute. He is in charge of the specialist Serious Fraud Office and the Crown Prosecution Service (CPS), which is headed by the Director of Public Prosecutions (DPP), not a political appointment. This is a national prosecution service, created by the Prosecution of Offences Act 1985 and it now undertakes most prosecutions. Many others are initiated by those government departments (central or local) and government agencies with statutory powers of prosecution. For instance, if you are caught poaching in a river, you may be prosecuted by the National Rivers Authority. Private citizens retain their right to prosecute, unlike in Scotland. The most serious offences, such as those under the Official Secrets Act, may only be undertaken by the Attorney General but it is rare for him to appear in court. He is normally represented by counsel.

The Law Commission recommended in a 1997 consultation paper that many of the "vast number" of offences where consent to prosecution is required of the Attorney or DPP are anomalous and the need for consent should be radically curtailed. See now *Consents to Prosecution*, LC 255.

The Decision to Prosecute

10-006 There is no obligation on a Crown Prosecutor to prosecute all offences. For instance, most young offenders (10–17) are cautioned for the offences they admit to. Once the police pass the file to the CPS, they apply the *Code for Crown Prosecutors 2000*, which requires a two-stage test. The prosecutor must first decide on the sufficiency of the evidence to provide a realistic prospect of conviction and then, only if that test is satisfied, ask whether it is in the public interest to go ahead with the prosecution. The Code is obtainable free from the CPS and changes made in this latest version are explained in the article by the DPP, David Calvert-Smith. A decision not to prosecute is judicially reviewable. See discussion by Burton and see especially, *R. v. DPP, ex parte Kebilene and Others* (1999, HL). The House confirmed that, "absent mala fides or an exceptional circumstance, the decision of the Director (to consent to a prosecution) is not amenable to judicial review", *per* Lord Steyn. A decision to prosecute can be challenged before the trial judge as an abuse of process, or form a ground of appeal, he said. The European Court of Human Rights has held, in a group of cases heard against the United Kingdom in May 2001: *Jordan, McKerr, Kelly and Shanaghan* that in certain exceptional instances, where parties might reasonably expect a prosecution, that the DPP must give reasons for not prosecuting. See discussion by Ferguson at (2001) 151 N.L.J. 808.

Victims can ask for judicial review of a decision to discontinue a prosecution *R. (on the application of Joseph) v. DPP* (2001) but the courts are loath to interfere. The DPP is not obliged to consult the victim but there have been repeated complaints by victims that they are not kept informed. The Government has promised in its 2001 white paper *Criminal Justice —*

The Way Ahead that by 2005 a victim will be able to track the progress of their case online.

The Crown Prosecution Service

Ever since the CPS was created, in 1985, there have been allegations that it is underfunded and that Crown Prosecutors are consequently over-worked and too many cases are dropped or lost through lack of preparation. A 2000 survey of the CPS exposed their lack of morale yet again and the issue was discussed in Parliament in December 2000. A statutory CPS inspectorate was created in 2000 and the Government announced new funding. The CPS was restructured into 42 areas by the Access to Justice Act 1999 and is in the process of developing criminal justice units and trial units, following the recommendations of the Glidewell report on the CPS, to work closely with the police in preparing cases for the magistrates' court. The DPP has announced, in 2001, that he supports the decriminalisation of a number of summary offences, such as road traffic offences. Like American "violations", they would be subject to fixed penalties. A 2001 report by Denman found extensive racism within the CPS and the DPP acknowledged the service was "institutionally racist" and announced a review of CPS case decisions for racism and sexism.

10-007

3. Bail

Most offenders who are arrested by the police are bailed by them for a court appearance at the next available court sitting of the magistrates' court. Bail may include conditions, such as a curfew, or specified residence, or exclusion from the environs of the victim's home, or surrendering of a passport and a surety may be required. Bail may be renewed by the clerk or magistrates, if the defendant is not dealt with at the first court appearance (see below). The offender has a right to bail under the Bail Act 1976, which reversed the common law presumption against bail so, if the police oppose bail and the offender contests this, a contested bail hearing will take place at the magistrates' court. Indeed, the court (magistrates' or Crown Court) must consider whether bail should be granted at each appearance. Where a court or constable grants or refuses bail or imposes conditions, they must give written reasons to the defendant (s.5). The defendant accused or convicted of an imprisonable offence need not be granted bail if the court is satisfied that there are substantial grounds for believing that the defendant, if released on bail, would

10-008

- fail to surrender to custody, or
- commit an offence, or
- interfere with witnesses.

The defendant need not be granted bail if the offence is indictable or triable either way and he was already on bail for another offence, or if the court is satisfied he should be kept in custody for his own protection or (child) welfare, or he is serving a custodial sentence or if there has not been time to obtain sufficient information to decided on bail, or if he has been arrested whilst on bail, or he is being remanded for a report and it would be impractical to make inquiries without keeping him in custody. Where the defendant is accused of a non-imprisonable offence, acceptable reasons for refusing bail are more limited. For instance, the accused need not be granted bail if he has previously failed to surrender to custody and the court believes he would "jump bail" again (Sched. 1).

10-009   Those convicted of or charged with manslaughter, murder, attempted murder, rape or attempted rape lost their right to bail under the Criminal Justice and Public Order Act 1994 but since the Crime and Disorder Act 1998, they may be granted bail in exceptional circumstances. This exception was added by the 1998 Act, in order to satisfy the requirements of Article 5 of the European Convention on Human Rights (liberty and security of the person). The Article provides that no one shall be deprived of his liberty save in specified cases, in accordance with a procedure prescribed by law. Article 5(3) limits pre-trial detention because a person shall be released pending trial unless the State can show "relevant and sufficient" reasons to justify continued detention, which requires the exercise of judicial discretion. This is why the 1994 Act, abolishing bail for certain offenders, was in breach of the Convention, which the United Kingdom Government accepted in *Caballero v. U.K.* (2000, ECHR). The impact of Article 5 on bail has already been the subject of a number of ECHR and domestic cases which there is not time to review here but see Burrow and also Archbold. In *R.v. Havering Magistrates' Court, ex parte DPP* (2000, QBD), the applicant argued that Article 5 had been breached at his hearing for breach of bail conditions, when the magistrates heard hearsay evidence. The Court held:

- If the process conformed with Article 5, it did not have to conform to Article 6 as well.
- The ECHR case law simply underlined that the defendant could not be deprived of his liberty without a fair opportunity to answer the basis on which the order was sought.
- In doing so it was essential to bear in mind the nature and purpose of the proceedings.
- A magistrate was required to come to a fair and rational opinion based on the material put before him.
- In doing so he must bear in mind the consequences to the defendant—loss of liberty (in the context of presumption of innocence).

- Article 5 did not require facts to be proven to the criminal standard of proof.
- The magistrate was not restricted to legally admissible evidence —it could be hearsay—so long as he took account of the quality of the evidence.
- The defendant had to be given a full and fair opportunity to comment on that material and to give oral evidence.

The defendant may renew his application for bail, if the magistrates refuse it, or appeal to a judge in chambers. Under the Bail Amendment Act 1993, the prosecution may appeal against a grant of bail by magistrates, to a judge in the Crown Court.

The Law Commission fears that three aspects of the law on bail may still require amendment or appeal, in the light of Art. 5, *e.g.*, English law's removal of the right to bail where the defendant has allegedly committed an offence while on bail. See further Law Commission Report LC269 (website). The 2001 white paper, *Criminal Justice—The Way Ahead*, promises new laws to tackle offending on bail and better information for courts. **10-010**

4. Summary Offences

The Criminal Law Act 1977 divided offences into three categories. First, offences triable only on indictment in the Crown Court. Secondly, offences triable only summarily in the magistrates' court. Thirdly, offences triable either way. The Criminal Justice Act 1988 added a fourth category, summary offences triable on indictment. **10-011**

As I pointed out in 1997, in *"An Essay on the Importance and Neglect of the Magistracy"*, in the twentieth century, Parliament repeatedly downgraded indictable offences to triable either way and triable either way offences to summary offences, thus shifting criminal business down onto the shoulders of the magistrates. Also, when new offences are created they tend to be summary or triable either way, thus guaranteeing that all of the first category and most of the second will be heard by magistrates. They now deal with about 97 per cent of criminal business from start to finish. It should be obvious from that statistic that magistrates' work is not all trivial, although many people imagine this to be the case, including, unfortunately, many judges and lawyers.

The most obvious summary offences are almost all Road Traffic Act offences; drunk and disorderly behaviour; assaults such as common assault; minor criminal damage cases and cases prosecuted by government departments or agencies. A summary case is usually begun by an information being laid before a Justice of the Peace requesting that they issue a summons to the person accused. The summons will require that **10-012** person to appear at a named magistrates' court, at a time stipulated, so that the case against him may be heard. The Road Traffic Act allows defendants to motoring offences to plead "guilty" by post, avoiding a court appearance.

Duty solicitors, private practitioners now funded by the Criminal Defence Service, are meant to be available, at each magistrates' court.

Speeding Cases Through the Court

10-013   The Home Office *Review of Delay in the Criminal Justice System*, 1997, "the Narey report" recommended various measures to speed criminal cases through the courts, responding to a concern that an "adjournment culture" pervaded most magistrates' courts, where magistrates would readily accede to all requests to adjourn the case, thus causing multiple appearances and consequent delay in most cases. Consequent upon the recommendations of its author, Martin Narey, sections of the Crime and Disorder Act 1998 are designed as time-saving measures. Under section 43, time-limits may be set for different types of case. Section 46 provides that where a person is bailed (by the police) to appear before a magistrates' court, the date set for his appearance should be the next available court sitting. This means someone arrested on a Thursday night can now expect to find themselves before the court on Friday morning. If they plead guilty, the expectation behind the Act is that they should normally be sentenced there and then. If they are likely to plead not guilty, their first appearance may take the form of an early administrative hearing, under section 50 of the Act, at which his eligibility for criminal defence may be determined. Such hearings may be conducted by the single justice or a justices' clerk, or a legal adviser (court clerk) acting under powers delegated by the JC. Section 49 lists powers that may be exercised by a single justice or clerk. These include a lot of judicial trial management powers which are likely to be exercised at a later hearing called a pre-trial review. For instance, at a EAH or pre-trial review, a clerk may renew bail on conditions previously imposed. I have expressed concern about giving these new judicial powers to clerks (see Chapter on magistrates).

10-014   A speedy first appearance is also required by Article 5 of the European Convention, discussed above. Article 5(3) says everyone who is arrested or detained shall be brought promptly before a judge and shall be entitled to trial within a reasonable time or to release pending trial.

The Guilty Plea

10-015   When the accused appears before the court, he is asked if he pleads guilty or not guilty. The vast majority of offenders plead guilty (see annual *Criminal Statistics*). If he pleads guilty, he may be convicted and sentenced immediately, unless the magistrates require more information on the defendant, in which case they will adjourn for the preparation of a medical or psychiatric report or a pre-sentence report, prepared by a probation officer or social worker. The Crime and Disorder Act 1998, section 53 provides that a member of the CPS staff who is not a Crown Prosecutor may prosecute guilty pleas in the magistrates' court.

Plea Bargaining

At any time prior to or during a criminal trial, it is common for a defendant to change his plea from "not guilty" to "guilty" to one or more counts. This results in what has become known as a "cracked trial". This wastes court time and public resources and, in relation to trial on indictment, was one of the concerns of the Royal Commission on Criminal Justice. It usually results from plea negotiations between prosecution or defence, which may be initiated by either side, commonly known as "plea bargaining". This means the defendant agrees to plead guilty in exchange for a concession by the prosecutor, such as a reduced charge (charge-bargaining) or a concession that the facts of the crime were not so serious as originally alleged (fact-bargaining). The defendant may also plead guilty in the hope of a reduced sentence. The Court of Appeal has long sanctioned a system of a 25–30 per cent "sentence discount", rewarding the defendant for pleading guilty but the case of *Turner* (1970) prohibited the trial judge becoming involved in a plea bargain to assure the defendant of a specific sentence discount. This prevented the development of a full-blown system of legally enforceable plea bargains, conducted in special hearings, before a judge, which exists in most of the United States. The Royal Commission said nothing about such pre-trial negotiations involving the judge but, in order to try and obviate the occurrence of cracked trials, recommended a "sentencing canvass", offering the defendant a graduated system of sentencing discounts: the earlier the plea, the greater the discount. Whilst acknowledging the danger that this might induce innocent people to plead guilty, the Commission, heavily influenced by the Bar Council's Seabrook Report (1992), concluded that this risk would not be increased by "clearer articulation of the long accepted principle" of sentencing discounts. Section 48 of the Criminal Justice and Public Order Act 1994 (now Powers of Criminal Courts (Sentencing) Act 2000) gives statutory recognition to the system of informal sentencing discounts and, indeed, makes it mandatory, by requiring the sentencing judge to take into account the timing and circumstances of a guilty plea and, if the punishment is accordingly reduced, to state so in open court. According to *Turner*, advocates are not meant to pressurise clients into pleading guilty and judges are not meant to offer specific discounts but cases decided by the Court of Appeal expose the frequency of breaches of these rules by judges and counsel doing secret pre-trial deals in chambers. One such case was *Dosseter* (1999), where the Court of Appeal reminded advocates that plea bargaining "forms no part of English criminal jurisprudence" (1999).

10-016

10-017   The Bar would like to see the system of plea bargaining formalised. My view is diametrically opposed. I do not want to see the English legal system going down this American route. I have set out a long list of reasons, in 2000. Not least of my objections are that:

- every piece of research into defendants discloses a subset who plead guilty while maintaining innocence, often induced to do so by the temptation of a lighter sentence;
- rewarding someone for pleading guilty is morally repugnant and hypocritical, since it punishes those who exercise their right to trial;
- before the 1994 Act, magistrates, who do 95 per cent of sentencing, managed without discounts so I cannot see why they should be expected to give them now;
- Scottish judges consider sentencing discounts immoral and inappropriate;
- research by Henham found that the application of the discount is erratic in both the Crown Court and in magistrates' courts.

10-018   In *Att.-Gen.'s References (Nos 80 and 81 of 1999)* (1999) and *R. v. Peverett* (2000), while the Court of Appeal deprecated the unsuitably light sentences the offenders had received, nevertheless refused the Attorney-General leave to refer them to the Court of Appeal as unduly lenient. Where the prosecutor (CPS) had made representations to the defendant on which he was entitled to rely and had acted to his detriment by pleading guilty, this could properly be regarded as having given rise to a legitimate expectation that the Crown (Att.-Gen.) would not subsequently seek to resile from those representations. In other words, the Court enforced the plea bargains, in fairness to the defendant, despite warning that it had long set its face against plea bargaining. See also *Jackson* (2000) where the judge had promised a sentence discount so the CA felt obliged to enforce it, despite the defendant's "appalling" driving record. The second was swiftly followed by new *Attorney-General's Guidelines on the Acceptance of Pleas* (2000), in which the Attorney reminds prosecutors that justice should be transparent. He goes so far as to say that where the case in not exceptional, it is the duty of the advocate to remind the judge of the Court of Appeal's decisions and disassociate himself from sentence discussions. This reflects concern over the number of Crown Court judges who flout *Turner*, let alone counsel. To my disappointment, Auld L.J. recommended a formalised system of graduated sentencing *discounts* (Criminal Courts Review, Chapter 10).

Pre-trial Disclosure in Summary Cases

10-019   There is no statutory scheme of disclosure for summary cases, as there is for triable either way offences, under the Magistrates' Courts (Advanced Information) Rules 1985 and for indictable offences under the

Criminal Procedure and Investigations Act 1996 (see below). The accused may make voluntary disclosure under section 6 of the Act. Nevertheless, many of those of us who comment on the criminal process have argued that Article 6 (fair trial) of the European Convention on Human Rights requires disclosure and no distinction should be made between summary trial and trial on indictment. The Attorney-General's Guidelines (see below) instruct prosecutors to disclose all evidence upon which the Crown proposes to rely. This is quite revolutionary and has been widely predicted to reduce the number of defendants electing jury trial, since one of the reasons for doing so used to be to force the prosecutor to disclose evidence, under the regime for trial on indictment, described below. Where magistrates hear an argument on public interest immunity prior to trial, they need not disqualify themselves from hearing the trial: *R. v. Acton Youth Court* (2001, QBD). This case applied *R v. Stipendiary Magistrate for Norfolk ex parte Taylor* (1997, QBD) which applied the same principle.

The Not Guilty Plea and Trial

If a plea of not guilty is entered, the prosecutor will outline the case **10-020** against the accused, then call witnesses to substantiate that accusation. They may be cross-examined by the defence. As in all criminal trials in England and Wales, the *onus of proof* is on the prosecution to prove the case against the person accused. The *quantum of proof*, sometimes called the *standard of proof* required is "proof beyond reasonable doubt". If the magistrates are left with a reasonable doubt they must acquit the defendant, since he is entitled to the benefit of any doubt.

It follows that at the conclusion of the prosecution case, the defendant, or his legal representative, may submit to the magistrates that there is "no case to answer". This submission means, simply, that the evidence produced by the prosecution does not show that the defendant has committed the offence with which he is charged. It is up to the prosecution to establish his guilt, not for him to convict himself out of his own mouth. If the magistrates uphold that submission the case is dismissed forthwith. If not, the full case for the defence is then presented to the court. Defence witnesses will be called, the prosecutor may cross-examine them and the magistrates will decide whether or not the evidence is sufficient for them to convict. If so, they may sentence the defendant. If they are considering custody or one of the alternatives, they will adjourn for a pre-sentence report. If they decide to acquit, the case is dismissed.

Magistrates can call for the assistance of their court clerk (legal adviser) **10-021** if the case raises issues of law or mixed fact and law and they can ask his advice on sentencing. This is explained in greater depth in the Chapter on magistrates. The maximum penalty open to the magistrates, unless a specific statute provides otherwise, is six months' imprisonment, and/or a £5,000 fine. If a defendant is convicted of two or more offences at the same hearing the magistrates have power to send him to prison for 12 months. They may send a convicted defendant to the Crown Court for sentencing, if they feel their powers are inadequate.

Appeals

10-022   If magistrates discover they have made a mistake, they may re-open a case to vary a sentence or order where it appears to be in the interests of justice to do so (Magistrates' Courts Act 1980, as amended). The convicted defendant has the right to appeal to the Crown Court on fact and/or sentence if he pleaded not guilty, or sentence only if he pleaded guilty. Disagreements between witnesses as to the story are disputes of fact. An appeal on a point of law may be made by the prosecution or defence "by way of case stated" to the Divisional Court of the Queen's Bench Division. For a summary appeal, the Crown Court is composed of either a circuit judge or a recorder accompanied by two magistrates. The decision of the court is by a majority and the judge has a second and casting vote if the members are equally divided. The magistrates must accept the judge's pronouncements on matters of law.

In its appeal court role, the Crown Court conducts a complete rehearing of the case. This means that a second trial takes place, since the parties and the witnesses will give their evidence again. The Crown Court then reaches its own independent conclusion. No jury is used in these appeal cases and there is no further appeal possible on fact in a summary case from the Crown Court. The Crown Court has a duty to give reasons for its decision on the appeal unless the reasons are obvious or the case is simple: *R.v. Kingston Crown Court, ex parte Bell* (2000, QBD) and see *R. v. Snaresbrook C.C., ex parte Input Management Ltd* (1999, QBD). If on the appeal a point of law is argued before the court, the court may, having given its decision, agree to state a case for the consideration of the Queen's Bench Divisional Court.

Notice that, although the convicted offender has a right to appeal against sentence, the prosecution has no right to appeal against an unduly lenient sentence, as they can from a Crown Court judge's sentence (see below). Some, including me, have argued that this is anomalous and occasionally victims or their families are outraged. One such case is reported in *The Times* on January 30, 2001. A hit and run driver, who drove over two miles with the dead man's body on the car roof, his arm dangling through the sun-roof, was given 160 hours of community service for careless driving.

The Divisional Court of the Queen's Bench Division

10-023   As has just been seen, an appeal on a point of law from the magistrates' court's decision or the decision of the Crown Court is heard here. This Court sat only in the Royal Courts of Justice in London but has just (2001) started sitting in Cardiff. The appeal is by way of "case stated". This means that the prosecution, or convicted person, or legal representative, asks the magistrates, or judge in the Crown Court to state a case for the consideration of the Divisional Court. This case is then prepared in writing by the judge or magistrates' clerk setting out the point of law which was raised, the decision of the magistrates and the reason why they decided it as they did. As magistrates' courts are not courts of record, this used to involve the clerk in composing reasons some months after trial, from his and the magistrates' memories but, as magistrates have been giving reasons since the Human Rights Act 1998 imported into English law the requirement for a reasoned judgment, stating a case will be a lot easier.

If the Divisional Court decides that the magistrates were wrong, it has three options: (i) it may reverse, affirm or amend the magistrates' decision; (ii) it may remit the case to the magistrates requiring them either to continue hearing the case, or to discharge or convict the accused, as appropriate; (iii) it may make such order as it thinks fit (Supreme Court Act 1981). Note that the prosecution has equal right of appeal here and may succeed in having the case sent back for the magistrates to convict.

The Queen's Bench Divisional Court also exercises the High Court's **10-024** supervisory jurisdiction over the functioning of magistrates' courts and the Crown Court in their dealings with summary cases. The judicial review of a case is so similar to an appeal by way of case stated that I have seen a High Court judge ask, two days into a hearing, which type of case he was hearing. The QBD has stated that it would prefer that convictions were challenged by way of case stated than by judicial review: *Chester v. Gloucester Crown Court* (1998). The use of the prerogative orders in the exercise of judicial review is considered below. Judicial review proceedings are not appropriate for sentencing appeals: *Allen v. West Yorkshire Probation Service* (2001, QBD) but the existence of a right of appeal to the Crown Court does not preclude a person convicted of offences by magistrates seeking judicial review where the complaint raised was of procedural impropriety, unfairness or bias: *R. v. Hereford Magistrates' Court, ex parte Rowlands* (1997, CA). A further appeal, subject to leave being obtained, is possible to the House of Lords. Such cases are rare. At the moment, there is glaring inconsistency between types of appeal available from the two courts of first instance (Crown and Magistrates'). Auld L.J. recommended harmonisation in his second report.

Post Appeal

The Criminal Appeal Act 1995 gives the Criminal Cases Review **10-025** Commission (described below) an unconditional power to refer a conviction or sentence imposed by magistrates to the Crown Court, to be treated as an appeal.

5. Offences Triable Either Way—Mode of Trial

10-026   The Magistrates' Courts Act 1980 lays down that for an offence triable either way, the magistrates' court shall hear representations from the prosecutor and the defendant as to the appropriate mode of trial. (The court has no discretion if the Attorney-General or the Director of Public Prosecutions seeks indictable trial.) Having heard the representations and considered all the circumstances, the magistrates may decide that the defendant should be tried on indictment. If so, that decision is final. If they consider that summary trial is appropriate the magistrates tell the defendant so, but offer him the right to elect jury trial. Experience has shown that the vast majority of defendants who have an option choose to have the case tried by magistrates.

As Home Secretary, Jack Straw twice introduced Bills designed to remove this right but they were both rejected by the House of Lords. The story of these Bills and their background is told in the Chapter on the jury. As I explain in that Chapter, his Conservative predecessor, recognising the sentimental attachment of the English to jury trial in criminal cases, decided it would be politically inexpedient to remove the defendant's right to opt for jury trial in all triable either way cases.

The Plea before Venue Procedure

10-027   Instead, he sponsored what is now section 49 of the Criminal Procedure and Investigations Act 1996 which requires the magistrates, before determining mode of trial in triable either way cases, to ascertain the accused's plea. Where he indicates a not guilty plea, they must proceed to deal with the case summarily. Where the accused pleads not guilty, they may choose to send the case up to the Crown Court or, where they decline to do so, they must still give the defendant the option of summary trial or trial on indictment at the Crown Court. In other words, if the defendant expresses an intention to plead guilty, he loses the right to opt for the Crown Court. The magistrates must hear the case but retain the right to send it up to the Crown Court for sentence, where they feel their own sentencing powers are too low. There is of course, nothing to prevent the accused from indicating a not guilty plea at this stage, then changing his plea to guilty at the Crown Court. In such cases, the section fails to achieve its desired objective. For further criticisms see Padfield.

The Committal

10-028   Where the justices choose to send the accused for trial in the Crown Court, or he so elects, he is committed for trial there in committal proceedings. This inquiry is an impartial investigation of the prosecution case. Written statements must be submitted to the examining magistrates. In effect this is committal by consent. The written statement of evidence must be signed; it must contain a declaration that the person making it believes it to be true and copies must be made available to the defendant. She is thus made fully aware of the case which she will have to meet at the trial. The procedure is dependent on the defendant's being represented. The Crown Court location is determined by the locality where the alleged criminal act took place and the accused person receives a written statement of the charge, "an indictment". An indictment may be made up of several "counts", or separate charges.

6. Indictable Offences (Offences that Have to be Tried in the Crown Court)

Committal Abolished — Section 51 of the Crime and Disorder Act 1998

After previous failed statutory attempts, this section removed commit-   **10–029**
tal proceedings for indictable offences. It came into force in January 2001, after pilot trials used to evaluate its practicality. It had been recommended by the Narey Report on delay, 1997, as well by the Royal Commission on Criminal Justice 1993. Narey found that indictable cases wasted much of their time in the magistrates' court. The pilot schemes proved successful, with an average reduction of seven weeks per case. From now on there will be a simple preliminary hearing in the magistrates' court, before two or three justices. Its purpose is to determine whether there is an indictable only offence charged and whether there are related offences which fall to be sent under section 51, to decide the defendant's remand status and deal with legal representation. Magistrates will usually hear a full bail application at such a hearing and may adjourn the hearing if there is insufficient information before them. It might also be adjourned at the prosecution's request if they seek to produce co-defendants. Provided certain conditions are fulfilled, magistrates are required to send the defendant to the Crown Court on related triable either way or summary offences. For detail, see O'Doherty.

Disclosure

The rules governing the disclosure of evidence are very complex, espe-   **10–030**
cially in relation to trial on indictment. They are now contained in the Criminal Procedure and Investigations Act 1996, the European Convention on Human Rights, Articles 5 and 6, considerable recent ECHR and English case law applying the Convention to the Act and now the new Attorney-General's Guidelines on Disclosure (2000) and appended Commentary. The complexity of disclosure rules is hardly surprising since they provide the very fulcrum on which the scales of justice

swing, balancing the interests of all of us, represented by the State, in securing the conviction of the guilty and the interests of a civilised democracy in ensuring that the innocent accused are acquitted, hence the case law and masses of surrounding commentary. As the Attorney-General says in his new guidelines "(a) failure to take action leading to proper disclosure may result in a wrongful conviction. It may alternatively lead to a successful abuse of process argument or an acquittal against the weight of the evidence".

One of the most controversial elements of the 1996 Act was its introduction of a requirement for pre-trial disclosure by the accused. This new requirement on the defence to disclose an outline of their story before hearing the prosecution's entire case (or risk the court's drawing adverse inferences) was said to breach the presumption of innocence. Defence lawyers also objected that the Act curtailed disclosure requirements on the prosecution, which had been governed by case law. The Conservative Government set out its proposals for the Act in a consultation document, "Disclosure", in 1995. They were concerned by the findings of the Royal Commission on Criminal Justice that the defence were gaining an unfair advantage over the prosecution by disclosure requirements which had become unduly onerous, following recent case law reacting to famous miscarriages of justice, such as the Birmingham six, Guildford four, Maguires, Kisko and Judith Ward. Defence lawyers could delay trial and put obstacles in the way of a prosecution by requiring the disclosure of more and more evidence yet the accused was still in the position of being able to ambush them with a surprise defence, at trial, thus securing an unwarranted acquittal.

10-031   The Act was immediately attacked as unfair on the defence and a potential breach of the Convention, which was not then binding in English law: see Murray, Leng and Redmayne. Since it came into force in 1997, its contentiousness has increased, as defence lawyers have made repeated challenges to the Act or practice under the Convention and there are widespread allegations of prosecution non-disclosure (see *The Times*, May 4, 1999) and an increasing number of prosecutions stopped by judges. One of the worst was a 2000 £5 million trial alleging police corruption and drug smuggling, in which the judge said the CPS disclosure certificate had "all the intellectual content of a fax sheet cover". The Attorney-General, in his commentary, explains that his new guidelines are a response to these concerns and an interim measure, pending a review of disclosure in the light of research commenced in 2000 to evaluate the working of the 1996 Act.

The regime under the Act and guidelines is now as follows:

- The prosecutor is under a duty to make "primary disclosure" to the accused of any evidence which, in his opinion, might undermine the prosecution case, or give a written statement that there is none. An example would be material which the defence could use in cross-examination, to seek the exclusion of evidence (Guideline 36), or material pointing to the involvement of another person in the offence (Guideline 37). Material must not be disclosed where the court has concluded, on an application by the prosecutor, that it is not in the public interest to disclose it (s.3).

- In the interests of justice, prosecutors may need to disclose significant information before their statutory duty arises in, for instance, bail proceedings (Guideline 34). This takes account of the Court of Appeal's decision in *Lee* (1999).

- In cases to be tried on indictment, the accused must then give a written defence statement to the court and prosecutor, setting out his defence in general terms and indicating on what matters and why he takes issue with the prosecutor. If this includes an alibi, he must give details of the alibi witnesses (s.5). The Attorney-General says a comprehensive defence statement helps the prosecutor identify what further material needs to be disclosed and helps trial management by focussing on the issues in dispute (Guideline 27).

- At this point, the prosecution must disclose any previously undisclosed material which might reasonably be expected to assist the accused's defence (secondary disclosure). Examples include scientific or scenes of crime findings and videos, or names of individuals who may have relevant information (Guideline 40). If the accused has reasonable cause to believe there is further material which should have been disclosed, he can apply for disclosure (s.8).

- The prosecutor has a continuing duty to keep under review whether further disclosure is necessary (s.9).

- Most controversially, the court or jury may "draw such inferences as appear proper in deciding whether the accused is guilty", in any case where the accused has failed to give defence statement or at trial puts forward a different defence, or makes a contradictory or defective written statement.

The Attorney-General's guidelines add the following:

- Fair disclosure is part of the fair trial requirement of Article 6 (of the Convention on Human Rights) but fairness means other interests need protecting, such as those of victims and witnesses. **10-032**
- The guidelines go beyond legislative requirements.
- Investigators should err on the side of recording and retaining material where they have doubts as to its relevance.
- Disclosure officers (police) must inspect all material.

- Where investigators seize volumes of material then do not use it, they should make it known to the accused and available for inspection.
- Prosecutors must be alert to the possibility of material unrevealed to them.
- In deciding what should be disclosed, prosecutors should resolve any doubt in favour of the accused.
- The prosecution advocate must keep under review until the conclusion of trial decisions regarding disclosure. This had been recommended by the Law Society and Criminal Bar Association.

The best recent critique of the above regime and explanation of whether it satisfies Convention case law from England and Strasbourg (ECHR) is provided by Plowden and Kerrigan. They draw attention to a statement by the ECHR in the leading case of *Rowe and Davies v. U.K.* (2000):

"It is a fundamental aspect of the right to a fair trial that criminal proceedings, including the elements of such proceedings that relate to procedure, should be adversarial and that there should be equality of arms between the prosecution and defence. The right to an adversarial trial means, in a criminal case, that both prosecution and defence must be given the opportunity to have knowledge of and comment on the observations filed and the evidence adduced by the other party. . . . In addition, Article 6(1) requires, as indeed does English law . . . that the prosecution authorities should disclose to the defence all material evidence in their possession for or against the accused . . ."

10-033   The ECHR warned, however, that "entitlement to disclosure of relevant evidence is not an absolute right". There are three competing interests that might lead to the withholding of evidence — national security, protection of witnesses, and preserving secrecy in police investigations. This was applied when the case came back to the Court of Appeal decision in *R. v. Davies, Rowe and Johnson* (2000). The authors provide a very useful survey of the law in 2001 and conclude, amongst other things, that the English regime for public interest immunity (PII), by which a prosecutor can apply to a trial judge not to disclose sensitive material, seems to be Convention compliant, according to the above case and recent cases of *Jasper v. U.K.* and *Fitt v. U.K.* According to these cases and *Brushett* (2000, CA) the vigilance of judges in examining contentious material to decide what should be disclosed and the continuing duty to review disclosure spare English law from falling foul of the Convention. See also Ashworth's comments on these cases. See more of these cases below, under appeals. *Rowe and Davis v. U.K.* was applied by the ECHR in *Altan v. U.K.* Here, the prosecution had denied at the trial that there was undisclosed relevant material yet it came to light before their appeal that that was not true. The prosecution successfully sought to exclude that evidence from the appeal on the ground of PII. The Court held that the trial had been unfair. The prosecution's failure to lay the evidence before the trial judge rendered the trial unfair, as the trial judge was in the best position to decide whether the non-disclosure of PII evidence would be unfairly prejudicial to the accused. In 2001, Auld L.J. suggested simplifying the disclosure tests and regime.

The Plea and Directions Hearing

At the Crown Court, the defendant (except in cases of fraud) has been 10-034 required, since the mid 1990s, to appear at a proceeding called a "plea and directions hearing", designed to prepare for trial and fix the trial date. In all class one or serious or complex cases, the prosecution provides a summary, identifying issues of law and fact and estimating trial length. The arraignment takes place at the hearing: the defendant enters a plea of guilty or not guilty to each of the charges. Following a not guilty plea, the parties are expected to inform the court of such matters as: witnesses, defence witnesses whose written statements are accepted, admitted facts, any alibi, points of law and special requirements for the trial (for example, live video links for child witnesses). If the plea is "guilty", the judge should, if possible, proceed to sentence the defendant, after hearing his plea in mitigation. This is a plea for leniency, allowing the defendant to argue any partial excuses or explanation for his admitted offences. If the judge or recorder is considering imposing a custodial sentence or non-custodial alternative, she may require a pre-sentence report to be prepared, or, where appropriate, a medical or psychiatric report. Since 1999–2000 various Crown Court centres have been abandoning oral PDHs in small class 4 cases and the issues are dealt with in writing.

Preparatory hearings are held before serious fraud trials and may be ordered in complex and lengthy cases, under the Criminal Procedure and Investigations Act 1996. The prosecution may appeal against a judge's ruling. Auld L.J. recommended a move away from pre-trial hearings towards standard timetables and co-operation between the parties.

Trial on Indictment

Arguments on points of law and acquittals by the judge

One of the big advantages to the defendant of a trial in the Crown 10-035 Court, over summary trial in the magistrates' court, is that the pre-trial legal argument stage provides a very realistic opportunity for the case to be dismissed on the order of the trial judge, in an ordered or directed acquittal. Indeed, over half of Crown Court acquittals occur before or during the trial, without a jury's ever being given an opportunity to bring in a verdict. This is one of the elements which contributes to the acquittal rate in the Crown Court being significantly higher than that in the magistrates' court. When the prosecution appear at court and offer no evidence, the judge orders an acquittal and one of the biggest factors causing this is the non-appearance of a crucial witness, or their retraction of evidence. Baldwin found that this was foreseeable in many such collapsed cases and the prosecution could have been withdrawn at an earlier stage. As a result of pre-trial legal argument, a court may stay an indictment as an abuse of process. Applications to Crown Court judges on this ground seem to be significant growth area in 2000–2001 and a Practice Direction on their conduct was issued in 2000.

A judge may direct an acquittal during the trial. Mostly, this happens at the close of the prosecution case when the defence have successfully invited the judge to find that there is not a sufficient case to convict the defendant, in a submission of "no case to answer". This may be decided on a point of law, or an assessment of the sufficiency of the evidence. Commentators suggest that the Convention will require judges to give reasons, which they did not do before 2000. The Law Commission Report on double jeopardy and prosecution appeals (No. 267, 2001) recommends that where the judge acquits at this point on a point of law, the prosecution should have a right of appeal against an acquittal. This will be introduced into a Criminal Justice Bill very soon, possibly in 2001, as it appears as a proposal in the 2001 white paper, *Criminal Justice—The Way Ahead*. Where a judge wrongly rejects a submission of "no case", the conviction will be regarded as unsafe by the Court of Appeal: *R. v. Smith* (1999, CA).

10-036   Also, legal argument may take place at any time in the trial, where the judge is asked to rule on a point of law or evidence in the absence of the jury, in a "*voir dire*" hearing (a trial within a trial). When the prosecution depends on poor quality, unsupported identification evidence, the judge must direct an acquittal. Otherwise, the judge's task is to consider, without usurping the jury's function, whether there is evidence upon which a reasonable jury could convict. Directed acquittals are again caused mainly by inadequate or untrustworthy witnesses but also by legal problems and evidential insufficiency (Baldwin). In *R. v. Brown* (2001), the Court of Appeal held that the judge is under a duty to keep under review whether to direct an acquittal, such power to be sparingly exercised, and should do so if satisfied that no jury on the evidence could safely convict. What a judge may not do is prevent the prosecution bringing their case because he thinks the defendant's defence is likely to be believed by the jury: *Att.-Gen.'s Ref. No.2 of 2000* (2001, CA). If the judge upholds the defence submission and directs an acquittal, the prosecution may not appeal and the Law Commission has recommended that this should not change (see now *Prosecution Appeals Against Judges' Rulings* (LC Report 269). Pattenden powerfully argues that this means that any wrongfully directed acquittal (and the numbers were found to be significant, by Block, Corbett and Peay) by the judge must go unchallenged, which is unfair for the victim, witnesses and public.

Prosecutors have much more extensive rights of appeal in some common law and European civil law jurisdictions. The Law Commission's final report, published in 2001, confirms their recommendations in the consultation paper, for which they received a high degree of support.

A judge may also stop a trial at any time, if he thinks adverse publicity may endanger the impartiality of the jury. This happened very controversially in 2001, to the trial of Leeds United footballers Lee Bowyer and Jonathan Woodgate, accused of beating an Asian student unconscious. The jury had already deliberated for 21 hours at the end of a nine-week trial, costing £8 million, when the *Sunday Mirror* published an interview with the victim's father, alleging that it was a racist attack. The judge reported the newspaper to the Attorney-General, who alone has the power to prosecute them for contempt.

Jury trial

If the plea is "not guilty" the court proceeds to swear in 12 jurors, who **10-037** will be responsible at the end of the trial for deciding whether the accused is guilty or not guilty. Once the jury is sworn in, the prosecution will open the case by outlining the facts and then calling the prosecution witnesses to give evidence to prove those facts. The defence can cross-examine all such witnesses. Undisputed evidence can be admitted by written statement. At the close of the prosecution case the defence counsel presents the defence case and calls witnesses for the defence, possibly including the defendant. These witnesses too can be cross-examined on their evidence. The accused is not required to give evidence. This rule is called the right to silence and is discussed below. The court has to decide whether the prosecution's accusation is proved beyond reasonable doubt. It does not hold an inquiry into the case. If it did do so, it would be forced to have the accused answer questions which were relevant to the circumstances of the alleged crime.

When the final speeches by the prosecution and defence counsel have been made, the judge "sums up" for the benefit of the jury. This summing-up is the last speech which the jury hear before they retire to consider their verdict. In it the judge has to balance the arguments of the prosecution and the defence, but leave the jury to decide on the issue of guilt, beyond reasonable doubt, of the accused.

As a result of the abolition of the requirement for a unanimous verdict by the Criminal Justice Act 1967, it is possible for the judge to accept a majority verdict of the jury, provided that there are not more than two in the minority. If there are three or more in the minority this is known as a "hung jury" and the trial is abandoned. It is then up to the prosecution whether to request a retrial. The judge will only stop this if he consider it an abuse of process. Normally prosecutions are abandoned after two juries have hung but there is nothing in law stopping a retrial. Hall has commented, in 2001, that it is anomalous that if an accused is ordered to be retried after a successful appeal, it is the Court of Appeal which decides on it but in this instance, the decision is that of the prosecutor. If the jury has dropped to 11 or ten in number there can be a majority verdict if there is not more than one dissenter. Every effort is made, however, to obtain a unanimous verdict and the jury must have been out for at least two hours before the judge is able to accept a majority verdict. If the verdict is "not guilty" the accused is immediately discharged; if the verdict is "guilty", after a plea in mitigation by his counsel, he will be sentenced by the judge. I return to the jury in the Chapter on the jury. I made a series of recommendations for restructuring jury trial in a 2001 report for Auld L.J. in his *Criminal Courts Review.*

The Right to Silence

10-038   Until the Criminal Justice and Public Order Act 1994, the defendant had a virtually unqualified two-stage right to silence, both in the police station and at trial. In court, this extended to the right not to be asked questions and the judge could comment on a defendant's exercise of the right but not adversely. The right was considered by the Criminal Law Revision Committee, in 1972, the Royal Commission on Criminal Procedure, 1981, and the Royal Commission on Criminal Justice, 1993, and it has long been a subject of controversy.

Proponents hail it as a major safeguard of the English legal system that the defendant cannot convict himself out of his own mouth. It leaves the burden of proof entirely on the prosecution. Opponents criticise it as a rule protecting the guilty. They believe it encourages the police to intimidate suspects into confessing and some have said that it is sentimental to argue that the accused should not be allowed to convict himself.

In 1987, the Home Secretary set up a working party to examine the effects of abolishing the right to silence but this was quietly disbanded at the peak of public concern over wrongful convictions, such as those of the Guildford Four and Birmingham Six. The 1993 Royal Commission considered the value and operation of the right to silence. The majority recommended that adverse inferences should not be drawn from silence at the police station and recommended retaining the existing caution (that is, the warning given by police before questioning by them). Only when the prosecution's case had been fully disclosed should the defendant be required to offer an answer to the charges made against him at the risk of adverse comment at trial on any new defence he then discloses or any departure from a previously disclosed defence (in other words, in the event of an "ambush defence").

10-039   The Criminal Justice and Public Order Act 1994 goes much further than this and, critics would say, effectively vitiates both stages of the right to silence. Sections 34–39 allow the court to draw "such inferences as appear proper" from the accused's failure to mention, under police questioning, any fact which he could have been expected to mention, or failure, under questioning, to account for any objects, marks or substances, or failure, under questioning, to account for his presence at a particular place, or failure to give evidence or answer questions at trial.

The new provisions on silence in the 1994 Act are one of the most heavily criticised and discussed areas of a provocative statute. The operation of the sections in practice has been the subject of critical comment. It is said that the sections offer no protection to the mentally disordered suspect and that the re-drafted police caution is so lengthy and complex that it is only fully understood by a minority of suspects. The Court of Appeal had already ruled, in October 1995, in three appeals against conviction on the grounds that trial judges had wrongly directed the jury on the effects of these sections. The Court of Appeal held (*R. v. Cowan*) that the trial judge was required to remind the jury of certain rules still protecting the defendant, for instance, that the burden of proof lay on the prosecution, that the defendant was entitled to remain silent, that an inference drawn from silence could not on its own prove guilt, that the jury had to be satisfied that the prosecution had established a case to answer before drawing any inferences from the defendant's silence and, finally, that if they concluded that his silence could only sensibly be attributed to the defendant's having no answer or none that would stand up to cross-examination, they could then draw an adverse inference. The Judicial Studies Board issued a specimen direction to juries for the use of judges in future trials (all such specimen directions can be read on the JSB website). It is confusing and complex.

Those who criticised these sections as being a breach of Article 6 of the **10-040** European Convention on Human Rights were disappointed by the case of *Murray v. United Kingdom* (1996), in which the European Court of Human Rights ruled, in respect of a similar provision in Northern Ireland, that there was no such thing as an absolute right of silence and it was only a matter of common sense to permit the drawing of adverse inferences where a defendant said nothing in the face of overwhelming evidence. The ECHR, nevertheless, considered legal advice crucial to a defendant who exercised his right to silence. The Attorney-General swiftly issued guidance in the light of this ruling and the Youth Justice and Criminal Evidence Act 1999 disapplies section 34 in cases where the suspect has not been allowed the opportunity to consult a solicitor prior to questioning.

The application of the 1994 Act's provisions on silence have continued to give rise to a stream of appeals to the Court of Appeal, not least because the relevant sections are so difficult to apply, in practice, that judges quite often mistakenly permit the jury to draw an adverse inference in cases where it is not applicable. This glut of cases has led Birch to argue that, on a cost-benefit analysis, section 34 should be repealed because it is "too expensive" It consumes too much judicial time at trial and on appeal. It "is a headache for the conscientious jury and a tool with which the slapdash, incompetent jury may wreak injustice" and "the gains in terms of cogent evidence are likely to be slight". In many appeals, the prosecution had a strong case at trial, without silence. The danger in these cases is if section 34 is wrongly applied, it may result in the quashing of an otherwise respectable conviction. On the other hand, some appeals have demonstrated that its application has persuaded some juries to attach considerable, misplaced significance to silence. She restates some "obvious" features of the section. For instance, if no facts are advanced at trial, the section has no application. Also, the section does not necessarily contemplate a silent interviewee, just one who refuses to answer some of the interviewer's questions. Then she explains some of the problems of interpreting and applying the section. The section permits the jury to draw "such inferences as appear proper" but what this means is not explained. (I would remind the reader that this applies to magistrates as well as juries.) Similarly undefined are what is a fact and what is relevant in terms of evidence relied on. Birch's article, incidentally, gives an excellent explanation of the moral and practical arguments surrounding the right of silence, as well as the history of section 34.

10-041   At the time of writing, 2001, the most important case on silence is *Condron v. U.K.* (2000, ECHR), the first case in which the European Court of Human Rights pronounced on the validity of section 34. See Ashworth's comment on the report in 2000 and Jennings, Ashworth and Emmerson and see cases in which it has been applied (*e.g. Betts and Hall*, 2000, CA). In this case, the applicants had stood trial in 1995 on charges of supplying heroin and possession with intent to supply. On the advice of their solicitor, they did not respond to questioning as they were suffering withdrawal symptoms. The judge permitted the jury to draw an adverse inference under section 34. The ECHR found a violation of Article 6(1) because the judge had left the jury at liberty to draw an adverse inference, even if they had been satisfied that the applicants remained silent for good reason on the advice of their solicitor. The CA had no means of knowing whether an adverse inference had played a significant role in the decision to convict. Four days later, the ECHR delivered their judgment in *Averill v. U.K.* (2000). In this Northern Irish terrorist case, the applicant was denied legal advice during the first 24 hours of his detention, which the Court held to be a violation of Article 6(1) but, following *Murray*, held there was no violation of 6(2) just because the judge had drawn an adverse inference from silence. They held that, while it would be incompatible with the right to a fair trial to base a conviction solely or mainly on an accused's silence, in appropriate circumstances, silence could be taken into account when assessing the persuasiveness of other prosecution evidence. The Court noted that the trial judge was not obliged to draw inferences from silence but did so in the exercise of his discretion and provided detailed reasons for his decision. Further, the

Court of Appeal scrupulously reviewed the reasons given by the trial judge and endorsed his decision. Jennings *et al.* draw the following conclusions from these cases:

- Legal advice is fundamentally important, especially where there is a possibility of adverse inferences.
- There may be other good reasons for remaining silent, apart from legal advice.
- A trial was not rendered unfair where adverse inferences were drawn from silence if the only reason was a professed policy of not speaking to the police.
- Adverse inferences may properly be drawn from silence where the situation clearly calls for an explanation. For instance, in *Averill*, his failure to account for his presence near the scene of a double murder and his failure to account for fibres on his clothing and in his hair justified such inferences.

See also, *McGee v. U.K.* (2000), where the ECHR found that depriving **10-042** the applicant of legal advice during the early stages of police interrogation was a violation of Article 6. It was only after he signed a confession that he was allowed to see a solicitor. From *R. v. Ali* (2001) it appears that the defendant satisfies section 34 if he prepares a statement containing all the facts he relies on at trial.

In research on the effects of a similar provision on silence in Northern Ireland, in 1990–1995, Jackson found that the change of law had resulted in a large decrease in cases where the defendant refused to testify. Nevertheless, there had, ironically, been a marked decline in the conviction rate.

The Privilege against Self-Incrimination

The privilege is not spelled out in Article 6 of the Convention but is a **10-043** developed element of ECHR jurisprudence. At the moment, there seem to be two sets of conflicting decisions of the Court on procedures which fall foul of the rule and they are commented on by Ashworth in "The Self-Incrimination Saga" *Archbold News*, June 27, 2001 and in a comment on *Henney and McGuinness v. Ireland* [2001] Crim.L.R. 481.

The Privy Council, on appeal in a Scottish case, *Brown v. Stott* (2000) held that section 172(2) of the Road Traffic Act, which asked a registered vehicle owner to disclose who was the driver of a car caught in a speed trap, did not breach the privilege because only a simple question is put, in the interests of public safety. This was a relief to prosecuting authorities in view of the number of drivers caught for speeding who were claiming a defence under Article 6. This was applied by the Divisional Court in *DPP v. Wilson*, confirming that an admission in answer to the statutory question may be used in evidence in a subsequent prosecution.

Ashworth expresses concern about the correctness of these decisions, especially that the latter case did not cite the ECHR decisions in *Heaney and McGuinnes v. Ireland* and *Quinn v. Ireland,* handed down after *Brown* in December 2000. In the former, the applicants had been convicted of a refusal to give police an account of their movements under Irish terrorist legislation. This was held to have been a breach of the privilege. The Court accepted that the privilege against self-incrimination was not absolute but held that the threat of imprisonment "destroyed the very essence of the right". The Court approved of *Funke v. France* (1993), where the sanction was only a fine. The last decision was *J.B. v. Switzerland* (2001), which ruled there was a breach by the tax authorities in requiring the applicant to furnish information about the source of income on pain of fines. Ashworth remarks on the strange distinction between these cases and the ECHR's attitude to the requirement to submit to blood and urine tests, which they have held do not breach the privilege.

Appeal

10-044   A convicted person may appeal from the Crown Court to the Court of Appeal (Criminal Division), with leave of the Court of Appeal or if the trial judge grants a certificate that the case is fit for appeal (Criminal Appeal Act 1968, s.1 as simplified by the Criminal Appeal Act 1995, s.1). He may appeal against sentence, with leave of the Court of Appeal (1968 Act, ss.9–11). Applications for leave to the Court of Appeal are normally considered on paper, by a High Court judge. If she refuses leave, the application may be re-heard by the Court of Appeal in open court. An appeal by way of case stated on a point of law may be made to the High Court (QBD Divisional Court). An application for judicial review is precluded "in matters relating to trial on indictment" but not in relation to other matters: Supreme Court Act 1981, section 29(3). There is case law on what matters may and may not be reviewed, for instance *R. v. Maidstone Crown Court, ex parte Harrow L.B.C.* and see especially *Kebilene* (1999, HL), referred to elsewhere in this book.

7. Powers of the Court of Appeal

Grounds

10-045   Section 2(1) of the Criminal Appeal Act 1995 amends the Criminal Appeal Act 1968 to set out new and simplified grounds upon which the Court of Appeal may allow a criminal appeal. The Court of Appeal:

"(a)   shall allow an appeal against conviction if they think that the conviction is unsafe; and

(b)   shall dismiss such an appeal in any other case."

Receiving Fresh Evidence

The Court of Appeal may "receive any evidence which was not **10-046** adduced in the proceedings from which the appeal lies" (Criminal Appeal Act 1968, as amended by the 1995 Act, s.4). The Court must, in considering whether to receive any evidence, have regard in particular to:

(a) whether the evidence appears to the Court to be capable of belief;
(b) whether it appears to the Court that the evidence may afford any ground for allowing the appeal;
(c) whether the evidence would have been admissible at the trial;
(d) whether there is a reasonable explanation for the failure to adduce the evidence at trial.

(Criminal Appeal Act 1968, section 23(2), as amended by section 4 of the 1995 Act, paraphrased).

In *Craven* (2000, CA), the Court held that, empowered as it was to receive fresh evidence and taking account of all the evidence before it, including evidence to which the jury might not have had access, should uphold a conviction, if they considered it safe. Thus a defect at trial, rendering it unfair, could be cured by a fair and proper consideration of the evidence on appeal. They applied the ECHR case of *Edwards v. U.K.* (1993).

As Duff (below) points out, a common reason for non-referral by the CCRC of a case to the Court of Appeal is that, although fresh evidence has come to light, there is no reasonable explanation why it was not adduced at trial (*CCRC Annual Report 1999–2000*). The prosecution are entitled to take account of new evidence at trial and can change their allegations: *Mercer* (2001, CA).

Referral to the CCRC

Section 5 of the 1995 Act gives the Court of Appeal a new power to **10-047** direct the newly created Criminal Cases Review Commission to investigate and report on any specified matter relevant to the determination of an appeal against conviction, where such an investigation is likely to result in the Court being able to resolve the appeal and where the matter cannot be resolved by the Court without such a reference.

Comment

The 1995 amendments to the Court of Appeal's powers all result from **10-048** the recommendations of the Royal Commission on Criminal Justice, 1993. These were a culmination of years of criticism from JUSTICE (1989, *etc.*), the House of Commons Select Committee on Home Affairs (1981), academics, M.P.s and many others. It was repeatedly said that the grounds of appeal in the 1968 Act were narrow and ambiguous, that the Court of Appeal interpreted their powers too narrowly, that they were too ready to uphold a conviction, even where they accepted there had been an irregularity at trial, and that they were too reluctant to admit fresh evidence.

The Act was designed to simplify the grounds of appeal so, for instance, it was decided in section 2 to make the ground for quashing an appeal simply a determination that it was "unsafe", instead of "unsafe or unsatisfactory", as the 1968 Act had read. The other list of grounds in the unamended Act were deleted, as it was thought that "unsafe" was a comprehensive enough term to cover all types of miscarriage of justice which should be quashed. Indeed, the Home Secretary and Minister of State, in introducing the Bill, assured Parliament that the new ground simply restated the existing practice of the Court of Appeal. All this is explained by Sir John Smith, in the *Criminal Law Review*. He warned in it, as he had Parliament, that "unsafe" needed clarification. He regretted that the Government was not persuaded by his argument.

Judicial Interpretation of "Unsafe"

10-049   Since then, the Court of Appeal has provoked more regret, by producing a series of contradictory cases on what errors at trial can render a conviction unsafe enough to merit quashing. Sir John explains the confusing result in his comment on *Rajcoomar* (1999, CA). In this case, where the defendant pleaded guilty after the judge wrongly rejected an abuse of process objection, the Court declined to quash the conviction, following *Chalkley* (1998), where they had held that their amended grounds for quashing were narrower than under the old law. The Court distinguished *Mullen* (1999), where they had held that "for a conviction to be safe, it must be lawful and, if it results from a trial which should never have taken place, it can hardly be regarded as safe". Sir John, commenting in the *Criminal Law Review* on these two and other cases, submits there is no proper ground for a distinction. In each case, it was assumed there was no doubt the defendant committed the offence charged but there was a fundamental procedural flaw so the conviction should have been quashed. Indeed the Court in *Mullen* (1999) considered the meaning of "unsafe" sufficiently ambiguous for them to apply *Pepper v. Hart*, to permit themselves to look at *Hansard* (parliamentary proceedings) to see what was the intention behind the amendment. We encountered this case in the Chapter on sources.

10-050   Unfortunately, there seem to be inconsistencies in the increasing batch of cases where the Court of Appeal has had to determine the meaning of "unsafe" in the context of the European Convention on Human Rights, fair trial requirement under Article 6. When the Court of Appeal in *R. v. Togher, R. v. Doran, R. v. Parsons* took into account (their words) the ECHR's judgment in *R. v. Davis, Johnson and Rowe* (2000) on disclosure, cited above, they held that they were required by the Human Rights Act 1998 to interpret the domestic legislation in a way compatible with the Convention, where possible. Although *Chalkley* suggested the safety of a conviction was to be considered irrespective of the trial process, they, in *Togher*, preferred the approach in *Mullen*. If a defendant had been had been denied a fair trial, it would almost be inevitable that the conviction would be regarded as unsafe. These cases were not mentioned by the Court of Appeal in *R. v. Williams* (2001). Here, the Court held that a mis- or non-direction must be significant in order to render a conviction unsafe. It leaves the problem of determining when a misdirection or non-direction is "significant". These precedents were, nevertheless mentioned in *R. v. Craven* (2001, CA), which held that whether there was such unfairness as to render a conviction unsafe depended on the vice which was said to constitute unfairness. If the verdict of the jury would not have been different then the trial was not unfair and the conviction not unsafe. If a defect at trial was cured on appeal then the defendant had received a fair trial under Article 6. In *R. v. Francom* (2000), the CA held they should approach the issue of safety of a conviction in the same way as the European Court of Human Rights. The last word at the time of writing appears in *R. v. A.* (2001), discussed in depth in the Chapter on human rights. It went further than these cases. The House of Lords held that a breach of Article 6 will *always* result in a conviction being unsafe.

The Nature of an Appeal to the Court of Appeal

It is important to understand that the Court of Appeal does not provide   **10-051**
a rehearing in criminal cases, unlike an appeal from a magistrates' court to the Crown Court. The limited powers of the Court of Appeal were spelt out in the successful appeal of the Birmingham Six in 1991, *R. v. McIlkenny and Others*, in a judgment read out by the judges in turn:

> "Nothing in section 2 of the Act, or anywhere else obliges or entitles us to say whether we think that the appellant is innocent. This is a point of great constitutional importance. The task of deciding whether a man is innocent or guilty falls on the jury. We are concerned solely with the question whether the verdict of the jury can stand. Rightly or wrongly (we think rightly) trial by jury is the foundation of our criminal justice system. . . . The primacy of the jury in the criminal justice system is well illustrated by the difference between the Criminal and Civil Divisions of the Court of Appeal. . . . A civil appeal is by way of rehearing of the whole case. So the court is concerned with fact as well as law. . . . It follows that in a civil case the Court of Appeal may take a different view of the facts from the court below. In a criminal case this is not possible . . . the Criminal Division is perhaps more accurately described as a court of review."

Further, the Court of Appeal may substitute a conviction for an alternative offence, or order a retrial, where it feels this is required by the interests of justice.

Retrials

10-052 A retrial has only been available since 1964. There are arguments for and against retrials. A retrial is preferable for the accused over an outright dismissal of his appeal. At least he gets another chance. On the other hand it is said retrials may be tainted by publicity, as the jury may have developed their own opinions over the first trial or appeal in a high profile case. This was unsuccessfully argued as inherently unsafe, in *Stone* (2001, CA). The Court of Appeal held that, following the successful appeal against conviction by Michael Stone for the highly publicised murder of Lin and Megan Russell, the question whether a retrial should be ordered where there had been extensive publicity had to be decided on a balance of probabilities whether he would suffer serious prejudice to the extent that no fair trial could be held. Stone was retried in 2001 and convicted by a second jury.

Also, the witnesses' memories will have faded and the element of surprise in cross-examination will be lost, as all witnesses will have become familiar with all the evidence. A retrial gives both prosecution and defence the opportunity to strengthen their case. One omission from the Act is that the power to order retrials under the 1968 Act, section 7 is left untouched, despite considerable debate, in the Royal Commission and elsewhere, over the circumstances in which it is appropriate to order a retrial. See Smith, 1995.

Attorney-General's References

10-053 The Attorney-General may, under the Criminal Justice Act 1972, refer a point of law to the Court of Appeal, on behalf of the prosecution, following an acquittal. The Court of Appeal simply clarifies the law for the future, leaving the acquittal verdict untouched. The point may then be referred to the House of Lords.

Appeals on Sentence

10-054 The defendant may appeal against the sentence imposed by the Crown Court to the Court of Appeal who may substitute any other sentence or order within the powers of the Crown Court, provided it is not more severe than originally. The Criminal Justice Act 1988, section 36 gives the Attorney-General new prosecutorial power to refer any "unduly lenient" Crown Court sentence to the Court of Appeal, who then have the power to quash it and substitute any sentence within the Crown Court's powers. This applies to indictable and some either way offences. The Attorney may then refer any such decision of the Court of Appeal up to the House of Lords.

Shute published an analysis of these appeals in 1989–1997 which disclosed that a disproportionate percentage of reviewed sentences had been imposed at the Old Bailey. The Old Bailey (Central Criminal Court) deals with some of the most notorious offenders in England and Wales.

Appeals to the House of Lords

A further appeal to the House of Lords is possible by the prosecution **10-055** or the defence but only if the Court of Appeal certifies that the case reveals a point of law of general public importance and either that court or the House of Lords grants leave (permission). There are very few criminal appeals heard by the House of Lords each year. There were six in 2000. In 2001, Auld L.J. suggested reconstituting the Court of Appeal and improving its procedures.

8. Post-Appeal: Resolving Miscarriages of Justice

Until 1996, the Home Secretary had power to refer cases to the Court **10-056** of Appeal but would not normally do this unless all avenues of appeal had been exhausted and there was fresh evidence upon which the Court of Appeal might decide that the conviction was unsafe and unsatisfactory (1968 Act, s.17). For example, this power was used in 1987 to refer the convictions of the Birmingham Six to the Court of Appeal and again in 1991.

The Royal Commission on Criminal Justice 1993, paying heed to the multitude of critics who complained that the Home Secretary was too reluctant to use his power to refer, recommended that it should be replaced by that of a criminal cases review authority, whose job it would be to investigate miscarriages of justice, in cases referred to them by the Court of Appeal, or drawn to their attention in other ways. Following this recommendation, section 17 was duly repealed in the 1995 Act, which created a Criminal Cases Review Commission (ss.8–25). The Commission is a body corporate, independent of Government, whose 11 members are appointed by the Crown on the advice of the Prime Minister. One third of them must be lawyers and two thirds must be experienced in the criminal justice system.

Under section 9, they have a very broad power to refer any conviction or sentence at any time after an unsuccessful appeal or a refusal of leave, to the Court of Appeal. The condition for their making a reference is that they "consider there is a real possibility that the conviction, verdict, finding or sentence would not be upheld" because of an argument or evidence not raised in the convicting court or an argument, point of law or information not raised prior to sentence. Section 13(2) provides an even wider power to refer any case which does not satisfy those conditions, in exceptional circumstances. When deciding whether to refer, the Commission has a duty to take account of representations made to them and they have wide investigatory powers. They may seek the Court of Appeal's opinion, direct an investigation by the police or any other relevant public body, require the production of documents, reports or opinions or undertake any inquiry they consider appropriate.

The 1995 Act preserves the prerogative power to pardon a convicted individual. This is a residual monarchical prerogative, exercised traditionally by the Home Secretary and section 16 gives him the power to refer any case under his consideration to the Commission for their opinion.

Critiques of the CCRC

10-057   For immediate critiques of the statutory powers of the CCRC see Malleson and Nobles and Schiff. Concern was expressed over the fact that the Commission would be using the police to investigate miscarriages of justice, some of which will have been caused by police malpractice. Modern examination of the working of the Commission and further critiques of its powers have more recently been made by James, *etc.*, and Duff. See now Nobles and Schiff 2000 and 2001.

The Commission reports on its work annually and the report can be obtained from its website. The Commission's first cases were 280 transferred from the Home Office and Northern Ireland Office when it started work in 1997 but it was rapidly swamped with over 3,000 in the next four years. It has only 57 staff and, despite an expansion from extra funding in 1998 its backlog is increasing. James *et al.* calculate that it receives four new cases per day while processing only two. Given the enormous backlog, the authors wonder, as I have always done, why precious resources have been prioritised towards clearing up wrongful hangings of those long dead, such as Derek Bentley, hanged in 1952, while possible innocents wait in prison for years. They examine suggestions made by the House of Commons Home Affairs Select Committee, in its 1998–1999 Report on the work of the Commission.

The most common critique of the statutory powers of the Commission, since its creation is that it is limited to referring cases where there is a "real possibility" the Court of Appeal will find the conviction unsafe. This seems to place the Commission in "an essentially dependent position" (Duff) and require them to apply "a parasitic standard" (Nobles and Schiff). The impact of this restriction is demonstrated in *R. v. Criminal Cases Review Commission, ex parte Porter* (1999, QBD). The applicant sought judicial review of a determination by the CCRC not to refer her case to the Court of Appeal because they considered it unlikely the Court would admit fresh evidence or quash her murder conviction. She argued that the Commission had sought to usurp the Court of Appeal's functions. In deciding on her case, and trying to predict whether the Court would be prepared to receive her fresh evidence, the Commission had reviewed a considerable number of Court of Appeal cases.

A Divisional Court led by Lord Chief Justice Bingham refused her **10-058** application, because applications to call fresh evidence depended on their peculiar facts and the CCRC had given detailed reasons for its view. Duff says this case shows the Commission is diverted from its principal task of investigating alleged miscarriages of justice into detailed analyses of the jurisprudence of the Court of Appeal in order to try and second guess its likely determination of a case, because of its anxiety to establish a "real possibility" that they will quash. Duff, a member of the Scottish CCRC, demonstrates, through hypothetical scenarios, just how difficult it can be for the Commission to decide on a reference. He is concerned at the over-legalistic approach of the English Commission, arguing that the members cannot have been expected to assess cases like lawyers, in, for instance, assessing the admissibility of evidence, because of the require-ment that some of them be laypeople. He suggests, for example, that where there is convincing *inadmissible* evidence of a miscarriage of justice, the CCRC should readily refer a case to the Home Secretary in the hope that he will apply the prerogative of mercy.

Between April 1997, when it started work, and October 2000, the Commission had made 100 referrals to the Court of Appeal. For the latest statistics on caseload, cases referred and outcome from the Court of Appeal, see the Annual Report on its website. Noteworthy cases con-sidered by the Commission receive a lot of press coverage (search *The Times* website or CD-Rom, for instance). At the time of writing, notori-ous cases considered by the Board and still pending are that of the A6 murderer James Hanratty, hanged in 1962, whose body was exhumed in 2000 for DNA tests and the case of Stephen Downing, sentenced for murder in 1973, as a semi-literate 17-year-old. The saddest aspect of this case, if the Court of Appeal ultimately accepts his conviction to be wrong, is that although his sentencing judge set a 17 year tariff, he spent a further ten years in prison because of his refusal to admit the offence.

In 2001, the Court of Appeal drew attention to what they perceive as a serious problem in interpreting the Commission's powers. In *R. v. Kansal*, they were clearly exasperated that the Commission had referred to them a 1992 conviction that was unsafe if Article 6 of the European Convention were applied. They thought they had no option but to declare the conviction unsafe but pointed out that asking them to apply the Convention retrospectively contradicted the normal approach of the Court of Appeal which was not to reopen convictions because of a change of the law since trial. Leaving aside the threat that they could be asked to reopen the convictions of Guy Fawkes and other historical figures, the consequences for the workload of the Court of Appeal and commission were alarming. For useful analyses of miscarriages of justice and the CCRC, see Nobles and Schiff 2000 and 2001.

The Royal Prerogative of Mercy

10-059   As explained above, the 1995 Act preserved this power, exercised by the Home Secretary, to release a sentenced prisoner. Jack Straw did this in 2000, where a prisoner in transit saved a life in a road accident.

9. More Effects of the Convention

10-060
- Defendants can use the Convention to challenge substantive law, as a defence, as an argument for a stay of proceedings as an abuse of process, to apply to quash an indictment, to found a submission of no case to answer and can use breach of Convention rights as a ground of appeal. Whether Article 6, fair trial, applied retrospectively caused a great deal of confusion in appeals until the House of Lords held in *R. v. Lambert* that Article 6(2) the presumption of innocence, did not apply to a conviction before the HRA 1998 Act came into force (October 2, 2000). On the other hand, the ECHR itself has applied the Convention retrospectively repeatedly. Examples are the cases on disclosure and on the privilege against self-incrimination.
- A hearing should be in public, unless there are pressing reasons to the contrary: *Riepan v. Austria* (2000).
- In *Gregory v. U.K.* (1997) the ECHR held the secrecy of jury deliberations did not render a trial unfair under Article 6. In this case, the jury had handed a note to the judge alleging that "racial overtones" had been shown by one of their members. The judge consulted both counsel and redirected the jury. The Court held that, in the absence of proof of actual or subjective bias, they had to consider the actions of the experienced trial judge who had observed the jury. The redirection had been sufficiently forceful, detailed and carefully worded to ensure the impartiality of the jury and dispel objective doubts.
- The above case does not resolve the problem of whether there is a breach of the Convention when the legal adviser (court clerk) retires with the magistrates. Opinion is currently divided between those of us who consider all advice should be given in open court and those justices' clerks and chief executives who consider this impossible. See further the new Practice Direction on the Role of the Clerk.

- On electronic surveillance, tapping and bugging, Article 8, guaranteeing the right to respect for private life, allows interference by the State only in limited circumstances, such as national security. The interference must be necessary and proportionate.
- On lawyer-client communications, the Court has held that the right to communicate in confidence is a basic right of Article 6(3)(c). This means police stations must allow detainees to speak to their lawyers in private over the telephone and our courts must consider how this affects seating arrangements in the courtroom and waiting areas in the court building.
- Adequate time and facilities to prepare for defence: the European Commission of Human Rights has held 17 days was sufficient to prepare for even a complex trial.
- On the right to legal representation, see the Chapter on legal services.
- Judgment is to be pronounced publicly and this right is unqualified. This means judgment has to be read in open court and publicly available: *Preto v. Italy* (1983).
- Costs: the refusal to order costs to a successful defendant violates the presumption of innocence in Article 6(2).
- Sentencing: the Convention has a significant impact on sentencing, which is outside the scope of this book. For example, controversy arose in 2001, when the Parole Board released on licence the killers of Jamie Bulger. This followed their application to the ECHR under Article 6 (*T and V v. U.K.*, 1999). Their trial judge, in 1993, fixed their sentence tariff at eight years, which was subsequently increased by the Home Secretary, Michael Howard to fifteen, because of "public concern". This was quashed in the High Court on judicial review but the Commission said the Home Secretary was not an "impartial" sentencer so this role was switched to the Lord Chief Justice, who fixed the tariff at eight years.
- The Court agreed that the formality and ritual of the Crown Court trial must have been intimidating and incomprehensible to 11-year-old children. Consequently, in 2000, the Lord Chief Justice issued a practice direction requiring that *youth trials* should take account of the age, maturity and development of the defendant. For instance, robes and wigs should not normally be worn. Further details of youth justice are outside the scope of this book.
- The Convention, not domestic law, determines whether proceedings are civil or criminal so default proceedings for fine and council tax defaulters will almost certainly be classed as criminal, despite contrary rulings by the English courts. The proceedings are argued to breach Article 6, as the magistrates' clerk acts as legal adviser to the justices as well as enforcement officer. The

Access to Justice Act 1999 shifts responsibility for fine enforcement from the justices' clerk to the chief executive but one court clerk could still be placed in this dual role. A challenge is pending before the ECHR: *Mort v. U.K.*

- Victims' rights: the Convention offers no specific rights. The Commission has held that it is not appropriate to recognise any role for a victim's family in sentencing a murderer, as they are not "impartial".

- The Youth Justice and Criminal Evidence Act 1999 was successfully challenged in the Court of Appeal within days of its coming into force. Section 41, which restricted the right of a rape defendant to question the sexual history of his alleged victim was found to be in breach of Article 6. On appeal to the House of Lords, their Lordships held that it was for the trial judge in each case to decide whether the proposed evidence and questioning were relevant and necessary for fairness. Incidentally, the same Act bans unrepresented defendants in rape cases from questioning victims. This has not been challenged.

- Delay: in *Howarth v. U.K.*, the ECHR found there had been a breach of the "reasonable time" requirement of Article 6(1), when proceedings lasted four years from arrest to sentencing appeal. This does not apply to delay between the commission of the crime and the prosecution, as can be seen from the multitude of child abuse cases since 1990, whose facts occurred in the 1970s or before. In *Att.-Gen.'s Ref.(No.2 of 2001)*, the Court of Appeal held that time started to run from when the defendant was charged or summonsed.

- Denial of a lawyer: the right to a fair trial is breached in advance of trial if the accused is detained without access to a lawyer for a long period. Here the accused was detained for over 24 hours before being given access to a lawyer: *Magee v. U.K.* (2000).

- Handcuffs: the LCD is concerned that when a prisoner is taken into court through a public area in handcuffs, there could be a breach of Article 3 (Prohibition of Torture: inhuman or degrading treatment).

- It was envisaged that the Convention would have the biggest impact in magistrates' courts. The LCD, in 2000, established a fast track group, to identify cases around the country which raised an important point. Justices' clerks and other legal advisers also have access to a human rights intranet. A group of defence lawyers has been formed to monitor human rights issues. It includes several lawyers' groups. The Law Officers set up an equivalent group for prosecutors.

- Because of the duty to give reasons, magistrates, whose courts are not courts of record, have started to give reasons for all their decisions. They have also recognised that these must specifically explain their decision. Tick-box reasons will not suffice so they now give fuller reasons for refusing bail than before 2000. *R. v. Denton* (2000, CA) held that a Crown Court judge should have given reasons. That had been a rule of English law for many years and was simply given added emphasis by Article 6.

- Bias: The Court must ascertain all the circumstances having a bearing on the suggestion of bias. It must then ask whether those circumstances would lead a fair-minded and informed observer to conclude that there was a real possibility or a real danger) the two being the same) of bias: *Re Medicaments and Related Classes of Goods (No.2)* (2001, CA).
- Trial in the absence of the defendant. Taking account of Convention and domestic cases, rules have been laid down in *R. v. Hayward* (2001, CA). See also *Purvis* (2001, CA).

10. Reform of Criminal Procedure

The Royal Commission on Criminal Procedure

A Royal Commission on Criminal Procedure reported in 1981 and many of its recommendations have been enacted. The Prosecution of Offences Act 1985, instituted a Crown Prosecution Service in place of prosecution by the police and the Police and Criminal Evidence Act 1984 introduced a comprehensive code of police powers and practices in the investigation of crime and amended the rules of evidence in criminal proceedings in certain respects. **10-061**

Royal Commission on Criminal Justice

In 1991, in response to public anxiety over a well-publicised series of miscarriages of justice, overturned by the Court of Appeal, including the cases of "The Guildford Four", "The Birmingham Six", the Maguires and others, which reflected very badly on the fairness of the English system of pre-trial procedure, trial and appeal, the Home Secretary and Lord Chancellor appointed a Royal Commission on Criminal Justice (RCCJ), which reported in 1993. Its terms of reference were to examine the effectiveness of the criminal justice system in securing the conviction of the guilty and the acquittal of the innocent and to examine in particular: **10-062**

1. the supervision by senior officers of police investigations;
2. the role of the prosecutor in supervising the gathering of evidence and arrangements for its disclosure to the defence;

3. the role of experts and the forensic science services;
4. access to experts and legal services by the defence;
5. the accused's opportunities to state his case;
6. the powers of the courts in directing proceedings, including the possibility of their having an investigative role during and pre-trial; uncorroborated confession evidence;
7. the role of the Court of Appeal;
8. arrangements for investigating miscarriages of justice when appeal rights have been exhausted.

The Commission decided against importing inquisitorial elements from foreign systems. They commissioned a great deal of research into the workings of the English and foreign criminal processes and examined many aspects of our system, from the point of police investigations, to the post appeal process. They made 352 recommendations, too many to summarise here, although most of the recommendations relevant to this book are discussed above. Some of their proposals were very far reaching and it is said that if they are all effected, they will tip the scales of justice in favour of the prosecution. Many recommendations have already provoked legislation, although not always in line with the Commission's wishes. Examples of this are certain sections of the Criminal Justice and Public Order Act 1994, the Criminal Appeal Act 1995 and the Criminal Procedure and Investigations Act 1996. Changes in practice have also followed, such as those required by the practice directions on plea and directions hearings.

The Human Rights Act 1998

10-063   This has had the biggest impact of any recent reform of criminal procedure as should be obvious from this Chapter and the Chapter on human rights.

Modernising the Crown Court

10-064   The Court Service, the independent agency which administers the Crown Court, produced a consultation paper in 1999, *Transforming the Crown Court*, with proposals to streamline Crown Court business and hearings. This was followed by a mandate, in 2000. One of the stated aims is to carry out 100 per cent of court service functions electronically, where possible, by 2008. It promises that the courtroom will be revolutionised by IT to support there oral presentation of evidence, by video links and on screen and the electronic recording of proceedings. As an effort to enhance "customer service", information and services will be increasingly available online and via call centres 24 hours a day and technology will be used to reduce the stress of court appearances for defendants and witnesses. The new central summoning system for jurors is part of these reforms (see Jury Chapter). They aim to reduce the unit cost of a Crown Court case and

210

reduce the time taken from transfer to the Crown Court to disposal, by improving case management. The new IT systems are being piloted at the Crown Court at Kingston from 2001 to 2005. Lord Justice Brooke, known for his keenness on IT, represents the judiciary in both the Modernising the Civil Courts and Modernising the Crown Court programme.

The Criminal Justice System Business Plan 2001–2002 announced a £525 million spending plan to effect these reforms in the Crown Court and similar reforms to victim and witness services and in reducing delay in the magistrates' courts.

Fraud trials are now being conducted as paperless trials, with all documentation scanned in and displayed electronically. The most famous example was the Maxwell trial, which took place in the special fraud trial suite of the Old Bailey in Chichester Rents, Chancery Lane.

The Criminal Courts Review and *Criminal Justice: The Way Ahead*

As described in the Chapter on criminal courts, Lord Justice Auld was given the task in 2000–2001, of reviewing the structure and procedures of the criminal courts. See his terms of reference on his website and look for his 2001 report there. Much of his Review recommends a rethinking of procedure.

10-065

In their 2001 white paper and the Queen's speech of the new administration in June 2001, the Government outlined plans to introduce Bills on a number of reforms to criminal procedure and evidence, some of which are listed above. Lord Justice Auld, somewhat annoyed about the pre-empting of his report, is hoping that they will heed suggestions before finalising their plans.

FURTHER READING ON CRIMINAL PROCEDURE

Archbold, published by Sweet and Maxwell, annually. This is probably the most comprehensive practitioner's manual on criminal procedure, mainly in the Crown Court.

10-066

Stone's Justices Manual, Butterworths. This annual multi-volume publication is the equivalent of *Archbold* for magistrates' court cases.

Blacksone's Criminal Practice.

J.R. Spencer, "The Case for a Code of Criminal Procedure" [2000] Crim.L.R. 519, which also gives a great potted history of trial procedure and references to excellent historical sources.

The Royal Commission on Criminal Justice Report, Cm. 2263 (1993).

Home Office:www.homeoffice.gov.uk.

Home Office, *Review of Delay in the Criminal Justice System*, 1997 (The Narey Report) See website.

N. Walker, "What does fairness mean in a criminal trial?" (2001) 151 N.L.J. 1240.

B. Emmerson and A. Ashworth, *Human Rights and Criminal Proceedings* (1999).

Human Rights Unit for the 1998 Act, the Convention, legal updates and excellent links: www.homeoffice.gov.uk/hract/.

The Criminal Courts Review website: www.criminal-courts-review.org.uk.

Burrow, "Bail and Human Rights" (2000) 150 N.L.J. 677.

Law Commission website www.lawcom.gov.uk.

Crown Prosecution Service, information 020 7796 8442, website: www.cps.gov.uk.

D. Calvert-Smith (2000) 150 N.L.J. 1494. See also O'Doherty, (2000) 164 J.P. 932.

M. Burton, "Reviewing Crown Prosecution Service decisions not to prosecute" [2001] Crim.L.R. 374.

P. Darbyshire, "The Mischief of Plea Bargaining and Sentencing Rewards" [2000] Crim.L.R. 895.

Attorney-General's Guidelines on the Acceptance of Pleas, December 2000, Legal Secretariat to the Law Officers' website, www.lslo.gov.uk.

S. O'Doherty "Indictable only offences—the new approach" (2000) 150 N.L.J. 1891 (on s.51).

The Criminal Procedure and Investigations Act 1996 and *Explanatory Memorandum* (Home Office).

The Attorney General's Guidelines on Disclosure (2000) www.lslo.gov.uk.

Murray (1996) 146 N.L.J. 1288; Leng [1995] Crim. L.R. 704; Redmayne (1997) 60 M.L.R. 79.

P. Plowden and K.Kerrigan, (2001) 151 N.L.J. 735, on disclosure.

A.J. Ashworth, comments on *Rowe and Davies v. U.K.* and *Jasper v. U.K*; *Fitt v. U.K.* [2000] Crim.L.R. 584.

N. Padfield, "Plea Before Venue" (1997) 147 N.L.J. 1369.

Judicial Studies Board website, includes all specimen directions to juries: www.cix.co.uk/~jsb.

D. Birch, "Suffering in Silence: A Cost–Benefit Analysis of section 34 of the Criminal Justice and Public Order Act 1994" [1999] Crim.L.R. 769.

Condron v. U.K. [2000] Crim.L.R. 679 and *Averill v. U.K.* [2000] Crim.L.R. 682 and Ashworth's comments thereon.

A. Jennings, A. Ashworth and B. Emmerson, "Silence and Safety: The Impact of Human Rights Law" [2000] Crim.L.R. 879.

M. Zander, "Silence in Northern Ireland" (2001) 151 N.L.J. 138, on Jackson's research.

R. Pattenden, "Prosecution Appeals Against Judges' Rulings" [2000] Crim.L.R. 971, discussing Law Com. Consultation Paper 158 (2000).

B. Block, *etc.*, " Ordered and Directed Acquittals in the Crown Court: A Time of Change" [1993] Crim.L.R. 971.

J. Baldwin, "Understanding Judge Ordered and Judge Directed Acquittals" [1997] Crim.L.R. 536.

Reports on the collapse of the Leeds footballers' trial: *The Times*, April 10, 2001.

J. Hall, "Hung Juries and Retrials" *Archbold News*, June 27, 2001.

JUSTICE, *Miscarriages of Justice*, 1989.

J.C. Smith, "The Criminal Appeal Act 1995: (1) Appeals Against Conviction" [1995] Crim.L.R. 920. Also, comment on *Rajcoomar* [1999] Crim.L.R. 728. and see his comments on *Chalkley* (1999) and *Mullen* (1999).

A.J. Ashworth, comment on *R.v. Davis, Johnson and Rowe* [2000] Crim.L.R. 1012.

S. Shute, "Who Passes Unduly Lenient Sentences?" [1999] Crim.L.R. 603.

M. Berlins, "Do We Need Two Appeal Courts" 1 *Poly Law Review* 1.

K. Malleson at "The Criminal Cases Review Commission: How Will It Work?" [1995] Crim. L.R. 929.

A. James, N. Taylor and C. Walker, "The Criminal Cases Review Commission: Economy Effectiveness and Justice" [2000] Crim.L.R. 140.

P. Duff, "Criminal Cases Review Commissions and Deference to the Courts: The Evaluation of the Evidence and Evidentiary Rules" [2001] Crim.L.R. 341, examining the arguments of Nobles and Schiff at (1995) 58 M.L.R. 299.

Annual Reports of the CCRC from their website: www.ccrc.gov.uk.

R. v. Criminal Cases Review Commission, ex parte Pearson [1999] Crim.L.R. 732, including comment by Sir John Smith.

Report House of Commons Home Affairs Committee Session 1998–1999, *The Work of the Criminal Cases Review Commission.*

Newspaper reports of alleged miscarriages of justice and editorial on Downing, (2000) 164 Justice of the Peace 909.

M. McConville and L. Bridges (eds), *Criminal Justice in Crisis* (1994): the fullest and best collection of critiques of the Royal Commission on Criminal Justice.

Criminal Justice System website (see annual reports): www.criminal-justice-system.gov.uk.

Criminal Justice: The Way Ahead (2001). See LCD website.

R. Nobles and D. Schiff, "The Criminal Cases Review Commission: Reporting Success?" (2001) 64 M.L.R. 280.

FURTHER READING ON MISCARRIAGES OF JUSTICE

On individuals:

(1994) 144 N.L.J. 634; (1996) 146 N.L.J. 1552; (1999) 149 N.L.J. 1017; (1998) 148 N.L.J. 667; (1998) 148 N.L.J. 1028, Woffinden, *The Times*, June 2, 1998; D. Jessel, *The Guardian*, November 19, 1996.

On Derek Bentley: D. Pannick, *The Times*, February 11, 1997.

10-067

Hanratty: B. Mahrendra, (2001) 151 N.L.J. 883.

On the Birmingham Six: *Counsel*, April 1991, p.8; (1990) 140 N.L.J. 160; L. Blom-Cooper, *The Birmingham Six and Other Cases* (1997, resulting in libel actions by the Birmingham Six).

Guildford Four: *Legal Action*, December 1989, 7; (1989) 139 N.L.J. 1441; (1989) 139 N.L.J. 1449.

The Winchester Three: (1990) 140 N.L.J. 164.

The Maguires: *The Times*, July 17, 1990 and other press coverage.

Stephan Kisko: *The Times*, February 18, 1992.

The Bridgewater Three: *The Times*, February 22, 1997 and other newspapers; *R. v. Home Secretary, ex parte Hickey and Others* (1997).

Generally:

JUSTICE, *Miscarriages of Justice*, 1989; *Remedying Miscarriages of Justice.*

Kirkby J., *Miscarriages of Justice—Our Lamentable Failure?* (1991, Child and Co. lecture, Inns of Court School of Law).

R. Buxton, "Miscarriages of Justice and the Court of Appeal" (1993) 109 L.Q.R. 66.

B. Woffinden, *Miscarriages of Justice.*

D. Jessel, *Trial and Error.*

R. Nobles and D. Schiff, *Understanding Miscarriages of Justice* (2001).

On victims, not dealt with in this Chapter: J. Broadhead, (2001) 151 N.L.J. 803 and see *Criminal Law Review* index.

11. The Adversarial Process

A contrast used to be drawn between the English legal system as "adversarial" and continental European systems, daughters of the French legal system as "inquisitorial". As we shall see, that comparison is far too crude and is now inaccurate. Many historians and sociologists attribute the rise of the adversarial procedure to the rise of lawyers, in the eighteenth century. The adversarial model of procedure, in its purest form incorporates the following elements.

11-001

1. The Judge as Unbiased Umpire

It used to be said that the essence of the role of the English judge, or magistrate, is that she acts as an unbiased umpire whose job it is to listen to evidence presented by both sides, without interfering in the trial process. This was often contrasted with the role of the *juge d'instruction*, the French first instance judge who performs an inquisitorial role in some trials, directing criminal investigations, cross-examining the defendant and compiling a dossier of evidence for the trial court. There is no comparable English equivalent. The court takes a much greater role in compiling the evidence and is involved at an earlier stage in the process. Similarly, the role of the German judge is to take an active part in the assembling of evidence and the questioning of witnesses, before and at trial. This is a rather crude comparison, not least because the European Convention on Human Rights provides that a fair trial must be adversarial and continental European jurisdictions have embraced the Convention in their law much longer than the United Kingdom. It used to be said that the English judge's role, especially in the civil trial as a non-interfering umpire, is a reflection of the English sense of fair play: each side has an equal opportunity to win the litigation "game" by convincing the judge of the merits of their argument, collecting good evidence and citing favourable case

11-002

authorities. The judge does not interfere in the presentation of evidence by examining and cross-examining witnesses. This is left to the parties or their advocates. The role of the judge was set down clearly by Lord Denning M.R. in *Jones v. National Coal Board* (1957, CA) and can be summarised thus: he should:

1. listen to all the evidence, only interfering to clarify neglected or obscure points;
2. see that advocates behave and stick to the rules;
3. exclude irrelevancies and discourage repetition;
4. make sure he understands the advocates' points;
5. at the end, make up his mind where the truth lies. If the judge interferes unduly in the advocates' speeches or adduction of evidence, it may constitute a ground of appeal. For a new statement on the judicial role in criminal cases, see *R. v. Tuegal* (2000, CA).

The parties controlled the evidence

The parties brought whatever evidence they saw fit to prove their case. The court would seldom limit it. Similarly, the parties would decide which and how many witnesses to call. The parties were able to "keep their cards close to their chest" pre-trial, which was sometimes likened to "trial by ambush". This, plus the complexity of English procedural rules, plus the rigid adduction of evidence by examination and cross-examination, meant that unrepresented parties were at a disadvantage and it was often the case that the best lawyer won.

The best case wins

It was said that the court's job was to determine the relative strength of the parties' cases, not to determine where the truth lay.

The principle of orality

Most cases were argued by word of mouth, from start to finish. This was a relic of jury trial but was elevated to the level of principle.

2. Erosion of the Adversarial Process

11-003   The last quarter of the twentieth century saw an erosion of this archetype at work in the English legal system:

- During 1991–1993, The Royal Commission on Criminal Justice considered whether the court should have an investigative role before and during the criminal trial. They did not recommend this but that:

"Wherever practicable in complex cases judges should take on responsibility for managing the progress of a case, securing its passage through the various stages of pre-trial discussion to preparatory hearing and trial and making sure that the parties have fulfilled their obligations both to each other and to the court." (Recommendation 254) and the 1995 practice direction on Plea and Directions Hearings in the Crown Court, described above, goes some way towards this aim.

- the Heilbron-Hodge Committee (1993) and Lord Woolf (1996) recommended an interventionist role for the civil trial judge and active case management is now the hallmark of civil procedure, with the judge controlling the speed and length of the civil case, limiting the evidence presented. For an excellent and entertaining analysis of the implications of this change in the judicial role see Mr Justice Lightman at (1999) 149 N.L.J. 1819.
- The interim report of the Civil Justice Review (1986) prompted the courts to require, by practice directions, that the parties exchanged witness statements, forcing them to lay some of their cards on the table. Openness was massively enhanced by the requirement for skeleton arguments and bundles to be exchanged and presented to the court.
- Skeleton arguments, bundles and use of witness statements have made a massive shift from oral case argument to arguments on paper with the judges and opposition reading pre-trial. No longer can a student observe court proceedings and expect to be entertained to a full story being told to the court. Oral argument has been limited in the United States since 1849 but until the 1990s, counsel dictated the length of trials by simply giving an estimate to the court. The Court of Appeal first introduced a requirement for skeleton arguments in 1989. See the comparative account of Leggatt L.J.
- In civil cases, since the new Rules have been in force, parties frequently share a single expert. Nevertheless, a judge (and jury) will still frequently find themselves having to decide between two experts in a criminal case (for example on psychiatric or forensic evidence). It may lead to a vital witness not being called who would have given penetrating evidence against both sides.
- Jolowicz considers that most judges want to do substantive justice in the case (get to the truth), not just procedural justice and that the Woolf reforms will help them to realise that objective, which is to be welcomed ((1996) C.J.Q. 198).
- Small claims in the county court have always been an exception to the adversarial stereotype. Research by Applebey (1978) showed some registrars (now called district judges) employed an

217

inquisitorial technique. Many of those who appear are unrepresented and, therefore, the progress of the case depends on the district judge being somewhat interventionist. The Civil Justice Review (1998) recommended that registrars (now district judges, since 1990) adopt a more standardised inquisitorial role in small claims.

* The plight of the unrepresented in criminal cases has been well documented in socio-legal research (Dell (1971); Carlen (1976); Darbyshire (1984)). Where a defendant is unrepresented, mostly in the magistrates' courts, he is wholly dependent on the goodwill and expertise of the bench or, more realistically, the clerk, to help him put his case and examine witnesses and explain what is being asked of him, for example, choice of venue in a triable-either-way offence. Some clerks are much more prepared and skilled to help than others.

11-004   Unrepresented parties in civil proceedings, known as litigants in person, have become a cause of concern in the 1990s. Their numbers are increasing, most probably because of the lack of availability of legal aid or its replacement. There were 88,000 litigants in person in 1999. This slowed proceedings, especially in the High Court. An example was the "McLibel" trial, the longest libel trial in legal history (1995–1996), where McDonald's burger chain sued two unrepresented defendants. High Court and Court of Appeal judges have become so concerned about their prevalence that they convened a working party, under Otton L.J., which reported in 1995. Their report points to the disadvantages suffered by litigants in person. They encourage the development of services offered by solicitors and barristers and they urge the Lord Chancellor to enhance the funding of the Citizens' Advice Bureau in the Royal Courts of Justice and to give serious consideration to the needs of such litigants. The Supreme Court has since taken further measures to assist them. For instance, in late 1995, a new Chancery Guide was issued, which includes a section specifically designed to help them and point them in the direction of further assistance. Lord Justice Otton initiated the introduction of judicial assistants to help judges research the law in cases where one or both parties was unrepresented. See further Applebey above. Since the Magistrates' Courts Act 1980, the court has been under a duty to help the unrepresented party, in family proceedings, to present their evidence.

FURTHER READING ON THE DEMISE OF THE ADVERSARIAL TRADITION

Leggatt L.J., "The Future of the Oral Tradition in the Court of Appeal" [1995] Civil Justice Quarterly 1.

12. Alternatives to the Civil Courts: Institutions and Procedures

This Chapter deals with alternative hearings for civil disputes, outside the court system. There is a big difference between the two sets of alternatives, however. With tribunal systems, Parliament has decided that certain disputes will not go to court but to an alternative forum. The litigant has no choice. With arbitration and ADR, on the other hand, it is the litigants who have chosen to use an alternative.

12-001

1. Tribunals

Function

Outside the court system, 130 bodies and sets of tribunals adjudicate on specialist civil disputes (*Review of Tribunals* website, 2000). They have a much greater caseload than the civil courts. The largest hears over 300,000 cases a year. Lord Irvine said they have "a colossal impact on the lives of well over 470,000 people every year" (speech to the Council on Tribunals conference, 2000, Press Notice 158/00, Lord Chancellor's Department (LCD) website and see annual *Judicial Statistics* for those for which the LCD is responsible, LCD website). They are sometimes referred to as "administrative tribunals", because many of them hear appeals by the citizen against an administrative decision, or, like the Civil Aviation Authority, they take the initial decision. As the State grew, throughout the twentieth century, through statutory schemes of administration, tribunals were created by those statutes. Tribunal systems exist to deal with agriculture, (*e.g.* Agricultural Lands Tribunal), regulating commerce, (*e.g.* Data Protection Tribunal, Financial Services Tribunal),

12-002

education, (*e.g.* Admission Appeals Panels, Special Educational Needs Tribunal), employment, (*e.g.* Employment Tribunals), land, (*e.g.* Lands Tribunal), social security and pensions, (*e.g.* Appeals Tribunals, Pension Appeal Tribunals), health, (*e.g.* Mental Health Review Tribunals, Vaccine Damage Tribunal) and taxation, (*e.g.* General Commissioners of Income Tax) and many other miscellaneous matters. Some of them deal with disputes between private citizens. Employment Tribunals hear employees' claims against employers, relating to unfair dismissal, redundancy and discrimination and Rent Assessment Committees hear landlord-tenant disputes. These are more like court-substitutes and there is no logical reason why the county court should not have been given this jurisdiction.

Characteristics

Creation

12-003   All tribunals are creatures of statute. They were decided by the Franks Committee (1957) to be "machinery for adjudication", in other words, court-like bodies, not part of the administrative set-up. The Franks Report said they should be run according to the principles of "openness, fairness and impartiality".

Composition varies

Some are composed of a lawyer alone and some have a lawyer chair and two laypeople. Characteristics can change as has recently been the case with those dealing with immigration and asylum and social security. Where laypeople are used, they normally represent certain interests, such as employers in general and employees in general in the employment tribunals or expertise, such as tribunals which include doctors, psychiatrists (Mental Health Review Tribunals) or accountants. Appointments are often made by the relevant department but the Lord Chancellor appoints the legally qualified chairmen of over 14 tribunals and the lay members of some (details in judicial appointments section of LCD website and see job advertisements in the law section of *The Times*). The tribunal committee of the Judicial Studies Board provides some training (see JSB website).

Procedure

Some have procedural rules contained in statutory instruments. The Council on Tribunals, below, publishes a model. Others have none. The employment tribunals, in 2001, imported the overriding objective of the CPR into their new rules. Case loads vary enormously. Whereas the Appeal Tribunals under the Social Security Act 1998 hear over 100,000 cases a year, the Sea Fish Licence Tribunal and the Antarctic Act Tribunal usually hear none.

Organisation

They are all administered separately. Tribunals concerned with tax, **12-004** state benefits and health problems are organised on a national basis but those which hardly ever sit tend to be central. Some tribunals have never been constituted. For instance, no Mines and Quarries Tribunal has ever been convened, since provision was made for it in 1954. In some cases, the relevant government department is responsible for administration. The LCD has responsibility for several.

Appeal

From most tribunals, there is no appeal on fact, except those with an appellate level. For instance, appeal lies from the Immigration Adjudicators to the Immigration Appeal Tribunal. Appeal on a point of law lies to the High Court or Court of Appeal from the decisions of some tribunals under various statutes If a tribunal acts outside its powers (*ultra vires*) procedurally or by taking an unreasonable decision, an aggrieved party can apply for judicial review (see the Procedure Chapter).

The Council on Tribunals

This supervisory body was created on the recommendation of the **12-005** Franks Committee. It consists of 10 to 15 part-time lay members and has to report annually to Parliament on the operation of tribunals and inquiries. If the Council wishes, it can submit a special report to Parliament at any time. It investigates complaints from members of the public, instigates its own examination of the way in which the system is working and assists the central government departments which are responsible for the membership of tribunals and for the procedural rules under which tribunals and inquiries are held.

Advantages and Disadvantages

The early tribunal systems were established by Labour and Liberal **12-006** governments to keep disputes out of the courts and the grasp of Conservative or conservative judges whom they distrusted but both Labour and Conservative governments kept creating new tribunals with increasing frequency in the second half of the twentieth century, for which different reasons are now articulated. Professor Wade, in his authoritative text *Administrative Law*, claimed they were cheap, speedier and more accessible than the courts. (Harlow, 2001, below, challenges the claim to these advantages as partially inaccurate.) More specifically, benefits are said to be these: the costs are negligible; there are no court fees and people can supposedly manage without lawyers; tribunals can give a fixed date for the hearing in contrast to courts; procedure is meant to be informal; tribunal members can assist the parties; their jurisdiction is limited so members become specialists, compared with a district, circuit or QBD judge who must be a "jack-of-all-trades"; they involve laypeople as adjudicators, like magistrates and the jury, because many tribunals consist of a lawyer chairman and two laypeople with specialist expertise. They are not bound by precedent but those tribunals with an appeal level, such as employment and immigration, have developed their own specialist sets of law reports, which effectively act as precedents.

Critics of tribunals point to their informality, lack of visibility, lack of precedent and consequent unpredictability as endangering a fair hearing. Worse, legal aid (now called legal help and legal representation) had only been made available before four tribunals until 2000 (Commons Commissioners, Lands Tribunal, Mental Health Review Tribunals, Employment Appeal Tribunal) so people had to pay for a lawyer privately or represent themselves. This is unfair in those tribunals which have become very like courts, because of the frequent use of private lawyers and because they have developed their own case law, such as employment tribunals. Research (*e.g.* Genn and Genn, 1989) showed that being represented at a tribunal enhanced the appellant's chances of success. The Citizens Advice Bureaux complained, in 1995, that tribunals were neither expeditious nor free from technicality, as proponents claimed. The Human Rights Act 1998 has prompted the Lord Chancellor to authorise the Legal Services Commission to extend publicly funded legal representation to more tribunals. In 2000, it was extended to hearings before the immigration adjudicators and Immigration Appeal Tribunal and in 2001, he announced an extension to proceedings before the VAT and Duties Tribunal, the General and Special Commissioners of Income Tax and the Protection of Children Act Tribunal. The Lord Chancellor explained to the House of Lords, "where a tribunal is dealing with penalties which the courts have decided are criminal,within the terms of the European Convention on Human Rights, or where the appellant reasonably argues that the penalties are criminal, provision for legal assistance will be provided, where the interests of justice require it". See Harlow, cited below.

12-007   Ironically, some tribunals have become so courtlike they have lost any advantage over the courts so arbitration is starting to be offered as an alternative. For instance, from 2001, parties can opt out of the overcrowded employment tribunals and into a new ACAS arbitration scheme for simple unfair dismissal claims. Formal pleadings, jurisdictional arguments, complex legal issues and cross-examination are banned and lawyers have no special status. Interestingly, in response to some of these concerns, the rules of employment tribunals have been changed in 2001. There has been the insertion of the overriding objective, similar to that of the Civil Procedure Rules 1998, the extension of cases management powers (again like the civil justice reforms and power to penalise an advocate with a costs order, again like the civil procedure reforms). This is somewhat ironic.

It has often been pointed out that their administration and their clerks are usually from the department whose decision is being appealed against so they appear to lack independence. From time to time, critics have called for a unification of courts and tribunals, *e.g.* Legal Action Group Conference, 1990.

Many critics condemned as cost-saving measures the reorganisation of social security tribunals in the Social Security Act 1998. Oral hearings were reduced, despite government statistics which showed the applicant's chances of success were greater with an oral hearing. Three-person tribunals were cut down, meaning the elimination of laypeople (see Adler, (1999) 6 *Journal of Social Security Law* 99 and *Legal Action*, September 1997). Many more criticisms have been articulated in 2000–2001.

Official Reviews

Tribunals have developed piecemeal and numbers increased significantly since 1960. Governments have created new ones rather than add jurisdiction to an existing one. Their growth has been questioned by The Committee on Ministers' Powers (1932), the Franks Committee on Administrative Tribunals and Enquiries (1957) and they have been under review in 2001 by the *Review of Tribunals* (Leggatt Committee). The Franks Report led to the 1958 Tribunals and Inquiries Act, consolidated in the 1992 Act, now the key statute. The 1958 Act, as well as setting up the Council on Tribunals, ensured reasoned decisions, provision for appeals on points of law to the High Court, that chairmen of most tribunals should be drawn from a panel of lawyers and that, wherever possible, procedural rules should apply.

12-008

The 2000–2001 review was prompted by the "haphazard growth of tribunals, complex routes of appeal and the need for mechanisms to ensure coherent development of the law" (Lord Chancellor Irvine, speech to the Council on Tribunals Conference, 2000, press release 158/00). The Review's terms of reference (paraphrased) are to ensure that:

- there are fair, timely, proportionate and effective arrangements for handling disputes, within a framework that encourages systematic development of the law and forms a coherent structure, with the superior courts, for the delivery of administrative justice;
- arrangements conform with the ECHR;
- there are adequate arrangements for improving people's understanding of their rights;
- arrangements for funding and management are efficient and pay due regard to judicial independence;
- performance standards are effectively applied and monitored.

The Review body published a 2000 consultation paper (see website) and proposed a series of benchmarks against which the achievement of fairness should be tested: independence from departments; accessible and supportive systems; suitable jurisdiction; simple procedures; effective and suitable decision-making process; proportionate remedies; speed; authority and expertise and cost effectiveness. They invited comments on these in the contexts of the ECHR, devolution and the Government's *Modernising Government* programme (white paper, 1999). For their detailed questions and the responses (2000) see the *Review* website.

12-009   Adler and Bradley (in Partington, 2001) identify these problems:

1.   No appeal is provided from some administrative decisions, yet 24 tribunals under the supervision of the COT are unused.
2.   The manner in which new tribunals are established and existing ones changed for short-term administrative or political reasons (social security—see Adler above and recently immigration and asylum) and the inability of the COT to stop this.
3.   The poor resources of those with small caseloads for such activities as selection, monitoring and training of chairmen and members.
4.   The weakness of the COT compared with government departments. With their small secretariat, no research capacity, inability to produce complete statistics and sporadic pre-announced visits to a handful of tribunal hearings, they are ill-equipped to fulfil their statutory duty to "keep under review the constitution and workings of tribunals" (Tribunals and Inquiries Act 1992).

They examine various proposals for reform and describe two models of unified tribunal systems from Australia and Quebec. Robson had proposed to the Franks Committee (1957) an Administrative Appeal Tribunal, which could generate a set of general principles, enabling the system to be more simple and coherent. The Whyatt Report (1961) proposed a general tribunal, modelled on a Swedish one, to deal with complaints where there was no specialist tribunal. The JUSTICE-All Souls Report (1988) had, however, rejected an administrative appeal tribunal, because of the sheer volume of work of the various specialist tribunals. They examined the Australian Administrative Review Tribunal, under development in 2001, two-tiered, with the first comprising a number of specialist review tribunals and the second a specialist panel to review first tier decisions raising substantial questions of law or mixed fact and law. They also examined the Administrative Tribunal of Quebec, established 1996, which has four divisions. Adler and Bradley then set out their proposals: a Unified Appeal Tribunal (UAT) consisting of ten specialist divisions. Existing tribunals would be brought into its framework and any future tribunals would be added. There would be a right of appeal from all government discretionary decisions. Panels would always comprise a legally qualified person and laypeople or specialists. Standard procedural rules would apply. Selection and training would be unified. Some training would be generic, such as on the implications of the ECHR for tribunal hearings and other training would be specialist. The UAT would require accommodation in all centres of population. Common services, such as clerking, secretarial support, IT, libraries, and publicity would be provided in the tribunal building. The UAT would be able to commission research. Appeal should be available on a point of law to the courts from the upper tier of the UAT. They conclude:

> "Those who consider our proposal as altogether too ambitious and too radical might stop briefly to consider what the state of the ordinary courts would be like if there were as many specialised courts as there are tribunals and if, every time Parliament created some new private law rights or new regulatory offences, a new civil or criminal court were to be created."

Harlow (in Partington, 2001) examines the implications of the ECHR **12-010** and E.C. law for tribunals. She argues that the requirements of Franks, (openness, fairness, impartiality, reasons) differ little from Article 6(1). She examines in some depth whether various different tribunals are likely to be required by Article 6 to provide publicly funded representation. She remarks that the Strasbourg court has not been generous in attitude, manifest in its case law, on legal aid. Article 6 rights arise where a person's civil rights and obligations are in issue but it is not possible to predict what Strasbourg will classify as a civil right. She thinks English administrative justice may possess an advantage over the continental model of specialist administrative courts. French administrative court procedures have been found to be in breach of the Convention on a number of occasions, with the adjudicators held to be insufficiently independent of the executive. She examines what elements of inquisitorial procedure are acceptable under the Convention and doubts that the practice of chairmen to help unrepresented parties to put their case would pass challenge. An Independent Tribunal Service, she considers, would strengthen the independence of the system and make it less vulnerable to challenge.

Thompson (in Partington, 2001) would like to see us remodel the COT on the Australian Administrative Review Council, now under creation, and charge it with monitoring the administrative justice system as a whole, including judicial review by the courts. It would facilitate training in administrative decision-making, perform a public educative function and report to Parliament and the devolved legislative assemblies. After this book was written, the delayed Leggatt Report was published, called *Tribunals for Users One System, One Service*, 2001. It recommended a unified, independent, user-friendly system. There is not the space to summarise its 361 recommendations here. See the Tribunals Review website.

2. Arbitration

12-011   Arbitration was the nineteenth century merchants' alternative to the expense and delay of the High Court. Arbitration is classified by some as a form of ADR but, as it is more formal, applies the law and results in a legally binding decision, most specialist ADR writers exclude it. It means the reference of a dispute to a third party or parties to decide according to law but outside the confines of normal courtrooms or procedure.

Arbitration may arise in one of three ways:

1. *By reference from a court*
   A judge of the commercial court may refer a suitable case to arbitration or herself act as arbitrator. The Lands Tribunal has a statutory power to act as arbitrator by consent. The small claims procedure in the county court used to be called arbitration because of the informal conduct of the cases by the district judges.

2. *By agreement after a dispute has arisen*
   For instance, if a contract has broken down, the parties might agree to refer their dispute to an arbitrator.

3. *By contract*
   Contracting parties may agree that, in the event of a dispute arising under the contract, they will refer it to an arbitrator to be appointed by, say, the president of their trade organisation. Most standard construction contracts include such a clause and the relevant nominating authorities include the Royal Institute of Chartered Surveyors and RIBA. Such clauses are common in commercial contracts and insurance. Examine your own household or vehicle insurance policy if you want to see an example of an arbitration clause to which you are, unwittingly, a party.

An arbitrator may be a specialist lawyer or, more likely, a technical expert in the subject in dispute. The Chartered Institute of Arbitrators has around 9,700 members in 2001, mostly non-lawyers. It provides training leading to qualification. Arbitrations here are now governed by the Arbitration Act 1996, Order 73 and a 1997 Practice Direction. Section 1(a) states that the object of arbitration is "the fair resolution of disputes by an impartial tribunal without unnecessary delay or expense" and 1(b) continues that "the parties should be free to agree how their disputes are resolved, subject only to such safeguards as are necessary in the public interest". Section 33 imposes a general duty on an arbitrator to act fairly. The arbitrator has both the right and the duty to devise and adopt suitable procedures to minimise delay and expense. Section 34 gives her absolute power over procedure. Once parties have voluntarily and validly submitted to arbitration, the courts will not normally entertain one party if they try and ignore this agreement and make a court claim. The court will normally order a stay or stop of proceedings, under section 9. The arbitrator gives a reasoned decision which is enforceable in court. There are three grounds on which an award may be challenged in court: jurisdiction, serious irregularity and on a point of law. The Act has been subject to considerable interpretation in case law. There is not the space to review it here but all leading cases have been reported in law report series such as the *All Englands*. Because many foreign arbitrations are conducted in London, difficult issues of private international law can arise. An example is described at (2001) 151 N.L.J. 122. Case law on arbitration has also been generated in the European Court of Justice, such as *Van Uden*, Case C-391/95.

Most disputes in shipping or aviation are referred to arbitration, as are those of multinational corporations. They are common in oil, gas, banking, commodities, insurance and securities. Arbitrations are very big, lucrative business to London's lawyers and accompany the use of London as an international commercial centre. Domestically, a number of specialist schemes exist, such as Professional Arbitration on Court Terms, run by the Law Society and Royal Institute of Chartered Surveyors as an alternative to courts determining lease renewal terms and commercial rents and the Personal Insurance Arbitration Scheme, one of over 80 small claims schemes administered by the Chartered Institute of Arbitrators, to provide arbitration under domestic insurance contracts such as holiday or car insurance. Under this scheme, the insurer is bound by the arbitrator's award but if the insured does not like it, he can have a second bite of the cherry by making a claim in the courts. Examples of barristers, trained as arbitrators, offering their services commercially to litigants, are Dispute Resolution by Barristers ((1999) 149 N.L.J. 515), Western Circuit Arbitration and Arbitration for Commerce and Industry ((1998) 148 N.L.J. 739). In 1999, the Chartered Institute of Arbitrators launched the London Arbitration Scheme, with an attempt to keep the cost proportionate (20 per cent) to the subject of dispute. **12-012**

Many cross-border disputes arose through the construction of the channel tunnel, for instance, a £1 billion claim by Eurotunnel against Trans Manche Link but they were often resolved by arbitration conducted through the International Chamber of Commerce in Paris. Other international arbitration bodies include the London Court of International Arbitration, the London Maritime Arbitration Association as well as centres in New York, Geneva, Stockholm and Hong Kong. It is estimated that Paris has the most international arbitrations but, since the nature of arbitration is private, there are no statistics.

12-013   Arbitration became popular because it had the advantages of being swift, arranged at a date to suit the parties, cheaper than court proceedings and more private. Obviously, this is desirable where time is of the essence, (e.g. a dispute about liability for damage to a perishable cargo) or the parties do not want their commercial secrets exposed in the courtroom. Sampson (1997), however, argues that, because of lawyer domination, arbitration has become "a mirror image of litigation", with complex parallel procedures to civil litigation. He quotes Sir Thomas Bingham M.R.:

> "the arbitration process, by mimicking the processes of the courts and becoming over-legalistic and overlawyered has betrayed its birthright by allowing itself to become as slow, as expensive and almost as formal as the court proceedings from which it was intended to offer escape".

The 1996 Act was meant to reverse this process, by giving powers to enable arbitrators to force the pace of arbitration. The advantages offered by civil litigation in the courts are: if one party believes the other's case has no substance, she can ask for summary judgment; further parties can be added if necessary; the arbitrator has no power to consolidate arbitrations in a multi-party action. There was no legal aid for arbitrations but this difference may disappear.

3. Alternative Dispute Resolution

12-014   This has been the fashionable development of the 1990s. Many British lawyers, most notably Lord Chancellor Mackay, who favoured public funding for family mediation, then Lord Chancellor Irvine, now in office, have taken an active interest in this American import, as a means of avoiding the public and private expense and the private pain of litigation.

ADR can be defined as any method of resolving a legal problem without resorting to the legal process. Experts consider that any subject can be referred to ADR but advisability depends on the parties' attitudes. Here are some of the alternatives to conventional litigation:

Early Neutral Evaluation

A neutral professional, often a lawyer or judge, hears a summary of each party's case and gives a non-binding assessment of the merits, which can be used as a basis for settlement or negotiation. Since a 1996 Practice Statement, the Commercial Court judges can offer this to parties appearing before them.

Expert determination
An independent expert is appointed to decide and her decision is binding.

Formalised Settlement Conference
Described at (1995) 145 N.L.J. 383.

Mediation
A mediator helps both sides to come to an agreement which they can accept. It can be evaluative, where the mediator assesses the legal strength of a case or facilitative, where the mediator concentrates on assisting the parties to define the issues. If an agreement is reached it can be written down and forms a legally binding contract, unless the parties state otherwise. If not, traditional civil litigation is still open so proponents consider it a "no lose" option for a lawyer. Acland, an expert writer and ADR provider called it "simply negotiation with knobs on" (*Gazette*, November 1995, 8).

Conciliation
The conciliator takes a more interventionist role than a mediator, in bringing the two parties together and suggesting solutions to help achieve a settlement. Incidentally, mediation and conciliation have been used in China for centuries. The United Nations Commission on International Trade Law provides a set of model rules.

Med-arb
Is a combination of, where the parties agree to mediate but if no settlement is reached, the dispute is referred to arbitration. The mediator may turn into an arbitrator.

Mini Trial
The hiring of an independent person to give a non-binding decision on the issue. Hiring retired judges to do this is common in the U.S. The *Judge Judy* television programme is a somewhat crude example.

Neutral fact finding
This is a non-binding procedure used for complex technical issues. A neutral expert is appointed to investigate the facts and evaluate the merits of the dispute. It can form the basis of settlement or negotiation.

ADR is not suitable for every claim. For instance, where the parties refuse to speak to one another, or where, as in most cases, the defendant is silent and judgment is ordered in default to the claimant. It is ideal where the parties must continue in a relationship, such as neighbours or businesses. Also, it can save years of nit-picking argument, generating thousands of pounds of costs in multi-party commercial disputes.

The Growth of ADR, Thanks to the Judges

12-015   By 1989, ADR was highly developed in the USA (see Brown, 1989). By 1992, the Law Society announced it was a priority in their continuing education scheme and it was favoured in the Heilbron-Hodge report on civil litigation, the Woolf Report, 1996 and was promoted by Lord Chancellor Mackay in all his speeches and his green and white papers on legal aid in 1995 and 1996. The LCD published a booklet *Resolving Disputes Without Going to Court*, designed to explain ADR to litigants. Nevertheless, although it was much discussed in law journals from 1989 and, from 1990, firms started offering it commercially (Centre for Dispute Resolution and ADR Group), many lawyers had still not heard of it even by 1997. Also, as had occurred in the USA, lawyers were hostile to it, (Shapiro, 1997). Its promotion in the United Kingdom is attributed to judges (see below), in both countries. Big commercial solicitors' firms have at last been the first lawyers to catch on to ADR, with a 1997 survey of the 200 top property law firms showing that 70 per cent regarded mediation as effective. By 1998, ADR was becoming popular in disputes involving professional indemnity, construction, international and personal injury. The Government, still keen to promote ADR, has announced, in 2001, that it will use ADR whenever possible. ADR will be considered in all suitable cases. ADR clauses will appear in standard procurement contracts and flexibility is promised in reaching agreement in compensation claims. ADR trainers have found that most people wishing to be trained as mediators are now lawyers but they have to drop the habit of aggressive confrontation, typified by the adversarial litigator and adopt an empathetic approach to focus on the interests of the parties (*Gazette*, 1997).

ADR may be private or court-annexed and, as I mentioned above, since lawyers have been slow to use ADR, it has been left to the judges to devise schemes for it. In 1993, the Commercial Court announced in a Practice Note that the judges would encourage ADR in suitable cases and a second one in 1996 permitted a judge to stay (suspend) a case to enable the parties to try ADR. Such orders are now made in about 30 per cent of cases. It allows a judge to conduct an ENE. The 1995 Practice Note on case management in the QBD and the Chancery Division requires the parties' solicitors to certify whether they have considered resolving the dispute by ADR and discussed this with their client. From 1996, the London Patents County Court offered litigants the alternatives of expert arbitration or fast-track mediation. From 1997, legal aid was available for the Central London County Court mediation pilot scheme (see below) and a court-linked mediation scheme was commenced in Bristol. Now, the Civil Procedure Rules 1998, Rule 1, places a duty on the court, as part of its active case management, to encourage the parties to use ADR, if the court considers it appropriate. The Court of Appeal set up an ADR scheme, whereby invitations to participate in the scheme are sent out in almost all final appeals. Also, judges many encourage it of parties seeking permission to appeal. Our judges have shown a resistance to making references to ADR compulsory, unlike their American counterparts.

Acceptance of court-annexed schemes has been disappointing. From **12-016** November 1998 to March 1999, parties in 250 Court of Appeal cases were offered mediation but both sides agreed to mediate in only 12. A mediation scheme was offered, virtually cost-free, at Central London County Court from 1996, for all contested cases above the small claims limit. Hazell Genn evaluated the scheme after two years. She found that in only about five per cent of cases both parties accepted mediation. The joint demand for mediation was lowest where both parties were legally represented. Interviews with solicitors revealed:

- widespread ignorance of mediation among lawyers;
- apprehension about showing weakness;
- litigant resistance to compromise.

Of those who mediated, 62 per cent settled and the settlement rate was highest where neither party was legally represented. Average settlement amounts were £2,000 lower than non-mediated settlements. Solicitors felt mediation had saved time but there was a common view that failure to settle at mediation increased costs. Some of the most successful mediators were barristers. Among Genn's conclusions were that mediation can magnify power imbalances and works best where parties are roughly equal and demand for mediation is very weak and lawyers play a crucial role in influencing demand.

In 1999, a survey of the top 500 companies in the North West, 52 per cent of respondents said their solicitors had not discussed with them the possibility of resolving a dispute through mediation (see LCD discussion paper). See also Goriely and Williams, 1997.

In 1999, concerned at the lack of uptake of ADR, the Government **12-017** (LCD) published a discussion paper to try and ascertain why. Exploring the possible reasons, they conceded that it was not easy to find out about different ADR services. There was no central register. Surveys showed public awareness of trade association arbitration schemes, utility regulators and ombudsmen seldom reached 50 per cent. Levels of awareness of ADR must be much lower. The Department wondered if government should do more to promote it. The responses were published but there is only the space here to examine very little of them. Fifty-one per cent of respondents had found benefits of ADR in time, cost or convenience. Benefits cited were: preserving or rebuilding relationships between disputants, privacy, flexibility, informality, stress reduction, the enabling of a win-win scenario, innovative solutions, greater client participation and the ownership of the process. Most thought that government should do more to promote ADR but that it should not be obligatory. The Civil Justice Council responded (see their website). They warned that Article 6 of the ECHR means that access to the courts cannot be excluded and thought the time was not yet right for ADR to be obligatory. They urged "a major educational push" to attract a wider public to the benefits of ADR and they annexed to their paper an account of the Canadian Disputes Resolution Fund.

Nevertheless, a critical core of big law firms have been attracted to mediation, the most popular form of ADR, in non-family cases. S.J. Berwin offered ADR to their clients from 1997 (and see 1997 *Gazette*). A breakthrough came in 1998, when a case funded by the Law Society and ADR group successfully challenged the Legal Aid Board's refusal to fund non-family mediation. (Lord Mackay (1994) had been against legal aid for out-of-court ADR because that might imply that lawyers' participation was necessary and their presence might make ADR legalistic. Further, there was a need for processes to broaden the issues beyond the law.) Now mediation can be funded by the Legal Services Commission. Nevertheless, the biggest boost to ADR, especially mediation, is bound to come from its promotion by Rule 1 of the CPR. A 2000 MORI survey of 180 law firms showed that, since the rules had come into force the previous year, 54 per cent said they were more likely to have been involved in mediation. Statistics from private ADR firms showed a big rise in mediation. For instance, the Centre for Effective Dispute Resolution claimed that in 2000–2001, 27 per cent of their mediations were ordered by the courts.

In 2001, the National Audit Office is expressing concern about the soaring cost of claims against the NHS (billions of pounds). They are considering mediation or a no-fault compensation scheme as alternatives (*The Times*, June 12, 2001).

Mediation in Family Cases

12-018   The limited success that ADR has had so far is in the area of mediation. Family mediation services have been offered, at least since the 1980s, by local authorities, charities and by the mid-1990s, by lawyers trained for the job and sometimes government funded. By 1996, Lord Woolf became the patron of the British Association of Lawyer Mediators, the founders of which had recognised a new market, which they did not want to let slip out of lawyers' hands. Notice, again, the judicial encouragement of ADR. Hundreds of lawyers attended mediation courses. Even specialist barristers chambers started offering mediation direct to the public. Lord Mackay's ill-fated Family Law Act 1996, had it been fully implemented, would have required legally aided divorcing parties to attend an information meeting on mediation. In 1997–1999, 14 pilot schemes were launched and over 7,500 people attended information meetings but monitoring by Professor Gwynn Davies (see LCD website/research) showed disappointing results. Although 90 per cent of attendees found the meetings useful, only seven per cent went on to mediation and 39 per cent reported that the meeting made them more likely to seek legal advice. The information meetings, especially group meetings were insufficiently personal. Most people attended alone, yet many of the options described required the commitment of both spouses. (Comment: obviously if the other party paid for private legal advice, nothing could compel them to turn up to such a meeting, which I suggest was a stunning oversight of the promoters of the Act.) The Law Society complained that the pilots caused delays in obtaining legal aid and, in the interim, some parents were denied child contact. A leader in *The Times* (December 18, 2000) pointed out that since people usually thought long and hard before seeking a divorce, the offer of mediation was, by then, redundant. Consequently, Lord Irvine decided, in 1999, not to implement that part of the Act. Nevertheless, in January 2001, Lord Chancellor Irvine announced a Government advertising campaign to promote family mediation, as Professor Davies' final research report in 2000 had exposed a lack of public awareness. Family mediation is now funded by the Legal Services Commission.

FURTHER READING ON TRIBUNALS

Review of Tribunals (2000), LCD consultation paper, www.tribunals-review.org.uk. and final report *Tribunals for Users One System, One Services* by Sir Andew Leggatt, 2001, on same website. **12-019**

M. Partington (ed.), *The Leggatt Review of Tribunals: Academic Seminar Papers* (University of Bristol, 2001).

H.Genn and Y. Genn, *The Effectiveness of Representation at Tribunals* (1989).

The Council on Tribunals, www.council-on-tribunals.gov.uk.

R. White, as below, Chapters 14, 15 and 16.

FURTHER READING ON ARBITRATION

Arbitration Act 1996, explained in the Law Society's *Gazette*, February 5, 1997, p.35. **12-020**

T. Sampson (1997) 147 N.L.J. 261.

M.P .Reynolds, *Arbitration*.

M. Yuille, Law Society's *Gazette*, November 5, 1997, p.25.

and ADR

M. Zander, *The State of Justice* (2000), pp. 35–38. **12-021**

Lord Mackay of Clashfern, *The Administration of Justice* (1994), Chapter 4.

Civil Justice Review.

LCD, "Alternative Dispute Resolution: A Discussion Paper", 1999 and "Summary of Responses", both on LCD website.

Several authors, Law Society's *Gazette*, November 5, 1997.

H. Brown, *Gazette*, December 20, 1989.

A. Acland, *Legal Action*, November 1995, p.8.

D. Shapiro, (1997) 147 426.

N. Nicol, *Legal Action*, September 1997, p.6 (on access to ombudsmen).

A. Connerty, (1997) 147 N.L.J. 1686.

T. Goriely and T. Williams, "Resolving Civil Disputes: Choosing Between Out-of-Court Schemes and Litigation—A review of the literature" LCD, 1997, LCD website/research.

J. Smerin, *Gazette*, November 11, 1998.

District Judge M. Trent, (1999) 149 N.L.J. 410.

R. White, *The English Legal System in Action*, pp. 241–244.

H. Genn, "The Central London County Court Pilot Mediation Scheme Evaluation Report" LCD website: www.open.gov.uk/lcd/research and *Legal Action*, August 1997, p.6.

Civil Justice Council website: www.open.gov.uk/civjustice.

H. Brown and A. Marriott, *ADR Principles and Practice.*

Centre for effective dispute resolution website: www.cedr.co.uk.

M. Lind, "ADR and Mediation—boom or bust?" (2001) 151 N.L.J. 1238.

Part IV: Professionals in the Law

13. The Legal Profession

1. Barristers and Solicitors

The main characteristic of the English legal profession is that it is **13-001**
divided into two, barristers and solicitors. This makes it unusual but not
unique, in world-wide terms. For centuries, each side has enjoyed certain
protected monopolies in legal services but, since 1985, most of these have
been abolished by degrees. This and the significant changes in the structure of legal services, wrought by the Access to Justice Act 1999, have left
some members of the legal profession feeling insecure.

The barrister is usually thought of primarily as an advocate. Until
1990, barristers had the virtually exclusive rights of audience as advocates
before all the superior courts. They are known as "counsel". In total there
were, in 2000, 10,132 barristers in practice. Senior judges in the English
legal system have, until now, been drawn exclusively from the ranks of
experienced counsel

The solicitor can be an advocate in the magistrates' court and county
court and may, since the Courts and Legal Services Act 1990 (CLSA),
apply for rights of audience at all levels but she is more familiar to the
public in her role as a general legal adviser. In 1999, there were over
100,000 solicitors' of whom around 79,000 held practising certificates.

Members of the public are able to call at a solicitor's office and seek **13-002**
advice, whereas a barrister can at present only be consulted indirectly
through a solicitor, except by specified clients. The solicitor is sometimes
likened to a general practitioner and the barrister to a consultant.

The analogy must not be taken too far, however, since the legal knowledge of the newly qualified barrister will not equal that of the senior partners of a firm of solicitors. Sometimes, the solicitor is more of a specialist
than the barrister. A 1991 survey showed that most solicitors consider
themselves specialists.

Apart from the barristers and solicitors in private practice, a large number of lawyers are employed in central and local government, in commerce and industry and in education. For instance, in 2000, there were 2,627 employed barristers.

2. Training

Barristers

13-003   A would-be barrister must first register as a student member of one of the four Inns of Court, Gray's Inn, Lincoln's Inn, Inner Temple and Middle Temple. They are close to the Royal Courts of Justice in London. The Inns, to one of which every barrister must belong, originated as colleges teaching the common law to advocates.

Detailed regulations govern entry to the profession. The general pattern is for the student to obtain a law degree and thereafter to undergo the one-year Bar Vocational Course (BVA). This training is provided by the Council of Legal Education and, since 1997, by several universities. On satisfactory completion of the vocational course, students are called to the Bar by their Inn of Court. Graduates who do not have a law degree have to take and pass a one-year course, before proceeding to the BVC. Students are required to attend their Inn of Court to dine. This is a relic of the Inns' collegiate function. However brilliant the student, she cannot be called to the Bar unless she has eaten all of her 12 dinners.

After call to the Bar, the student has to undergo a process known as pupillage. This involves understudying a junior counsel in day-to-day practice for a period of 12 months. Students entering employment may undergo pupillage as an employee. From 2001 all barristers are required to undertake continuing professional development.

Solicitors

13-004   The usual method of entry is a law degree and then a one-year Legal Practice Course. Provision is made, however, for non-law graduates and mature students to qualify as solicitors by undergoing a one-year educational stage before the LPC. After this, the student must serve as a trainee in a firm of solicitors for two years. All solicitors must, since 1998, undergo regular "continuing provisional development" by attending non-examined training.

When the student has completed the training contract he may be "admitted" by the Master of the Rolls formally adding his name to the roll of officers of the Supreme Court. He may not practice without an annual practising certificate individually issued by the Law Society. In order to obtain a practising certificate the solicitor has to comply with very detailed regulations governing solicitors' accounts and be insured through a managing general agency or approved insurer.

Problems in Entering the Legal Profession:
Numbers, Cost and Discrimination

Entry to the profession is expensive and notoriously difficult for disad-   **13-005**
vantaged groups.

Numbers

Law graduates escalated in the 1990s, to over 12,500 per year. In
1999, 6,285 students enrolled on an LPC course. 4,827 new traineeships
were registered, (*Trends in the Solicitors' Profession*, 1999). More people qualify as solicitors than there are available training places. Research conducted by the Policy Studies Institute for the Law Society, tracking the
progress of 4,000 law degree and CPE graduates from 1993, showed
that, by 1997, 25 per cent of LPC graduates still did not have training
contracts. They found a bias against women, ethnic minority applicants,
those from new universities and from less privileged backgrounds, irrespective of academic performance. City recruits were 16 times more
likely to have graduated from Oxbridge than a new university, (*The Law
Student Cohort Study*). Non-whites have to make more applications than
their white counterparts. The 1999 Law Society Statistics show that 19.4
per cent of students enrolled in 1998–1999 were ethnic minority. Only
5.5 per cent of solicitors with practising certificates are minority. This is
partly because non-whites have only started entering the profession in
large numbers recently but also because of difficulties in entering the
profession. Of those entering the LPC in 1998, 75 per cent of whites but
only 45 per cent of minorities obtained a training contract. Attitudes of
the profession were attacked as favouring white males, by Cherie Booth
and senior minority solicitors, in 2000. Discriminatory attitudes were
exposed in *Discriminating Lawyers*, by Phil Thomas (2000). In 2001, a
scheme was launched by the Law Society, a charity, government and law
firms to help ethnic minority students find training places.

Entry to the Bar is more difficult. It is overcrowded, with many forced   **13-006**
out of practice. The workload of the criminal Bar (half the Bar) declined
in the 1990s and the Bar feared a reduction in civil work because of the
Access to Justice Act 1999. In 1998, there were 2,704 applicants through
the Bar's CACH clearing house for places on the BVC. One thousand,
four hundred and fifty were accepted. 1,842 applicants chased 800 pupil-
lages. (Not all sets of chambers offering pupillage participate in the PACH
scheme, 27 per cent taking applications direct.) Only a fraction of pupils
are taken on as practising tenants. Fewer than three per cent of those
graduating with a law degree or the CPE will secure a tenancy.
Discriminating Lawyers found that while 66 per cent of male Oxbridge graduates secured pupillage, only ten per cent from new universities did. Bar
statistics reveal a high turnover in the first five years (General Council of
the Bar *Annual Report*, 1997).

COST

In 2000, the average fee for the LPC or BVC was over £5,000. The PSI *Cohort* study showed that 64 per cent of LPC graduates had an average debt of £7,000, three years after finishing the course. Ironically, the PSI report found that professional sponsorship was most likely to go to those from well-off families. Seventy-four per cent of Oxbridge graduates received LPC funding, compared with 3 per cent from new universities. Sixty per cent of trainees were paid below the Law Society minimum, with the disabled, non-Oxbridge graduates and those from state schools paid the least.

At the Bar, things are worse. Local authority discretionary grants, which used to fund many through the Bar exams (80 per cent of students in 1987) have almost dried up (under 10 per cent in 1997). One 1970s recipient was Cherie Booth who said the current expense of going to the Bar discriminates against the poor (1997 Bar Conference).

13-007   A 1998 Bar Council report showed that new barristers had debts of £15–25,000. In *Edmonds v. Lawson* (2000) the Court of Appeal held that a pupillage contract is not a contract of employment within the National Minimum Wage Act 1998. The year's pupillage is unpaid. Some are given an allowance by their chambers and the Bar Council recommends £10,000 p.a. but this rests on the goodwill of chambers. Pupils may not earn fees until the second six months. Those fees are often paid late. Many cannot survive, because their earnings are less than their chambers rent. Hence, many drop out of the Bar within the first five years, with large debts. In 2001, the Bar Council voted to introduce compulsory financial awards to pupils of £10,000 p.a.

For new lawyers, work can be hard. The 2000 report of the PSI *Cohort* study showed a third of trainee solicitors regularly worked over 50 hours a week.

3. Organisation

13-008   The organisation of the two branches of the legal profession is the responsibility of two quite independent sets of governing bodies.

Barristers

The Inns of Court

13-009   The Inns are administered by their senior members, Benchers. The student is called to the Bar at her Inn. The Inns, historically, had a collegiate function in training new barristers. They now provide the dining system and own and administer valuable property in the Temple area from which most of London's practising barristers rent their chambers.

The General Council of the bar (known as "the Bar Council")

This is the professional governing body of the Bar. It comprises elected barristers and those representing the Inns, circuits and specialist Bar associations. The Bar Council performs similar professional functions to the Law Society. It lays down the Bar's Code of Conduct and administers the system for disciplining errant barristers and it represents the bar as a trade union. In addition, the six court circuits have their own Bar Associations, as do specialist barristers. The Council's informative website explains all aspects of the organisation and the profession.

Junior Counsel and Queen's Counsel

All practising barristers, however old, are junior counsel unless they **13-010** have been designated Queen's Counsel (Q.C.). There are some 1,072 Queen's Counsel in practice, of whom 82 are women. The status is bestowed by the Queen on the advice of the Lord Chancellor. Annually, the Lord Chancellor's office issues an invitation to junior counsel to apply. The change of status is, financially, something of a speculation. Once appointed, the Queen's Counsel is expected to appear only in the most important cases. She is known as a "Leader" because she is often accompanied by one, and sometimes two, junior counsel. There used to be a rule called the Two Counsel Rule whereby a Q.C. had to pay a junior to appear as an assistant in court. This was abolished in 1977, following criticism by the Monopolies and Mergers Commission but it is still widely followed in practice. The practice has been the subject of repeated criticism and scrutiny and regulations inspired by the Lord Chancellor's Efficiency Commission on Criminal Practice have made serious inroads into the practice from November 1988. The practice was further restricted, in the Crown Court, in 2000. The process of becoming a Queen's Counsel is called "taking silk", referring to the fact that the new status involves a change from a stuff gown to a silk gown. The Lord Chancellor has set out details of the eligibility criteria for Q.C.'s in *Silk 2002* (current at the time of writing). Candidates should appear regularly before the courts of England and Wales, the ECJ or international courts. They will normally have been barristers or solicitors for ten years, with at least five years' advocacy experience in the higher courts. This means that solicitor-advocates were not considered suitable until about 1999. The Lord Chancellor grants silk only to practitioners who display these attributes: intellectual ability; outstanding ability as an advocate; high professional standing and respect; maturity of judgment and balance; a high quality practice based on demanding cases (paraphrased).

The Lord Chancellor makes widespread "consultations" with the judiciary and the profession. He discusses the candidates with the Law Officers and heads of division. Rejected applicants are not given reasons but may discuss their application with the Lord Chancellor's staff. Statistics reveal that very few women and ethnic minorities apply. In 2000, of 506 applicants, only 53 were women and 24 ethnic minority. The Lord Chancellor appoints around six honorary silks per year. In 2000, silk was conferred on Nelson Mandela. Successful candidates are invested in the House of Lords in full ceremonial dress.

13-011   The Adam Smith Institute published a strong attack on the silk system, in Reeves' 1998 report, *Silk Cut*. They recommended silks should be abolished, for these reasons:

- The term "junior" for other barristers is misleading.
- The annual "silk round" occupies seven civil servants.
- Those employed in local authorities, the CPS and industry are not eligible.
- Very competent barristers may seldom appear before the consultant judges.
- Silks are about ten per cent of the Bar. This keeps able juniors out.
- The office has become the route to extremely high earnings. Clients are lured into extra expense because they think that employing a silk will enhance their chances of success.
- Eire is the only other E.U. Member State with silk system.
- Judges have criticised the waste of public money in using silks.
- Despite the abolition of the Two Counsel Rule, silks rarely appear alone.
- Although silks are meant to be selected for their outstanding competence as advocates, the European Court of Justice has criticised the written submissions of British lawyers as unduly long and repetitive.
- Without silk, a free market in advocacy would prevail, with reputations dependent on competence.
- An archaic and misleading title is bestowed upon relatively few practitioners, which does nothing to enhance legal services.

In February 1999, over 100 M.P.s, led by Andrew Dismore, started campaigning for the abolition of silk. At the 1999 silk ceremony, the Lord Chancellor defended the award of silk as "the kite-mark of quality", enabling lawyers and clients to identify the leading members of the profession and to identify likely candidates for the Bench. In April 2000, when no solicitor-advocate of the six who applied was granted silk, the Law Society President condemned the rank of Q.C. as a perk for barristers. Since 1995, when they could first apply, only four solicitor-advocates have been awarded the rank, of 33 applicants. In his speech at the 2001 silk ceremony, Lord Irvine defended the appointment process for Q.C.s, insisting it was fair and open but, unexpectedly, in the Bar's October 2000 annual conference, they voted overwhelmingly to reform the system of selecting Q.C.s.

Since 1995, there has been increasing concern expressed in the press **13-012** over the earnings of silks, especially silks funded by the State for criminal defence, because they fix their own fees. This is said to be a gross abuse of public funds. The Home Secretary and Lord Chancellor have both voiced concern, the Lord Chancellor pointing out, in 1998, that the top one per cent of jury trials absorbed 24 per cent of the total criminal legal aid budget. In 1998, the Law Lords conducted their own inquiry into the level of fees charged by counsel for appearances before them. They criticised the Lord Chancellor for attacking "fat cat" barristers and releasing details of Q.C.s' earnings to the media, yet failing to exercise his right to object to large bills at taxation hearings. The Bar responded by calling for fixed fees in criminal cases. Judges have joined in this criticism. Mr. Justice Lightman, speaking to the Chancery Bar in 1998, said "it must be a matter of grave concern if leaders of the first rank charge fees beyond the range reasonably affordable by ordinary litigants but fees which their wealthy and powerful opponents can afford. There is then no equality before the law." A 2000 survey of barristers' earnings found 26 "silks" earned over a million pounds a year and in 2001, *The Lawyer* published a survey showing silks lost as many cases as they won, in 2000. For three years running, a survey of barristers earnings has shown a large gap between the earnings of the elite and many of the junior Bar. Also, those working on publicly funded cases earn half as much as barristers doing privately funded work.

An elite group of barristers, known as Treasury Counsel, are briefed to appear for the Government in public law cases and for the prosecution in top criminal cases in the Old Bailey. In recent years this system has suffered two accusations. The first was a complaint that the selection system was secretive and discriminatory, favouring white males from a limited background and that Treasury Counsel are overpaid. A former circuit judge, in a report to the Attorney-General in 2000, said they were often paid twice as much as the judges before whom they appeared. See further discussion on "Fat Cat Lawyers" in the Legal Services Chapter.

THE BARRISTER'S CLERK

It is normal for a "set" of barristers in chambers to share a clerk as a business manager and it is said that the clerk can make, or break, the barrister. The barrister's clerk arranges work and negotiates the fee unless it is a publicly funded case paid for by the Community Legal Service Fund or Criminal Defence Service. There is an Institute of Barristers' Clerks, which represents clerks' interests. In October 2000, *The Independent* reported that some clerks earn up to £350,000, far more than most barristers.

Solicitors

13-013 **The Law Society**

Solicitors are, by statute, professionally regulated by the Law Society which is controlled by an elected body consisting of a Council and President and they are assisted by a full-time Chief Executive and a large Secretariat. For non-statutory purposes, membership of the Law Society is voluntary. The Society publishes the Law Society's *Gazette*. The Office for the Supervision of Solicitors and Solicitors' Disciplinary Tribunal deal with alleged professional misconduct by solicitors. The Tribunal is made up of solicitors and lay members appointed by the Master of the Rolls. The Tribunal has power to strike the name of the offending solicitor off the Roll, or they may suspend a solicitor from practice, or administer a reprimand, order payment of a penalty of up to £5,000 or order the solicitor to pay certain costs.

The mechanism for handling client's complaints is described on the Law Society's website. Since the 1979 Royal Commission on Legal Services Report, there has been growing governmental concern over the ability of the solicitors' profession to regulate themselves. Independent surveys exposed poor quality work. A 1995 *Which* survey tested the quality of advice given to researchers posing as clients. In a variety of legal problems, only a small minority of solicitors gave the correct advice. A 2000 Consumers' Association survey found many vulnerable people felt they received a second class service and again in 2001, *Which* criticised solicitors' services.

In the meantime, the Law Society was failing to cope with a mounting backlog of complaints. In 1996, it replaced the discredited Solicitors' Complaints Bureau with the Office for the Supervision of Solicitors (OSS) but this had no effect. At the time of writing it is considering replacing this with yet another complaints mechanism but this may be too late. In 1999, the Legal Services Ombudsman, appointed under the Courts and Legal Services Act to oversee the complaints process, described OSS complaints handling as "spiralling out of control". In 1998, the Lord Chancellor warned the Law Society that he would ask Parliament for statutory power to take over the regulation of solicitors from the Law Society and this was granted in the Access to Justice Act 1999. In 1999, in a speech to the Law Society conference he described their handling of complaints as "lamentable". In January 2001, LCD Minister David Lock gave a final written warning to the Law Society that it would lose its "privilege" of self-regulation if it did not radically improve matters by the summer (LCD press release 1/01) but, by July 2001, the Legal Services Ombudsman repeated this warning. She was satisfied with the OSS's handling of complaints in only 57 per cent of cases.

13-014 Law Society Practice Rule 15 requires solicitors' firms to provide an in-house complaints procedure. Research by a Bristol University team in

1998 found 80 per cent of clients sampled had not been told of such a procedure, as required, and the procedure was seldom, if ever used and the operation of the process was criticised by other researchers in 2000 (150 N.L.J. 416). Another academic, Avrom Sherr, produced a damning report on the solicitors' complaints procedures in 1999 (*Willing Blindness? —Complaints Handling Procedures*). In 1998, a Channel 4 *Dispatches* programme uncovered various dishonest solicitors who had been found guilty by the Solicitors' Disciplinary Tribunal of fraud or mishandling clients' money and who continued to practice.

To make matters worse, the Law Society is involved in another scandal. Vice-President Kamlesh Bahl, who would have become the first female president, resigned in 2000 and brought an action for race and sex discrimination against the Society, which she won in 2001 although a complaint has been made to the OSS that she lied on oath.

At the time of writing, 2001, the Law Society are still arguing about how to reform themselves.

The Institute of Legal Executives

The body which represents qualified "para-legals" employed in solicitors' offices is the Institute of Legal Executives, which has its own examination system for admission as an Associate or a Fellow of the Institute. The routine work of a solicitor's office is largely carried out by legal executives and they are significant fee earners in many practices.

4. *Work of Barristers and Solicitors*

Barristers

Most barristers are professional advocates. As such, a barrister must be **13-015**
capable of prosecuting in a criminal case one day and defending an accused person the next; or of preparing a skeleton argument and taking the case for a claimant in a civil action one day and doing the same for a defendant the next. In this way barristers claim to attain a real degree of objectivity and independence becoming specialists in advocacy.

In practice there is a great deal of paperwork involved in the pre-trial stages of a case, particularly where skeleton arguments have to be prepared. Additionally, barristers will often be asked, by solicitors or other professionals, to give written advice on a particular legal matter. this is known as "taking counsel's opinion". Indeed, some barristers who specialize in planning law, tax law or employment law may do most of their work from their rooms or chambers, or home, in documentary form and only occasionally appear in court.

Over half of practising barristers work in London. The remainder operate from around 60 provincial centres.

Barristers are not allowed to form partnerships, other than overseas, but may share the same set of chambers and also frequently share a clerk. It often happens that court hearings overlap or are fixed for the same day and then another barrister usually in the same chambers, has to take the case at short notice. This is called a "late brief". See discussion below.

From a low point of 1,919 barristers in 1960, the Bar has increased in size each year and does not seem to have been affected by enhancing solicitors' rights of audience, as described below. Their work has diversified in parallel with solicitors' work. The enforcement of the Human Rights Act in 2000 has provided a substantial opportunity for a new and broad field of specialist advice which is much in demand.

13-016   The Access to Justice Act 1999, while seen as threatening some publicly funded work, has permitted quality civil rights chambers to gain legal services contracts for the first time, with the Legal Services Commission, in the same way as firms of solicitors. Like solicitors, the Bar have developed their own *pro bono* scheme, some of which is directed to working with Community Legal Service volunteers on welfare law advice.

In 2000, the Bar launched BarMark, its own quality assurance standard, granted by the Bar Council and certified by the British Standards Institution.

Solicitors

13-017   The trend is towards having several solicitors in partnership or, since 1992, incorporated companies and towards ever larger firms or consortia of firms and this trend will increase, from 2000, because of the requirement for contracts for legal services, explained later. This gives them the opportunity to specialise to some extent so that whilst one partner may spend all his time on family work, another will deal with litigation, another with probate and trusts and so on. In some of the larger London firms there are more than 100 partners who are highly specialised.

Most large London firms are now multi-national partnerships. Solicitors export a significant element of their services to foreign clients. A 1999 Law Society survey showed legal services contributed £791m to the United Kingdom's invisible earnings. Solicitors' main specialisms in 2001 are these:

Commercial work
City solicitors advise on company formation and organisation, taxation, insolvency, intellectual property, pensions, insurance, contracts and financial regulation.

Domestic conveyancing
This means transferring the legal title to property. The 1979 Royal Commission on Legal Services (RCLS) found this to be the "bread and

butter" fee earner of many firms, especially as solicitors enjoyed a monopoly. The financial recession from 1989 forced solicitors to look for other work, however.

Selling property

As solicitors saw some of their conveyancing work disappear to estate agents and institutions, some solicitors started selling property.

Family law

The divorce rate and growth in legal aid caused an expansion of this work since 1980. The Children Act 1989 permitted children to be legally aided. A 1997 Law Society survey showed that women solicitors spent more time on family work. In 1999, the Society launched a Family Law Panel. Members must be committed to non-confrontational negotiation.

Probate

The survey showed a decline, since 1989, in the number of solicitors involved in the administration of deceased persons' property. Solicitors' monopoly over probate work was abolished by the Courts and Legal Services Act 1990 and this has led to competition from independent practitioners.

Employment

The survey demonstrated this to be a growth area in the 1990s.

Social welfare

Solicitors have been notoriously poor in providing advice on welfare **13-018** law, such as housing and state benefits. The RCLS criticised this gap in provision. Now, solicitors' firms who seek a Community Legal Service contract must show they can provide advice in welfare benefits.

Criminal law

This was another big growth area in legally aided work since 1980, with the expansion of the duty solicitor schemes into magistrates' courts and police stations and the increase in the proportion of defendants who are represented. The survey showed that the number of solicitors involved declined in the period 1989–1997.

Accidents and personal injury

Specialist litigators have developed since 1980, often legally aided, sometimes involving multi-party actions, with multiple claimants, such as industrial disasters or the negligent release of new drugs. The survey showed that personal injury cases provided the biggest increase in fee earning time since 1989.

Consumer protection

Although the small claims civil track is designed to be used by the litigant in person, many choose to be privately represented.

Individual financial advice

This relates to investments, insurance and pensions. The 1997 survey showed that one sixth of practitioners regularly conducted personal bankruptcy and debt work. Many are registered under the Financial Services Act.

Pro bono work

This means providing legal services free of charge. The Solicitors Pro Bono Group was formed in 1997, with funds donated by big city law firms, several of whom had established *pro bono* units. A 1998 survey showed that, on average, solicitors gave 37 hours a year.

International practice

English law firms have offices in around 40 foreign countries. The Rights of Establishment Directive 98/51 (implemented 2000) makes it easy for solicitors to open up offices in other Member States of the European Union. After three years they will have the right to acquire the title of lawyer in the foreign state.

Advocacy

13-019   Solicitors all have rights of audience before magistrates' courts and county courts. Additionally, they may qualify for an advocacy certificate in the higher courts.

Multi Disciplinary Partnerships

By 2001, solicitors were still banned from forming a partnership with a member of another profession. The 1979 RCLS supported the ban. The Conservative government's green paper, *The Work and Organisation of the Legal Profession* (Cm. 570, 1989) viewed it as an unnecessary restriction on competition and section 66 of the Courts and Legal Services Act 1990 removed the statutory prohibition. The Law Society nevertheless maintained its opposition, arguing that MDPs would undermine the network of solicitors' firms, threaten client confidentiality and create conflicts of interest. The 1997 survey showed that over half of solicitors thought that MDPs were inevitable. At the time of writing, 2001, the ban was being challenged in the European Court of Justice as a breach of competition law but, ironically, since the Law Society was about to permit MDPs in 2001, it was advised that legislation would be needed to permit them.

5. Professional Etiquette

Both barristers and solicitors are closely restricted in their professional **13-020** conduct by the supervision of their respective governing bodies. The former prohibition on advertising has been relaxed to enable a solicitor to advertise in newspapers and on radio and television. Barristers were precluded from advertising until the 1990s. Currently a barrister only meets the lay client when the solicitor, or solicitor's representative, is present, so building up the isolation, as well as the objectivity, of the barrister. In order to prevent barristers gaining unfair advantage by cultivating the friendship of solicitors, there used to be a rule which prevented a solicitor and barrister in a case from having lunch together.

Barristers and solicitors are required to dress formally when appearing in court; for a barrister this involves wearing wig and gown, since without these he cannot be "seen" or "heard" by the judge. Solicitors wear a gown but no wig. The wearing of wigs has become more controversial since the emergence of solicitor-advocates' full right of audience, granted under the CLSA 1990. Solicitor-advocates want to wear wigs but by 1996, the Lord Chancellor has not permitted this. In a 2000 vote, most barristers chose to retain wigs, as enhancing the dignity and solemnity of court proceedings and a formal sign of the advocate's status and importance in the courtroom. This is despite the fact that Lord Chief Justice Woolf thinks they are outmoded and Lord Irvine L.C. has expressed his distaste for wigs in civil disputes and has dispensed with all his ceremonial garb for his appearances as speaker of the House of Lords. (See debate in *The Times*, July 10, 2001).

There used to be a rule, articulated in the 1969 case of *Rondel v. Worsley* **13-021** (HL) that barristers could not be sued for negligent work in court, or in preparation of court work. In *Arthur J. S. Hall & Co. v. Simons* (2000), the House of Lords abolished this protection as no longer in accord with public policy and being out of line with the liability of other professions, such as doctors, and with lawyers in other European Union states. They reviewed the reasons which had supported the rule, such as the cab rank principle, which they thought had not had much impact, and the public policy rule against re-litigating an issue which had been before the courts. It had also been supported as ensuring that barristers would respect their duty to the court. The House dismissed all these reasons, preferring the argument that there would be benefits in ending the immunity. It would end the anomalous exception to the basic premise that there should be a remedy for a wrong. There was no reason to fear a flood of actions against barristers. It tended to erode confidence in the legal system if advocates, alone among professional men, were immune from liability for negligence.

A corollary of this immunity was the rule that barristers did not sue for their fees because, historically, barristers were not contractually bound to solicitors but were paid an *honorarium*, or gift for services rendered. (This used to be deposited in the pocket in the back of the gown, as it was thought ungentlemanly for barristers to soil their hands with money. The pocket remains.) The Courts and Legal Services Act 1990, section 61, permitted barristers to enter into binding contracts but the Bar Code of Conduct still prohibits this. Periodically, young barristers campaign to be allowed to sue for their fees, as slow-paying solicitors cause cash-flow problems which make developing a career at the Bar a financial strain.

Finally, one result of the division of the legal profession is that no one can practise as both a barrister and a solicitor at the same time although it is now possible to be doubly qualified. Provision has, however, been made for transfer from one profession to the other and it has become easier over the years especially since the Access to Justice Act 1999.

6. The Abolition of the Professions' Monopolies: Bar Wars

13-022   Since the mid-1970s, people have questioned the desirability of allowing the legal profession to preserve its ancient monopolies. In the eyes of others, they are restrictive practices, limiting consumer choice and allowing lawyers to overcharge. Notice how both sides of the profession have passionately defended their monopolies on the ground that they best serve the public interest.

The Abolition of the Solicitors' Conveyancing Monopoly

13-023   The conveyancing monopoly was one of the reasons for the establishment of the Royal Commission on Legal Services, 1976–1979. Under the Solicitors Act 1922, unqualified persons were prohibited from conveyancing for gain. The Royal Commission found most solicitors' practices derived 40 to 60 per cent of their gross fee income from it. Critics complained that it allowed solicitors to overcharge. They operated a scale of fees which meant that, for conveying an expensive property, however simple the work, they earned a large fee. Solicitors defended their monopoly by claiming that their training, professional ethics and compulsory indemnity insurance all protected the public.

The Commission disappointed all critics by recommending the preservation of the monopoly but the Consumers' Association promoted Austin Mitchell M.P.'s House Buyers' Bill, in 1993, designed to abolish it. He withdrew the Bill in 1994, when the Thatcher government assured him they would introduce similar legislation. To them, monopolies were all undesirable, as stifling competition in the free market and thus limiting consumer choice. The Farrand Committee was established, to examine the system of conveyancing. They recommended a system of licensed conveyancers a scheme enacted in the Administration of Justice Act 1985.

Solicitors perceived a much greater threat, from conveyancing by banks and building societies. The Building Societies Act 1986 gave the Lord Chancellor the power to permit this but it remained unimplemented throughout the 1980s. The Law Society complained that such a practice would create conflicts of interest. Lord Mackay, the Conservative Lord Chancellor, addressed this question in one of his three 1989 green papers, *Conveyancing By Authorised Practitioners* (Cm. 572, (1989)). It proposed a simplified framework, replacing the 1986 Act. The paper denied solicitors' allegations that the public would be unprotected. Lending institutions would only be permitted to do conveyancing by using employed solicitors and licensed conveyancers. Solicitors continued to argue that the public would suffer from conflicts of interest, being persuaded to have their conveyancing done by their mortgage lender, who probably also sold them their house. They claimed that "unfair competition" from banks and building societies would extinguish most firms of high street solicitors, thus denying the public easy access to legal services. The Government refined its plans in a 1989 white paper, *Legal Services: A Framework for the Future* (Cm. 740, (1989)). They proposed to add further safeguards for the public against conflicts of interest. This resulted in the Courts and Legal Services Act 1990, sections 34–53, which provides the regulatory machinery for licensed conveyancers.

Most importantly, section 17(1) articulates the Conservative philosophy **13-024** enacted in their reforms of legal services and abolition of lawyers' monopolies: the statutory objective of the Act:

"The development of legal services in England and Wales (and in particular the development of advocacy, litigation, conveyancing and probate services) by making provision for new or better ways of providing such services and a wider choice of persons providing them, while maintaining the proper and efficient administration of justice."

Consequences of the Abolition

- Solicitors relaxed their advertising ban.
- Conveyancing costs fell.
- Solicitors began selling houses, getting their own back on estate agents.
- The Law Society identifies and promotes new areas of work for solicitors. The profession has expanded each year.
- Solicitors have had to promote themselves through "client care". They have launched a succession of schemes to identify those solicitors' firms satisfying set criteria. The latest Law Society

quality mark, current in 2001, is Lexcel.
- Solicitors attacked the Bar's monopoly over rights of audience in the higher courts.

Abolition of the Probate and Litigation Monopolies

13-025   Solicitors' monopolies over probate and litigation work were protected by the Solicitors' Act 1922. They were abolished, in a similar way, by the Courts and Legal Services Act 1990, which permitted institutions and legal executives to offer probate services.

As for litigation, solicitors did not fuss about the abolition of this restrictive practice. The Bar has been contemplating for decades whether ordinary clients should be permitted to directly access a barrister, who would then conduct all the litigation and not just the advocacy element. They have progressively permitted barristers to access certain groups of clients direct. This scheme is now called BarDIRECT. In the meantime, the Access to Justice Act 1999 has eased the procedure by which a body may be authorised to grant litigation rights and section 40 makes the Bar Council and the Institute of Legal Executives "authorised bodies", under the 1990 Act, whose members have the right to conduct litigation. Explaining this section, in the consultation paper, *Rights of Audience and Rights to Conduct Litigation in England and Wales*, the Lord Chancellor simply stated that the Government had no firm view on rights to conduct litigation so it is now up to those barristers who wish to be able to litigate to persuade the Bar Council that permitting this and unlimited direct client access to them would be desirable. In 2001, the Legal Services Consultative Panel recommended to the L.C. that employed barristers should be allowed to conduct litigation.

Abolishing the Bar's Monopoly over Rights of Audience

13-026   Since county courts were created by the County Courts Act 1846, solicitors have had rights of audience before them. In magistrates' courts, the vast majority of advocates are solicitors. In 1998, I asked the Law Society, the Legal Aid Board and the Lord Chancellor's Department to estimate what proportion of solicitors appeared in the magistrates' court and they all agreed it was about half. Solicitors may also appear in most tribunals, as may laypeople, such as Citizens' Advice Bureaux workers and other charity workers. Others who have rights of audience include employees of central and local government and other public bodies. For example, employees of the Customs and Excise Department prosecute VAT offenders in magistrates' courts. Additionally, individuals have a right to represent themselves. This is thought of as an important civil right.

Solicitors, then, are by far the most prolific of advocates but the public's image of the typical advocate has always been the robed and bewigged barrister because, until 1990, they had a monopoly over rights of audience in the Crown Court and all superior courts (except for the Crown Court in five localities remote from barristers' chambers and except for defence solicitors in appeals from magistrates' courts and committals for sentence). The cases dealt with in the superior courts are, generally, more complex, time consuming and, importantly, lucrative.

The Royal Commission on Legal Services (1976–1979)
Solicitors asked the Royal Commission to extend their rights of audience to the Crown Court (at the very least). To the Bar's relief, the Commission concluded that an extension would be against the public interest. Their reasons are worth studying because they are still argued now, in defence of a separate Bar:

13-027

- It would destroy the livelihood of the junior Bar (90 per cent of the Bar), who derived 30–50 per cent of their income from criminal work.
- If it resulted in the development of substantial solicitors' advocacy practices, each specialising in representing either prosecution or defence, this would lead to the loss of the advantage of independence.
- If solicitors were given general rights, it might lead to the development of large, specialist firms, which would be against the public interest.
- County court trials, which solicitors were used to conducting, could not be compared with jury trials, which required the skills of public speaking, a detailed knowledge of the law of evidence and the ability to cross-examine.
- The majority of solicitors' practices were not geared to providing advocacy services. Most solicitors could not absent themselves from their offices for most of the working day, sometimes for days on end.
- Even if solicitors were only given the right to appear in guilty pleas in the Crown Court, this could still threaten the livelihood of the young criminal Bar. Also, the "offender requires the highest possible standard of representation which can only be provided by a specialist advocate" (para. 18.58).
- Such a change would be a step nearer to a fused legal profession, which the Commission did not favour.

Thatcherite attack on restrictive practices
In the week that the Government announced a review the conveyancing monopoly, the Law Society retaliated by launching a campaign for rights of audience in all courts. To the scandalised amusement of the press,

13-028

the two sides of the profession waged a bitter public debate. By 1986, the Law Society had crystallised details of their campaign in a document called "Lawyers and the Courts: Time for Some Changes". It proposed a new career structure, with every lawyer receiving a common education, then a period in general practice, at the end of which all would enjoy the same right of audience in all courts. The Bar would be reserved for specialists, upon completion of further examinations. Direct access to the Bar would be permitted. The Bar's reaction was hostile.

The Marre Report

To take the heat out of the atmosphere, the two sides established the Committee on the Future of the Legal Profession, (the Marre Committee) in 1986. They recommended extending solicitors' rights of audience to the Crown Court, with an advisory board in each circuit recommending to the Law Society which solicitors should be licensed to appear.

The green papers

The next significant watershed was the Lord Chancellor's publication, in 1989, of three green papers. The paper on *The Work and Organisation of the Legal Profession* acknowledged the case for restricting rights of audience:

- Judges work without legal assistance, therefore rely on the strength and adequacy of advocacy.
- Judges need to trust advocates not to mislead the court.
- Judgments create precedents. Judges look to advocates to cite all relevant authorities. "The presentation of cogent legal argument is a highly skilled task requiring not only a knowledge of the law but also constant practice in advocacy."

Therefore, rights of audience should be restricted to those who are properly trained, suitably experienced and subject to codes of conduct which maintain standards.

13-029 Then Lord Chancellor Mackay dropped his bombshell, making himself the instant enemy of judges and the Bar:

"The basic premise is that the satisfaction of such requirements should, for the future, alone be the test for granting rights of audience; and not whether an advocate happened by initial qualification to be a lawyer, whether a barrister or a solicitor, and whether in private practice or employed." (in the green paper).

A system of advocacy certificates, general and limited would be established, with professional bodies determining whether candidates had satisfied the relevant requirements, such as passing exams. The Lord

Chancellor, after consulting the judges, would determine which professional bodies would have the power to grant rights.

Judicial hysteria

The Bar and judiciary launched verbal open warfare on Lord Chancellor Mackay. The Bar Chairman said "the proposals will remove the control of justice from the judges and entrust it to civil servants". This would give rise to "grave constitutional dangers". Predictably, he argued "the general public will be the loser and so will justice."

Judges warned of an imminent constitutional collapse. Lord Chief Justice Lane called the green paper "one of the most sinister documents ever to emanate from government". He warned, famously: "oppression does not stand on the doorstep with a toothbrush moustache and a swastika armband". Judges threatened a one-day strike if Lord Chancellor Mackay would not allow them extra time to respond. High Court judges called the proposals "a grave breach of the doctrine of the separation of powers" (response issued on May 23, 1989). The long-term effect might be to "impair the competence, integrity and trustworthiness of advocates and, as a result, significantly damage the quality of justice in this country." Judges sought to emphasise that they had, for centuries, enjoyed the prerogative of deciding who appeared before them. They were affronted that this power would pass to a government minister, the Lord Chancellor.

Solicitors retorted that judges were using a double standard, forgetting that solicitors were already advocates in the lower courts.

The Courts and Legal Services Act 1990

The Lord Chancellor followed these proposals with a white paper, *Legal Services: a Framework for the Future*, the precursor of the Courts and Legal Services Act 1990 which established a new system for granting rights of audience. What was enacted was a watered down version of what Lord Mackay wanted. He had been forced to capitulate to the judges' demands. (This, according to Lord Chancellor Irvine, in 1998, proved to be the scheme's downfall.) While section 27 provided that "appropriate authorised bodies" could grant rights of audience, section 29 required them to be subjected to such a cumbersome machinery for approval, as to be almost unworkable. Further, they had to gain approval for the tiniest alterations to their codes of conduct, if these affected rights of audience. The Lord Chancellor was statutorily compelled to seek the advice of the Lord Chancellor's Advisory Committee on Legal Education and Conduct (ACLEC) a quango created by the Act, and of the Director General of Fair Trading, before taking a decision jointly with the four "designated judges", the Lord Chief Justice, Master of the Rolls, President of the Family Division and Vice-Chancellor. Each of the judges could veto a proposed rule change.

13-030

Effects of the 1990 Act: solicitor-advocates

By 1994, only 15 solicitors had applied for qualification. By June 1998, there were only 624 solicitor-advocates, out of 70,000. This could be because of the cost and palaver of taking the course and exams. Some solicitors, with many years' advocacy experience in the magistrates' court could see little point in making this effort which would place them in no better position than a newly qualified barrister.

13-031 ACLEC commissioned research by teams from the Universities of Westminster and Bristol.

They found:

- Most solicitors with higher court rights qualified through being former barristers.
- Of all qualified solicitors, few had ever acted as a higher court advocate.
- Several factors inhibited Crown Court advocacy: lack of certainty over trial dates, where the Bar's flexibility and freedom from paperwork gave them an advantage; the low volume of work and length of trials and remuneration.
- Small criminal litigation firms could not afford to develop in-house advocacy practices.
- Personal injury and professional negligence solicitors did not believe in-house advocacy would improve the service to their clients.
- In general commercial litigation, solicitors regularly exercised their county court rights. Since the county court limit was already £50,000, extended rights of audience were an irrelevance.
- Specialist family lawyers already conducted their own advocacy as a matter of routine. High Court appearances in family cases were extremely rare.
- Solicitors did not like being stigmatised as abnormal advocates, by, for example, not being allowed to wear wigs.

In the meantime, by 1993, work for the youngest barristers was dropping, because of a reduction in case load of the criminal courts and competition in the magistrates' courts from freelance solicitor-advocates (especially in London) who acted as agents for other solicitors. Solicitors preferred to use them because, unlike the Bar, they were prepared to guarantee an appearance and would not return a brief at the last moment. Experienced solicitors were more skillful than new barristers and solicitors understood legal aid forms. (N. Gillis, (1993) 143 N.L.J. 1373.)

13-032 In 1998, ILEX, the Institute of Legal Executives, was designated under the Act to grant rights of audience to its members, in civil matters before a district judge, in county court or magistrates' family business, in tribunals and in coroners' courts. The Chartered Institute of Patent Agents applied to become an authorised body, in 1998.

Rather surprisingly, given the judicial backlash over audience rights in the higher courts, not much fuss was made when the Crime and Disorder Act 1998 stepped outside the regime set up by the 1990 Act to grant audience rights to laypeople employed by the CPS in the magistrates' court. Those involved in magistrates' courts received the news cynically, however, claiming that the real reason for this new liberality was cost cutting.

The "sorry saga" of employed lawyers

The 1990s saw the Law Society and the CPS in a frustrating struggle to gain higher court rights of audience for employed solicitors and for barristers employed by the CPS. To cut a six-year long story short, proponents argued that it was bizarre to deny rights of audience to someone like the Director of Public Prosecutions, as soon as she took up her appointment, when she was an eminent Q.C. in independent practice and, in any event, CPS employees prosecuted successfully in the magistrates' courts and employed solicitors could argue cases in the county court and tribunals. The opponents, led by the Bar, argued that it was against the public interest to allow prosecutions to be undertaken by state prosecutors. The interest of justice would benefit from the use of independent, private practice solicitors and counsel, hired by the CPS. (T. Holland (1996) 146 N.L.J. 450; D. Pannick, *The Times*, July 4, 1995; N. Ley (1995) 145 N.L.J. 1124; (1998) 148 N.L.J. 1082, 1295.) Nigel Ley was concerned that CPS employed lawyers believed that their conviction rate was one of the indicia of their performance and would be reluctant to do anything to risk an acquittal, whereas independently hired barristers were free from the dictation of the CPS in deciding whether and how to proceed with a prosecution. The "sorry saga" of employed lawyers' attempts to gain audience rights is recounted in lurid detail in an annexe to Lord Chancellor Irvine's paper, below. The Bar Council provoked anger among non-practising barristers in 1998, when it decreed that they did not have any rights in courts or tribunals, unless they obtained a special waiver.

Labour's Disgust with the "Sorry Saga"

In June 1998, Lord Chancellor Irvine produced a consultation paper, **13-033** *Rights of Audience and Rights to Conduct Litigation in England and Wales* (Lord Chancellor's Department website). If his predecessor's 1989 green papers were a bombshell, then this and its accompanying package of reforms were a rocket, designed to propel the Bar from the Dickensian era to the modern day. The language of his foreword to the paper betrays his exasperation over the failure of the 1990 Act to achieve Lord Mackay's objective of opening up rights of audience:

"there remain features of the way the [legal] profession is organised which the Government believes stifle innovation and maintain rigid structures, limiting consumer choice and increasing the expense of going to law. One particular example is the restriction on the right to appear in the higher courts as an advocate; members of the public often complain that they are required to hire two lawyers, where one would do. . . . The 1990 Act was intended to allow solicitors to obtain the right to appear in any court, thus increasing the public's choice of advocate; it was also intended to allow employed lawyers, such as Crown Prosecutors, to appear in the higher courts. However, there has been continuing opposition to these changes, both before and after the Act was passed, with the result that the Act has achieved virtually nothing. Eight years on, nearly all advocates in the higher courts are barristers in private practice.

The failure of the Act's good intentions and the inadequacy of the mechanisms it put in place to extend rights of audience are best illustrated by the sorry saga of the Law Society's attempt to obtain rights of audience in the higher courts for employed solicitors, which is set out in this paper. After a prolonged gestation of six years to-ing and fro-ing, advice and counter-advice, referrals backwards and forwards, a Byzantine procedure produced a mouse of reform: employed solicitors were allowed to appear in substantive proceedings in the higher courts, provided they were led by a lawyer in private practice.

The Government is not satisfied that the present state of affairs is in the public interest. . . . Our view is that all qualified barristers and qualified solicitors should in principle have the right to appear in any court."

13-034 This extract neatly summarises the argument of the consultation paper. Additional arguments were:

- Rights of audience needed to be restricted because the consequence of using an untrained advocate might be to adversely affect the client, any other party involved in the case and the wider public, as tax payer.
- Solicitors already appeared in £50,000 county court cases and in complex, high value cases, in High Court chambers.
- It was irrational that barristers lost their rights of audience on becoming employed and regained them when they returned to private practice. The suggestion that CPS lawyers were insufficiently independent was belied by the fact that most prosecutions occur in the magistrates' court, where they have full rights of audience.
- As for the argument that barristers provided high quality

advocacy, there were already concerns about the standard of private barristers' advocacy. The Public Accounts Committee survey showed that, at some Crown Court Centres, 75 per cent of CPS instructions had been returned. In a third of these cases, there was concern about the experience level of the new barrister who handled the case.

- The argument that junior barristers must be allowed to cut their teeth prosecuting in the Crown Court was inconsistent with arguments that the independent Bar provided uniformly high quality advocacy which employed barristers could not attain.

- The Government believed that barristers should be employed because of their merits, not because they have a monopoly.

- The professional bodies should retain the right to impose reasonable conditions and rules of conduct on the exercise of rights of audience.

- The Lord Chancellor should have the power to call in any such rule, as running counter to the general principle or statutory objective of the 1990 Act, for example by unduly restricting rights of audience.

- Rights of audience should be portable. Once a person has qualified, he should carry that qualification to any other branch of the profession.

- ACLEC was too large and had failed to further the statutory objective of the 1990 Act of developing new or better ways of providing legal services and a wider choice of persons providing them. It had cost £1 million per year to run. The unwieldy approval procedure had also frustrated the objects of the Act, as illustrated strikingly by the six-year delay and problems caused in the Law Society's application for higher court audience rights for employed solicitors. ACLEC should be replaced by a small "Legal Services Consultative Panel", to be called on by the Lord Chancellor for its expertise.

- Applications for approval as an authorised body should be made to the Lord Chancellor, who would have to have regard to the judges' advice but not be bound by it, as would approval for rule changes.

- Following the abolition of ACLEC, the LCD would take over organising the standing Conference on Legal Education, which provided a forum for the providers of academic and vocational education and the professional bodies.

The Lord Chancellor crystallised his plans in his 1998 white paper, *Modernising Justice,* which accompanied the Access to Justice Bill (now the 1999 Act) and explained its background.

Comments On Lord Irvine's proposals

13-035   Michael Zander, from his experience conducting the Royal
Commission's *Crown Court Study*, reiterated the concern that barristers
employed by the CPS would cast an insufficiently independent eye over
prosecutions ((1998) 148 N.L.J. 969).

The Law Society, of course, welcomed the proposals.

The Bar Council, by now claiming to "support open competition in the
provision of advocacy and litigation services" (Heather Hallett, then
Chairman of the Bar) produced a 50-page report setting out their own
proposals, including such extravagant plans as that the decision as to who
could appear as advocates "should be decided on a majority vote of
the four most senior judges and the Lord Chancellor, having consulted
the rest of the senior judiciary" and ensuring solicitors advise clients
on the best choice of advocate, by outlawing "tying in" arrangements
between advocates and solicitors.

A telephone survey by a big city solicitors firm, Linklaters, of 151 companies and merchant banks, showed 73 per cent supported solicitor advocacy.

Sydney Kentridge Q.C. was concerned over the constitutional aspects
of the proposals. He objected:

". . . if these proposals take effect, the rights of audience in the High
Court and Court of Appeal will be determined and controlled not by
the judges of England and Wales but by a Cabinet Minister. The judiciary will no longer have the power to decide who may appear in front
of them . . . only a mere right to be consulted. Such a removal of power
and function from the judiciary, (exercised by judges in this country for
some hundreds of years) and transferring such power and function to
the executive, would constitute a quiet constitutional revolution."
(*Counsel*, December 1998, p.24).

Supporting his argument with case law he said determining rights of
audience was a royal prerogative, delegated to judges, who, in turn, had
delegated their disciplinary power over the Bar to the Inns of Court and
Bar Council. He drew an analogy with threats to the Bar from central
government in the South African apartheid era. Barrister Robin de Wilde
reiterated the same points ((1998) 148 N.L.J. 1424) and traced judicial regulation of rights of audience back to 1280, when the City of London courts
regulated those who might appear as barristers according to standards of
advocacy. By 1292, barristers were regulated, trained and selected by their
Inn of Court. He threatened a "totalitarian regime". Similarly Lord Steyn,
a Law Lord, complained that this proposal was a breach of the separation
of powers, (Kalisher Lecture, 1998). Michael Zander agreed that the real
agenda was for Lord Irvine to take control ((1998) 148 N.L.J. 1084).

The judges of the Court of Appeal and High Court and the Council **13-036** of the Inns of Court all commented. The High Court judges reiterated their objections to Lord Mackay's 1989 green papers, that the proposals were "a grave breach of the separation of powers". The Court of Appeal complained that the Lord Chancellor's role was anomalous, as a cabinet minister and head of the judiciary. The Inns of Court agreed with Sydney Kentridge (cited by Lord Ackner, a retired Law Lords, at (1998) 148 N.L.J. 1512). David Pannick Q.C. found these arguments unpersuasive because:

> "[p]arliament can and does intervene to regulate the administration of justice in all other respects. It does so because the public interest is most effectively, and democratically assessed by those we elect rather than by barristers who have been appointed to the bench . . . judges have no right to decide, and no expertise that qualifies them to decide, what the public interest requires in a policy context where there are competing considerations. . . . The special pleading of judges and barristers has had no persuasive effect on laypeople, save to reinforce their low opinion of the legal profession." (*The Times*).

When the Bill was later debated in the Lords, speeches from lawyers and judges took up most of the seven-hour second reading debate. Retired judges reiterated that the Bill was constitutionally offensive and Lord Falconer retorted that they were wrong in asserting the judiciary had, historically, regulated rights of audience. A string of Acts going back to 1836 showed rights of audience had frequently been regulated by Parliament.

The Access to Justice Act 1999

Unmoved by the protestations of the Bar and judiciary and backed by **13-037** the Office of Fair Trading, Lord Irvine introduced his Access to Justice Bill in December 1998, embodying intact his proposals on rights of audience. It was accompanied by the white paper *Modernising Justice* and an explanatory memorandum, both available on the LCD website. Part III of the Act introduces the following scheme:

Section 36 replaces sections 31 to 33 of the Courts and Legal Services Act 1990. It grants rights of audience to every barrister and solicitor in all proceedings, subject only to the qualification regulations and rules of conduct imposed by their professional bodies.

Section 37 nullifies any restriction on the rights of audience of employed advocates, including lawyers employed by the CPS and section 38 provides the same protection for employees of the Legal Services Commission.

Section 39 makes advocacy rights portable so a barrister, for example, no longer has to give up audience rights on converting to be a solicitor.

Progress Since the 1999 Act

13-038   Both the Law Society and the Bar Council were forced to change their rules by July 2000 to comply with the Act and permit higher court audience rights to employed barristers and the Law Society produced a new scheme designed to make it much easier for solicitors to train for higher court audience rights. Even trainee solicitors can begin working for advocacy certificates. Nevertheless, by 2001 there were still under 1,100 solicitor advocates, only 151 of whom had full audience rights.

Law Lords Scott and Bingham, in autumn 2000 started a campaign to get judges to sit "unrobed" in all interlocutory hearings and appeals from the county court and to permit all solicitors rights of audience in such hearings.

Direct Access to the Bar

13-039   One remaining restrictive practice is the rule, self-imposed by the Bar Council, that clients must approach a barrister via a solicitor, in most cases. The Office of Fair Trading condemned this practice, in 2001, as against the public interest. The public were forced to pay for two lawyers where one (the barrister) would do.

7. Fusion: do we Need Two Professions?

13-040   The legal profession in England and Wales is unusual in world-wide terms, the two sides of the profession being characterised and preserved by their respective monopolies and restrictive practices. Because those have been torn down since 1985, the question is automatically raised whether, if all lawyers can do, or qualify to do, everything now, the professions will eventually merge, fuse and, if so whether that will serve the public interest. Barristers have always argued that giving rights of audience to solicitors will sound the death knell to the Bar. As we have seen, Lord Mackay took no notice of this argument and endeavoured to open up rights of audience in the 1990 Act. As Lord Irvine pointed out, in 1998, however, civilisation as we know it has not ended in the 1990s. Indeed, numbers of independently practising barristers have increased every year since 1990. The Royal Commission on Legal Services and many other individuals have discussed the feasibility and desirability of a fused profession. Here are the pros and cons.

Arguments against a Divided Profession

13-041   *Expense to the client*, "two or three taxi meters": why should the client pay for two barristers to argue his case in court, if it is a serious case meriting a Q.C. and a junior, accompanied by a solicitor's representative? Why not just let the client hire one lawyer to do everything, instead of paying for three "taxi meters" clocking up a huge bill, hour by hour? Professor Michael Zander provoked the establishment of the Royal Commission on Legal Services in 1976 by famously making this argument, most fully explored in his book, *Lawyers and the Public Interest* (1968).

Inefficiency, failures in communication

Some witness suggested to the Royal Commission that the present structure caused this; because of the distance between barristers and solicitors, written instructions sent to counsel were often inadequate. Barristers were reluctant to complain.

Returned briefs

Very frequently, a solicitor sends a brief to chambers marked for a named barrister. At the last minute, the brief is returned because the barrister is otherwise occupied. The solicitor then has to find another barrister or permit the brief to be passed on to another barrister in the same chambers who may be a stranger to him or the client. This causes frustration to the solicitor, denied the choice of original barrister and may destroy the client's confidence (see Mackenzie at (1990) 150 N.L.J. 512). The solicitor may have reassured the client of the best of service from the named barrister yet the client is faced with a stranger at the doors of the court. Many defendants complained of the shoddy service they received after meeting their barrister on the morning of trial, in Bottoms and McClean's *Defendants in the Criminal Process* (1976) and *Standing Accused* (1994) by Mike McConville *et al.* Zander and Henderson's *Crown Court Study* for the Royal Commission on Criminal Justice (1991–1993) provided statistics which illustrated how bad the problem is. In 66 per cent of contested cases, the CPS said the barrister who appeared at trial was not the barrister originally instructed. In most cases, the CPS learned of the change of barrister at the last minute. In eight per cent of cases where there was a change of barrister it was said to cause a problem. As for defence barristers, in 48 per cent of cases, the barrister at trial was not the one originally instructed and in the majority of such cases, the solicitor was informed on the day before, or on the day of hearing. In 60 per cent of cases, the defendant either saw no barrister or a different one before trial. In 17 per cent of cases, the solicitor said the original barrister would have been better than the substitute.

In 1997, research by the National Audit Office showed that CPS briefs **13-042** had been returned in 75 per cent of the cases sampled and new counsel was judged to be inappropriate in almost a third of these. In 1998, the CPS inspectorate published a report on child witnesses, heavily critical that briefs were returned in half of all child abuse cases.

The Legal Action Group, in evidence to the Royal Commission, argued that the "detachment" which the Bar claims to be an advantage is seen by the client as ignorance of his case and circumstances. Public confidence in the legal system suffers.

Arguments Against Fusion

Free from interruptions by clients

13-043   Barristers can concentrate on the specialist matters, benefiting from the fact that another lawyer has already identified the issues and sifted out the relevant facts.

Jury advocacy

This is a specialist type of advocacy, requiring special skills akin to those involved in public speaking. These skills require regular practice. There may be grave consequences to the client. Emotions run high. The barrister is accustomed to this environment and can provide the necessary detachment.

Loss of choice

If the profession were fused, leading barristers would join large firms of solicitors and so the ability to brief them would be lost to all other solicitors. Under the present system, clients in the remotest areas or with the most complex problems still have access to the best barristers. Solicitors under a fused profession would not readily refer a client to another firm. Access to advocates would be reduced. Most firms of solicitors have few partners. They could not absent themselves from the office for days on end appearing in court. It is therefore important that solicitors have access to barristers to provide services which they could not.

Advocacy

In a fused system, there would be a drop in quality of advocacy, which would damage not just the interests of the client but the administration of justice. Standards would decline because the specialist knowledge of the Bar would be diluted. Specialisms need regular practice. The Bar can fairly claim to be specialist advocates.

Cost effectiveness

13-044   The present system is more cost effective. Under a fused system, it would be more expensive to have a solicitor to represent the client as solicitors' overheads are larger.

Orality

English practice rests on the principle of oral hearing, which demands well prepared, experienced practitioners. This point, like those below, was made by F.A. Mann ((1977) 98 L.Q.R. 367). It is no longer as valid as it then was. Now, skeleton arguments must be prepared in all cases brought before all civil cases and in most appeals.

Procedure
English procedure requires a single and continuous hearing, which requires time and undivided attention that few solicitors could afford.

Judicial unpreparedness
In England and Wales the principle of *curia novit legem* applies. This means that counsel submits the law to the court, which is assumed to know nothing. Counsel has a duty not to mislead the court. Such a system requires specialist knowledge and experience, intensive preparation and much training. If we required judges to research and prepare the law in each case, we would require many more judges.

Comment

These are good points in relation to advocacy in the higher courts but firstly, they ignore the fact that most advocates are solicitors and, since Mann wrote, the county court deals with some very important civil cases, where solicitors have rights of audience. Really Mann's arguments support the existence of specialist advocates, not a divided profession, bolstered by all the monopolies and restrictive practices lawyers enjoyed in his day.

13-045

Further, the notion that solicitors generally choose the best advocate for the job, from amongst the pool of barristers sounds great in theory but, as we have seen, in the routine of the Crown Court, both prosecution and defence briefs end up, more often than not, with a barrister who was not the one originally selected.

8. Race and Gender Discrimination

There is not the space in this book to recount the sad litany of race and gender discrimination in the legal profession but see the website accompanying this book at www.sweetandmaxwell.co.uk/academic

13-046

FURTHER READING

The Law Society's *Annual Statistical Report*.
P. Thomas, *Discriminating Lawyers* (2000).
General Council of the Bar, *Annual Report*.
The Policy Studies Institute, *Law Student Cohort Study*.
Access to Justice Act 1999 and *Modernising Justice*, 1998, the white paper which explains it (LCD website: www.lcd.gov.uk).
The Lord Chancellor, *Silk 2002* (title changes annually), LCS website.

13-047

D. Pannick, "Why the silk's purse won't survive" [2001] P.L 439.

P. Reeves, *Silk Cut* (1998) for the Adam Smith Institute.

Law Society's *Gazette*, available online, free.

Counsel.

The Lawyer.

The Solicitors Journal.

Report of the Royal Commission on Legal Services (1979) Cmnd. 7648.

G. Davis, etc., (1998)148 N.L.J 832, on solicitors' in-house complaints procedures.

A. Scher, *Willing Blindness? Complaints Handling Procedures* (1999).

Research from Bristol and Westminster: G. Davis *et al.* (1997) 147 N.L.J. 212.

M. Zander, (1998) 148 N.L.J. 1422; and (1997) 4 *International Journal of the Legal Profession* 167.

"Lord Chancellor Debunks Criticism of Queen's Counsel Appointment Process", press release 156/01.

B. Mahendra, on silks, at (2001) 151 N.L.J. 449. See also F. Gibb and D. Pannick on silks, *The Times*, April 10, 2001.

F. Gibb, "£1m-a-year QCs lose as often as they win" *The Times*, March 19, 2001.

F. Gibb, "Rumpoles fall behind law's fat cats" *The Times*, April 14, 2001.

14. Judges

1. Who are Our Judges and how are They Appointed?

Appointment, Selection and Qualifications, According to Statute and Current Policy

The Courts and Legal Services Act 1990 bases eligibility for the judi-   **14-001**
ciary on rights of audience. This means that barristers are eligible for
every judicial appointment but solicitors may only be appointed as High
Court judges if they are solicitor-advocates with a High Court qualification, as defined by the Act. Lord Irvine, the Lord Chancellor, explains
current policy, the application procedure and job specifications, in great
detail, in Annex A to the *Judicial Appointments Annual Report 1999–2000*
(LCD website). The scheme is as follows:

General policy
1.   Appointments must be made on merit, regardless of ethnic origin,
      gender, marital status, political affiliation, sexual orientation, relig-
      ion or disability. This illustrates the Lord Chancellor's acute sensi-
      tivity towards constant criticism of the composition of the
      judiciary—that it is too narrow, being overwhelmingly white, male
      and upper or middle class. The Lord Chancellor asked Sir Leonard
      Peach to report on the system of selecting silks (Q.C.s) and judges
      and Sir Leonard reported in 1999 (*Appointment Processes of Judges and
      Queen's Counsel in England and Wales*, LCD website). Some of his find-
      ings are mentioned below. Appointments are administered by the
      Judicial Group of the Lord Chancellor's Department (LCD).
2.   "The Lord Chancellor will have regard to comments . . . received
      from judges and members of the profession . . .".

267

3.   "Applicants will have demonstrated possession of the following skills and attributes in their professional careers and in their service in part-time and/or full-time judicial office":

legal knowledge and experience and knowledge of evidence and procedure; a high quality of effectiveness in any part-time appointment; a high level of professional achievement; intellectual and analytical ability; sound judgment; decisiveness; communication and listening skills; authority and case management skills; integrity and independence; fairness and impartiality; understanding of people and society; maturity and sound temperament; courtesy; commitment, conscientiousness and diligence.

Applications

14-002   Applications are required for all appointments up to the level of circuit judge. Judicial posts are advertised, along with detailed job specifications. This reform was effected by Lord Mackay from 1994. Prior to this there was no organised application procedure. Lord Irvine advertises for High Court judges, since 1998 but reserves the right to invite practitioners onto the High Court Bench.

Consultation about candidates

Comments on potential judges are collected confidentially. In the case of the most senior judicial appointments, the Lord Chancellor consults with senior judges. All High Court judges and above are consulted on appointments to the High Court. Each year, comments are sought on applicants for recorderships and the circuit bench, from listed members of the judiciary and some representatives of the legal profession.

Interviews

Those applying for inferior judicial posts (circuit level) are interviewed by a serving judge, a departmental official and a "specially selected and trained" lay member.

Work shadowing

The scheme of "work shadowing" encourages practitioners to accompany working judges, before deciding whether to apply.

Statutory and policy criteria for appointment

I include the correct forms of address (for the key to which judges sit in which courts, see the court structure map):

Lords of Appeal in Ordinary (colloquially known as "Law Lords"), e.g. The Right Honourable Lord Phillips of Worth Matravers

These are appointed by the Queen on the advice of the Prime Minister, who is likely to seek the advice of the Lord Chancellor, Law Lords and senior judges. A Law Lord must have held high judicial office for two years, or a Supreme Court qualification for 15 years (meaning Supreme Court audience rights, under the Courts and Legal Services Act 1990), or Scottish or Northern Irish equivalent. In practice, they are generally appointed from the Court of Appeal, the Scottish Court of Session or the Court of Appeal in Northern Ireland. One exception is Lord Slynn, who was a judge in the European Court of Justice. Incidentally, the Lord Chancellor is entitled to sit in judgment with the Law Lords and Lord Irvine sat four times in 2000. The same applies to ex-Lord Chancellors.

The Heads of Division (Master of the Rolls, Lord Chief Justice, Vice-Chancellor and President of the Family Division), e.g. The Right Honourable Lord Phillips of Worth Matravers, or Phillips M.R.

These are appointed by the Monarch on the advice of the Prime **14-003** Minister. (The Queen takes no part in the choice and the Prime Minister is advised by the Lord Chancellor.) Recruits must be Lords Justices of Appeal (and most are) or qualified as such.

Lords Justices of Appeal, e.g. The Right Honourable Sir John Grant McKenzie Laws, or Laws L.J., or Lord Justice Laws

These are appointed by the Monarch on the advice of the Prime Minister, who receives advice from the Lord Chancellor, who normally consults senior members of the judiciary. They must have a ten-year "High Court qualification" or be judges of the High Court, which is the normal route.

High Court Judges, e.g. The Honourable Sir Roger John Laugharne Thomas, or Thomas J., or Mr Justice Thomas

These are appointed by the Queen on the advice of the Lord Chancellor. They need a ten-year High Court qualification or to have been a circuit judge for at least two years. Around half of appointments are made from circuit judges and the rest are mainly barristers who have practised for 20 to 30 years and are Q.C.s, according to the LCD website. The Courts and Legal Services Act 1990 made solicitor-advocates eligible for appointment.

Deputy High Court Judges

These are appointed by the Lord Chancellor, under the Supreme Court Act 1981, section 9(4). Lord Irvine continues his predecessors' policy of testing out most High Court judges by appointing them to sit part-time. In 2000, there were 205 deputies.

Retired Judges

The Lord Chancellor has power to authorise retired superior judges to sit part-time until their 75th birthday. In 2000, around 26 retired judges were authorised.

Circuit Judges, e.g. Judge Charles Elly

These are appointed by the Queen on the recommendation of the Lord Chancellor, under the Courts Act 1971. They must have a ten-year county court or Crown Court qualification, or be a recorder or have been in full-time office for three years in another judicial capacity. The Lord Chancellor will normally consider only applicants who have sat as recorders for at least two years and are aged 45–60. Once appointed, they may sit at the Crown Court or county court. Most hear both civil and criminal cases and they may be authorised to hear family cases. Some sit full-time in the specialised jurisdictions, such as chancery or mercantile cases. Experienced circuit judges may be requested to sit in the High Court (Supreme Court Act 1981) or in the Criminal Division of the Court of Appeal.

Deputy Circuit Judges

14-004   These are appointed by the Lord Chancellor from among retired judges. In 2000, there were 35.

Recorders, e.g. Cherie Booth Q.C.

These are part-timers appointed by the Queen, on the recommendation of the Lord Chancellor for a renewable period of five years. Appointees must have a 10-year Crown Court or county court qualification. They sit in the Crown Court and/or the county court, handling less serious matters than a circuit judge. They are required to sit for at least 15–30 days per year, of which at least 10 days should be in one continuous period. The Lord Chancellor will not normally appoint anyone below the age of 35. Note that the post of assistant recorder was abolished in 2000. This was the Lord Chancellor's response to the Scottish case of *Starrs v. Procurator Fiscal* (1999) where the Court held that a judge with no security of tenure was not "independent" within the meaning of the European Convention on Human Rights so the system of part-time sherrifs was unlawful.

District Judges, e.g. District Judge Gold

These are appointed by the Lord Chancellor and sit full-time in the county courts or district registries of the High Court, disposing of 80 per cent of all contested civil litigation. The statutory qualification is a seven-year general qualification, meaning barrister or solicitor. The Lord Chancellor normally only considers applicants who have been serving deputy district judges for two years, aged 40–60.

Deputy District Judges
These are appointed by the Lord Chancellor, for a probationary period of 18 months. They are normally aged 35–65. They sit part-time for 20–50 days per year.

Masters and Registrars of the Supreme Court
These mainly deal with interlocutory (pre-trial) High Court work, as trial managers. Taxing masters tax costs in Supreme Court work. They are normally appointed aged 40–60, from the ranks of deputy masters and registrars. They must have a seven-year general qualification.

Current Composition

Up-to-date judicial statistics can be found by clicking on the "judges"   **14-005**
button on the Lord Chancellor's website. They demonstrate that women, solicitors and members of the ethnic minorities are not reflected in the judiciary in the proportions in which they populate the legal profession. At the time of writing, 2001, there were no women Law Lords. The first and only female head of division was Dame Elizabeth Butler-Sloss (appointed in 2000). There were two female Lords Justices of Appeal (of 35), eight female High Court judges (of 107) and 45 female circuit judges (of 573) There are only two solicitor High Court judges and none above that rank and only one non-white High Court judge and six non-white circuit judges.

Social Background
Further, the narrow social and educational background of judges has been most famously attacked by J.A.G. Griffith in successive editions of his book *The Politics of the Judiciary.* Innumerable surveys are cited by him, all demonstrating that the senior judiciary is dominated by Oxbridge graduates, educated at the top public schools (fifth edition, 1997, at 18).

In 1999, the Labour Research Department accused the Labour Government of failing to have had an impact on the composition of the judiciary. They examined 692 judges, including the 85 appointed or promoted since Labour came to power in 1997 and found:

- Most of the newly appointed or promoted were white males. Women in 1999 accounted for six per cent of the judiciary and ethnic minorities for one per cent.
- 79 per cent of those newly appointed or promoted had been to public school and 73 per cent were Oxbridge graduates. These figures were worse than for the judiciary as a whole. Overall, 69 per cent were public school educated and 64 per cent went to Oxbridge.

Labour had had an impact on the age profile of judges. The average age on appointment or promotion since 1997 was 55, compared with 60 for the judiciary as a whole The average age of the Law Lords remained at 66, the same as in 1997 and 1994. (Press Release, June 1, 1999, Labour research website.)

Criticisms: are Lord Chancellors Giving us "Weasel Words"?

14-006   It is said that the traditional system of secretive selection of judges, from a limited pool of practising advocates, operated by one man, the Lord Chancellor, acting on the opinions of the judiciary and the profession, has produced a Bench which is far too narrow, in terms of class, education, age, gender and ethnic background. The scheme set out above has been repeatedly attacked, by academics, left-wing politicians, the pressure group JUSTICE, the Law Society and women and minority lawyers' groups. The most thorough exposure of these views is collected in the House of Commons Home Affairs Committee, third report for the session 1995–1996, *Judicial Appointments Procedures Volume II, Minutes of Evidence and Appendices* (1996), to which I shall refer as JAP. Here I examine the issues, in more detail.

Can and should judges be drawn from a wide section of the community?

Lord Mackay did not think so, "It is not the function of the judiciary to reflect particular sections of the community, as it is of the democratically elected legislature" (JAP, 130). He added that he expected composition would broaden over time. J.A.G. Griffith cynically attacked this sentiment as these "weasel words" (at 261). Lord Irvine appears to take a different view from his Conservative predecessor: "I believe that the judiciary should be a microcosm of the community that it serves." (interview on the *Today* programme, March 21, 1999).

The System of "Secret Soundings"—"Comment Collection"

Traditionally, in England and Wales, aspirants did not apply for a job as a judge, especially for the superior judiciary, meaning High Court judges and above. They were invited to put themselves forward by the Lord Chancellor, whose civil servants gathered files of fact and opinion on potential judges and kept candidates under constant review. This is because the senior jobs were limited to the Bar. The Bar was so small, around 1000, until 1960, that the Lord Chancellor was presumed to know all the candidates personally. By 1990, many candidates for recorderships and the circuit judiciary applied and some were still invited but there was no standard application form other than for district judges.

14-007   Lord Hailsham L.C. endeavoured to make the recruitment and appointment system less secretive and, in the 1980s, published his selection criteria. Lord Mackay made countless speeches urging more women and ethnic minorities to put themselves forward. In 1994–1995 he dramatically opened up the recruitment and selection system by advertising inferior judicial posts and introducing interview panels. As for the superior judiciary, by convention, until 1998, candidates did not apply.

The problem is that, despite all the reforms outlined above, effected by these three Lord Chancellors, the L.C. is still heavily reliant on these ongoing consultations with judges, as explained above. They are referred to by critics as "secret soundings", to the irritation of the Lord Chancellor, who values them. The Judges' Council, in their evidence to the Home Affairs Committee defended the system:

> "judges see and hear most of the potential candidates before them, day in, day out, from a position in which they are uniquely well placed to assess their professional competence and personal qualities, and to compare them with competitors in the field." (219).

The Equal Opportunities Commission, in their evidence, expressed "a major concern" over such soundings:

> "Selection for appointment should depend on an objective assessment of the applicant's skills and abilities. Given the predominance of men in the senior ranks of the judiciary, the bar and the solicitor's profession, there is an increased risk of stereotypical assumptions being made with regard to "female" as opposed to "male" qualities and aptitudes. It is therefore the Commission's view that the practice of canvassing opinion is certain to risk introducing impressionistic and subjective factors into the recruitment process." (at 211).

If consultation is to continue, then those consulted should at least receive training.

Most critics made the simple point that any system which relies on the say-so of a limited group is inevitably open to members of that group selecting people like them. As Chris Mullin M.P. retorted:

> ". . . it appears to be self-perpetuating does it not? They all know each other, many of them went to school together, most of them were at university together and they have no doubt known each other all the time dining in their various Inns of Court. They are males aged between 55 and 66 on average . . . and they appear to move in very limited circles." (at 5)

The Law Centres Federation called the Bar and the judiciary "in effect a self-perpetuating oligarchy or clique" (at 227) The Association of

Women Barristers urged that the system should be abolished (at 193). The Law Society said the system disadvantaged those who were not from the standard background for judges and perpetuated the weight given to advocacy skills. They wanted it replaced with a system of objective tests and interviews, such as is used in civil service recruitment (at 229). The Bar Association for Commerce, Finance and Industry (employed barristers) called the system "wholly indefensible in the 1990s" (at 204). The Association of Women Solicitors opposed the system because it disadvantaged women and solicitors who were unlikely to appear before and, consequently, be known to serving members of the judiciary and it placed undue emphasis on advocacy skills. The African, Caribbean and Asian Lawyers' Association said that the composition of the judiciary reflected neither the British population nor the legal profession.

14-008   The accusation that the system perpetuates a clique was strikingly illustrated by research undertaken on behalf of the Association of Women Barristers. Examining 104 High Court Appointments made during 1986–1996, 70 (67.3 per cent) came from a set of chambers of which at least one ex-member was a judge during the consultation period. Only 58 of 227 sets of London chambers produced judges, of which seven sets produced an astonishing 30 appointees. Of the 131 sets outside London, they produced only seven judges. The 104 appointees, from a pool of 8,800 barristers replaced over two thirds of the judges, yet came from roughly the same chambers as those they replaced (J. Hayes, (1997) 147 N.L.J. 520).

Sir Leonard Peach (1999) suggested that each candidate should nominate three referees and this is now done. They are consulted separately from the other consultees. Otherwise, Sir Leonard expressed his confidence in the system. This disappointed all critics, especially the Law Society, who repeated their condemnation of the "secret soundings" system, as they call it as "fundamentally flawed" and an "old boys' network". The report did, however, recommend that the consultations system be supplemented with alternative methods of evaluating an applicant's suitability, such as one-day assessment centres and psychometric and competence testing (see comment by Malleson, (2000) 150 N.L.J. 8). The Lord Chancellor, in September 2000, announced that work would commence on a pilot for an assessment centre, following recommendations by a Bar Council and Law Society working party. He also accepted the need for wider advertising, better aptitude testing and an easier route from other judicial roles. In June 2000, Kate Malleson and Fareda Banda reported to the Lord Chancellor on *Factors affecting the decision to apply for silk and judicial office* (see LCD website). It exposed widespread dissatisfaction with the selection process, especially among women, solicitors and minorities, who felt particularly disadvantaged by the consultations

274

process and resented the apparent elite group of barristers' chambers. Many repeated the call for a Judicial Appointments Commission.

Restricting judicial appointments to those with rights of audience
The gist of the above criticism, that those who do not appear before **14-009** the right judges will not be selected, is compounded by the law itself (Courts and Legal Services Act 1990) which bases all judicial appointments on audience rights. This excludes most solicitors (most lawyers) from appointment directly to the High Court and all those with purely academic qualifications from all judicial appointments. The Judges' Council defended this restriction:

> "Successful advocates must develop and exhibit the ability, founded upon sound judgment, to evaluate the strengths and weaknesses of their opponent's case as thoroughly as their own. . . . In addition, the administration of justice in England and Wales depends upon lawyers who appear before the court owing their paramount duty to the interest of justice, and not advancing arguments or evidence which are improper, mendacious or corrupt." (JAP, 219).

Certain groups have long argued that prowess as an advocate, standing in court arguing one side of a case, does not demonstrate the skills needed of a judge, to sit quiet and give an impartial hearing to both sides and fair judgment. For instance, JUSTICE has always been opposed to the restriction of judicial eligibility to advocates:

> "The best drama producers may not be the best critics; the best players do not necessarily become the best referees. In particular the strong combative or competitive streak present in many successful advocates is out of place on the bench." (*The Judiciary in England and Wales*, 1992.)

The Law Society argued that the emphasis on advocacy "actually impairs the selection of the best candidates". Full-time advocates suffered the disadvantage of a lack of experience of dealing with clients directly, or of conducting litigation, which could lead to "a rather unworldly approach". (JAP, 234–235).

Other jurisdictions do not limit the judiciary to practising advocates and use is made of academics as judges in the highest courts. Thinking of the qualities needed of judges in the Court of Appeal and the House of Lords, they spend most of their time considering and developing points of law. Academic lawyers devote their whole careers to developing expertise in specialist areas of the law.

The present Lord Chancellor has accepted some of these criticisms. As a result of the Peach Report and Banda and Malleson's research, he re-wrote the appointment criteria to emphasise that he does not regard advocacy experience as an essential requirement for appointment to judicial office (see criteria in *Judicial Appointments Annual Report 1999–2000*).

The emphasis on silk

Around half of High Court judges are recruited from Queen's Counsel. This system is opposed by solicitors, women and ethnic minorities because, as explained in the Chapter on lawyers, they allege that it disadvantages them, again because of the emphasis on advocacy and also because appointments to silk are massively unrepresentative of such groups, again because the method of recruitment to silk is based on what they call "secret soundings" with the senior judiciary.

The exclusion of solicitors

14-010   They have long been the most persistent of critics of the judicial appointment system. Prior to the Courts and Legal Services Act, solicitors were only eligible for appointment up to circuit level. This brought about the criticisms that the system was unfair on solicitors and produced too narrow a pool of potential judges. The Act has made very little difference since, in 2001, there are still only two solicitor High Court judges. This is hardly surprising, as only a handful of solicitors have higher court audience rights, by 2001.

In the early 1990s, the Law Society's *Gazette* carried several critical articles and the Society published a discussion document urging that the system be subjected to a complete overhaul. The emphasis on advocacy meant that solicitor candidates, minorities and women were overlooked. It was they who urged the devising of a list of judicial qualities as formal selection criteria, which Lord Mackay eventually published in 1994. Solicitors stridently opposed the consultation system. Further, they complained that the published selection criteria still placed too much emphasis on career success and income. The requirement for part-time sitting prior to full-time appointment was too lengthy and should be made more flexible, as short blocks of sitting were disruptive of solicitors' practices and that other judicial appointments, such as tribunal chairman, district judge and stipendiary magistrate did not seem to be a stepping stone to the circuit bench. Appointments, they said, should be made or recommended by a judicial appointments commission (see below), from as wide a pool of candidates as possible, who all felt equally encouraged to apply, according to selection criteria which did not unnecessarily disadvantage any group.

14-011   Both Lord Mackay and the present Lord Chancellor, Lord Irvine remained unmoved by these criticisms. By October 1999, solicitors had become exasperated in the lack of progress toward reforming the judicial appointment system and the Law Society announced they were boycotting the "consultations" system. In other words, if solicitors were consulted on potential candidates, they would not offer an opinion. Lord Irvine condemned the Law Society's action as a "disservice to its members", in his press releases, speeches and *Judicial Appointments Annual Report 1999–2000*. In that report, he emphasised that 47 per cent of new appointments went to solicitors but acknowledged these were not the senior appointments. In October 2000, the Law Society reiterated all their criticisms in a report again calling for an independent judicial appointments system (summary in press release, Law Society website).

Racial minorities — is the appointments system discriminatory?

Geoffrey Bindman wrote a provocative article in the *Gazette* suggesting that the system was indirectly discriminatory and thus illegal, under the Race Relations Act 1976 (February 27, 1991). Bindman cited the Commission for Racial Equality's code of practice for employers, which recommended against recruitment through the recommendations of the existing workforce where the workforce was predominantly from one ethnic group and the labour market multi-racial. Recruitment by word of mouth was a common cause of discrimination. Lord Mackay refuted this criticism, sending the Law Society's president counsel's opinion (a barrister's expert opinion) to the effect that the article was "wrong in law and fact". He said he could only reach his objective of increasing the number of women and minorities on the Bench if he could find a sufficient proportion of them in the practising profession of the appropriate age and standing.

The present Lord Chancellor seems equally frustrated at the low numbers of minorities applying for judicial appointment. At the Minority Lawyers' Association Conference in November 1997, (speech on the LCD website) he reiterated Prime Minister Tony Blair's embarrassment that there were no black superior judges and only one per cent non-white circuit judges. He explained that only about one per cent of barristers of 15 years' call, the group eligible for High Court appointments, were minority. The root cause of the problem, he said, was long-term discrimination on both sides of the legal profession: "I cannot solve all the problems by myself. The professions need to ensure their houses are in order." Black lawyers remain cynical, because of the continuing lack of non-white judges. There was a reduction in the proportion of ethnic minority practitioners appointed in 1999–2000 to 4.2 per cent from 5.4 per cent but in the *Annual Report 1999–2000*, the Lord Chancellor points out that, of lawyers with over 20 years' experience, the group from which most judges are appointed, under four per cent are minority.

The exclusion of women

Again, the statistics quoted above speak for themselves. As for the **14-012** circuit bench, recruitment was examined by Sally Hughes for the Law

Society in 1991, in *The Circuit Bench — A Woman's Place?* She challenged the excuse made, by Lord Mackay above, that the numbers of women on the Bench will naturally increase as the number in practice increases. Examining two cohorts of barristers, she found that women took longer than men to be appointed to the Bench and were recruited from a much narrower age range. Their late appointments could not be accounted for by maternity leave. Of the 173 circuit judges appointed during 1986–1990, only 4.6 per cent were women. The majority of women judges surveyed thought that, although some had suffered discrimination early in their careers, the judicial appointments system did not discriminate against women. Nevertheless, many women had had low career expectations and one third had been invited to apply, without having put themselves forward. This was consistent, said Hughes, with employment research which showed that women were less likely to apply for promotion and more inclined to accept initial rejection. Thus she concluded that to restrict appointments to applicants (as transpired in 1994–1995) would damage the recruitment of women.

By 1995, the Law Society reported that there had been a rapid improvement in the number of women assistant recorders but there was little sign of improvement at higher levels. This showed that the Lord Chancellor's recruitment drive was working but changes would have to be made much lower down the system to develop the careers of women and minorities, if there were to be real impact. (JAP, 232–233.)

The Association of Women Solicitors complained that the requirement to sit part-time for several years was a double bind for women solicitors. They might annoy their business partners by disrupting their practice and reducing their earning capacity shortly after taking a career break or maternity leave. The judicial atmosphere was unwelcoming to women. Women were disadvantaged by the existence of male clubs, where judges and barristers lunched. The Inns of Court and freemasonry provided opportunities for male barristers to fraternise with judges.

Some of their recommendations, and those of other parties have since been followed, such as open advertising and reformed selection criteria (partly satisfied in 1995) and the removal of obstacles to employed barristers (in the Access to Justice Act 1999).

14-013 In his *Annual Report 1999–2000*, the Lord Chancellor reported that 26.9 per cent of those appointed through open competition in that year were women, compared with 23.5 per cent the previous year. (See now Hale.)

Gays and lesbians

Martin Bowley, president of the Bar Lesbian and Gay Group, had a sorry personal tale of prejudice to tell the Home Affairs Committee. He had been informed that he was not appointed to the Bench because this was against the Lord Chancellor's policy "since [homosexuals] were particularly vulnerable to public and private pressures". This bar was dropped in 1994. The LCD judicial appointments group staged a recruitment event at the Lesbian and Gay Law Conference 2000.

Freemasons
    Where a judge is suspected of being a freemason, it is sometimes alleged that he has favoured "brothers" appearing before him, as barrister, solicitor, Crown prosecutor, police witness or one of the parties. The problem of alleged bias is exacerbated by the fact that, unlike common membership of a golf club, membership of the freemasons is much more difficult to discover. Furthermore, they have secret signals with which to greet one another. In the context of judicial appointments, there is a further concern that aspirant barristers who are freemasons (all male) have a special relationship with recommending judges who are also masons.
    The House of Commons Home Affairs Committee, in 1997, reported **14-014** on its investigation into *Freemasonry in the Police and the Judiciary.* (Third Report 1997. All quotations are from the minutes of evidence.) In evidence, the United Grand Lodge of England refuted all allegations of bias or corruption, especially the frequent allegation that masons owe an allegiance to their fraternal oath which overrides their professional duties or ethics and the judicial oath. The Judges Council (at 113) and Lord Chancellor Mackay could see no cause for concern. It was disclosed that 32 senior freemasons were judges, in 1997, plus an unknown number of more junior freemasons. The Law Society and the Association of Women Barristers argued that judges and senior police officers should not be freemasons. Liberty (at 114) detailed one case alleging corrupt masonic connections. They said they knew of many such instances. The Association of Women Barristers (at 109) listed "a significant number" of legal Masonic Lodges. Lord Chancellor Irvine has since required all incoming judges to publicly disclose membership of the freemasons. The Lord Chancellor, in 1998, asked over 5,000 existing judges to voluntarily declare whether they were freemasons. Two hundred and forty-seven judges admitted they were and 64 declined to answer.

The joint working party on equal opportunities in judicial appointments and silk
    This was set up in 1997, consisting of representatives of the Bar Council, Law Society, and minority lawyers' groups. It reported to the Lord Chancellor in 1999, making 42 recommendations aimed at increasing numbers of women and ethnic minorities applying for silk and judicial appointment. Many of these have already been implemented or are accepted or under consideration by the L.C., following the Peach report (see Annex D to the *Judicial Appointments Annual Report 1999–2000* and compare with p.20 of the report. It is well worth reading).

Why Should the Judiciary be More
14-015 ## Representative?

Many have argued that an imbalance in the judiciary will warp the administration of justice itself. For instance, David Pannick argues "the quality of judicial performance would be improved if more of the bench enjoyed the experience peculiar to more than half the members of our society" (*The Times*, July 30, 1996). Barbara Hewson, of the Association of Women Barristers listed examples of gender bias in judicial and tribunal decisions (*The Times*, September 17, 1996) and advocated the research and educational work of gender bias task forces, such as exist in the United States ((1997) 147 N.L.J. 537), where the National Judicial Education Program identified three types of gender bias: stereotypical thinking about the nature and roles of men and women, how society values women and men and myths about the social and economic realities of women's lives (and see McGlynn at (1998) 148 N.L.J. 813).

Since the massive growth of judicial review, in the 1980s and 1990s, and especially since the passage of the Human Rights Act 1998, it has been argued that our judicial appointment process should be much more open to public scrutiny, since judges' decisions frequently have political repercussions and, in enforcing the European Convention on Human Rights, the courts will become constitutional watchdogs and the Law Lords will effectively constitute a constitutional court. For this reason, John Patten, a former Conservative Home Office Minister, argued that all judicial appointments should be publicly advertised and subjected to a powerful lay selection process, with an annually updated register of interests and public hearings before the appointment of a Law Lord, as occur when a new U.S. Supreme Court Justice is appointed (*The Times*, March 16, 1999).

The Roles of the Lord Chancellor and Prime Minister in Appointing Judges
14-016

As Griffith has said, in *The Politics of the Judiciary*, "The most remarkable fact about the appointment of judges is that it is wholly in the hands of politicians" and he traces the history of political patronage, judicial appointments as a reward for political services. Nevertheless, as Drewry points out,

> "even the sternest critics of the present arrangements would surely have to concede that any vestige of the old party political "spoils" system that prevailed until the early part of this century has been eradicated. Above all the *neutrality* of judges is underpinned by the strong commitment to the constitutional principle of judicial *independence*, which is regularly reaffirmed by politicians of all political parties as an essential pillar of the rule of law. "

Anyway, the debate about the political background of judges

"has been overtaken in the last couple of decades by the transforma-
tion of party political ideology and the social class structure. Even if
one accepts that judicial ideology may over the years have displayed
some sympathetic resonance with traditional Conservative values,
many of those values were displaced or distorted in the 1980s or 1990s
by New Right free market radicalism, and Margaret Thatcher's and
John Major's ministers were often given a very hard time by the
courts." (Comment [1998] P.L. 1.)

Critics remained concerned, however, about the role of the Prime
Minister and Lord Chancellor. Griffith says whether the P.M. merely
accepts the Lord Chancellor's advice on senior appointments will depend
on the personalities of the two but Rozenberg insists that Margaret
Thatcher vetoed some of Lord Mackay's suggestions (JAP, p.273).
Brazier, in evidence to the 1995 Select Committee, articulates the concerns of many about the overwhelming power of the Lord Chancellor in
most appointments:

• The concentration of power in the hands of one person, without
  the benefit of a structured system of advice, is unsatisfactory. The
  present system lacks openness, relies on unstructured questions to
  advisers of unknown identity. There is no accountability to
  Parliament.
• The increasing size of both branches of the profession means the
  Lord Chancellor cannot have adequate knowledge of all potential candidates. (The JUSTICE report said that, some 50 years
  earlier, with a Bar of 1500 and under 100 judges, the Lord
  Chancellor was personally involved in choosing judges.)

Concern arose again in 2001, over the apparent conflicts of interest that
may arise from the Lord Chancellor's position in all three organs of
government: legislature (as speaker of the House of Lords), executive (a
minister) and head of the judiciary. Lord Irvine solicited donations to
Labour funds from lawyers. Conservatives said this was an abuse of his
power over those lawyers who aspired to judicial appointments and many
critics renewed their wider criticism of the Lord Chancellor's tripartite
constitutional position (*The Times*, February 20 and 22, 2001 provides
excellent analysis).

The Call for Sweeping Reform—a Judicial Appointments Commission

The suggestion has frequently been made that a commission of lay   **14-017**
persons and others should either advise the Lord Chancellor in judicial
appointments or replace him.

Reiterating their call for such a body, with powers stretching beyond appointment, JUSTICE, in 1992, suggested it should be responsible for recommending all judicial appointments, including tribunal members and magistrates, all judicial training, career development of the circuit judiciary, performance standards and complaints. The Commission would comprise 13 members: seven lay persons, two judges and four lawyers. Visible and real independence from the executive and judiciary would be crucial. The proposal was designed to secure a more diverse bench.

In supporting such a Commission, the Law Society said, in evidence to the Home Affairs Committee, that its advantages would be:

- distancing individual appointments from ministerial control;
- assisting in formalising selection procedures and criteria to reflect good recruitment practice and
- assisting in achieving public confidence in the objectivity and even-handedness of the selection process (JAP, 237).

In their evidence, the Judges' Council rejected such reasoning as "misguided" and introducing politics into the selection process.

The Society was supported by Professor Brazier. He noted that the Liberal Democrats and the Labour Party, then in opposition, favoured a Commission. The Labour Party set out its plans for a Commission in several policy documents, including *Access to Justice*, 1995 and *A New Agenda for Democracy*, 1997, although the proposal did not appear in the party's 1997 election manifesto. Those commentators above were disappointed when, in October 1997, Lord Chancellor Irvine announced that he had decided not to established a Commission (LCD press notice, October 9, 1997, LCD website). Instead, he announced some of the reforms listed above and promised to consider establishing an ombudsman for those aggrieved by the appointments process and a system of performance appraisal.

14-018   In the meantime, two discussion papers, by Thomas and Malleson had been commissioned by the Lord Chancellor's Department Research Secretariat, under the joint title, *Judicial Appointments Commissions — The European and North American Experience and the Possible Implications for the United Kingdom* (summarised on the LCD website). Kate Malleson reviewed U.S. and Canadian models and found there was no strong evidence to suggest that the use of commissions as opposed to other appointment methods had any significant effect on the make-up of the judiciary in terms of competence or representativeness. A more important variable might be their approach to the appointment process. The experience in Ontario suggested that active attempts to recruit under-represented groups could have a significant effect on the type of judges appointed. She found that public confidence in the use of commissions is generally very high.

Examining continental European appointment systems, Cheryl Thomas drew attention to differences in the appointment processes that explain differences in judicial composition. Women made up a significant proportion of the judiciary in most of the countries examined and at least half of incoming judges in France, the Netherlands, Germany and Italy. She explained that, as recruitment there is through public examination based on university-level knowledge of the law, women normally fare better than men. She concluded:

"Recruitment of judges later in their professional career, as occurs in common law countries, tends to bring into play social forces which reduce women's chances: family commitments and professional discrimination. Civil law, bureaucratic-style judiciaries have favourable employment conditions for women (maternity leave, flexible working hours, etc.,) and the judiciary is seen as a positive career choice for women law graduates." (Full report, LCD Research Series 6/97, p.21).

Nevertheless, she suggested that the continental practice of involving lower ranking judges in judicial appointments commissions, may also encourage an increase in the appointment to the bench of women, minorities and other less traditional types. It shifts the criteria for appointment and lessens the influence of legal elites who tend to favour the status quo.

In 1999, Sir Leonard Peach recommended to the Lord Chancellor that **14-019** he appoint a Judicial Appointments Commissioner and a number of Deputy Commissioners. A Commissioner was appointed in 2001. He will not advise on appointments but keep the appointments process under constant review and publish an annual report. Critics were disappointed at Sir Leonard's suggestion. The Law Society repeated its call for a commission to select judges, which was open and independent of government (see (1999) 149 N.L.J. 1851). The Association of Women Solicitors and other groups agreed with this criticism. In July 2000, Lord Steyn became the first Law Lord openly to call for a commission, a call repeated by the Society of Labour Lawyers. The Law Society, in support of their attack on the current selection system, point to Hazel Genn's study, *Paths to Justice*, 1999, which disclosed that the public think that judges are old and out of touch.

A More Radical Suggestion—a Career Judiciary

Most continental civil law countries have developed a career judiciary. **14-020** Modern descriptions of a sample of systems are given in Thomas's discussion paper, cited above. Generally speaking, most judges are recruited at a very young age, soon after graduating in law. They are selected like civil servants, by competitive examinations, which sometimes include psychological and fitness testing, as well as legal knowledge, which results in women being the majority of recruits. The new recruit must attend courses at judicial college and then starts off at the bottom of the judicial ladder and may, if successful, be promoted through the ranks to the senior judiciary. It is common to require continuing education and further examinations. Some judges are selected from amongst practising lawyers but this is the exception. A portrait of such judges in France is drawn in an article by Adam Sage (*The Times*, December 1, 1998), who claims that judges are young, radical and middle-class.

From time to time, it has been fashionable to suggest a career judiciary here. Most witnesses before the Home Affairs Committee, discussed above, did not mention such a radical plan but the Law Society, as explained above, did favour recruitment by competitive, civil service-type examinations. The Judges' Council rejected the suggestion on the basis of profound differences between common law systems and the legal systems of continental Europe.

The Committee agreed with Brazier's opinion that the judiciary was already a career, in the sense that a career path of a judge may involve sitting in courts of a progressively higher rank. Nevertheless, the Committee firmly rejected any move to a career judiciary in this country.

Kate Malleson argues ((1997) 60 M.L.R. 655) that, since 1970, the judiciary has undergone a process of formalisation which has resulted in the creation of a form of career judiciary for the following reasons: the judiciary has expanded massively; the majority of work in the criminal courts (she means the Crown Court) is currently carried out by part-time recorders, many of whom are seeking promotion. This must strongly influence their behaviour. Significantly, performance appraisal had, thus far, only been introduced to monitor the suitability of part-time judges for promotion. The formalisation of training and the issue of bench books of model directions, she sees as undermining the culture of individualism that formerly thrived within the judiciary. In her 1999 book, *The New Judiciary*, she argues that the growth in size of the judiciary and the expansion of its policy-making role are leading to radical change in the role of the judiciary. The book is the most modern analysis of the judiciary.

2. *Training*

14-021   We lack the systematic form of judicial training and examinations which are a universal requirement for continental judges. It is often said that our system of recruitment direct from practising professional advocates is the antithesis of training.

The Fear of Undermining Judicial Independence

For centuries, judges have resisted the suggestion that they undergo **14-022** training on the ground that it might undermine their "judicial independence". One of the most famous books written by a judge about judging is Lord Devlin's *The Judge* (1978). In it, he delivers a 20-page tirade against a 1976 Home Office Consultative Working Paper suggesting the introduction of judicial training. Here are some extracts:

> "when in 1948 I was appointed to the High Court. . . . I had never exercised any criminal jurisdiction and not since my early days at the Bar had I appeared in a criminal court. I had never been inside a prison except once in an interviewing room. Two days after I had been sworn in, I was trying crime at Newcastle Assizes . . . for centuries judicial appointments have been made on the basis that experience at the Bar is what gives a man the necessary judicial equipment . . . where the independence of the judges may be touched or appear to be touched, it is a good thing to have a protocol. Protocol should, I think, decree that in the acquisition of background information a judge should be left to his own devices" (pp. 34–35).

The sentiments are typical of judges of the old school. He thought training belonged on the continent. Nevertheless, the Judicial Studies Board was established in 1979.

Malleson challenges the claim that judicial training and performance **14-023** appraisal pose a threat to judicial independence. (M.L.R., cited above). She notes that judges use the objection of threat to their independence as a sort of trump card to play when opposing any innovation in the judiciary but they fail to explain what they mean by judicial independence. Certainly, in opposing the establishment of the Board, they meant freedom from control by the executive, or interference by any outsider, such as an academic director of studies. For this reason, the Board is run by judges. Its President is always a High Court judge; its Director of Studies is a seconded circuit judge and many of its committee members and trainers are judges. The introductory statement on the website asserts:

> "The JSB enjoys a considerable degree of autonomy from its parent Department, the Lord Chancellor's Department, in deciding the need for and nature of judicial training. This independence for training purposes is an important part of wider judicial independence."

Malleson points out, however, that judges perform a dual function: a constitutional role as one branch of the State counterbalancing the interest of the executive and Parliament and a distinct social service role carried out in their day-to-day work in the courts. Training and performance appraisal, she says, are not matters which affect the constitutional position of the judges, "they are concerned with the way in which legal services are provided to the public" (at 660) and are much more likely to bring pressure to bear on the decision of a judge in a particular case but, as JUSTICE said in the 1992 report cited above, "Judicial independence has never justified substandard justice. . . . Judicial independence is constrained by the principle of good administration, for which someone or some body must be accountable to Parliament" (at 4). Training and performance appraisal (see below), she concludes, do not pose any threat, if they are confined to updating the law and questions of how judges handle cases before them (such as fair dealing between the parties and handling delicate issues sensitively).

The Current Training Regime

14-024   Here, I summarise the training regime established by the Judicial Studies Board (JSB) at the time of writing. It can be obtained from the Annual Report on the JSB website.

Recorders

Before sitting in the Crown Court, a recorder is required to attend a four-day residential induction course run by the JSB, which consists of lectures, sentencing and summing-up exercises, under the supervision of a tutor judge, a mock trial and a session on equal treatment. Appointees will also visit two penal establishments, meet probation officers and undertake a period of sitting-in with a circuit judge in a Crown Court, for five to ten days. Once sitting alone, a tutor judge will observe and report on the new recorder. The Criminal Conference provides a day's training, 18 months after appointment.

Criminal continuation seminars

These are three-day residential courses, attended every three years by circuit judges, recorders and newly appointed High Court judges. They have recently included such topics as mentally disordered offenders, vulnerable witnesses and the Parole Board. Seminars for judges specialising in serious fraud and in sexual offences have also been provided.

Circuit sentencing conferences

14-025   These are one-day annual conferences organised by the circuit Presiding Judges and attended by every circuit judge and recorder on the circuit. The 2000 theme was sentencing and the Human Rights Act.

Civil induction seminars

Before sitting in the county court, recorders, assistant recorders and deputy district judges are required to attend a residential four-day induction course, where judges work in small syndicates, studying topics such as damages, court practice, equal treatment and poverty. The appointee must also sit in with a circuit judge and a district judge.

Civil continuation seminars

These are two-day sessions attended by circuit judges, recorders and assistant recorders, once every three years. Recently they have included topics such as jury trials in the county court, housing law and an update on contract and tort.

Family judges

Similarly, the JSB organises induction and continuation courses in private and public family law, for nominated family law circuit, district and deputy High Court judges, who attend in three-year cycles. The President of the Family Division held a residential seminar on the Children Act for Family Division Liaison Judges and Designated Family Judges. Conferences were held for potential nominated care judges and seminars were held on the Family Law Act 1996 and the Housing Act 1996.

Special seminars

These are organised on an *ad hoc* basis. For instance, when the Children Act 1989 was passed, a training programme was organised for all relevant judges. From 1997, all civil judges have been given access to justice seminars on such topics as case management, the civil justice reforms and ADR.

When ethnic minority awareness training was devised, all inferior judges were subject to it. It is now part of equal treatment training. An Equal Treatment Bench Book was issued to all judges in 1999. The Human Rights Act required the JSB to launch a massive training programme for all judges, which is ongoing.

Criticism

Since the JSB was established, the basic training offered to new judges has been criticised for its inadequacy, by new judges and outsiders. A 1993 BBC2 documentary, *Inside the Wig: Thinking Like a Judge*, exposed the defects of the system. David Pannick, then an assistant recorder, commented that a four-day course was "inadequate to provide more than a basic knowledge of the ever-growing intricacies and absurdities of the criminal law, including procedure, evidence and sentencing". He advocated an informed debate on whether there should be a Judicial Training College at which new recruits would spend rather longer than four days (*The Times*, May 11, 1993). Solicitor Tony Holland, Past President of the Law Society and member of the JUSTICE committee on the judiciary found the programme a demonstration of inadequacy. "No-one seemed to question this at all. In a sense it was like a Mad Hatter's tea party, with

14-026

no-one understanding why the system was the system . . . bright tax lawyers would run a mile from such an ordeal were it not for the pension and the knighthood . . . three and a half days is enough to sentence a man to 10 years in prison." (((1993) 143 N.L.J. 895 and see p.27).

The Bar Council, in evidence to the Home Affairs Committee, favoured greater use of specialist judicial appointments, as did the Chancery Bar Association (JAP, 205). Most new appointees were expected to try criminal cases in the Crown Court, whatever their background, whereas applicants with experience in family or civil cases should be permitted to try those cases when first appointed.

JUSTICE expressed concern at the management of the JSB. They thought a professional director of studies should be appointed, first, because the scale of the job required a professional approach and secondly because relying on judges taking time off their judicial duties was a waste of scarce judicial resources (1992 report, as above).

The Call for Judicial Performance Appraisal

14-027   Recently, critics have called for some form of performance appraisal, possibly linked with training. For instance, the Royal Commission on Criminal Justice, 1993, said: "We are, however, less satisfied that adequate monitoring arrangements are in place and find it surprising that full-time judges seldom if ever observe trials conducted by their colleagues." (para. 98).

One outspoken proponent was Judge Derek Holden. He was persuaded in favour of such a scheme when he was President of the Independent Tribunal Service. The seven regional chairmen were responsible for monitoring the 1,000 legally qualified tribunal chairmen. The results, argued Judge Holden, were useful in a monitoring system, providing an important basis for promotion or the renewal of an appointment. Such a monitoring system could become part of a training exercise (*The Times*, November 9, 1993).

Judicial performance appraisal was part of Labour policy prior to their election to power in 1997. Since then, it has been extended from tribunals to the lay magistracy, since 1998, then extended to deputy district judges and, following the recommendation of Sir Leonard Peach, it will be extended to all part-time appointments, from 2001. Sir Leonard also advocated self-appraisal, which the Lord Chancellor says he supports (*Annual Report 1999–2000*).

3. Removal

14-028   It is thought that to make them easily removable would threaten judges' independence, subjecting them to political interference. Thus, superior judges enjoy a formidable security of tenure. Under the Act of Settlement 1700, they may only be removed following a motion by both Houses of Parliament. No English judge has been removed in this way.

Removing and disciplining inferior judges (that means circuit judge and below) is the Lord Chancellor's job. Under section 17(4) of the Courts Act 1971, he "may, if he thinks fit, remove a circuit judge from office on the ground of incapacity or misbehaviour". Under this statute's predecessor, a Liverpool county court judge, William Ramshay was removed, following endless complaints and an unseemly battle with the press. The 1971 Act was used to remove Judge Keith Bruce Campbell, in 1983, following his conviction for smuggling 125 litres of whisky and 9,000 cigarettes, on a yacht he shared with his co-defendant, a car dealer.

Inferior judges often resign before they can be removed. Circuit Judge Angus MacArthur resigned from the Bench in 1997, shortly before being convicted for his third drink-driving offence and jailed for 28 days. He had been reprimanded by Lord Mackay, following his second conviction, in 1993, who had warned him that he would be removed following a third offence. Also in 1997, a recorder, John Reeder Q.C. received a five-month jail sentence for drink-driving. Reeder had resigned as a recorder prior to sentence. In 1998, commentators were critical when Lady Justice Butler-Sloss was offered retraining instead of being prosecuted for careless driving after a crash which left a passenger with facial injuries. The problem with cases where judges receive lenient treatment is that the public may perceive judges to be above the law.

There is no statutory definition of "misbehaviour" so it is up to the **14-029** interpretation of the Lord Chancellor of the time. In 1994, Lord Chancellor Mackay wrote to the Lord Chief Justice, setting out what conduct he regarded as misbehaviour. He asked that any judge convicted of a criminal offence, other than parking or speeding, should write to him. He said drink-driving was "so grave as to amount *prima facie* to misbehaviour". The same would apply to offences of violence, dishonesty or moral turpitude. In the same letter he warned:

> "The public expects all judges to maintain at all times proper standards of courtesy and consideration. Behaviour which could cause offence, particularly on racial or religious grounds, or amounting to sexual harassment, is not consistent with the standards expected of those who hold judicial office. A substantiated complaint of conduct of that kind . . . is capable of being regarded as misbehaviour."

Discipline Short of Removal

It is not unusual for the press or an M.P. to make a public complaint **14-030** about the outcome of an individual case. Commonly, the complainant will call for the judge's resignation or demand that the Lord Chancellor investigate the matter. Normally, Lord Chancellors steadfastly resist such clamour. They respond that the courts provide an appeal mechanism to consider whether a decision is inappropriate and that for the Lord Chancellor to interfere would be a breach of judicial independence. There are occasions, however, where judges make unfortunate remarks in or out of court, or behave in a way which the Lord Chancellor deems inappropriate but which does not amount to misconduct. There are no powers of discipline, short of removal and there is no formal complaints system. Complainants write to the Lord Chancellor, or the Lord Chancellor hears in some other way of bad behaviour. The LCD Judicial Correspondence Unit handle the complaints. The judge in question is given the opportunity to comment. The Lord Chancellor may, if he sees fit, write a letter of reprimand to the judge. A famous example of this was a reprimand delivered by Lord Hailsham to Mr. Justice Melford Stevenson for describing the Sexual Offences Act 1967 as "a buggers' charter".

The present Government is very keen to enhance the image of the judiciary so, from the present Lord Chancellor, a judge can expect a swift reprimand for off the cuff remarks which can be interpreted as unjust, insensitive or politically incorrect. The *Judicial Appointments Annual Report 1999–2000* reveals that seven judges were reprimanded in 1999–2000. For instance, in 1999 Old Bailey Judge Graham Boal made a sexist, racist, homophobic joke against the judicial appointment system in an after dinner speech at the annual dinner of the Criminal Bar Association. Lord Irvine gave other examples of his reprimands to judges for racist remarks in his speech at the launch of the Judicial Studies Board's *Equal Treatment Benchbook* in 1999 (see website).

14-031   In 1988, Lord Chancellor Mackay suspended the Kilmuir Rules, which had prevented judges speaking out in public. This was taken advantage of by Judge James Pickles, who courted media attention at every opportunity, culminating in the development of his own chat show. One day, in 1990, he went too far. He called a press conference in a Wakefield pub, in which he discussed a Court of Appeal case which had criticised him and called the Lord Chief Justice "an aged dinosaur". This was too much for the tolerant Lord Mackay. He released his letter of "serious rebuke" to the press, in which he sought loyalty to the Court of Appeal and instructed the judge to stop taking substantial fees for his media appearances. After his retirement, in 1991, he became *The Sun's* star columnist, styling himself "Judge Pickles", a title he was no longer permitted to use.

If a judge makes offensive remarks in court and the Lord Chancellor chooses not to act, there may be little the sufferer can do. If justice is impeded and the insulted or aggrieved party also loses the case, then there may be a ground for appeal but, if a witness or juror is insulted, she has no redress. Judges are immune from defamation actions for things they say in court. One judge notorious for his outspoken remarks, Alan King Hamilton, called a jury back into court to see a defendant sentenced, to teach them a lesson for their audacity in acquitting his co-defendants. He said they had acquitted on evidence that would not confuse a child and excused them for life from further jury service. Considering how important it is for judges to be seen to be fair, alert, sensitive and in touch with the social mores and moral climate of the day, it is a source of concern that there are so many outrageous judicial blunders that find their way into the newspapers.

Should we Have a Judicial Ombudsman?

The powerlessness of litigants, lawyers and witnesses in the face of such behaviour has led to calls for a formal complaints and discipline scheme. For instance, in their 1972 report, *The Judiciary*, JUSTICE called for a judicial ombudsman, to investigate complaints. They cited the example of Sweden as a success. In their 1992 report, *The Judiciary*, JUSTICE suggested that their proposed Judicial Commission would provide an independent mechanism for reviewing the professional conduct of judges and considering complaints.

14-032

4. Judicial Independence

Constitutional theorists, notably Locke in the seventeenth century and Montesquieu in the eighteenth, praised the separation of powers as a guarantee of democracy. The concentration of governmental power of more than one type—legislative, executive and judicial—in the hands of one person or body, is considered dangerous. Some written constitutions try to guard against this. In the British constitution there is no point in looking for a separation of powers, despite some rather unfounded Victorian notions and modern judicial statements to the contrary (such as the oft-cited assertion of Lord Diplock in *Duport Steels v. Sirs* (1980)). All we can hope for is a system of checks and balances that allows one organ of government to be kept in check by the others.

The controversial entities of the English legal system seem to be the Lord Chancellor and the Attorney-General, as they hold power in all three organs of government. Robert Stevens remarked, in his 1993 book, *The Independence of the Judiciary*, "nothing underlines the atheoretical nature of the British Constitution more than the casualness with which it approaches the separation of powers". Nevertheless, the judiciary enjoys some measure of independence from interference by politicians and outsiders and there are controls to stop political activity by judges. The concept of judicial independence seems to contain the following, in addition to security of tenure as described above.

14-033

High salary, fixed by non-governmental body. High pensions

Judicial salaries were, historically, meant to be high to keep judges above corruption. (See modern salaries on LCD website.) Judges' pensions are fixed at half their salary.

Freedom from interference with decision-making

Again, it is a hallmark of dictatorships and extreme regimes that the Government tells the judges how to judge. Judicial freedom in this sense includes the discretion to conduct procedures as they see fit. An attempt by Lord Mackay to persuade Sir John Wood, President of the Employment Appeal Tribunal, to drop preliminary oral hearings, in some cases, because of the backlog of cases was heavily criticised.

Independence to manage the courts

The extent to which the judges should run the courts and judicial business is one of the most controversial elements under this heading. Judges think they should be in control and that this is vital for judicial independence. Increasingly, however, governments have sought to increase executive control over court management and expenditure and judges have been publicly objecting to this, often in hysterical terms, throughout the late 1980s and 1990s. They are fond of quoting early American constitutionalist, Alexander Hamilton, writing in *The Federalist* (No. 78), who described the judiciary as the weakest and least dangerous department of government, although they normally omit to attribute the quotation. (See for instance, Purchas, below, quoting Lord Hailsham, quoting Diplock.)

14-034   Professor Ian Scott described two alternative models for judicial administration, a judicial-centred model and an executive-centred model. In the former, the judiciary have complete control over the administration of the courts. Modern judges complain that we are moving too far over towards an executive-centred model. Sir Francis Purchas has spoken and written at length of the threat to judicial independence (for instance, in the 1993–1994 *New Law Journal*). Sir Francis repeatedly likened developments to the Nazi regime. The argument had started in 1987, with Lord Browne-Wilkinson V.-C. complaining of the "widespread dissatisfaction amongst litigants caused by the use of county court judges and members of the Bar sitting as deputy High Court judges to try 29 per cent of all High Court civil cases in 1985". ([1998] P.L. 44). Lord Chief Justice Lane then Lord Chief Justice Taylor publicly attacked Lord Mackay in 1991 and 1992. Judge Harold Wilson ((1994) 144 N.L.J. 1453) objected to the takeover of court administration by civil servants of the Court Service. This rather astonishingly harks back to the era prior to the Courts Act 1971, when the county court judges (around 90) managed their own affairs, with the help of a registrar, claiming the system had worked well. This may well have been the case at county court level but at assize level, judicial-centred case management was archaic and producing lengthy delays. Until 1972, we had the bizarre set-up of each assize judge being followed around by all relevant paperwork, clerks and other functionaries from one assize town to another. A day was set aside for travelling (from the days of horse-drawn transport) and a day for unpacking and during all this the court was incommunicado to all court users. The element of the judiciary which has managed to cling on to managerial independence at local level is the magistracy, as we shall see.

The Rule against Bias

In *Re Pinochet Ugarte* (*The Times*, January 18, 2000), the House of Lords **14-035** extended the rule that a judge was automatically disqualified from a hearing in which he had a pecuniary interest to cases where the judge was involved personally, or as a director of a company, in promoting some cause. In *Locabail v. Bayfield Properties* [2000] All E.R. 65, the Court of Appeal observed that *Gough* had not met with universal approval and would have to be slightly modified in accordance with the Human Rights Act 1998. In June 2000, the Lord Chancellor published guidance to judges on outside interests on his website, following *Locobail*. The last word and binding precedent on the bias test is set out in *Re Medicaments and Related Classes of Goods (No. 2)* (2000, CA) by Lord Phillips M.R. (as paraphrased in *The Times* law report, February 2, 2001):

> "The Court first had to ascertain all the circumstances which had a bearing on the suggestion that the judge was biased. It then had to ask whether those circumstances would lead a fair-minded and informed observer to conclude that there was a real possibility, or a real danger, the two being the same, that the tribunal was biased. The material circumstances would include any explanation given by the judge under review as to his knowledge or appreciation of those circumstances. Where that explanation was accepted by the applicant for review it could be treated as accurate. Where it was not accepted, it became one further matter to be considered from the viewpoint of the fair-minded observer. The court did not have to rule whether the explanation should be accepted or rejected, rather it had to decide whether or not the fair-minded observer would consider that there was a real danger of bias notwithstanding the explanation advanced."

FURTHER READING

David Pannick, *Judges* (1987).
House of Commons Home Affairs Committee: *Third Report 1995–1996,* **14-036**
  Judicial Appointments Procedures, Volume II, abbreviated in the text above.
JUSTICE, *The Judiciary in England and Wales* (1992).
Robert Stevens, *The Independence of the Judiciary* (1993).

J.A.G. Griffith, *The Politics of the Judiciary* (5th ed., 1995).

Kate Malleson, *The New Judiciary* (1999).

Lord Chancellor's Department website, www.open.gov.uk/lcd. Click on "Judiciary" for details of those in office, including statistics on race and gender; the *Judicial Appointments Annual Report*; appointment details, job specifications, the Peach Report on the appointment system, etc. Click on "Speeches" for many enlightening speeches by the Lord Chancellor and other judges. Click on "Research" for relevant research, *e.g.* Banda and Malleson.

Judicial Studies Board website, www.cix.co.uk/~jsb. The *Annual Report* gives current training details.

The Times Law Section on Tuesdays carries job advertisements for judges.

The Law Society website, www.lawsociety.org.uk carries press releases attacking the judicial appointments system. It also provides access to all *Gazette* articles attacking the appointment system. Search for "judicial appointments".

Dame Brenda Hale, "Equality and the Judiciary: why should we want more women judges?" [2001] P.L. 489.

D. Williams, "Bias, the judges and the Separation of Powers" [2001] P.L. 45.

T. Legg, "Judges for the New Century" [2001] P.L.

Lord Devlin, *The Judge*.

Part V: Laypeople in the Law

15. Magistrates

1. Laypeople in the Legal System

The English legal system is unique, in worldwide terms, in making such **15-001** extensive use of laypeople as decision-makers, as magistrates, jurors and tribunal members. This is partly the product of history but is now justified as keeping the law in touch with the public affected by it. There are over 30,300 lay magistrates and they are by far most important judges in the English legal system because, along with professional magistrates, district judges (magistrates' courts) called here DJMCs, they deal with over 97 per cent of defendants to criminal charges, from start to finish and 95 per cent of all sentencing; they have a powerful family jurisdiction and deal with other civil business and they administer most of the liquor licensing system. For most people, an appearance in court means an appearance before the magistrates. Despite this, most law books give the impression that magistrates' jurisdiction is trivial. The law itself has been developed around judges' and Parliament's false assumption that most criminal cases are dealt with by judge and jury. This is a big mistake, as I have pointed out elsewhere ("An Essay on the Importance and Neglect of the Magistracy" (1997)).

2. Appointment and Removal

Magistrates, or lay justices, Justices of the Peace, are appointed by the **15-002** Crown on the advice of the Lord Chancellor (or the Chancellor of the Duchy of Lancaster, in Lancashire, Greater Manchester and Merseyside). Each area has a Commission from the Crown. Magistrates must live within 15 miles of its boundaries. The Lord Chancellor (L.C.) or C.D. receives recommendations for appointment from 109 advisory committees. They are composed mainly of magistrates but the L.C. now requires that a third are non-magistrates. Since 1999, members have received standard training. Any adult can apply to be a magistrate. Qualities required by the L.C. are "good character, understanding and communication, social awareness, maturity and sound temperament, sound judgment and commitment and reliability" (" How to become a magistrate" and *Judicial Appointments Annual Report 1999–2000*, LCD website, Chapter 5, summarising *Lord Chancellor's Directions for Advisory Committees on Justices of the Peace*, 1998).

All candidates undergo a two-stage interviewing process, meant to ascertain if they possess these necessary qualities and judicial aptitude. The committee must have regard to the number of vacancies and the "the Lord Chancellor requires that each bench should broadly reflect the community it serves in terms of gender, ethnic origin, geographical spread, occupation and political affiliation" (*Directions* para. 8.1).

Lay justices receive no remuneration. They are, however, entitled to travelling expenses and to certain subsistence payments and a loss of earnings allowance but this allowance by no means compensates those who operate small businesses. Few justices claim their allowances (Morgan and Russell, below).

Criticism of the Appointment System

15-003   The overwhelming problem with the magistracy is its lack of diversity. Some say that this is partly caused by the fact that magistrates select new magistrates, although the 2000 report of the L.C.'s Equality Working Group refutes this (see below). Even the Magistrates' Association called this system a "self-perpetuating oligarchy" (in evidence to the House of Commons Home Affairs Select Committee in its report on *Judicial Appointments Procedures*, 1995). Committees are given no advertising budget and only now are they being systematically trained in interview techniques. They occasionally advertise for applicants in local media. They also circulate local political and community organisations. (For expansion, see "For the New Lord Chancellor—Some Causes of Concern about Magistrates" 1997.) The L.C. ran the first national recruitment campaign for a month in 1999. It aimed to destroy the stereotype that magistrates are white and middle class, not ordinary people. Magistrates' courts organise open days to publicise their work and the Magistrates' Association runs a "Magistrates in the Community" campaign, addressing schools and local groups and they participate in a national mock trial competition, in an endeavour to demystify the magistracy and attract applicants.

The Problem of Achieving a Balanced Bench

15-004   Successive Lord Chancellors have boasted that the magistracy represents the community. This is not the case. Like many before me, I have argued, using the support of statistics and research, that it is predominantly Conservative, white and middle class (see "Concern" above). Unlike others, I am also concerned that magistrates are too old. For the most modern analysis, see Morgan and Russell's research, 2000, cited below.

Age

"In theory, you can become a magistrate at 21. In practice nobody is ever appointed before 27" (Rosemary Thomson, then chairman of the Magistrates' Association in evidence to the Home Affairs Committee, as above). Two fifths of lay justices have retired from full-time employment (Morgan and Russell). Since the peak age of offending is around 18 for males and 15 for females, this makes a double generational difference between the bench and the accused. Since I wrote "Concern", the Lord Chancellor has made it clear that this does not bother him. Indeed, he has raised the maximum age for new magistrates from 60 to 65, in the hope of achieving a more socially balanced bench. DJMCs are younger (Morgan and Russell, 2000).

Social class

Successive studies, cited in my 1997 article, have shown the bias towards the middle classes and towards certain occupational groups and this is confirmed by Morgan and Russell, who found the magistracy to be "overwhelmingly drawn from managerial and professional ranks" (at viii). Various reasons have been identified for this. People who travel in their jobs may be unavailable to sit. People who run small businesses may find the loss of earnings allowance inadequate. Insufficient blue collar workers are attracted to apply (see evidence of the Magistrates' Association and others to the Home Affairs Committee, in 1995). Despite the fact that their jobs are protected, it may be that people fear they will be sacked for taking time off to be a magistrate, or will irritate work colleagues. A story is told by one magistrate of how he resigned his job because his employer denied him the seven days' leave he needed to train as a new magistrate and expected him to fulfil many of his bench sittings from annual leave (*The Magistrate*, February 2001). Lord Chancellor Irvine recognises this problem of social imbalance. He has tried to replace the committees' obligation to select a politically balanced bench with a mechanism for establishing a socio-demographic mix but his 1998–1999 consultation exercise to this effect was unsuccessful. His *Annual Report 1999–2000* expresses his continued endeavour to find ways of securing a socially balanced bench.

Race

The precise racial balance of the Bench is unknown but it is obvious   **15-005**
that, historically, it has under-recruited minorities. There is a shortage of applications from minority groups. This contrast is visible in court, where non-whites are over-represented among defendants and victims.

This is especially acute in areas of minority population concentration (for detail see "Concern" cited above). Recognising this, Lord Mackay, the Conservative Lord Chancellor, then Lord Irvine, have tried to compensate by appointing more non-whites than there are in the population at large, culminating in the appointment of 8.6 per cent of new justices in 1999–2000 (*Annual Report*). See now the 2000 report of the Equality Working Group, discussed below. Morgan and Russell found the Bench was ethnically representative of the population at national level (2000).

Disability

The Equality Working Group (below) reported a shortage of applications from disabled people.

Gender

15-006   Many commentators have complained in the past that the magistracy is overwhelmingly male. This is patently not true, as I pointed out in 1997 and as can be seen at a glance from the statistics. As of January 2000, there were 30,308 lay justices, of whom 14,764 were women. It is true that most DJMCs are male.

In response to the report of the Stephen Lawrence Inquiry, the Lord Chancellor's Department set up an audit of its procedures to assess whether they provide equality of opportunity and support diversity. An Equality Working Group was established to seek ways of encouraging applications from all sections of society, eliminating discrimination and producing a diverse Bench. See 2000 Report on the LCD website. They praised the efforts of the Lord Chancellor to foster a nationally co-ordinated approach to recruiting a diverse bench in a fair way but made various recommendations, including that the LCD should do the following:

- Explore ways of attracting media attention to raise the magistracy's profile among underrepresented groups.
- Train committees to distinguish between positive action and positive discrimination.
- Communicate zero tolerance of discrimination.
- Copy the Territorial Army model of presenting awards to local employers who allow their staff time off to be magistrates.
- Consider how to change people's attitudes to colleagues who take time off to serve.
- Guide committees in targeting recruitment campaigns to underrepresented groups.
- Develop an integrated national strategy to replace the present piecemeal one.
- Make court buildings more accessible for disabled magistrates.

- Find out why justices resign. It seems to be because they cannot fulfil the sittings required so guide benches on how to be flexible to accommodate such justices.
- Ensure dress codes are not culturally biased.

In 2001, Auld L.J. recommended, in *The Criminal Courts Review* that efforts should be made to ensure benches are more broadly reflective of the communities they serve.

Removal

The Lord Chancellor can remove the name of any magistrate from the Commission, under the Justices of the Peace Act 1997. This is rarely done but is usually because a magistrate refuses to enforce a particular law, such as prosecutions arising from public demonstrations, or for personal indiscretion, such as conducting an obvious extra-marital affair with another magistrate. Magistrates retire at 70. Their names are placed on a supplemental list so they can no longer sit on the Bench but can deal with minor matters and so retain the status of a Justice of the Peace. **15-007**

3. Training

Lay justices are non-lawyers. They need to understand basic procedure, the rules of evidence, in outline, the elements of the law they commonly apply and how to behave appropriately in court. Training is organised locally and has been the responsibility of Magistrates' Courts Committees (MCCs) and justices' clerks. Consequently, the quality of it differed from court to court, dependent on local attitudes and how much the Committee was prepared to spend (see my book *The Magistrates' Clerk*). Under the Magistrates' New Training Initiative, developed centrally by the Judicial Studies Board (JSB), since 1998, newly appointed magistrates are trained to achieve four basic competences: applied understanding of the framework within which magistrates operate and the abilities to follow basic law and procedure, think and act judicially and work effectively as a team member. They are assisted by a mentor and appraised by a trained appraiser. During the first two years, this includes 11 mentored sittings and one appraised sitting. The technical content mainly consists of an introduction to practice and procedure, punishment and treatment. This is the basic minimum. Justices wishing to sit in the youth court or on the family panel undergo extra specialist training. After three years, magistrates must undergo further training every three years. The further training includes court chairmanship and, since 1996, is a pre-condition for those justices wishing to chair proceedings. Justices selected for the Youth Court or family panel undergo extra **15-008** courses. The LCD and, latterly, the Judicial Studies Board have been applying more uniformity to training. The Board now has a magisterial committee (see the JSB *Annual Report* on their website). All newly elected Bench Chairmen attend a two-day course organised by the JSB on their pastoral and disciplinary role, press liaison and working with others involved in magistrates' courts. New acting DJMCs receive a two-day training course and must observe a full-time DJMC in court for a week. DJMCs receive two half days' continuation training per year. Like other judges, magistrates take part in specialist national training campaigns such as those introducing equal treatment, the Human Rights Act 1998 and the Crime and Disorder Act 1998. The Equality Working Group recommended positive action to encourage underrepresented groups to train for specialist panels and to chair the bench in court. In 2001, Auld L.J. recommended that the JSB should be responsible for devising and resourcing magistrates' training.

4. Organisation

15-009   There are now 367 magistrates' benches. Since April 2001, when the Access to Justice Act came into force, radically reducing their number, there are 42 magistrates' courts committees, including a new Greater London Magistrates' Courts Authority consisting of magistrates, which manage these courts. MCCs spend the budget allocated by central and local government on staff, administration, recruitment to the bench and training for magistrates and clerks. Since magistrates' courts have long been locally organised, outside the ambit of centralised departmental control over all other courts, one of their hallmarks has long been their individual, sometimes idiosyncratic, differences in practice, procedure and interpretation of the law. In 2001 Auld L.J. recommended that MCCs be replaced by a central executive agency, administering all courts. (*Criminal Courts Review*). An Inspectorate was established in 1994, assessing quality of service at magistrates' courts and it aims to identify and disseminate good practice. The Police and Magistrates' Courts Act 1994 also provided for the appointment, by each committee, of a "justices' chief executive", who is the line manager of all the other local justices' clerks and staff. Nationally, the Magistrates' Association speaks for the magistrates as a collective body.

Lay justices sit in pairs or groups of three (legal maximum). In the Youth Court, three justices of mixed gender sit, or one district judge, or a mixed bench. Youth justices are drawn from a specially trained panel, as are family court magistrates but they must also hear adult criminal cases. Collectively, magistrates are known as "the Bench" and they are addressed as "Your Worships". The Chairman of the Bench is annually elected.

5. District Judges (Magistrates' Courts), Formerly Known as Stipendiaries

DJMCs are full-time professionals, with a seven-year general qualification, as defined by the Courts and Legal Services Act, section 71. According to current policy, they will normally have sat as deputies, part-time for at least two years and their performance as such will have been assessed and their sittings observed. There were, in 2001, 92 DJMCs in England and Wales and 171 deputy DJMCs. Deputies are part-timers, normally barristers, solicitors or justices' clerks, aged 35–55. Newly appointed deputies must observe full-time DJMCs for five days and attend a brief training course. Historically, although most cases in Outer London and the provinces are heard by justices, most cases in Inner London have, for the last three centuries, been dealt with by professionals, or "stipes" as they are still colloquially known. They were appointed locally. In the provinces, this was to meet increased caseloads, since professionals deal with cases more speedily than justices. The Royal Commission on Criminal Justice, 1993, recommended that there should be a more systematic approach to the role of stipendiaries and a unified stipendiary bench was created by the Access to Justice Act 1999 when stipendiaries were removed. **15-010**

6. Magistrates' Clerks

Both lay and stipendiary magistrates are advised by magistrates' clerks. The chief clerk at each court is called the justices' clerk. A justices' clerk may be in charge of more than one Bench and the nationwide trend of the last two decades has been to amalgamate Benches under one clerkship. In 2001, there were 130 justices' clerks, all of whom were professionally qualified. The clerks' staff, like the justices' clerks, are appointed/employed and paid by the magistrates' courts committees and under the supervision of the justices' chief executive. Of course, since many justices' clerks are in charge of more than one court and since most courts have more than one courtroom in session at a time, the justices' clerk necessarily delegates advisory functions to her assistants. They are called court clerks, or legal advisors, of whom there are around 1,800, and, until 2010, they need not be professionally qualified, although around 1,200 are. Delegated legislation in 1980 required that, if not professionally qualified, court clerks should be law graduates or equivalent, or possess a special clerks' Home Office diploma in magisterial law, or be qualified by five years' experience before 1980. A 1985 survey of court clerks' qualifications showed that only about 28 per cent of them were professionally qualified and about half were diploma holders. **15-011**

This leads to the curious situation where, in a third of provincial court-rooms, the court clerk advising the lay justices is not professionally qualified. More anomalous is the fact that in Inner London, where most cases are heard by DJMCs, they are often advised by professionally qualified clerks. The nationwide situation remains patchy, dependent on whether the local magistrates' courts committees have pursued a policy of recruiting professionals. In 1999, the LCD introduced delegated legislation, requiring that, by 2010, all court clerks should be professionally qualified as barristers or solicitors. To the disappointment of someone who had been campaigning for this for many years (see *The Magistrates' Clerk*), the over 40s were exempted, because some areas are so dependent on unqualified clerks that they would not all be able to qualify in time. More disappointingly, those who were in post 1998 have now been exempted from qualification. There remain benches where most legal advisors are not professionally qualified.

Magistrates are dependent on their clerks for legal advice in court. Section 78 of the Police and Magistrates' Courts Act 1994 provides that, in doing so, the justices' clerks and court clerks are independent and not subject to the direction of the magistrates' courts committee or the new breed of "super clerks", the justices' chief executive. In 2000, a new Practice Direction on the Role of the Clerk was issued.

Concern over the Clerks' Powers

15-012   In "A Comment on the Powers of Magistrates' Clerks" [1999] Crim.L.R. 377, I raised the following concerns:

- Under the Criminal Justice and Public Order Act 1998, extensive pre-trial judicial powers may be delegated to a single justice or justices' clerk, exercisable in an early administrative hearing or pre-trial review (as suggested by the Narey Report, *Review of Delay in the Criminal Justice System*, 1997). This means court clerks, in reality, because justices' clerks delegate almost all of their powers. In the Lords' debate on the Bill, the Lord Chief Justice expressed the same concern: clerks are not judges. Magistrates should be doing the judging.

- In the Access to Justice Act 1999, the job of fine enforcement was transferred to justices' chief executives. This is only a partial solution to the problem of fine defaulters' courts, where the clerk was both prosecutor and legal advisor. The arrangement has been challenged in the European Court of Human Rights, as a breach of Article 6, fair trial.

- The Act abolished the criminal legal aid means test because the Lord Chancellor lost patience with court clerks' inefficiency at applying it, after the Audit Commission found wide scale errors for the seventh year running. Clerks will grant representation under the new criminal defence service scheme and still apply the merits test. My research into clerks in the 1970s and later research showed that these Widgery criteria on criminal legal aid, now criminal defence are open to highly subjective interpretation, resulting in different rates of grant from court to court.

7. History

Most people consider that a royal proclamation in 1195, which set up **15-013** keepers of the peace to assist the sheriff in the maintenance of law and order, was the origin of the justice of the peace. Clearer evidence comes from statutes in 1327 and 1361 under which "good and lawful men" were to be "assigned to keep the peace", holding administrative rather than judicial authority, and like the present-day justice, not legally qualified and acting part-time. The title Justice of the Peace was first used in the 1361 statute. In 1363, a statute required four quarter sessions to be held annually, and gradually the power to deal with criminal cases was added to the administrative work. From 1496, justices were permitted to try the minor (summary) criminal cases locally at petty sessions, instead of at quarter sessions, so giving rise to magistrates' courts as courts of summary jurisdiction, as they now are. When quarter sessions were replaced by the Crown Court, magistrates retained their role, hearing appeals alongside a circuit judge. Magistrates were the local government until elected authorities were created under the Local Government Acts of 1888 and 1894. Traces of this are still in the statutory one-third membership of magistrates on local police authorities and in their licensing function.

8. Should Lay Justices be Replaced by Professionals?

Three major new reports, among others, mean that we can now reach **15-014** a better informed opinion on this question. Despite repeated assurances to the contrary by the Lord Chancellor, lay justices think he is plotting to replace them with professionals, whose numbers have steadily grown over the 1990s. This has often resulted from a recommendation by the Magistrates' Courts Service Inspectorate (see Sanders, below, at 13). In research reported in *The Role and Appointment of Stipendiary Magistrates*, 1995, Seago, Walker and Wall aimed to examine the function of stipendiaries. They found:

- Very few courts had rules for allocating work to stipendiaries.
- There was a striking difference between the work of stipendiaries and acting stipendiaries, who were kept away from more legally and evidentially complex cases allocated to the former, especially provincial ones.
- Metropolitan stipendiaries appeared to be almost twice as quick to hear contested cases as provincial stipendiaries.
- Most of their judicial work was general list cases but they also heard long trials (especially those lasting more than a day) or complex or highly publicised trials and they had a heavier case-load than lay justices.
- Stipendiaries dealt with all types of work more speedily than lay justices. One provincial stipendiary could replace 32 justices and one metropolitan stipendiary could replace 24 justices.

In discussing the future role of stipendiaries, the authors suggested that pressure could be relieved on the Crown Court. "Consideration could be given to an enhanced jurisdiction (up to two to three years' imprisonment) for a trial tribunal consisting of a stipendiary and two lay magistrates" (p. 145). (See their 2000 *Criminal Law Review* article for a very useful analysis of the role of stipendiaries.)

15-015 In 2000, a major research project was undertaken for the Home Office and Lord Chancellor's Department. It is reported in *The Judiciary in Magistrates' Courts* by Morgan and Russell. Its aims were to investigate the balance of lay and professional magistrates and the arguments in favour of that balance. Apart from the findings on composition, above, they were:

- Lay justices sat on 41.4 occasions per year on average. Additionally, they spend a full working week on training and other duties. They sat in threes, except in 16 per cent of cases, when in pairs.
- All professionals sat in court around four days a week. They rarely sat with lay justices.
- Their finding on stipendiaries' work allocation was the same as Seago *et al.* Stipendiaries' time was concentrated on triable either-way rather than summary cases.
- Stipendiaries heard 22 per cent more appearances than lay justices. If their caseloads were identical, they could deal with 30 per cent more appearances.
- Stipendiary hearings generally involved more questioning and challenging.
- Stipendiaries showed more command over proceedings and would challenge parties responsible for delay. People applied for fewer adjournments before stipendiaries and were less likely to be granted them.

- Lay justices were less likely to refuse bail or use immediate custody as a sentence.
- Court users had more confidence in stipendiaries. They were seen as more efficient, consistent in decisions, questioning appropriately and as giving clear reasons.
- Lay justices were more often judged better at showing courtesy, using simple language and showing concern to distressed victims. Lawyers admitted to preparing better for stipendiaries.
- Few members of the public had heard there were different types of magistrate. Most thought lay justices would be better at representing the views of the community and sympathising with the defendants' circumstances but that stipendiaries were better at making decisions on guilt and innocence.
- One stipendiary could replace 30 lay justices. Doubling stipendiary numbers would cut down court appearances but increase the prison population. The net cost would be about £23 million per year.

In 2000–2001 the Institute for Public Policy Research commissioned a MORI public opinion poll on the magistracy and then asked Andrew Sanders to compare the skills and experience which lay and professional magistrates bring to the bench. His 2001 paper, *Community Justice — Modernising the Magistracy in England and Wales* reports the following:

- The MORI poll found a third of respondents did not know the majority of magistrates were laypeople and hugely underestimated the proportion of cases heard by magistrates. Only 29 per cent thought magistrates did a good job and 61 per cent thought they were out of touch. Forty-nine per cent were unhappy that magistrates were legally untrained. Forty-two per cent would be more confident in a mixed panel and 52 per cent in dealing with more serious offences.
- Sanders concludes that the skills of both professional and lay magistrates, sitting as a mixed bench are needed in deciding complex cases: legal skills to apply the relevant law to the facts; social skills to assess character and judge honesty and managerial and administrative skills. Panel decision-making is preferable to sole decision-making. Justice should be transparent and accountable. This is promoted by lay participation. Public confidence needs to be safeguarded and increased.

There are many more reports or comments on the magistracy but there is not room to summarise them here. References can be found in these three reports.

FURTHER READING
15-016 Elizabeth Burney, *J.P.: Magistrate, Court and Community* (1979).
Penny Darbyshire, *The Magistrates' Clerk* (1984).
"An Essay on the Importance and Neglect of the Magistracy" [1997] Crim.L.R. 627.
"For the New Lord Chancellor—Some Causes of Concern About Magistrates" [1997] Crim.L.R. 861.
"A Comment on the Powers of Magistrates' Clerks" [1997] Crim.L.R. 377.
Sir Thomas Skyrme, *The Changing Image of the Magistracy* (1979).
History of the Justices of the Peace (1991).
John Raine and M. Willson, *Managing Criminal Justice* (1993).
Martin Narey, *Review of Delay in the Criminal Justice System* (1997) Home Office website, www.homeoffice.gov.uk.
House of Commons Home Affairs Committee, Third Report, Session 1995–1996, *Judicial Appointments Procedures Volume II* (HMSO, 1996).
Peter Seago, Clive Walker and David Wall, *The Role and Appointment of Stipendiary Magistrates* (1995).
Seago *et al.*, "The Development of the Professional Magistracy in England and Wales" [2000] Crim.L.R. 631.
Rod Morgan and Neil Russell, *The Judiciary in the Magistrates' Courts* (2000), LCD website, www.lcd.gov.uk.
Judicial Appointments Annual Report 1999–2000, LCD website.
Report of the Equality Working Group (2000), LCD website.
The Judicial Studies Board Annual Report 2000, JSB website, www.cix.co.uk/~jsb.
Andrew Sanders, *Community Justice* (2000) IPPR.
See generally, the LCD website under "magistrates" and "speeches".
The Justice of the Peace journal.
The Justices' Clerks' Society website www.jc-society.co.uk.
The Magistrates' Association website.
Annual *Judicial Statistics*, Chapter on The Judiciary, LCD website.
The Magistrate.

16. The Jury

1. "The Lamp that Shows that Freedom Lives"

As illustrated by the adulation of Lord Devlin, quoted above, this **16-001** ancient institution arouses strong emotions in the hearts of the English and Welsh, as it does with the Americans and many others living in common law systems which are daughters of the English legal system. This is because, for centuries, jury trial was central to our legal systems. The use of ordinary people as factfinders in civil and criminal cases was and is perceived by some as the only democratic way of organising a legal system. What most people do not realise, as the opinion surveys cited in the last Chapter show, is that 97 per cent of defendants to criminal charges are dealt with by magistrates. Of the remainder who appear before the Crown Court, most plead guilty so fewer than one per cent of defendants receive a jury trial. (For detail, see discussion below and Darbyshire, 1997.) As for civil cases, the jury had almost died out by the beginning of the twentieth century. By 2001, fewer than 400 civil cases a year are heard by juries.

2. Selection of Jurors

Summoned at Random

The Juries Act 1974, as amended, specifies that every adult, aged **16-002** 18–70, who is on the annual electoral register and who has lived in this country for at least five years is qualified to serve as a juror. The Act goes on to detail many disqualifications and exemptions. For example, members of the legal profession and clergymen are ineligible. Offenders who have been sentenced to prison or an alternative, or detention or youth custody of three months, in the last ten years, are disqualified, as are those placed on probation within a five-year period and people currently on bail. A person sentenced to imprisonment or youth custody for five years or more is permanently disqualified. Members of the armed forces, doctors and those over 65 may be excused from jury service as may members of religious organisations, whose tenets or beliefs are incompatible with jury service. The court has a discretion to release a person from jury service, or defer it if cause is shown.

Selection from the electoral register is now done randomly by computer, by the Central Summoning Bureau, based in Blackfriars, since late 2000. Before the 1980s, jury summoning officers were given the freedom to select jurors from the electoral register, as they chose, and this led to some selecting alphabetically whilst others selected street by street. Even now there remain several factors destroying randomness. Most obviously, the electoral register is not accurately representative of the population because of mobility, house moves, death and, latterly, because of people declining to register, in an attempt to evade the council tax. It was up to the summoning officer which electoral register she used and thus which area the jurors would come from. In the 1980s, there were complaints from black defendants that jurors were summoned from white areas. Judges have resisted most attempts to artificially construct mixed race juries but in one trial the judge ordered an adjournment and, in another, ordered a jury be summoned from a different district, in the hope of selecting a mixed jury. The Royal Commission on Criminal Justice 1993, recommended that prosecution or defence be enabled to apply to the judge, pre-trial, for the selection of a jury containing up to three people from minority communities. Darbyshire *et al.* reiterated this recommendation in their paper for Lord Justice Auld's Criminal Courts Review and he adopted this recommendation

16-003   The group summoned to attend at a particular Crown Court location is called "the panel", from which juries are selected for trials over a certain period (usually two weeks) and the prosecution at this stage may exercise a problematic form of scrutiny known as "vetting" and then prosecution and defence may exercise rights to challenge. It must be understood, however, that vetting and all types of challenge are *extremely rare*, since the late 1980s.

Vetting

16-004   Controversy arose during the highly publicised Official Secrets Act trial in 1978, known as the "ABC Trial" (because of the three defendants' surnames: Aubrey, Berry and Campbell). *The Times* exposed the fact that successive Attorneys-General, using prerogative power, had been secretly vetting the backgrounds of potential jurors in this and other politically sensitive trials and trials involving professional gangs. The Attorney-General revealed his guidelines on vetting. In 1980 the two divisions of the Court of Appeal gave rather conflicting rulings on the legality of jury vetting. In *R. v. Sheffield Crown Court, ex parte Brownlow*, the Civil Division, led by Lord Denning, unanimously ruled jury vetting by the police to be illegal but the case was closely followed, in the Criminal Division, by *R. v. Mason*, in which police vetting had taken place, as part of the routine in Northamptonshire. The Court held police vetting was supportable as common sense.

In response, the Attorney amended the guidelines, enhancing controls over vetting and distinguishing between (a) vetting carried out by the police and (b) "authorised checks", requiring his personal consent:

1. Police may make checks against criminal records, to establish that jurors are not disqualified.
2. "Authorised checks" are now to be carried out only with the Attorney's permission, following a recommendation by the DPP. The DPP decides what part of the information disclosed should be forwarded to the prosecution (note: not the defence). Except in terrorism cases, such checks will not now be carried out in politically motivated cases. In, for example, official secrets trials, vetting will only be permitted where national security is involved and the hearing is likely to be *in camera*.
3. The Attorney will consider and, in other cases, the Chief Constable may consider, defence requests for information revealed on jurors. The Royal Commission On Criminal Justice 1993, recommended the routine screening of jurors for criminal convictions. In 1997, I asked the Conservative Attorney-General, Sir Nicholas Lyell, how often he authorised vetting. He had never heard of vetting and asked me to explain it, suggesting that the practice is very rare.

Challenges to the Array

All parties have a common law right, preserved by section 12(6) of the **16-005** Juries Act 1974, to challenge the whole panel, on the grounds that the summoning officer is biased or has acted improperly. For example this was attempted in *Danvers* (Crown Court, 1982) by a black defendant, on the grounds that the all-white jury did not reflect the ethnic composition of the community.

Challenges by the Prosecution

The prosecution may exclude any panel member from a particular jury **16-006** by asking them to "stand by for the Crown" without reasons, until the whole panel, except for the last 12, is exhausted. Reasons, "cause", must be given for any further challenges but, with panels often consisting of 100 or more, the prosecution rarely needs to explain its challenges. The

Roskill Committee recommended the abolition of this right but the Government declined to include it in the Criminal Justice Bill 1986.

The Attorney-General announced, in 1988, that the prosecution's right to stand a juror by without giving reasons would now be limited to two instances: to remove a "manifestly unsuitable" juror or to remove a juror after authorised vetting. This goes some way towards responding to complaints over the imbalance between prosecution and defence rights of challenge.

Challenges by the Defence

16-007   Once the jury are assembled in court, the judge invites the juror to step down if she knows anyone involved in the case. The defence may then challenge any number of potential jurors for cause, (*i.e.* good reason acceptable to the judge) but what is an acceptable "cause" has been qualified by a 1973 Practice Note issued by the Lord Chief Justice, who stated it was contrary to established practice for jurors to be excused on grounds such as race, religion, political beliefs or occupation. This followed a trial of alleged anarchists called "The Angry Brigade", where the defence had requested the judge to ask people to exclude themselves if, for example, they were members of the Conservative Party or if they had relatives in the police force or serving in the forces in Northern Ireland.

It is also clear that the reasons must be those known to the defence and should not normally be ascertained by examining the potential juror in court. In other words, no practice exists such as the "*voir dire*" system in the United States, where potential jurors are examined by psychologists and other professionals to discover any prejudices. There have been occasional, well-publicised exceptions, however, in the 1980s, where the judge has permitted examination of jurors on their affiliations or beliefs, notably in cases involving black defendants. In the 1995–1996 Maxwell brothers' fraud trial, potential jurors were questioned on their views of the evidence because of prejudicial pre-trial publicity.

Until 1989, the defence could make a certain number of peremptory challenges, that is, challenges without reasons. This number was reduced from seven to three in the Criminal Law Act 1977 and was abolished by the Criminal Justice Act 1988. This resulted from the Conservative Government's belief that the right to peremptory challenge was being abused by defence lawyers, deliberately trying to skew the jury and from the recommendation of the Roskill Committee on fraud trials (1986) that it be abolished. This leaves a gross imbalance between prosecution and defence rights of challenge.

Excusal by the Judge

16-008   Under the Juries Act, section 10, the judge may discharge from service any juror about whom there is doubt as to "his capacity to act effectively as a juror" because of physical disability or insufficient understanding of English. Additionally, judges have a common law discretion to discharge jurors and they occasionally interpret this quite broadly. For example, the whole panel was discharged in a controversial 1979 anarchists trial and the eventual jury were discharged for life, after acquitting most of the defendants.

3. Function of the Jury

The purpose of having the jury is to enable the decision on fact to be taken by a small group from the community, rather than for it to be left entirely in the hands of the lawyers. Thus, in criminal cases tried at the Crown Court, the guilt of the person accused has to be established to the satisfaction of ten of the 12 jurors beyond all reasonable doubt. Remember that this applies to fewer than one per cent of defendants to criminal charges, because only three per cent are tried in the Crown Court and, of these, most plead guilty and merely appear before the judge for sentence. After hearing the judge's "summing up" of the evidence they retire and consider their verdict in private. On the pronouncement of that verdict by the foreman of the jury, the accused is found either "guilty" or "not guilty". If "not guilty" the defendant is acquitted and is free to leave the court; if "guilty" he is convicted, and the judge sentences him. The judge will first hear the criminal record of the prisoner and then a plea in mitigation of sentence, which is made by defence counsel. The jury has no part to play in the decision as to sentence. Equally the jury has no part in decisions which are concerned with law or legal procedure. A judge will often have to ask the jury to retire, so that she can hear arguments on and decide on a point of law.

16-009

The Decline of the Civil Jury

The civil jury declined massively in the twentieth century. Although a jury of eight may be called in the county court at the discretion of the judge, in practice this is rare, except in the one growth area for jury trials since 1990, tort actions against the police. Jury trial is also available in certain cases in the Queen's Bench Division but jury trials here and in the county court only amount to a few hundred per year. In the following tort actions there is, by section 69 of the Supreme Court Act 1981, a right to jury trial: libel, slander, malicious prosecution, false imprisonment and fraud. Even here jury trial can be refused if a prolonged examination of documents, or accounts, or a scientific or local investigation, or other complex material is involved. In all other cases, the judge has a discretion to allow a jury trial. The trend away from jury trial in civil cases has been comparatively rapid since, as recently as 1933, 50 per cent of cases

16-010

involved a jury. In *Ward v. James* (1966) a five-judge Court of Appeal decided that trial by judge alone should be the usual mode of trial. The most important reasons for the disuse of the civil jury are the inconsistency in damages awards and exorbitant figures for damages which sometimes result. Recent examples of this include the award of £600,000 libel damages to Sonia Sutcliffe, ex-wife of the "Yorkshire Ripper", against the publishers of *Private Eye*, which led Ian Hislop to comment: "If this is justice, I'm a banana". This was later reduced to £60,000. The Courts and Legal Services Act 1990, section 8 provided for rules to empower the Court of Appeal to substitute its own award of damages. It has obviously been easier to achieve consistency in the scale of damages for personal injuries because they are left to the judges. Throughout the 1990s, however, juries have continued to make outlandishly high damages awards in the defamation actions of the rich and famous, much to the exasperation of the judiciary. Notice the disgust expressed in the words of the Master of the Rolls, in December 1995, in *John v. Mirror Group Newspapers*, an appeal in which the Mirror group succeeded in getting the Court of Appeal to reduce to £75,000 the jury's award of £350,000 to Elton John, for alleging that he displayed symptoms of an eating disorder at a Hollywood party:

> "It is in our view offensive to public opinion, and rightly so, that a defamation plaintiff should recover damages for injury to reputation greater, perhaps by a significant factor, than if that same plaintiff had been rendered a helpless cripple or an insensate vegetable. The time has in our view come when judges, and counsel, should be free to draw the attention of juries to these comparisons."

Also in 1995, a jury award of £750,000 damages made to Graeme Souness, against his ex-wife for calling him a "dirty rat" in *The People*, was settled, pending appeal to the Court of Appeal for £100,000. In 1996, four large awards of damages against the Metropolitan Police in jury trials for action such as false imprisonment provoked the Metropolitan Police Commissioner to call for judicial guidelines to be set down for juries in these cases, similar to those in defamation cases.

In a 2001 case, the Court of Appeal showed itself less reluctant to overturn a civil jury verdict than a criminal one. In *Grobbelaar*, it overturned an £85,000 damages award to former Liverpool goalkeeper for a defamation action in which the jury were persuaded that he had been falsely accused of match fixing, despite strong video and audio-taped evidence of his taking bribes.

Coroners' Juries

16-011   The coroner, whose task it is to inquire into sudden death and treasure trove (usually the ownership of finds of metal detector enthusiasts) can and in some circumstances must, call a jury for the inquest. The coroner's jury, after hearing the evidence, return a verdict as to the cause of death and the coroner must record this verdict.

4. Majority Verdicts

For centuries, the English legal system required that the verdict of the jury in both civil and criminal trials should be unanimous. If unanimity could not be achieved then a re-trial was necessary. In the 1960s there was increasing criticism of this requirement, particularly on the part of the police who pointed out that one member of the jury if "nobbled" by the defendant or his supporters could cause a re-trial by simply refusing to agree with the other 11 jurors in a criminal case. The Criminal Justice Act 1967 permitted a majority verdict of 10–2 to be accepted by the judge in a criminal case, or 10–1, or 9–1 if one or two jury members had been discharged. The jury must spend at least two hours seeking to achieve unanimity. If the verdict is "guilty" the fact that it is a majority verdict must be disclosed. Majority verdicts were permitted in civil cases from 1972 and all the provisions concerning majority verdicts have now been consolidated in the Juries Act 1974.

16-012

5. Jury Secrecy

The secrecy of jury deliberations is protected in English law. They deliberate alone in the jury room and disclosure of those deliberations is a contempt under The Contempt of Court Act 1981, section 8. The application of that section is so broad as to preclude bona fide research into jury decision-making, frustrating would-be socio-legal researchers and reform bodies. The Royal Commission on Criminal Justice, 1993, recommended its abolition, as did the Law Commission, in their 1995 annual report but Auld L.J. disagreed, in the *Criminal Courts Review* 2001.

16-013

6. Rights of Jurors

Jurors may claim travelling expenses, a subsistence allowance and a financial loss allowance. This is intended to compensate the jurors for loss of earnings, or childcare, or employing someone to run their business. The low allowance by no means compensates many employed people. Jury service is obligatory and personal inconvenience, such as having to cancel a holiday, may be no excuse. Medical evidence, or compelling business reasons, are possible methods of escape. The excusal rate varied greatly from court to court, until 2000, depending on the policies of the summoning officers. Since September 2000, the Central

16-014

Summoning Bureau have been compiling a database of common requests for excusal, in the hope of developing a nationwide excusal policy. The majority of people try to escape jury service. (Airs and Shaw, Home Office, 2000). By December 2000, the Bureau had also found that many people simply ignore jury summonses. In London, they summon six times as many people as they need for jury service and in the rest of England and Wales, they have to summon four times as many (Darbyshire, Maughan and Stewart, 2001). Following our recommendations Auld L.J. recommended eliminating the categories of ineligible and inexcusable as of right (*Criminal Courts Review* 2001). See our work on the Review website. The complexity of modern crime, producing cases that may last months, presents difficulties in finding 12 persons able to give up sufficient of their time. For the 1995–1996 Maxwell brothers' fraud trial, scheduled to last six months, 800 people were summoned. Seven hundred were excused on the ground of unavailability.

An interesting historical survival is the rule that jurors cannot be punished if they bring in a perverse acquittal contrary to the direction of the judge. This was laid down in Bushell's Case in 1670 where two Quakers were charged with tumultuous assembly. The jury were ordered to convict, but instead returned a verdict of "not guilty". The judge sent the jury to prison until they should pay a fine by way of punishment. On appeal, it was held that the fine and imprisonment could not be allowed to stand. The Ponting trial of 1985 saw a jury bring in a verdict of "not guilty" in an Official Secrets Act case where a conviction had been expected. This freedom to ignore the law and resort to their consciences, is called "jury equity" and in the United States "nullification". There are many more modern day examples. For instance, there have been several acquittals of defendants in the 1990s who have used cannabis to relieve the pain of such illnesses as muscular sclerosis. Auld L.J. recommended, in the *Criminal Courts Review*, that the law should be declared that jurors have no right to acquit in defiance of the law or in disregard of the evidence.

7. History

16-015   During its long history, the jury has completely changed its role. Nowadays, every effort is made to ensure that the jury have no prior knowledge of the case, and will be able to reach their verdict entirely on the evidence presented at the trial. Originally, however, the jury's role was a combination of local police and prosecutor. Centuries before a paid police force were created, the responsibility for law and order lay with the community. This meant the local "jury" arresting suspected offenders, and then bringing him before the visiting judge visiting and swearing, like prosecution witnesses, to the guilt of the accused. There was nothing unusual in this use of local representatives in the early community. It can be seen also in the local inquiries which led to the creation of the Domesday Book, and the system of inquisitions post mortem, the inquiry held on a death as to the ownership of the lands and goods of the deceased. Throughout the Middle Ages juries were used in the settlement of civil disputes concerning the ownership and tenancy of land and the right to an advowson (the right to present to the living of a church).

It was only very gradually and with the passage of centuries that the use of the jury as uninvolved judges of fact developed. Even then the original concept continued to exist and this led to the existence of a grand jury and a petty jury. The grand jury of 24 members met only at the start of assizes or quarter sessions in order to find a true bill of indictment against the accused. Since the accused had previously undergone the preliminary inquiry by magistrates, who had heard the prosecution case and had decided to commit the accused for trial, the decision of the grand jury became a complete formality. It was fully abolished by the Criminal Justice Act 1948. United States jurisdictions retain the grand jury to indict the accused in certain cases. The petty jury, trial jury, of 12 members emerged in the thirteenth century to take the place of trial by ordeal, which the ecclesiastical authorities then saw fit to condemn. It became increasingly distinct in its functions from the grand jury, although it long maintained its composition from local witnesses of fact deciding matters from their local knowledge. It was the fifteenth century before the petty jury assumed its modern role in criminal trials as judges of fact.

In civil cases the jury appears to have had its origin in the Assizes of Clarendon in 1166, and the Assizes of Northampton in 1176, establishing the grand and petty assizes. Here again the jury was at first called to decide a case from its local knowledge, and only with the passage of time did it become an impartial judge of the facts. The system allowed for trial to be in two parts. The local jury would hear and deal with the case, then send their findings to the judges at Westminster where the judgment would be given.

8. *Controversies Surrounding the Jury*

There is an ongoing debate between civil libertarians and others   **16-016**
about several issues surrounding the jury, all of which are very interconnected:

1. The pros and cons of retaining the jury and jury equity;
2. Randomness; representatives; jury vetting—its desirability and constitutionality; the fairness of prosecution and defence challenges.

Should the Jury be Retained and does it Inject Layperson's "Equity" into the Legal System?

16-017

PRO (a) The jury rouses strong emotions and seems to be defended by some historians, civil libertarians, politicians, judges and laypeople as the last bastion of civil liberties. For example, Lord Devlin hailed it as a guardian of democracy:

> "no tyrant could afford to leave a subject's freedom in the hands of his countrymen. So that trial by jury is more than an instrument of justice and one wheel of the constitution: it is the lamp that shows that freedom lives." (Trial by Jury (1966))

and Blackstone called the jury "the glory of English law . . . the liberties of England cannot but subsist so long as this palladium remains sacred and inviolate" (*Commentaries* (1768)). It is argued that the jury acts as a check on officialdom, on the judge's power, and a protector against unjust or oppressive prosecution, injecting jury "equity" by deciding guilt or innocence according to a feeling of justice rather than by applying known law to facts proven beyond reasonable doubt: for example Kalven and Zeisel in "The American Jury" (*New Society* (1966)),

> "It represents also an impressive way of building discretion, equity and flexibility into a legal system. Not least of the advantages is that the jury, relieved of the burdens of creating precedent, can bend the law without breaking it."

(b) Additionally, jury supporters argue that a decision by 12 laypeople is fairer than one by a judge alone, since it is likely that 12 people will cancel out one another's prejudices.

CON (a) The importance of the jury system is overrated. For example, when given the choice, being charged with a criminal offence "triable either way", the vast majority of defendants (about 80 per cent) choose to appear before magistrates (source: annual *Criminal Statistics*) and, of the remainder, who opt for, or are sent to, the Crown Court, over 80 per cent plead guilty to one or all charges and thus are not tried by jury but just sentenced by the judge. This point was noted by the Royal Commission on Criminal Justice, 1993, following Home Office research by Hedderman and Moxon. It was one factor influencing the Commission to recommend that the defendant should be deprived of the right to insist on jury trial in triable either way cases. (Recommendation 114.)

(b) The rate of use of civil juries has declined massively since the nineteenth century, as explained above. By now, civil juries are rarely used (under 200 trials per year) and examining the reasons why people do not opt for them gives an idea of the drawbacks of jury trial. The Faulks Committee (1974) recommended that juries should no longer be available as of right in defamation actions because, *inter alia*:

1. Judges were not as remote from real life as popularly supposed.
2. Judges gave reasons, whereas juries did not.
3. Juries found complex cases difficult.
4. Juries were unpredictable.
5. Juries were expensive (jury trial is more time-consuming, as explanations have to be geared for them, not a judge).

Additional reasons given by the anti-jury lobby for the unpopularity of civil juries are:

6. They seldom take notes, are not encouraged to do so and may not be able to remember all the evidence. Thus, they are likely to be swayed in the jury room by the more dominant characters' interpretation or recollection of events and to be more vulnerable to persuasive rhetoric than a judge. Their difficulty in understanding evidence is most acute in fraud trials and was considered by the Roskill Committee on Fraud Trials in 1986. Fraud trials are notoriously long (sometimes over 100 days), expensive and highly complicated. The Committee said:

> "The background against which the frauds are alleged to have been committed—the sophisticated world of high finance and international trading—is probably a mystery to most or all of the jurors, its customs and practices a closed book. Even the language in which the allegedly fraudulent transactions have been conducted will be unfamiliar. A knowledge of accountancy or bookkeeping may be essential to an understanding of the case. If any juror has such knowledge, it is by chance" (paragraph 8.27).

The Committee recommended the jury be abolished in complex criminal fraud cases and be replaced by a Fraud Trials Tribunal of a judge and two lay members. Their remarks on the anomalous (as they see it) use of the jury epitomise the view that the significance of the jury is overrated (paragraph 8.21).

> "Out of all the citizens (possibly some three million) who, in the course of any year, find themselves in difficulty with the law, only a small portion (32,000 in 1984) will be tried by a jury. The underlying logic of this situation we find puzzling in the extreme. If society believes that

trial by jury is the fairest form of trial, is it too costly and troublesome to be universally applied? . . . But if jury trial is not inherently more fair, given its extra cost and trouble, what are the merits which justify its retention? Society appears to have an attachment to jury trial which is emotional or sentimental rather than logical."

This debate was revived in 1992, following the Guinness trial and the Blue Arrow fraud trial, the longest trial in legal history, lasting over a year and again in 1996, following the acquittals after the Maxwell trial. The suggestion was revived by Labour Home Secretary, Jack Straw, in 1998. See "Juries in Serious Fraud Trials", the consultation paper, on the Home Office website. In 2001, Auld L.J. reiterated the recommendations that in serious and complex frauds, the judge should be able to orders trial by a judge and two lay members like The Fraud Trials Tribunal, recommended by the Roskill Report (above).

(d) The notion that the jury applies its own equity has no substance. Baldwin & McConville in *Jury Trials* (1979) found no evidence that juries acquitted people in the face of unjust prosecution. On the contrary, perverse verdicts, (*i.e.* verdicts against the weight of the evidence, as assessed by professional observers and assessors) occurred at random. The jury thus had the disadvantage of being unpredictable.

(e) Twelve laypeople are easily swayed by the eloquence of a barrister against the weight of the evidence, and the average intelligence of such a group of citizens, called to attend against their wishes, leaves them ill-equipped to cope with the complexity of many of the cases in which they have to give a verdict.

See further pros and cons of the jury in Findlay & Duff, *The Jury Under Attack* (1988) and Darbyshire (1991).

16-018 **Arguments about Randomness, Representatives, Jury Vetting and the Rights of Challenge**

The legal sources of definitions of the notions of randomness and representativeness are difficult to discover. They do not appear in the Juries Act 1974, which significantly qualifies randomness but there are statements elsewhere.

The Report of the Departmental Committee on Jury Service (The Morris Committee, 1965): "a jury should represent a cross-section drawn at random from the community" and the 1973 Practice Note by the Lord Chief Justice "a jury consists of twelve individuals chosen at random from the appropriate panel". (Now superseded by the 1988 direction.) Note: this does not imply that the panel should be random. Further, the *obiter* statement of Lord Denning in the *Brownlow* case (1980, above) reviewed the two "rival philosophies" as he called them, of our random jury and the highly selected American jury. He stated:

"Our philosophy is that the jury should be selected at random from a panel of persons who are nominated at random. We believe that twelve persons selected at random are likely to be a cross-section of the people and thus represent the views of the common man. Some may be moral. Others not. Some may be honest. Others not . . . The parties must take them as they come."

Lawton L.J., however, in *Mason* (1980, above) rejected as "misconceived" the argument that, on a true construction of the Juries Act 1974, every person who was not ineligible or disqualified should be permitted, as of right, to sit as a juror.

Challenges, like the statutory exclusory rules, destroy randomness and, for this reason, the Roskill Committee recommend their abolition. It is sometimes argued that civil libertarians are contradictory in supporting randomness, yet complaining that defence rights of challenge have been whittled away (see above). The focal point of their objection, though, is the imbalance between prosecution and defence rights.

9. Current Plans to Reduce Jury Trial

Withdrawing the Right to Elect Jury Trial

As explained in the Procedure Chapter, in cases of medium seriousness, **16-019** "triable either way", where the magistrates express no preference as to mode of trial, the defendant has the right to choose his mode of trial, by magistrates in the magistrates' court or judge and jury in the Crown Court. This is called "the right to elect" jury trial. Governments have been thinking of removing this right since the Royal Commission on Criminal Justice recommended they do so in 1993 (Ch. six, paras. 4–19). Drawing conclusions from Home Office and other research on mode of trial decisions by magistrates and defendants, they concluded that the system was not being used as intended. They found that, while defendants often opt for Crown Court trial in the belief that their chances of acquittal are greater, they nevertheless change their plea to guilty at the Crown Court; that defendants often opt for Crown Court trial in the mistaken belief that, if convicted, the Crown Court judge will impose a lighter sentence than magistrates and that magistrates send a number of cases to the Crown Court where the defendant ultimately receives a sentence within the magistrates' own sentencing powers. They recommended that the defendant should no longer have the right to insist on jury trial. Where prosecution and defence could not agree on mode of trial, the decision should be referred to the magistrates. The Commission was subject to academic criticism, especially by Warwick Professors McConville and Bridges, alleging that it had misinterpreted the Home Office research.

Nevertheless, the (Conservative) Home Office published a consultation document, *Mode of Trial*, in 1995. In it, they outlined various options designed to shift more cases from the Crown Court to the magistrates' courts. They pointed out that national mode of trial guidelines issued by the Director of Public Prosecutions had already gone some way towards achieving this. They sought opinions on three other options: the reclassification of more offences as triable only summarily, the withdrawal of the defendant's option to insist on jury trial in the Crown Court and a requirement that the defendant enter the plea before the trial/hearing venue is chosen. The Government chose to enact the third and least draconian of these options. Given the sentimental attachment of the English to jury trial in criminal cases, it would be politically inexpedient to remove the defendant's right to opt for jury trial in all triable either way cases. Instead, section 49 of the Criminal Procedure and Investigations Act 1996 requires magistrates, before determining mode of trial, to ascertain the accused's plea. Where he indicates a not guilty plea, they must proceed to deal with the case summarily. Where the accused pleads not guilty, they may choose to send the case up to the Crown Court or, where they decline to do so, they must still give the defendant the option of summary trial or trial on indictment at the Crown Court. In other words, if the defendant expresses an intention to plead guilty, he loses the right to opt for the Crown Court. The magistrates must hear the case but retain the right to send it up to the Crown Court for sentence, where they feel their own sentencing powers are too low.

16-020   Before this plan could take effect, however, The Narey Report (M. Narey, *Review of Delay in the Criminal Justice System*, Home Office website) was published in 1997 and reiterated the recommendation that the defendant's right to elect be removed. New Labour replaced the Conservatives three months later. In 1998, the Labour Home Secretary, Jack Straw, published "Determining Mode of Trial in Either Way Cases —A Consultation Paper" (Home Office website). In it, he set out the familiar arguments on abolishing the defendant's right to elect jury trial, as follows:

For abolition

- The right is not ancient. It only dates from 1855 and has nothing to do with Magna Carta.
- Twenty-two thousand defendants elected for Crown Court trial in 1997 but most changed their plea to guilty, after significant inconvenience and worry to victims and witnesses and considerable extra cost.
- By definition, elected cases are those which magistrates have determined are suitable for themselves. The mode of trial decision should be based on objective assessment by the court of the

gravity of the case, not the defendant's perception of what is advantageous to him, such as a greater prospect of acquittal.

- It is questionable whether defendants opt for jury trial to defend their reputation, as nine tenths of those electing already have previous convictions.
- Most defendants elect because they want to delay proceedings, to apply pressure to the Crown to accept a guilty plea to a lesser offence, or to deter witnesses or to put off the evil day.
- Few other jurisdictions allow the defendant such an element of choice, (*e.g.* Scotland).

Arguments in favour of the status quo
- The right helps to promote confidence in the criminal justice system.   **16-021**
- Whereas magistrates, in applying *The National Mode of Trial Guidelines*, are broadly concerned with the seriousness of the offence, it is the defendant's reputation which the public sees as a justification for continuing to allow the election.
- When people who have never been accused of a crime defend the right, it is usually on the basis that they would want such a right if they were charged with something of which they were innocent.
- It is assumed that Crown Court trial is fairer. Defendants mainly elect because they rightly believe they have a higher chance of acquittal.
- Some arguments go to the merits of trial by jury, for example, the jury's capacity to acquit contrary to legal proof of guilt.

One proposal in the paper was to take away the right of those defendants who had previous convictions and who had, therefore, already lost their reputations. Consequently, Jack Straw introduced into the House of Commons the Criminal Justice (Mode of Trial) Bill, in 1999. This would have abolished the defendant's right to elect, placing the mode of trial decision in the magistrates' hands. The prosecutor and accused would have had a right to make representations. The Bench would have to take into account the nature of the case, whether the circumstances make the offence serious, whether magistrates' sentencing powers would be adequate, whether the accused's livelihood or reputation would be damaged and any other relevant circumstances. The magistrates could take account of the defendant's previous convictions. In small cases of theft, where the sum involved was under £5,000, the magistrates would be obliged to treat it as an offence triable only summarily.

The Bill attracted much criticism, notably from the Bar, the Law   **16-022**
Society, the Society of Black Lawyers and from civil rights groups such as

the Legal Action Group. LAG argued the following (*Legal Action*, September 1998):

- The main reason defendants opt for jury trial is that they rightly see their chances of obtaining justice in the Crown Court as significantly higher. In 1997, 62 per cent of defendants who pleaded not guilty to some or all counts were acquitted. Having a professional judge oversee the case was as important as having a jury. Thirty-eight per cent were acquitted because the judge discharged the case and a further 16 per cent on the judge's direction.
- Electing jury trial brings into play a range of other safeguards, such as greater disclosure of the prosecution case. (This point was also made by many other commentators.)
- Removing the right to elect would significantly disadvantage black defendants. They more frequently elect for the Crown Court. Research indicates that this results in more of them being acquitted or having the charges against them dropped.
- Removing the right ignores the effect that other procedural changes will have in minimising defendants' manipulation of the system.
- The suggestion that defendants elect jury trial to put off the evil day is not borne out by research.
- Delays would increase, caused by mini-trials on venue.
- In opposition, Jack Straw had called the proposal "short-sighted".

Wolchover and Heaton-Armstong added ((1998) 148 N.L.J. 1614, and see 150 N.L.J. 158):

- It is the inherent superiority of jury trial which makes it essential for defendants to elect for it.
- The Labour party is normally associated with protection of civil liberties.
- A defendant who delays a guilty plea to obtain some advantage cannot expect the same sentence discount as one who pleads earlier and, since 1986, advocates have had a duty to warn defendants of this.
- Tactical elections will continue to decline because of the "plea before venue" procedure and because of section 48 of the Criminal Justice and Public Order Act 1994, which allowed the sentencing court to take account of the timing of the guilty plea.
- As experienced defence counsel, they denied that defendants caused delay to "put off the evil day". On the contrary, the most frequent and obvious cause of a last minute plea was the defendant's loss of courage.

- The argument is about the loss of a traditional common law right.
- Loss of liberty is no less serious for an habitual thief than loss of good name for someone with no previous convictions.

Courtney Griffiths Q.C. (*Counsel*, April 1999) added:

- Research by the Runnymede Trust, 1990, showed that, whereas under one third of white defendants, given the option, elected for jury trial, 45 per cent of black defendants elected.
- This is an intelligent choice. Only two per cent of magistrates are non-white. Home Office research at Leicester magistrates' court showed white defendants had a substantially better chance of being granted bail and were less likely to receive immediate custodial sentences than blacks. (Incidentally, when the research was completed in 1999, it showed the reverse. Magistrates acquitted more Asians and blacks than whites. McConville and Bridges however, completed another unpublished study which indicated the opposite and the Attorney-General, Lord Williams of Mostyn, conceded in a House of Lords debate, in 2000, that there is evidence of overcharging of ethnic minority defendants.)

Both the Bar and Law Society oppose the plan to abolish the right to **16-023** elect. A number of other commentators emphasised that jury trial is inherently superior to summary trial, especially as listing for a Crown Court trial triggered a much more careful review of the case by the CPS, which would often result in dropping the case or reducing the charges. This also implied that, if magistrates were to decide on mode of trial, they would be doing so on inadequate information. Further, at the Crown Court, a professional judge reviews the strength and admissibility of the evidence, whereas magistrates are both fact-finders and arbiters of the law. Nigel Ley ((1999) 149 N.L.J. 1316) drew attention to the fact that magistrates do not take notes of evidence or give reasons, that defendants in theft cases were often refused legal aid, and that now criminal defence solicitors in magistrates' courts were often ignorant of the law, as were magistrates' clerks. Some critics pointed out that magistrates' courts are seen as police courts, or magistrates are seen as part of the Establishment and magistrates are not as socially and ethnically diverse as the jury.

A *New Law Journal* editorial ((1999) 149 N.L.J. 549) argued that there were other ways of cutting down the cost and length of jury trials, such as reducing jurors to six, to have them sit in the magistrates' court and let lay justices do the sentencing, to cut out the opening statement and permit the judge to sum up only on law.

This first Bill was heavily defeated in the House of Lords, in January 2000. The Home Secretary replaced it with the Criminal Justice (Mode of Trial) Number 2 Bill, which was again defeated in the Lords in autumn 2000. Discarded was the requirement that justices consider the impact of a conviction on a person's reputation or job before they decide on mode of trial and added was a right of appeal against the magistrates' decision to the Crown Court. This did not satisfy the critics. Michael Zander and Lee Bridges ((2000) 150 N.L.J. 366, 855) said that not allowing the court to take account of the defendant's reputation or livelihood was even worse. Some pointed out that the new right of appeal would add to delay. Prior to the 2001 election, the Home Secretary insisted that he would use the Parliament Acts to push though a third Bill. This has only been done five times before. Many thought the timing of such a Bill inappropriate, in the middle of Lord Justice Auld's comprehensive review of the criminal courts. In his Review (2001), he reiterated the recommendation that the right to elect jury trial should be removed. He added, however, that the defendant should, in serious cases, be entitled to opt out of jury trial by choosing trial by judge alone. We discussed this in our 2001 paper for him and I have long argued for this change in the law (1991and 1997 and my evidence to Auld L.J).

The Criminal Courts Review

16-024   Apparently not content with all the legislative changes which followed the 1993 Royal Commission and the Crime and Disorder Act 1998 which enacted most of Narey's recommendations, the Labour Government commissioned Lord Justice Auld, in 2000, to commence another wide-ranging review of the criminal process. He is due to report in 2001 but, at the time of writing, a general election is in the offing and he is delaying publication. Students can view his terms of reference and report on the Review's website. As you can see from his Chapters on the jury (5) and the trial (11) he adopted many of our recommendations listed below.

10. Jury Research

16-025

Lord Justice Auld commissioned Darbyshire, Maughan and Stewart to conduct a review of the findings of jury research published up to 2000. This was updated to 2001. Our principal findings, reviewing thousands of pieces of jury research in the common law world, were published in *What Can the English Legal System Learn from Jury Research Published up to 2001?* Here is a summary of our findings and recommendations which you can also read, more fully, in a short article in the *Criminal Law Review* 2001:

1. Juries in England and Wales could be made more representative by cutting down the lists of those statutorily excluded or excused from service and by selecting jurors from more lists than just the electoral roll, such as DVLC, DSS, phone lists and mailing lists.

2. Most people try to avoid jury service, often because of childcare or work commitments. Reducing service to a week from two weeks would increase the acquittal rate so we do not recommend it. Instead, the timing of service could be made more flexible and loss of earnings could be paid to another carer (say, another relative) to look after children or an elderly dependent.

3. Lack of representativeness is a cause for concern because some personal characteristics appear to relate to verdict preferences and contribution to deliberations. For example, men participate more in deliberations and young people recall more instructions and more evidence. Race affects trial verdict so we endorsed the RCCJ's recommendation that the judge could order inclusion of three black or Asian jurors in a racially sensitive case.

4. Jurors judge witnesses by their demeanour in court but this is a questionable indicator of truthfulness. Expert evidence should be provided on the reliability of eyewitness and other evidence.

5. Jurors are frustrated over missing pieces of evidence they are not allowed to hear. They get confused by multiple charges or multiple defendants and sometimes argue in the jury room over the details of evidence. They seldom take notes but should be encouraged to take brief notes to help stay awake.

6. If judges continue to sum up the evidence, they should not recite it.

7. Juries have a great deal of difficulty in understanding and applying judicial instructions. They should be rewritten by psycholinguists, taking account of the large body of research from the USA.

8. Jurors should be given written instructions on the law and pre-deliberation instructions, where possible, as it is illogical and difficult for jurors to receive instructions on what evidence is important *after* they have heard it, as they now are. Certain basic instructions could be pinned on the jury room wall.

9. Juries have immense difficulty in understanding the quantum of proof "beyond reasonable doubt". When judges explain it to mean "sure", many jurors look for absolute proof of guilt, which is impossible. The word "sure" should be eliminated from the judges' explanation of BRD.

10. Juries should be instructed to discuss the evidence before voting as this makes them deliberate more thoroughly.

11. Criminal trial juries may be required to give reasons, if jury trial is to satisfy Article 6 (fair trial) of the European Convention on

Human Rights. In this case, we should study how such a system works in Spain and consider copying English civil procedure, whereby advocates and the judge agree a series of questions for the jury. Juries will need access to the transcript of evidence.

12. Many people resent giving up time for jury service and the abiding memory of most jurors is boredom, waiting for a trial or for legal argument to take place in their absence. In long trials, the jury trial should proceed in the mornings, while jurors are more alert and legal argument in the afternoons.

13. Heat, cold, boredom and their passive role may reduce jurors' arousal levels. Court managers should check courtroom temperatures and jurors should have breaks.

14. Small discomforts all irritate jurors. Court personnel should be more responsive and polite to them.

15. Jury service can be emotionally and physically stressful.

16. In long trials, we should copy the USA system of sitting two or more "alternates" alongside the real jury, in case of illness or indisposition.

17. Jury trial should be abolished in serious frauds. We guess most of the public would be indifferent to this and most people loathe sitting on such juries.

FURTHER READING

16-026 Lord Devlin, *Trial By Jury* (1966).

John Baldwin and Mike McConville, *Jury Trials* (1979).

William Cornish, *The Jury* (1968).

"The Roskill Report" *Fraud Trials Committee Report* (1986) HMSO.

Findlay and Duff, *The Jury Under Attack* (1988).

Darbyshire, " The Lamp that Shows the Freedom Lives—is it worth the candle?" [1991] Crim.L.R. 740.

Mike McConville and Lee Bridges, *Criminal Justice in Crisis* (1994).

M. Narey, *Review of Delay in the Criminal Justice System* (1997, Home Office website).

"Determining Mode of Trial in Either Way Cases—A Consultation Paper" (1998, Home Office website, www.homeoffice.gov.uk).

"Juries in Serious Fraud trials—A Consultation Paper", 1998, Home Office website.

Jennifer Airs and Angela Shaw, "Jury Excusal and Deferral", Home Office Research and Statistics Directorate Research Study No. 102, 1999, Home Office website.

Neil Vidmar (ed.), *World Jury Systems* (2000).

The Criminal Courts Review website: www.criminal-courts-review.org.uk.

Penny Darbyshire, Andy Maughan and Angus Stewart, *What Can the*

English Legal System Learn from Jury Research Published up to 2001? Penny Darbyshire's website at Kingston University, www.kingston.ac.uk~S025 or via the Review website and click on "juries research".

It is summarised in "What can we learn from Published Jury Research? Findings for the Criminal Courts Review 2001" [2001] Crim. L.R.

Part VI: Access to Justice

17. Legal Services From 2000

If the Rule of Law states that everyone should be equal before the law **17-001**
then, I would argue, this implies that everyone should have equal access
to the law and to justice. Further, the law presumes that we all know the
law so I would suggest that one of the requirements of a civilised modern
democracy must mean promotion of and access to information on our
legal rights and duties. As we will see, there has been much use of the
phrase "access to justice" in the 1990s. This means, broadly: being able
to make full use of legal rights, through adequate legal services, *i.e.* advice,
assistance and representation, regardless of means; also, the ability to
make full use of the court structure and rights of appeal.

Those issues are dealt with in this Chapter and in the Procedure Chapter,
in relation to the adversarial process (for example, the Woolf reforms).

Before the twentieth century, although there were various schemes for
providing representation to the poor, these were not put on a systematic,
statefunded basis until civil legal aid was introduced during World War
II, for the armed forces and later for the civilian population. In the 1940s,
the Rushcliffe Committee considered how best to provide legal services
for those who could not afford them. They declined to introduce a
National Legal Service, along the lines of the NHS because while it was
in the interests of the nation that its citizenry should be healthy, it was not
in the nation's interests that they should be litigious. Instead, they settled
on the model of delivery of services through the private practice lawyer
claiming a fee from the State. Indeed, when civil legal aid was created,
the Law Society administered it. Criminal Legal Aid arrived later and
legal advice and legal service were added to the other schemes, also delivered primarily through private practice lawyers. By 1988 the various
schemes for these different types of legal aid were put on a systematic
basis in one statute, the Legal Aid Act 1988. At the same time lawyer's
fingers were taken off the purse strings. The Legal Aid Board was created
to fund and manage the civil legal aid scheme and legal advice. Criminal

legal aid was always dispensed by the criminal courts, normally the court clerks in magistrates' courts. All types of aid were available only to those who passed a means test, those who could afford to contribute being required to do so. The means tests were different for each of the three and civil legal aid and criminal legal aid were subject to merits tests.

Despite all of this provision, sociologists and lawyers in the 1960s and 1970s exposed the phenomenon to "utmost legal need", which occurs when someone has a legal problem which goes unsolved. The causes of unmet legal need were identified and exposed (see below) and alternative legal services were developed in the attempt to respond. By the 1980s and 1990s, the legal aid budget was increasing out of control, with a smaller percentage of the population eligible for it. When New Labour were elected, in 1997, they devised this radical new scheme, explained here. I come back to the background of the new scheme after describing it.

1. The Access to Justice Act 1999 — Replacing Legal Aid from 2000

17-002   Civil legal aid was largely replaced, in April 2000, by the new legal services scheme, provided for in the Access to Justice Act 1999. Criminal legal aid was replaced by criminal defence services, also provided for in the Act, in April 2001. This replaces the framework for legal aid established by the Legal Aid Act 1998. The Lord Chancellor, who is responsible for legal services, explained his plans for these schemes in a white paper, *Modernising Justice*, which was published alongside the Access to Justice Bill, in December 1998 and in numerous consultation papers and speeches. All can be found on the LCD website. Up-to-date detail can be found in the Legal Services Commission's publications.

The Legal Services Commission

This was established by section 1 of the Access to Justice Act. It replaced the Legal Aid Board as the body administering what is now the replacement for legal aid. It consists of seven to twelve members, appointed by the Lord Chancellor, according to their knowledge of social conditions, work of the courts, consumer affairs and management. Section 2 allows for replacement with two bodies, one civil and one criminal. Section 3 empowers the Commission to make contracts, loans, investments, undertake inquiries and advise the Lord Chancellor.

Community legal service

17-003   Section 4 requires the Commission to establish and fund a Community Legal Service (CLS) "for the purpose of promoting the availability to individuals of services of the descriptions specified . . . and, in particular, for securing (within the resources made available) . . . that individuals have access to services that effectively meet their needs". Section 4(2) describes these services as: providing information about the law and the legal system and the availability of legal services, advice and help in preventing, settling or resolving disputes and enforcing decisions. Section 4(4) provides that everyone involved in the CLS should have regard to the desirability of promoting improvements in the range and quality of services provided by the CLS and in making them accessible and appropriate to their nature and importance and of achieving the swift and fair resolution of disputes. The Commission has a duty, under section 4(6), to find out about the need for and provision of services, plan what needs to be done and help other bodies to plan how to use resources to meet those needs. The Commission is empowered to set and monitor standards and provide accreditation schemes for service providers (s.4(6)–(8)). Under section 5, the L.C. provides the budget for the Commission to maintain a Community Legal Service Fund. They must aim to secure value for money. The Commission may fund services by entering into contracts, making grants and loans, establishing bodies to provide services or itself provide services, etc., (s.6). They may provide different services for different areas of England and Wales and the L.C. may direct them to provide particular services.

The funding code

Under section 8, the Commission must prepare a funding code, subject to the L.C.'s approval, setting out the criteria under which it is prepared to provide services and providing the form and content of applications for funding. Section 10 provides for regulations as to when recipients should pay fixed fees or contributions for legal services and section 11 provides that costs ordered against a funded individual should be kept to a reasonable amount, taking into account his resources and making allowances for his clothes, furniture and tools of trade.

The criminal defence service

Under section 12 the Commission must establish a Criminal Defence Service (CDS) for the purpose of securing that individuals involved in criminal investigations or criminal proceedings have access to "such advice, assistance and representation as the interests of justice require". It can set up an accreditation and monitoring scheme and fund such advice and assistance as it considers appropriate, by making contracts, grants, loans or establishing and maintaining advice and assistance bodies, or employing people to provide advice and assistance. It can fund advice and assistance by different means in different areas of England and Wales (s.13). The scope of section 13 had to be clarified by the

Criminal Defence Services Act 2001, to ensure that it covered existing services, like the duty solicitor scheme and ABWOR (assistance by way of representation) ensuring that a person appearing in criminal proceedings could be given emergency representation. Under section 14, the CDS has a duty to fund representation in criminal cases to people who have been granted a right to it under the Act. Section 15 provides that the represented individual may select any representative to act for him but it may be from a prescribed group but regulations may not provide that only a person employed by the Commission or a body maintained by the Commission may be selected. Under section 16 the Commission must prepare a code of conduct for its employees and funded providers, which includes a duty of non-discrimination and duties to the court, etc. Under section 17, where anyone is represented in a criminal court other than a magistrates' court, the court may ask them to pay for some or all of their representation. Under Schedule 3, the criminal courts are empowered to grant representation.

Conditional fee agreements

17-004   Under Part II of the Act, headed "Other Funding of Legal Services', Conditional Fee Agreements (CFAs), as provided for by the Courts and Legal Services Act 1990, are defined, in section 58(2) as "an agreement with a person providing advocacy or litigation services which provides for his fee and expenses, or any part of them, to be payable only in specified circumstances". (Of course the specified circumstances normally mean a success fee is paid only if the lawyer wins the case.) Conditions are prescribed: agreements must be in writing, must satisfy regulations and must relate to proceedings specified by the Lord Chancellor. They are prohibited in relation to criminal proceedings and virtually all family proceedings. Section 29 provides that insurance premiums for policies insuring against the risk of losing the case may be recovered in costs awarded by the court.

Legal services consultative panel

Section 35 abolishes ACLEC, the Lord Chancellor's previous advisory committee. The L.C. had criticised the body in his paper on rights of audience. He thought it had too many people, cost too much (£1million p.a.) and had succeeded in obstructing rather than furthering the statutory objective of the Courts and Legal Services Act 1990, to open up competition in the provision of legal services. It is replaced with a small Legal Services Consultative Panel, appointed by the L.C., with "the duty of assisting in the maintenance and development of standards in the education, training and conduct of persons offering legal services by considering relevant issues in accordance with a programme of work approved by the Lord Chancellor and, where the Consultative Panel considers it appropriate to do so, making recommendations to him". They are obliged to advise the L.C. when he calls on them.

Rights of audience

Sections 36–48 are one of the most provocative bits of the Act but the most exciting for all lawyers who are not practising barristers, because they open up rights of audience to employed barristers and to solicitors. They stem from the L.C.'s frustration at the lack of progress in opening up rights of audience, one of the stated aims of the Courts and Legal Services Act 1990. This reform is explained in depth in the Chapter on lawyers.

Modernising justice

This white paper, published alongside the Access to Justice Bill in December 1998, explains not just the framework in the statute, above, but the reasoning behind it and more detail on proposed policy to effect the Government's plans to radically overhaul legal services. Chapters 2, 3 and 6 cover legal aid and legal services. The full document, available on the LCD website, is worth reading, as it gives a more holistic picture of the legal services scheme which is still (2001) in the process of implementation and it tells us about law and policy, of which the new framework is, of course, a mixture. The Government had identified these problems in the old legal aid scheme:

17-005

- inadequate access to quality information—poor co-ordination in services;
- inability to control and target legal aid;
- restrictive practices and cumbersome court procedures. They intended to replace legal aid with a community legal service.

The legal advice sector had grown randomly.

The CLS would:

- develop a system for assessing needs and priorities and monitoring standards;
- co-ordinate plans of various funders;
- treat the advice sector and advice by lawyers under one budget.

A new Legal Services Commission would:

- develop local, regional and national plans to match provision to needs;
- report annually to the L.C.;

- manage CLS fund, which will replace legal aid in civil and family cases;
- make contracts, fund traditional or other types of provider;
- take account of local views;
- develop partnerships with local authorities, *etc.*

The interim project in 1999 was to:

- develop systems for assessing need;
- develop core quality criteria;
- build a CLS website on legal advice;
- launch four pioneer partnerships.

The LSC would develop a quality system by

- integrating it with the existing franchising system;
- kitemarking non-lawyers.

As for the legal profession, the Government would:

- cut restrictive practices;
- improve standards;
- make legal services more affordable through:

    — legal insurance
    — regulating cost
    — expanding provision for conditional fees.

Chapter 6 on criminal defence said the Government's objectives were to:

- ensure a fair hearing, by putting the defendant on an equal footing with the prosecution;
- protect the interest of the defendant;
- maintain the defendant's confidence and effective participation.

The CDS must reflect domestic law (PACE) and international law (Article 6 of the European Convention on Human Rights). Weaknesses of present system, said the Government, were:

- cost;
- the lawyers' pay framework was outdated because of:

    — inappropriate financial incentives
    — a few disproportionately expensive cases

- the means test was flawed. Note that the Lord Chancellor has scrapped any requirement for the recipient of criminal defence services to pay for some or all of his legal services, except that a Crown Court judge may order a defendant to pay some or all of the costs of representation. The L.C. scrapped the means test because magistrates' clerks were so bad at administering the legal aid means tests and were castigated by the Public Accounts Committee in 1998 for squandering legal aid money for the previous seven years.
- the legal aid scheme was highly fragmented.

Fundamental reform was necessary. The Government would replace legal aid with a Criminal Defence Service. It would:

- be separate from CLS, with a separate budget;
- but both run by the Legal Services Commission;
- cover all services provided under legal aid;
- develop more efficient ways of procuring services, through:
  - — contracts with accredited private practice lawyers, replacing franchising;
  - — salaried defenders on the model piloted in Scotland;
  - — restricting client choice to a duty solicitor or accredited solicitor;
- abolish means testing, targeting rich defendants;
- in 1999, establish pilot contracts for representation in youth courts.

The Legal Services Commission replaced the Legal Aid Board in April 2000 and the Criminal Defence Service was established by April 2001.

2. *Developing the New Legal Services Model in Practice*

The Legal Services Consultative Panel provided its first advice to the Lord Chancellor, on proposed changes to rights of audience, in April 2000.   **17-006**

Thirteen Regional Legal Service Committees were established in 1997–1998 and published their *Assessment of Need for Legal Services* by July 1999. They had organised their priorities. How they assess need is explained in *Legal Action*, July 1999. They identified particular groups suffering from an unmet need for legal services: those living in rural areas, the elderly, people with mental health problems, people whose first language was not English and those appearing before employment tribunals.

The New System for Civil Cases

The community legal service

17-007   In May 1999, the Government published a consultation paper on how they would develop this institution (LCD website). It made the following points:

- People need basic information and advice on rights and responsibilities, not necessarily to go to court.
- 6,000 professionals (lawyers) and 30,000 volunteers at Law Centres and other advice centres, such as Citizens' Advice Bureaux, *etc.*, provided this for £250 million pounds per year. (By March 2000, the junior minister said their estimate was that about a billion pounds per year was spent on legal services.)
- This is enough but service is fragmented and unco-ordinated.

The paper gave case studies demonstrating how difficult it was for people with certain problems to obtain satisfactory advice. The lack of an effective referral network meant people got initial advice and were sent away so the new legal services network should include:

- lawyers
- professionals outside private practice
- advice workers
- para-legals with specialist knowledge, *e.g.* Trading Standards Officers
- volunteers in Citizens' Advice Bureaux, *etc.*

The CLS should provide information, advice and assistance. The need for legal services varies geographically. Research disclosed no area where strategy had been developed jointly by different funders. Time was wasted by advice agencies demonstrating the quality of their services to their different funders. For instance, one Asian women's group had ten funders. Forty per cent of its manager's time was spent on reporting to them. Quantifying need was difficult. Statistics indicated the unmet need for legal services resulted not from inadequate provision but from "lack of access to appropriate adequate help of adequate quality".

The Legal Services Commission is the new co-ordinating body. It took over and developed the Legal Aid Board's responsibilities in 2000. It works with "Community Legal Service Partnerships", targeting funds to local needs. They bring together different funders and providers of legal and advice services to organise funding and delivery with the aim of meeting the needs they have identified. Pioneer partnerships were developed in six local authority areas, in 1999, bringing together the local authority, Legal Aid Board and local providers of legal services. The report on these pioneer projects is on the LCD website and gives a good idea of how they go about assessing need. By October 2000, there were 142 partnerships and by 2002, the whole country should be covered.

Core criteria were developed for the legal service providers' quality **17-008** mark from 1999. A legal services website was being developed, from 1999 but the Government acknowledged, in the consultation paper, that *Guardian* research in 1999 showed only two per cent of social classes D/E are online. Historically, this group has been identified as suffering from unmet legal need.

The CLS was officially launched in April 2000, replacing the Legal Aid Board. One of its first acts was to deliver to every home in Cornwall (one of the pioneers) an information card on how to get good legal advice. This would be extended nationwide. The CLS fund replaced the previous civil and family legal aid budget.

Contracting

The introduction of general civil contracting brought a massive shift in funding of legal services. Whereas any solicitor could apply to give legally aided services but few non-solicitor agencies could, providers of legal help are now limited to those who have a contract with the Legal Services Commission to deal with a specified number of cases. To get this, an advice agency or firm of solicitors must demonstrate they satisfy the quality criteria, based on an audit. For instance, they need to show that they have a satisfactory management system, that staff work is closely supervised and they had to have computerised systems by August 2000. The Commission must spend around a tenth of its budget on contracts with providers in the not-for-profit sector.

The predecessor to contracting was the franchising system, introduced **17-009** by the last Government by about 1994, whereby providers could get a franchise to provide services from the Legal Aid Board but did not have to do so. Franchised firms and agencies were already subject to rigorous quality criteria and auditing so they became the first contracted providers. A provider may have a general civil contract, a family contract, if on the family panel, or a controlled work contract, in areas such as immigration, mental health, community care, public law and actions against the police. Every contracted supplier gets regular payments based on monthly reports to the LSC. Their work is audited by inspection of sample files. Contracted legal advisers can call specialist telephone lines for free help in advising clients. For instance, *Shelter* provides training courses and advice on homelessness, possession proceedings, security of tenure and disrepair; the Public Law Project provides help on human rights, the Joint Council for the Welfare of Immigrants provides training and advice to contracted advisers on immigration and nationality law and asylum. The first barristers' chambers to be awarded a contract for advice and representation in employment, immigration and housing law was 2 Garden Court, Temple. Contractors should not take on more cases than are authorised under their contract but if an expensive case takes them beyond their prescribed limit, the CLS will pay for work actually and reasonably done.

Contracts can only be granted to fulfil a perceived need so in 2001, there was an excess of applicants for contracts in immigration work and the LSC announced that applicants would have to demonstrate that they would fulfil a particular need.

Funding certificates can be granted to firms without the relevant contract in special cases. For instance, if a non-contracted solicitor has been working privately for a client and then that person becomes eligible for CLS funding, the solicitor may apply.

The funding code—setting out types of legal service the Government is prepared to fund

17-010   This was launched at the same time, having been approved by Parliament. It replaced the old civil merits test for legal aid. Obviously, the Lord Chancellor has the flexibility, under the 1999 Act, to alter the list of what services can be funded, from time to time. This is the scheme in 2001. It provides seven levels of service, which may be provided in different ways and may attract different eligibility and remuneration.

- legal help
- help at court (these replace the old legal advice and assistance, under the legal aid scheme)
- approved family help (general help or mediation)
- legal representation (investigative help or full representation)
- support funding (either investigative or litigation support)
- family mediation
- such other services as are authorised by the Lord Chancellor.

Legal help, help at court and certain types of representation are classified as controlled work and can only be carried out by lawyers or legal advisers with a general civil contract (a contract with the LSC as an accredited provider). These providers are fully responsible for granting and withdrawing help in these cases. Funding for most cases requiring representation, approved family help and support funding will be granted by a certificate awarded by the Commission. The General Funding Code applies to any application for funding. In addition, there are category specific criteria which apply to very expensive cases, judicial review, claims against public authorities, clinical negligence, housing, family, mental health and immigration cases.

Eight categories of service are excluded, under Schedule 2 of the

Access to Justice Act so people will have to pay for them privately, for instance, by persuading a lawyer to act under a conditional fee agreement, or get help from a charity, or a CAB, or from a lawyer acting *pro bono*, or will be left to represent themselves:

- personal injury, apart from clinical negligence, death or damage to property. Even personal injury claims suitable for a conditional fee agreement (CFA) may not receive funding
- conveyancing
- boundary disputes
- wills
- trust law
- defamation
- company or partnership law
- other business matters.

Applying the Code criteria means considering the prospects of success **17-011** of the case and the cost-benefit. The *prospects of success* are evaluated for those clients applying for funding for representation. This means the likelihood of a successful outcome in the proceedings. Generally, at least a 50 per cent prospect of success is required but funding may be granted to borderline cases if, for example, the case has overwhelming importance to the client, has a wider public interest, is a human rights judicial review, involves housing possession, domestic violence or children. The Code provides various cost benefit tests, which usually mean comparing likely cost with likely damages obtainable. This replaces the merits test, under the old legal aid scheme.

Investigative help and representation will be refused if the case is suitable for a CFA. Support funding is provided for under the Code. It tops up privately funded personal injury claims, for instance to fund an initial investigation into the claim to establish whether it is worth proceeding under a CFA.

The Lord Chancellor announced the *priorities* of the new CLS, such as special Children Act proceedings, civil proceedings where the client is at real and immediate risk of loss of life or liberty, social welfare issues which enable people to climb out of social exclusion, domestic violence, child welfare and serious proceedings against public authorities. Public interest is a new consideration under the Code. Cases with a wider public interest have preferential treatment under the Code so even if a case falls into an excluded category it may qualify, even if it has only borderline prospects of success. Significant human rights cases are prioritised. Special applications for funding often concern representation in inquests following deaths in custody, for example.

The Lord Chancellor set up a specific budget for very high cost cases, where costs are likely to exceed £25,000. These are considered by the Special Cases Unit of the Commission. Each of these cases has a special contract and there must be a case plan and fully costed stages. For example a public law Children Act case involving several children and requiring expert reports, or a multi-party action or an action against the police might fall into this category.

17-012   Personal injuries, for which legal aid had been available, were removed from the scheme, because the Government thinks that most of these cases can be funded through conditional fee agreements. This was highly controversial. Clinical negligence cases and actions against the police for tort remain within scope of the new fund.

Funding for tribunal cases and ADR

Note that funding is now extended to representation before the Immigration Adjudicators and the Immigration Appeal Tribunal, the Protection of Children Act Tribunal, the VAT and Duties Tribunal and the General and Special Commissioners of Income Tax, whereas legal aid had not been available under the old pre-1999 Scheme. The only ADR specifically provided for is mediation but this is likely to be extended and will generally now be funded under legal help or representation. For instance, Early Neutral Evaluation can be funded in this way. Arbitration can be funded, whereas it could not have been provided under the old legal aid scheme. The Commission actively encourages the wider use of ADR, especially in the field of clinical negligence. If a funded client refuses an offer by the other side to enter ADR without good reason, the Commission may limit funding on the case.

Financial eligibility limits

These are updated by regulations, every April, as were the old legal aid means tests. Only clients with very low incomes and capital are entitled to fully funded legal services. Those whose income or capital fall above certain limits will have to pay a contribution towards certain (but not all) legal services, assessed according to means. This is the same as the old legal aid scheme. The Access to Justice Act preserves the statutory charge. This means that the CLS may place a first charge on any property recovered or preserved in funded proceedings or settlement. The logic behind this is to ensure people pay towards the cost of their cases if they are able; it encourages people to act reasonably and not to incur excessive legal costs and it puts them in a similar position to a privately paying client.

17-013   The Lord Chancellor proposes altering the financial conditions by October 2001, which he estimates will make five million more people eligible for legal advice. The Government proposes to increase eligibility limits further later.

One of the worrying aspects for a private person litigating against a funded client is that they will not normally recover their costs from the CLS fund, even if they win the case. This was the case under the old legal aid scheme and Lord Denning M.R. called this "the ugly, unacceptable face of British justice", in *Thew v. Reeves* (1981, CA). An exception will be made if the private client can demonstrate "severe financial hardship". In 2001, the Lord Chancellor is proposing changing this to "financial hardship". This will not apply to businesses or corporate bodies so they may still suffer.

Funding review committees and costs appeals committees

These are made up of independent lawyers who consider appeals against refusal of funding and issues of costs.

Conditional fee agreements

Legal representation or investigative help will not be granted in cases suitable for a CFA. A conditional fee agreement means, for example, a no-win, no-fee contract or a contract whereby the lawyer gets a higher fee if he wins the case. Distinguish it from a *contingency fee agreement*, which is illegal here but well known in the United States, whereby the lawyer takes a percentage of any damages won. Conditional fees were permitted by the Courts and Legal Services Act 1990 but widened in scope in April 2000, when three sets of rules came into force providing the new framework for CFAs. All civil proceedings may be funded by CFAs, except specified family proceedings. The maximum success fee which can be contracted for is 100 per cent.

The Quality Mark

This was launched in April 2000. It is a symbol which the accredited quality providers are allowed to display. This includes over 6,000 solicitors' offices, Citizens' Advice Bureaux and other advice centres. All franchised firms carry the Specialist Help Quality Mark. In 2001 Quality Marks were developed for mediation, telephone helplines and the best of the many legal advice websites, as well as the Bar. Holders of the Specialist Quality Mark are what used to be called franchises. **17-014**

Just Ask!

The CLS website was launched in April 2000, providing a directory of legal services. The Citizens' Advice Bureaux provides some advice online but the LAG warned that the plans, outlined in *Modernising the Civil Courts*, to access court services online will disadvantage some groups. In 2001, the LCD and the DTI announced three online debt advice projects.There is an increasing number of businesses offering free online legal advice, such as www.freelawyer.co.uk and www.legal-café.co.uk. These are not part of the CLS.

CLS information points

Available in 300 libraries by October 2000 and in 2001, a series of information leaflets was published to provide information on dealing with specific legal problems.

Telephone advice lines

17-015   These are being developed. Cardiff Law School provides one for travellers but it is funded by charity.

Litigants in person

These were reported on as long ago as 1995, by Lord Justice Otton. A CAB was located in the Royal Courts of Justice to help them but it is underused. It was reported on for the LCD by Plotnickoff and Woolfson, see LCD website. Otton suggested legal assistants to help judges with legal research in these cases. The number of L-I-Ps is increasing.

The New System in Criminal Cases

17-016   In 2000–2001, the Government published several consultation papers on the CDS, which was be launched in April 2001 (see LCD website). They announced proposals to develop a system of *public defenders* directly employed by the Legal Services Commission but clients will generally be able to choose between them and any private practice lawyer, except in cases like serious fraud, where they would be limited to specially qualified lawyers. The first four heads of Public Defenders' Offices were introduced as pilots in March 2001. The scheme will be piloted in six places for four years and will be the subject of a full review headed by Professors Lee Bridges and Avrom Scherr, two of the most eminent experts in the field of legal services.

After consultation, a professional Code of Conduct was approved by Parliament in March 2001. It seeks to guarantee minimum standards of behaviour. It imposes duties to:

- protect the interests of the client,
- act with integrity and independence,
- act with impartiality and avoid discrimination,
- respect confidentiality,
- the court,
- avoid conflicts of interest,
- not to offer or accept certain payments.

It also contains rules in relation to:

- their relationship with the legal profession,
- change of legal representative,

- withdrawal of legal representative
- public interest disclosure,
- excessive caseload,
- standards of conduct.

From April 2001, all solicitors' firms undertaking publicly funded criminal defence have to have a franchise (contract) with the CDS. Only solicitors working to quality standards are eligible for a contract. Solicitors working under a contract are now paid agreed monthly amounts, with claims set off against payments. A serious fraud panel was established in May 2000. From 2000, the Commission is piloting individual case contracts in "Very High Cost Criminal Cases", which will be controlled in the same way as very high cost civil cases. Solicitors are required to notify the Commission in all cases likely to cost £150,000 to defend or to last 25 trial days or longer.

Following consultation, the Government refined its proposals on choice of representative in February 2001. Defendants are allowed to make a reasonable change at any time. The decision will remain in the hands of the court because the judge or magistrates will be free from any accusation of economic interest.

Means and merits test

As announced in *Modernising Justice*, although there will be an "interests of justice" merit test (*i.e.* that the case is more than trivial), there is no means test for representation in the magistrates' court. The Crown Court has power to make a Recovery of Defence Costs Order of up to the full amount of defence costs at the conclusion of the case. Investigations into the defendant's means are undertaken by the Legal Services Commission. The aim is to identify defendants who may have the means to contribute, including criminal assets. The defendant's assets may be frozen pending the outcome of trial. A spouse's assets are taken into account if it appears assets have been deliberately moved. This tactic was the norm under the old legal aid scheme, which explains why many very wealthy fraudsters were granted legal aid. **17-017**

3. Background to the Reforms — Why was Legal Aid scrapped?

Throughout the 1990s, both the Conservative Government then their Labour successors were seriously concerned that something radical had to be done to reform the provision of legal services. Why? **17-018**

- The cost was "spiralling out of control", according to the Conservative Lord Chancellor, Lord Mackay, legal aid was the only demand-led draw on the Treasury. Some years in the 1990s, the cost rose by around 20 per cent, despite the fact that fewer people were being legally aided. See Gray and Fenn for an interesting statistical analysis of the sharp increase in cost per case. The Children Act 1989, providing separate representation for children and the development of *duty solicitor schemes* in police stations and the magistrates' courts were items which accelerated the cost increase and the public were concerned that a few cases cost millions of pounds when apparently wealthy defendants, such as the Maxwells, were legally aided.

- Unmet legal need was identified by research in the 1970s and never satisfied by 2000. It was caused by:

  - the high cost of legal fees
  - fear of lawyers, fear of cost
  - lawyers' lack of training and unwillingness to serve poor clients' needs for advice in welfare law
  - the inaccessibility of lawyers' offices to poor or rural clients
  - the creation of new legal rights without the funding to enforce them
  - people's ignorance that the law could solve their problem
  - the fact that the legal aid scheme omitted certain services, such as representation at tribunals.

- Funders were unco-ordinated. Legal aid was designed to deliver legal services through the medium of private practice barristers and solicitors so alternative legal services, listed below, received very little of the huge budget and they were dependent on a precarious mix of sources, such as charities, local authorities and other government departments.

- Criminal legal aid was administered unevenly. Research showed that the Widgery criteria, merits test was applied differently between magistrates' courts and the Audit Commission criticised them eight years running for failure to apply the means test properly. Kenneth Noye was convicted of murder at the Old Bailey in 2000. An inquiry was held into why he was granted legal aid when he was so apparently wealthy, largely as a result of a life of crime. A Court Service inquiry led to the resignation of one official and the disciplining of another.

- Fat cat lawyers, as the present Lord Chancellor calls them, were charging the Legal Aid Board exorbitant fees (see below).

In 1999, Hazell Genn published the most modern survey of how people solve their legal problems: *Paths to Justice*, summarised at (1999) 149 N.L.J. 1756. She found that people were generally extraordinarily ignorant about their legal rights and obligations.

Comment: the present Government's scheme was quite visionary. It was first announced in the Labour party policy paper, *Access to Justice*, in 1995. They had the simple idea of finding out how much money was spent on legal services in England and Wales and working out what legal needs were and how they could best be fulfilled, whether through private practice lawyers or alternatives.

4. *"Alternative"* Legal Services

Because the shortcomings of the legal aid scheme and the causes of **17-019** unmet legal need were identified since the 1970s, alternatives to private practice were developed to try to meet that need. These can no longer be seen as alternatives because they have just been absorbed into mainstream state-regulated provision and CLS funding. Lord Chief Justice Bingham gave a neat list of these alternatives in the Barnett Lecture in 1998 (LCD website):

- 53 Law Centres, deliberately established in poor areas, with a shop front image, where employed lawyers and para-legals provide advice and representation on such matters as welfare law and immigration. They have been established since 1973 but have always suffered from vulnerable funding. Those financed by local authorities found they were biting the hand that fed them, when they acted for groups suffering bad public housing. Law centre funding was sporadic and sometimes they would have to close temporarily.
- 700 Citizens' Advice Bureaux.
- 800 independent advice centres, covering diverse areas, some times providing legal services themselves and sometimes making referrals. Examples are the Child Poverty Action Group, Shelter, Youth Access, the Money Advice Association, Dial UK (disability advice), Mind, the Refugee Legal Centre, etc. Lawyers often provide advice free at evening advice centres but would need to make a referral if substantive legal help was needed.
- *Pro Bono* groups of both solicitors and barristers, newly organised in the 1990s, where professionals pledge to give their service free to some clients. The *Free Representation Unit*, a group of Bar students prepared to represent claimants in appearances before tribunals, etc., was established in the 1970s.

In addition, the Conservative administrations of the 1990s had devised various other ways of enhancing access to justice, which have been expanded under the new scheme:

- Conditional fees, as described above but in a limited sphere.
- Simplifying the law (plain English) and making court procedures simpler and cheaper and providing good advice leaflets and a CAB in the Royal Courts of Justice to help people represent themselves.
- Encouraging ADR (alternative dispute resolution, discussed in another Chapter), the cheaper and quicker resolution of disputes, out of court.
- Encouraging private legal expenses insurance.
- Duty solicitors, funded under the legal aid scheme, to provide emergency help and representation in police stations and the magistrates' courts.

5. Evaluation of the New Legal Services Scheme

17-020   When reading evaluations of the new scheme, especially in newspapers and the weekly law journals, I would invite the reader to bear in mind the following, which I have observed from studying the legal professions' behaviour for thirty years:

1. The Law Society and Bar Council are not just regulatory bodies, they are trade unions.
2. They are very efficient at promoting their members' financial interests.
3. Their publicity machinery is very powerful. The press is always flooded with comments from the profession when any change is proposed which affects them.
4. They oppose most changes.
5. They argue that what they want is in the public interest.
6. Their professional monopolies have maintained a stranglehold over legal services throughout the twentieth century and their professional bodies mainly defend the interests of private practice lawyers.
7. All of this is illustrated graphically in the Chapter on lawyers, exemplified by what Lord Chancellor Irvine has called the "sorry saga" of their behaviour over rights of audience since the ineffective Courts and Legal Services Act 1990.

Conditional Fees

Development up to 1998

Speculative litigation was illegal under the common law offences of **17-021** champerty and maintenance, abolished 1967, or unenforceable in English law from the Statute of Westminster 1275 until the Courts and Legal Services Act 1990, section 58 enabled the Lord Chancellor to make rules permitting conditional fee agreements. In Scotland it has long been permissible for a lawyer and client to conduct litigation on a speculative basis, by entering a straight "no win, no fee" agreement. In the United States, however, a variety of contingency fees is permissible, the most common being that the lawyer will take a percentage of the sum recovered. No other jurisdiction operates an extensive contingency fee system and the English distaste for it was expressed by Blackstone in his *Commentaries on the Law of England* (1765):

> "This is an offence against public justice, as it keeps alive strife and contention, and perverts the remedial process of law into an engine of oppression" (quoted in Lord Mackay's green paper).

The Royal Commission on Legal Services, 1979, decided that any contract between lawyer and client which gave the former an interest in the case was against the public interest but the Civil Justice Review 1988 and the Marre Report 1988 thought the issue should be re-examined. In 1989, Lord Chancellor Mackay published a green paper, *Contingency Fees*, setting out the options. As with his other 1989 green papers on legal services reform, and most other things Lord Mackay did, it provoked a very hostile reaction from the judiciary. Section 58 was enacted in the face of opposition from seven Law Lords, the Master of the Rolls, a former Lord Chancellor and Attorney-General and the Law Commission. Note that the section did not permit contingency fees, a percentage of the damages but "no win, no fee" contracts, with the lawyer permitted to take a percentage uplift in the event of winning the case, above the normal fee, provided the client had been informed. Judicial opposition was again in force as Lord Chancellor Mackay's delegated legislation permitting CFAs was being debated in the Lords in 1995. This Conditional Fees Order permitted CFAs in personal injury, insolvency and human rights cases. Lawyers could charge a maximum uplift of 100 per cent above the normal fee, with no statutory cap on the percentages of damages recovered that this could constitute.

In their 1995 policy paper, "Access to Justice", written by Paul **17-022** Boateng, the Labour Opposition condemned CFAs as "at present, little more than a gimmick designed to mask the chaotic state of the legal aid scheme and the court service". When his colleague Lord Irvine adopted

CFAs as one of the main elements of his legal services policy, two years later, as Lord Chancellor, he was repeatedly reminded of these words. Indeed, even in opposition, at the 1996 Bar Conference, Lord Irvine suggested that legal aid might be refused in cases where a conditional fee agreement was deemed to be more appropriate. Nobody much noticed that until he said it again, as Lord Chancellor, at the 1997 Law Society conference. The speech was not interpreted as the Lord Chancellor intended, with commentators concentrating on the suggested cutbacks of legal aid, many hysterically warning of "the death of legal aid", rather the extension of CFAs and the announcement of the Community Legal Service, which Lord Irvine had sought to emphasize. Newspapers, even *The Times*, depicted disabled plaintiffs who had succeeded in legally aided claims but who would not qualify for aid under the new regime. The Lord Chancellor was taken aback by these "savage and grave allegations" (see *Gazette*, December 1997). LCD Minister Geoff Hoon and Lord Irvine defended these plans in a number of publications:

> "Under our current arrangements, access to the civil courts is open only to the very poor and the very rich. . . . This is not right. It is not just. . . . I cannot see how it is fair to allow only very poor people to sue under legal aid when most of those in work—whose taxes fund legal aid—could not do so themselves.
>
> By extending no-win, no-fee arrangements to all money recovery civil proceedings, except family cases, justice becomes available to all. Legal help will become affordable in disputes with banks, builders and insurance companies, provided the lawyer judges that the merits of the case justify a conditional fee agreement.
>
> . . . Modernising legal aid is a real challenge. Civil legal aid has tripled in cost in six years to £671 million. The income received by lawyers has risen on average by 20 per cent a year over the same period. At the same time, the number of cases supported has fallen. . . . There is no extra money for legal aid. So we need to extract the maximum value from the money we have. If good alternatives to legal aid exist . . . those alternatives should be used. For too long, legal aid has been abused. Too many weak cases supported by legal aid have been taken on . . . conditional fees will make lawyers look harder at the cases which are brought to them." (1997).

17-023   The speech and articles proved an explosion of reaction from lawyers in print, which the Lord Chancellor was able to take into account when, in March 1998, he spelled out the Labour Government plans in "Access to Justice with Conditional Fees". This consultation paper reiterated the points made by Hoon and added:

- The risk of litigation should be shared by lawyer and client.
- The Government would be able to redirect funds to securing basic rights in housing, social security and judicial review.
- Legal aid would be delivered through contracts.
- Weak cases would be removed from the legal aid system by toughening the merits test. Public interest litigation would be specially funded.
- The use of legal expenses insurance would be widened (Lord Mackay had been keen on this).
- The introduction of conditional fees would be monitored.
- The success fee and insurance premium (against losing the case) would be recoverable from the losing party.
- The high success rate of legally aided cases results from oppression. Legal aid should not be used to blackmail defendants. Medical negligence should be limited to experienced lawyers because these cases have a very low success rate. Legal aid would be removed once conditional fees develop.
- Defendants will still be eligible for legal aid.
- All personal injury actions would be removed from legal aid immediately.

This prompted hundreds of articles in the legal journals and newspapers and over 200 formal responses to the LCD, mainly representing organisations. The LCD published a summary of responses:

- Most people supported extending CFAs, except for defamation proceedings. Concern was expressed about using them where monetary damages were not the objective, where risk is difficult to assess, where there are complex technical issues and for child litigants and those with a mental disability. The success fee should be regulated.
- A variety of monitoring arrangements were suggested.
- Most people supported making the success fee recoverable from an unsuccessful defendant and most thought insurance premiums should be recoverable.
- Most people, however, did not support the proposal to exclude some proceedings from legal aid. There was particular concern over its withdrawal from cases involving children or the mentally disabled. Solicitors were worried that they would not be able to fund the cost of investigations or the insurance premiums for clients. Some banks thought the policy could cause the collapse of some law firms. Many respondents, notably the Bar and the Law Society supported the idea of a Contingency Legal Aid Fund, to which successful litigants would contribute, which would pay the

353

costs of unsuccessful litigants. (Lord Mackay had mooted this idea.)

17-024 Other noteworthy comments made in print were:

- The paper contained no proposals for reducing the cost of family or criminal legal aid, yet these took two thirds of the budget (Mears).
- CFAs would not cover defendants yet there were about as many aided defendants in contract disputes as plaintiffs (Mears).
- Many people made the point that Lord Chancellor relied on the success of CFAs in personal injury claims yet it was well known that these were straightforward.
- Lord Ackner referred to the negative findings of research by the Policy Studies Institute on 197 CFA cases. It identified two problematic areas crucial to the success of CFAs, the estimation of risk and the calculation of the uplift. From the litigant's perspective, CFAs were not working well. The average uplift was 43 per cent so litigants were being "ripped off".
- Chapman of the Legal Action Group, said the withdrawal of aid from personal injury cases was poor value for money; the cost to the litigant would be three times as much as the Government would save per case.
- Hodges thought that if litigants were allowed to recover their success fees from the defendants they defeated, this would significantly reduce the risk to plaintiff and lawyer so legal aid blackmail could be replaced by CFA blackmail. Insurance companies warned of extra expense to them (as defendants) causing the cost of premiums of all insurance to inflate. The Forum of Insurance Lawyers complained that a windfall of extra fees would be paid to successful solicitors in uplifted fees for no good reason.
- Prais, Capper and others described what they considered to be a better system for legal services in Germany, with extensive private legal insurance and fixed fees for legal services.

Nevertheless, moving swiftly, the Government introduced the Conditional Fees Order 1998, which came into effect that July, extending CFAs radically, to all civil cases except family cases. The Access to Justice Act 1999, sections 27–31 amended the Courts and Legal Services Act 1990 to define CFAs and litigation funding agreements much more carefully and permitted the recovery of the success fee and the insurance premium in costs against the losing party and the Conditional Fee Agreements Regulations 2000 prescribed detailed requirements for the CFA contract. Collective CFAs were permitted from 2000.

Living with CFAs

In *Nothing to Lose?* researchers Yarrow and Abrams (1999) reported that **17-025** clients found CFAs confusing. They did not understand success fees. Sometimes they did not understand the solicitor would get nothing if the case was lost. Clients found the solicitor would not let them drop the case, because the insurance policy would not pay out the solicitor's fees. Nevertheless, clients did not mind paying the success fee.

Research by the Legal Aid Board (1999) indicated that solicitors were good at estimating the chances of success of a case.

Experienced medical negligence lawyers are concerned about the inadequacy of insurance to cover litigation they are involved in but Mahendra quotes research by Barton which suggests that cases with merit have a higher success rate under CFAs and weak cases are more promptly abandoned.

In 2001, CFAs are still receiving negative reports. Wignall points out some anomalies in CFAs between barristers and solicitors; academic researchers Moorhead and Scherr raise ethical questions in relation to the lack of understanding of the client over the risk they are taking, especially of paying costs if they pull out and McGill and Crosby point out that, in contrast with the Access to Justice Act 1999, the European Court of First Instance has ruled that insurance premiums are not payable as part of a person's costs; both the Master of the Rolls, Lord Phillips, who chairs the Civil Justice Council, and the Law Society are worried that costs under the new civil justice scheme are not working well because of disputes about who should fund CFAs. The last tranche of research by Yarrow, *Just Rewards?* reveals that solicitors are using CFAs to overcharge.

In a very important interpretive case in the Court of Appeal, *Callery v.* **17-026** *Gray*, July 2001, Lord Chief Justice Woolf, who designed the Civil Procedure Rules, Lord Phillips M.R., who is worried about costs arguments and CFAs and Brooke L.J. tried to make some sense of the mess of litigation over who pays for success fees and insurance premiums in small claims resulting from traffic accidents. They heard argument from seven Q.C.s and five other barristers. They had to interpret section 29 of the Access to Justice Act and Rule 44.12A of the Civil Procedure Rules on costs in pre-action settlements. They decided it was quite reasonable for the lawyer and client to enter a CFA at the initial stage of the claim. There was no need to wait for the defendant's response. They gave a highly purposive interpretation to the new regime. The purpose was to achieve access to justice for people who could not afford it so it was an inevitable consequence of government policy that defendants should be subjected to additional costs. Defendants, with the help of the court, should be able to limit success fees and insurance premiums to a reasonable amount. Their Lordships thought that a reasonable success fee in cases like this which had a 98 per cent rate was 20 per cent. They could not work out what was a reasonable insurance premium so directed an inquiry by a costs Master and would judge on that issue later.

Research by accountants Stay Hayward suggests law firms "cherry pick" cases for CFAs, as was feared by critics ((2001) 151 N.L.J. 1078).

Conclusion

CFAs are proving so complex and problematic that I would predict they will be abandoned eventually in favour of contingency fees.

Contracting/Franchising

17-027   The idea of limiting legal aid provision to lawyers who held exclusive block contracts was first mooted in the Conservative Government's *Legal Aid Efficiency Scrutiny*, in 1986 and met fierce opposition. It gave the Legal Aid Board the power to make contracts in the 1988 Legal Aid Act and adopted the less provocative notion of franchising. The Board offered fixed term, renewable contracts to franchisees to deliver certain categories of legal services, for example in family law, housing and so on. Franchisees had to satisfy certain requirements, such as an effective management infrastructure, non-discrimination, the capacity to offer advice in welfare benefits, an adequate library and efficiency in keeping clients informed. Hostility continued from the Law Society throughout the first half of the 1990s. They warned that clients would be confused. Approaching a solicitor for advice on two topics, they might be sent away on one. By 1996, only 1,300 firms were franchised. The Lord Chancellor rewarded franchisees with higher fees, increasing four years running, and swifter legal aid payments. This was seen as divisive and as obviating the need for block contracting as firms would be forced to apply: (1995) 145 N.L.J. 405. Eventually, franchises were granted to more diverse types of provider, such as Citizens' Advice Bureaux. The present scheme goes much further than this, however. By limiting legal service providers to those with contracts, it is reverting to the Conservative proposals of 1986. Firms were given just a few months to apply for a franchise to deliver legal advice, in 1998. Again, this scheme was initially opposed by the Law Society, who denounced the contract documentation as unreasonable.

Again, this provoked condemnation from private practice lawyers who said that limiting providers to those who won contracts would exclude many firms of solicitors, such as small ethnic minority practices ((1999) 149 N.L.J. 398). This would deprive the public of access to justice, as firms turned them away. In November 1998, a few weeks before the application deadline, 220 minority practitioners met at the Law Society. Only two were franchised and 20 had applied. The Legal Aid Board (now LSC) had to put back the application deadline. Complaints are now being made that this prediction has become a reality (*The Times*, July 4, 2000).

The same performance was repeated over criminal services contracts. By March 2001, bearing in mind the April deadline, under 100 of the 3,400 firms who did criminal legal aid work had signed a contract under the new scheme. A fees rise had been offered and a simplified means of claiming fees and eventually, the Law Society withdrew its opposition and encouraged solicitors to enter contracts.

Solicitors continue to complain. Gibbons says the Legal Services **17-028** Commission is undermining the goodwill of the profession. It just wants a body of automatons,

> "whose members can fill out forms, tick boxes and administer themselves to death. . . . It is unfortunate that the Government has learnt nothing from its treatment of nurses, GPs and teachers, all professions which are now suffering severe problems of recruitment."

There is widespread anecdotal support of his complaints of excessive bureaucracy, first of the Legal Aid Board and now of its replacement, the Commission. A letter in support told an astonishing tale of money wasting stupidity. If I could add my own anecdote, my friends are partners in one of the first firms to be franchised and so are not hostile or new to these contracts. In April 1998, they were told to expect a Legal Aid Audit of their files in October 1998, cancelled plans they had made, accordingly and were still waiting 18 months after the appointed date, two of the audit team having had nervous breakdowns. In May 2001, I watched the friend spending hours one weekend checking through forms her assistant solicitors had completed. She pointed out that if they wrote the figure 4 in the box denoting dependents instead of "four", her firm would not get paid.

Solicitors also complain that they have to turn away clients, as the new reforms force them to cherry pick clients (see *The Times*, July 4, 2000).

Very occasionally, some practitioners take a more balanced view. Venters concludes that the criminal block contract pilot scheme has worked well for her firm although she does have reservations about the cost of installing IT, unfixed fees for experts, unnecessary bureaucracy and lawyers' remuneration.

Collins, head of the CDS at the Legal Services Commission, defends **17-029** criminal contracting against Gibbons' accusations, mainly on the basis of the aim to ensure quality provision, for instance, the requirement for experienced supervisors to check the work of members of staff. He reminds readers why legal advice at police stations can now only be given by accredited representatives:

> "The requirement that advice only be given by accredited representatives was not universally welcomed, and some saw it as an unnecessary

interference with the professional judgment of practitioners. On such grounds is much opposed. However, research has shown the scheme to have made real improvements in the quality of service to the public in this vital area and we are pleased to note from the article that this now seems to be widely accepted. However, research has shown that the performance of solicitors themselves in giving police station advice can fall short of that provided by those who are accredited: it is not sufficient to merely rely on the basic qualification of being a solicitor to assure quality of advice.

It should be recalled that it was often criminal defence solicitors who believed themselves to have an excellent reputation, and considered supervision to be unnecessary, who were deploying unqualified representatives in the police station whose poor standards led to the need for the accreditation scheme."

I have quoted this at length because it articulates the aim of restricting publicly funded legal services to quality providers who are accountable. If anything, the quotation understates the mischief that had to be remedied. As Bridges and many others have pointed out, the uncontrolled growth of legal aid since 1960 was linked to the massive increase in lawyers. Under the old legal aid scheme, any lawyer could provide legally aided services at the State's expense, with no quality assurance, no inspection of case files and very little accountability. The rest of us who are paid out of the public purse expect some quality control and accountability for our remuneration. Think about the tight state control over school teachers and the police. Quality control over university lecturers is becoming equally onerous.

17-030   Research such as that reported in *Standing Accused* exposed just how appalling the state of criminal defence by some solicitors and barristers was. Barristers would appear in court having done no case preparation and not knowing the client from Adam. Solicitors would send the office cleaner to sit behind counsel in court. Mostly when someone asked to see a duty solicitor in a police station they would not get a solicitor but just anyone the contracted solicitor chose to send. I read sections of this book aloud to my students because it tells such horror stories. This book and many police investigations uncovered widespread fraud by some firms of solicitors who thought nothing of sending a secretary to sit behind counsel in court and charging the legal aid Board for a trainee solicitor. The complaints about poor lawyers continue. The Royal Commission on Criminal Justice, 1993, found most defence counsel did not meet their client until the morning of trial. The National Audit Office complained in *Handling Crown Court Cases* (1997) that 75 per cent of a sample of prosecution briefs were returned and counsel of inappropriate quality took on a third of those cases. In 1998, the CPS reported that only one in ten barristers saw child abuse cases right through their process. Half of briefs were returned by the original barrister. In 2000 Judge John Crocker, resident judge at Isleworth Crown Court, publicly complained about inefficient and ill-prepared barristers.

Further, I would endorse *Standing Accused's* findings on the quality of qualified defence lawyers from my own observation. I have spent many hours of my adult lifetime researching or casually observing courts of all types all over England and Wales and I have been entertained to some cringeworthy performances by lawyers who are ignorant of the law or procedure, rude to the court, incompetent advocates or just plain waffly. I have timed a Law Lord yawn once every 90 seconds at a silk repeating everything the Law Lords had read in his printed case and I have seen Lord Chief Justice Bingham and fellow judges cast their eyes to the sky, as when an aged silk demanded another one and a half days to bore the Court of Appeal into a stupor.

Research on legal advice under the contracting scheme was published **17-031** after a two-year study by the Institute of Advanced Legal Studies in 2001. It examined 80,000 cases in 100 solicitors' offices and 43 not-for-profit agencies and found

- quality of advice depended on the time spent and experience of the adviser;
- there need to be further improvements in quality;
- organisations in the not-for-profit sector take longer to carry out their work than solicitors but give higher quality advice;
- referral levels are poor and consistently late;
- contractees need to address problems experienced by clients in gaining access to their advice.

Fixed Fees

Apart from grumbling about contracting, lawyers have complained bit- **17-032** terly over the curb on their fees in publicly funded cases. In 1992, Lord Chancellor Mackay sought to introduce fixed fees in magistrates' courts. This was fiercely opposed and subject to judicial review by an application from the Law Society. Both sides called in management consultants to support their arguments (see Bridges). The Law Society won and standard fees were introduced in 1993. Solicitors maintained, in evidence to the Royal Commission on Criminal Justice, 1993, and sometimes still do maintain, that the amount they are paid does not allow them to provide an adequate service. LCD research confirms the solicitors' warning that this would affect the work performed on a case.

They claimed it would reduce the number of solicitors undertaking criminal cases. In an excellent statistical analysis, Bridges showed their argument lacked evidence and historical context. The growth in legal aid, especially in magistrates' courts, he pointed out, was linked to the rapid growth of the profession, in the 1970s and 1980s. On lack of quality, he thought this had more to do with solicitors' inability to keep abreast with legal developments through having small case loads. His arguments are entirely pertinent in 2001.

Even in the late 1990s legal aid was an important source of income. According to the Law Society *Annual Statistical Report* 1999, it accounted for 14.8 per cent of gross fees in 1997–1998 and 78 per cent of solicitors' offices received at least one payment for legally aided work. A 2000 survey of solicitors in family work found some survived on very low rates of pay (*Setting Up*, Nuffield Foundation), however, and the Law Society complained that some firms with CLS contracts were disinclined to take on publicly funded work because of dissatisfaction with rates of remuneration. In a November 2000 speech Lord Irvine responded that he was listening and negotiating with the Legal Services Commission.

"Fat Cats"

17-033   By the mid 1990s many newspapers were making a scandal out of the high earnings of some barristers in legally aided cases. At the Bar Conference in 1995, Lord Woolf criticised the high level of fees charged in civil cases. He called for a move to fixed fees, alleging wasteful practices, including separate unnecessary representation, unnecessary use of two counsel, unnecessary use of solicitors to sit behind counsel and undue prolixity. Still concerned about the cost of criminal legal aid, Lord Chancellor Mackay's departmental legal aid division warned the Bar of the intention to fix fees for civil legal aid work. The bar response was hostile and uncooperative. Lord Irvine, then shadow Chancellor, expressed concern, at the Bar Conference, 1996 in over the cost of a few very expensive criminal cases. He repeated this at the Bar conference in 1999:

> "I have and will bear down on excessive fees in the high cost cases which swallow up so much of our budget. Criminal legal aid is privileged because of our international obligations to provide it, but it must not be exploited. It cannot be right that 40 per cent of our criminal legal aid budget is swallowed up by a mere one per cent of cases. These excessive fees get legal aid a bad name and stand in the way of one of my key aims . . . to restore legal aid to the status of a popular public social service, so highly regarded for its economy and efficiency that it can compete for scarce resources with the most valued public social services" (speech on LCD website).

An example of this is the Maxwell Brothers' trial which cost over £14 million in legal aid fees.

17-034   In 1997, in response to parliamentary questions and to the anger of the Bar, the LCD issued league tables of the top 20 recipients of legal aid fees. A number earned over £400,000 for Crown Court work in 1995–1996. Lord Irvine, defending court fee increases in 1997, attacked the price of lawyers as the deterrent to going to law. He told the House of Lords

"there are a significant number of Q.C.s who earn a million pounds per annum and many who would describe half a million pounds in one year as representing a very bad year for them. . . . Fat cat lawyers railing at the inequity of court fees do not attract the sympathy of the public." (*The Times,* July 15, 1997).

Home Secretary Jack Straw reiterated the attack at the 1997 Bar Conference. In June 1999, *The Times* claimed a deal was about to be announced. In October, the Law Society joined in, calling for tight control of Q.C.s' fees in criminal cases. In October, the Bar published its response to the Legal Aid Board's paper "Ensuring Quality and Controlling Cost in Very High Cost Criminal Cases". A 1999 survey showed a big gap in earnings between Q.C.s and other barristers and that 34 per cent of Bar earnings were publicly funded by the Legal Services Commission. In November 1999, the Lord Chancellor announced regulations to tighten the criteria regulating the assignment of Queen's Counsel or more than one advocate in publicly funded cases, as he had planned to in *Modernising Justice,* 1998. The regulations were in force from September 2000. Orders may now only be made for two counsel or a Q.C. if the defence case involves substantial novel or complex issues of law or fact which could not be adequately presented without a Q.C. and either the prosecution has senior counsel or the defence case is exceptional. In January 2000, the Legal Aid Board proposed a Special Cases Unit to control fees in high cost civil cases. This received a hostile reaction from both the Bar and the Law Society. In July 2000, the Lord Chancellor announced a 10 per cent cut in fees for publicly defended criminal work, to reduce disparity between prosecution and defence fees, giving the profession until September 2000 to respond. He also proposed to reduce rates in family cases. These were vigorously opposed by the Bar in their October 2000 conference. The Bar Chairman threatened that the profession would end up with "half-decent lawyers practising in the commercial fields". In summer 2001, the Bar was still objecting to these proposed cuts in fees but in October 2001 the graduated fees scheme was introduced, including an integrated payment scheme for prosecution and defence lawyers.

I have related this chronology at length because it shows that, although two successive Lord Chancellors have been determined to get a grip on barristers' and especially Q.C.s' fees for publicly funded work, they have

17-035

failed. In 1997, a *Legal Action* editorial demanded: "If government ministers think that Q.C.s earn too much money, then let them do something about it. . . . Ministers have the means to bring down prices for government work." They said they had previously drawn attention to the high level of some Q.C. fees and the relative overcompensation of barristers in comparison with solicitors:

> "Furthermore, the Lord Chancellor is the market-maker for the work of all Q.C.s. He appoints them. He thereby regulates the numbers. . . . If the Lord Chancellor would grasp the nettle and abolish Q.C.s, then senior counsel would be paid at a level dictated by a wider market. The government would save money: so too would the public."

In 1997, solicitor Arnold Rosen put forward a powerful argument on this area of "exquisite privilege":

> "As if by magic potion, the day after a barrister places the letters QC after his or her name, the fees rise. Can such higher fees be justified when paid for by the tax-payer—not the client? . . . The Criminal Bar and the silks, in particular, have managed to cultivate an assumption which, when analysed, I believe to be false. The assumption is that silks earning £400,000 a year from the Legal Aid Fund could, unless retained by legally assisted parties go and earn it elsewhere. Where else? The entire Criminal Bar is a completely artificial market."

The Community Legal Service

17-036   The Law Society and others continued to lobby against the Lord Chancellor's new scheme, especially as the Access to Justice Bill was passing through Parliament. Even the Civil Justice Council found a list of defects in the scheme established in the Access to Justice Act 1999. Three hundred amendments were secured, many in response to these concerns. The Law Society launched an expensive and graphic press campaign against the plan in spring 1999. It depicted a photograph of a crying child suffering from bad housing, a beaten woman and a black man, who had been falsely imprisoned and discriminated against. Lord Irvine retaliated with a furious press release, pointing out that all those groups would still get funded legal services under the new scheme.

In 2000, the Consumers' Association published research on people's experiences with getting help, especially those in vulnerable groups. It showed (1) concern about lack of commitment and poor communication from lawyers (2) community centres and law centres gave the best help. (3) a lack of advisers in areas like social security, housing, disability discrimination, employment and immigration ((2000) 150 N.L.J. 725).

The Criminal Defence Service

1. *Public defenders*   **17-037**
    United Kingdom lawyers are well aware of the image of the
    American public defender providing a second class service to
    criminal clients and this has coloured much of the response to the
    LCD consultation paper on public defenders in 2000, "Criminal
    Defence Service: Establishing a Salaried Defence Service and
    Draft Code of Conduct, etc.". The Government reiterated that:

    > "(w)e believe that the twin objectives of value and excellence
    > can best be achieved within the CDS through a mixed system
    > of service provision, consisting of contracted private practice
    > lawyers and lawyers employed directly by the Legal Services
    > Commission."

    They explained their piloting plans and that the offices would
    be staffed so they could represent clients from the police station
    through to the Crown Court. Salaried defenders, offices would be
    block funded and would have to build up their own clientele. They
    listed the benefits of their proposed scheme, drawing for support
    from evaluations of schemes abroad: quality, better value for
    money, lack of profit motive, availability of information on the
    supply of CDS, positive pressure on private practice cost and
    quality and flexibility. They also looked in twice as much depth at
    the drawbacks.
    The Justices' Clerks' Society expressed concern over too close
    a relationship building up between employed prosecutors and
    defenders. This, coupled with targets could lead to an increase in
    plea bargaining. James Morton, (*The Times,* June 20, 2000) warned
    that "if it does take off, it will substantially undermine the private
    criminal practice" (and see Gibbons). Minister Lord Bach
    addressed such fears, in introducing the first four Public
    Defenders, in March 2001. Reiterating that this was not the
    Government's purpose, he commented "(w)e intend to open six
    offices during the first phase of the four-year pilot . . . compared
    with 2,800 franchised firms able to enter contracts".
    The Bar Council, defending private practice barristers as   **17-038**
    usual, naturally opposed salaried defenders. Following the
    Scottish experience, they predicted "the CDS will be a disaster
    in terms of budgetary control", if the Scottish experiment in
    public defenders was a model. They criticised the Government
    for going ahead with a pilot scheme here without taking
    account of the evaluation of the Scottish pilot, to be published
    in 2001. From the foreign evaluations of public defender

systems, cited by the Government, they pick out the negative comments. The same points are repeated by Frazer in an article reproduced in *The Times* and the N.L.J. Tellingly, however, he quotes in support from "McConville's" *Standing Accused* (1994) which he clearly has not read, since he cites it as an article. It also has three other authors. This should tell us something about the quality of argument of some private practice barristers. A *New Law Journal* editorial claims that talented and ambitious people will not stay as salaried defenders, because of poor promotion prospects. It considers ominous the Government's "mutterings" about its duty to secure value for money. The Legal Services Consultative Panel responded to the draft code of conduct for public defenders in some detail. On the general principles and structure, it emphasised the need to assure quality and independence. "The Crown Prosecution Service provides an example of the systemic problems that can occur if this is not built into the service from the beginning." The service will need to build in mechanisms to prevent overload, ensure proper training and support and "instil a culture that is robust enough to prevent it simply becoming part of the funding or case management strategy of the Legal Services Commission or Court Service".

2. *The means test*
May cease to be a problem as it will be applied in so few cases. The LSC is far better resourced to conduct means investigations than court clerks. Court clerks had no way of checking whether defendant's statements on means were true.

3. *The merits test for legal aid*
If this is going to be an interests of justice test, it will be subject to the same subjective interpretation as before. See my 1999 article on this. My research published in 1984, in *The Magistrates' Clerk* showed wide variations in the interpretation of the interests of justice test between courts and clerks. This finding was repeated by other researchers later.

FURTHER READING

17-039 *Modernising Justice*, the LCD 1999 white paper, which accompanied the Access to Justice Bill 1998, which provides a holistic picture of the new structure of legal services, which is still in the process of being implemented. It sets out the provisions of the framework legislation but, more usefully, the practical detail: www.lcd.gov.uk.
The Access to Justice Act 1999, www.hmso.gov.uk.

"Rights of Audience and Rights to Conduct Litigation", LCD consultation paper, 1998, see website.

The Legal Services Commission: www.legalservices.gov.uk. See, especially, their *focus* news magazine.

The Community Legal Service: www.justask.org.uk.

M. McConville, L. Bridges, J. Hodgson and A. Pavlovic, *Standing Accused* (1994).

LCD, *Contingency Fees*, Cm. 571 (1989).

B. Sahota, "Exploding the myths of conditional fees" (1995) 145 N.L.J. 592, summarising the judicial opposition to CFAs and the solicitors' arguments in favour. See also M. Napier in *The Times*, July 11, 1995.

D. Bedingfield, "The contingency fee system in America" (1993) 143 N.L.J. 1670, in defence and J.D. Zirin, against, in *The Times*, February 18, 1997.

The Labour Party, "Access to Justice—Conference 1995".

G. Hoon, "Access to justice—the reality not the slogan" (1997) N.L.J. 1611.

LCD, "Access to justice with conditional fees—a consultation paper" 1998.

Comments on conditional fees see Mears, (1998) 148 N.L.J. 486; Hodges, (1998) 148 N.L.J. 917; Tunkel, (1997) 147 N.L.J. 1784; Leech, (1996) 146 N.L.J. 1774; Ackner, (1998) 148 N.L.J. 477; Chapman, *Legal Action*, April 1988, at 6; Zander, (1997) 147 N.L.J. 1438; the reply to Zander is worth reading because it explains how success fees are calculated— (1997) 147 N.L.J. 1488; (1998) 148 N.L.J. 360; Prais, (1998) 148 N.L.J. 101 and (1999) 149 N.L.J. 1372; Pleasance (for the LAB), "Can solicitors pick winners?" (1999) 149 N.L.J. 138; Capper, (1998) 148 N.L.J. 1402; the Bar's Response to "Access to Justice with conditional fees, 1998; Bawdon on Yarrow and Abrams' research, (1999) 149 N.L.J. 1890; Mahendra, (2000) 150 N.l.J. 1013; Moorhead and Scherr, (2001) 151 N.L.J 274; Wignall, (2001) 151 N.L.J 355; McGill and Crosby, (2001) 151 N.L.J. 14; Yarrow, *Just Rewards?* summarised at (2001) 151 N.L.J. 750; P. Kunzlick, (1999) 62 M.L.R. 850.

On the Community Legal Service: *Legal Action* throughout 1997–1999. See especially LAG's plan, *Justice: redressing the balance*, summarised in *Legal Action*, November 1997, 6.

See review articles after its first year at (2001) 151 N.L.J. 998, 613.

J. Gibbons, "The Death of a Profession" (2000) 150 N.L.J. 1366 and letters, (2000) 150 N.L.J. 1610. See also (2001) 151 N.L.J. 749. Reply by Collins, for the CDS, at (2000) 150 N.L.J. 1520.

J. Venters, "Issues for Practitioners" (on contracting) *Legal Action*, August 1999, at 9.

Legal Aid Board, "Reforming the civil advice and assistance scheme: exclusive contracting—the way forward" 1998.

LCD press releases.

A.Gray and P. Fenn, "The Rising Cost of Criminally Legally Aided Cases" (1991) 141 N.L.J. 1622.

L. Bridges, "The Fixed Fees Battle", *Legal Action*, November 1992, at 7.

L. Bridges, "The Professionalisation of Criminal Justice" *Legal Action*, August 1992, at 7.

"Legal aid top 20 infuriates Bar", (1997) 11 *The Lawyer*, issue 8, at 1 and further articles on Q.C.'s earnings in *The Times*, September 28, 2000; (2000) 150 N.L.J. 1133; *The Times*, July 3, 1999.

S.I. 2000/1876 The Legal Aid in Criminal and Care Proceedings (General) (Amendment) (No.2) Regulations 2000 regulate the use of two counsel or a Q.C. in the Crown Court.

F. Gibb, "Legal aid cuts 'will drive away best barristers'", *The Times*, October 16, 2000.

Editorial, "Cuckoos and Counsel" *Legal Action*, June 1998, at 3.

A. Rosen, "An artificial market" (1997) 147 N.L.J. 630.

"Criminal Defence Service: Choice of Representative", 2000.

"Criminal Defence Service: Code of Conduct for Salaried Defenders employed by the Legal Services Commission", 2000 and "— Responses to the Consultation Paper" 2001, LCD website.

"The Legal Service Consultative Panel's Response to the LCD's Consultative Papers", 2000, LCD website.

J. Gibbons, "The Value of Nothing" (2001) 151 N.L.J. 858.

The Bar Council, "Criminal Defence Service, Appendix A: Salaried Defenders: Lessons for the U.K.", Bar Council website, www.barcouncil.org.uk.

C. Frazer, (2001) 151 N.L.J. 670.

Editorial, (2000) 150 N.L.J. 923.

P. Darbyshire, "A Comment on the Powers of Magistrates' Clerks" [1999] Crim.L.R. 377.

H. Genn, *Paths to Justice—What People Do and Think About Going to Law*, 1999, summarised at (1996) 146 N.L.J. 1756.

National Association of Citizens' Advice Bureaux: www.nacab.org .uk.

Law Centres Federation: www.lawcentres.org.uk. See annual reports.

LCD, "Legal Aid for the Apparently Wealthy", 1994.

See new articles in "the justice debate" in *Legal Action* 2001 and regular articles in *Legal Action* and *The Gazette*.

Index